Fodor's

TENTH **New** EDITION

Philadelphia and the Pennsylvania Dutch Country

Packed with details that will make your trip

The must-see sights, off and on the beaten path

What to see, what to skip

Vacation itineraries, walking tours, day trips

Smart lodging and dining options

Transportation tips

Key contacts, savvy travel advice

When to go, what to pack

Clear, accurate, easy-to-use maps

Books to read, videos to watch, background essay

D0104496

Fodor's Travel Publications, Inc.
New York • Toronto • London • Sydney • Auckland
www.fodors.com/

Fodor's Philadelphia and the Pennsylvania Dutch Country

EDITOR: Linda Cabasin

Editorial Contributors: Robert Andrews, Bob Brooke, David Brown, Joyce Eisenberg, Audra Epstein, Janis Pomerantz, Barbara Ann Rosenberg, Heidi Sarna, Helayne Schiff, M. T. Schwartzman (Gold Guide editor), Dinah A. Spritzer, Janet Bukovinsky Teacher.
Editorial Production: Stacey Kulig
Maps: David Lindroth, *cartographer*; Steven K. Amsterdam, *map editor*
Design: Fabrizio La Rocca, *creative director*; Guido Caroti, *associate art director*; Jolie Novak, *photo editor*
Production/Manufacturing: Mike Costa
Cover Photograph: H. Mark Weidman

Copyright

ISBN 0–679–03405–6

10th Edition

Special Sales

CONTENTS

Maps

ON THE ROAD WITH FODOR'S

WE'RE ALWAYS THRILLED to get letters from readers, especially one like this:

It took us an hour to decide what book to buy and we now know we picked the best one. Your book was wonderful, easy to follow, very accurate, and good on pointing out eating places, informal as well as formal. When we saw other people using your book, we would look at each other and smile.

Our editors and writers are deeply committed to making every Fodor's guide "the best one"—not only accurate but always charming, brimming with sound recommendations and solid ideas, right on the mark in describing restaurants and hotels, and full of fascinating facts that make you view what you've traveled to see in a rich new light.

About Our Writers

Our success in achieving our goals—and in helping to make your trip the best of all possible vacations—is a credit to the hard work of our extraordinary writers.

Bob Brooke, who updated the Lancaster County chapter, lives outside Philadelphia in Malvern and has traveled to more than 60 countries, covering places as diverse as Hong Kong and Mexico. He is the author of six books and writes frequently about Lancaster County and the Amish. His articles have appeared in many publications, including *British Heritage* and *Travel Mexico.* In addition, he's a regular contributor to the *Philadelphia Business Journal.*

A newspaper editor, travel writer, and tireless adventurer, **Joyce Eisenberg** has trekked through the poppy fields of northern Thailand and dined on emu and crocodile in Australia. But like Dorothy in *The Wizard of Oz,* she says, "There's no place like home." For her, that home is Philadelphia, which she loves for its unpretentious small-town feel and big-town cultural attractions. This year she updated Chapter 1 and rewrote much of Chapter 2, Exploring Philadelphia. She lives with her husband and two children, who

contribute to the city's cultural scene; her son is a member of the renowned Philadelphia Boys Choir; her daughter is a dancer and actress-in-training at the Walnut Street Theater's school.

Freelance writer **Janis Pomerantz** put her interests in shopping, nightlife and the performing arts, and sports to good use in her updates of those chapters. A native Philadelphian, she has traveled to places from Hong Kong and Thailand to Mexico and Israel, but she'd still rather be in Philadelphia.

Barbara Ann Rosenberg, who rewrote the Dining chapter this year, is a food and travel writer who keeps on top of the local dining scene. (Her frequent indulgences in Philadelphia restaurants are beginning to show!) Among the national magazines she writes for frequently is the *Robb Report.* She also serves as the editor of the *Restaurant Report,* a monthly publication about the hospitality industry in Philadelphia and the surrounding area.

Janet Bukovinsky Teacher, who updated the Gold Guide, Lodging, Side Trips, and Bucks County chapters, was a senior writer for *Philadelphia* magazine for many years before she decided to begin a freelance career. She makes her home in Philadelphia but loves to search out new places around the region.

A University of Pennsylvania graduate, New York–based Fodor's editor **Linda Cabasin** liked Philadelphia so much she married a local boy. She believes a visit to the area is always a good idea, whether it's to take in the Flower Show, study the paintings of Thomas Eakins at the Philadelphia Museum of Art, or stroll in the conservatories at Longwood Gardens.

We'd also like to thank **Leslie Squires** and **Michael Squires** for providing ongoing updates on matters from history to festivals.

New This Year

This year we've added terrific Great Itineraries that will lead you through the best of the city, taking into consideration how long you have to spend. Joyce Eisenberg has also added new neighborhood tours in Philadelphia to make it easier to explore some popular areas: the galleries and historic buildings of Old City, the posh environs of Rittenhouse Square, and trendy Manayunk. Both dining updater Barbara Rosenberg and shopping updater Janis Pomerantz expanded the coverage of Manayunk in their chapters, reflecting the growing appeal of its restaurants, galleries, and shops. Barbara Ann Rosenberg revamped the dining listings to reflect what's freshest and best on the fast-changing restaurant scene—with suggestions on where to find everything from great hoagies and cheap eats to superlative French fare.

We're also proud to announce that the American Society of Travel Agents has endorsed Fodor's as its guidebook of choice. ASTA is the world's largest and most influential travel trade association, operating in more than 170 countries, with 27,000 members pledged to adhere to a strict code of ethics reflecting the Society's motto, "Integrity in Travel." ASTA shares Fodor's devotion to providing smart, honest travel information and advice to travelers, and we've long recommended that our readers consult ASTA member agents for the experience and professionalism they bring to the table.

On the Web, check out Fodor's site (www.fodors.com/) for information on major destinations around the world and travel-savvy interactive features. The Web site also lists the 85-plus radio stations nationwide that carry the *Fodor's Travel Show,* a live call-in program that airs every weekend. Tune in to hear guests discuss their wonderful adventures—or call in to get answers for your most pressing travel questions.

How to Use This Book

Organization

Up front is the **Gold Guide,** an easy-to-use section divided alphabetically by topic. Under each listing you'll find tips and information that will help you accomplish what you need to in Philadelphia and the Pennsylvania Dutch Country. You'll also find addresses and telephone numbers of organizations and companies that offer destination-related services and detailed information and publications.

The first chapter in the guide, **Destination: Philadelphia and the Pennsylvania Dutch**

Country, helps get you in the mood for your trip. New and Noteworthy cues you in on trends and happenings, What's Where gets you oriented, Pleasures and Pastimes describes the activities and sights that really make Philadelphia unique, Great Itineraries helps you make the best of your time, Fodor's Choice showcases our top picks, and Festivals and Seasonal Events alerts you to special events you'll want to seek out.

The Exploring chapter is subdivided by neighborhood; each subsection recommends a walking or driving tour and lists neighborhood sights alphabetically, including sights that are off the beaten path. Other chapters are arranged in alphabetical order by subject (dining, lodging, nightlife and the arts, outdoor activities and sports, shopping, and side trips).

After the complete coverage of Philadelphia, you'll find separate chapters on Bucks Country and on Lancaster County, Hershey, and Gettysburg. Each of these chapters covers exploring, dining, lodging, nightlife and the arts, outdoor activities and sports, and shopping, and ends with a section called **A to Z,** which tells you how to get there and get around and gives you important local addresses and telephone numbers.

At the end of the book you'll find **Portraits,** a wonderful essay about the Amish way of life, followed by suggestions for any pre-trip research you may want to do, from recommended reading to movies on tape with Philadelphia or the Pennsylvania Dutch Country as a backdrop.

Icons and Symbols

★   Our special recommendations
✕   Restaurant
⊡   Lodging establishment
✕⊡   Lodging establishment whose restaurant warrants a detour
⟁   Campgrounds
☾   Good for kids (rubber duckie)
☞   Sends you to another section of the guide for more information
⊠   Address
☎   Telephone number
☉   Opening and closing times
💰   Admission prices (those we give apply to adults; substantially reduced fees are almost always available for children, students, and senior citizens)

Numbers in white and black circles that appear on the maps, in the margins, and within the tours correspond to one another.

Credit Cards

The following abbreviations are used: **AE**, American Express; **D**, Discover; **DC**, Diners Club; **MC**, MasterCard; and **V**, Visa.

Don't Forget to Write

You can use this book in the confidence that all prices and opening times are based on information supplied to us at press time; Fodor's cannot accept responsibility for any errors. Time inevitably brings changes, so always confirm information when it matters—especially if you're making a detour to visit a specific place. In addition, when making reservations be sure to mention if you have a disability or are traveling with children, if you prefer a private bath or a certain type of bed, or if you have specific dietary needs or other concerns.

Were the restaurants we recommended as described? Did our hotel picks exceed your expectations? Did you find a museum we recommended a waste of time? If you have complaints, we'll look into them and revise our entries when the facts warrant it. If you've discovered a special place that we haven't included, we'll pass the information along to our correspondents and have them check it out. So send us your feedback, positive *and* negative: E-mail us at editors@fodors.com (specifying the name of the book on the subject line) or write the Philadelphia and the Pennsylvania Dutch Country editor at Fodor's, 201 East 50th Street, New York, NY 10022. Have a wonderful trip!

Karen Cure
Editorial Director

Philadelphia and Vicinity

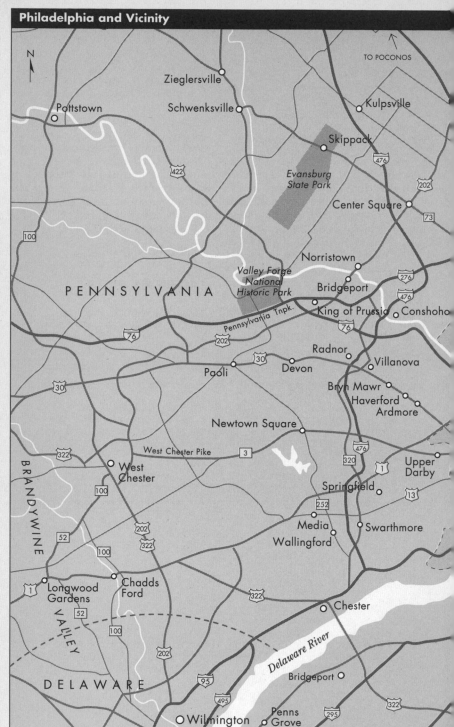

N

TO POCONOS

Zieglersville

Schwenksville

Pottstown

Kulpsville

Skippack

422

Evansburg
State Park

476

202

Center Square

73

100

Norristown

Valley Forge
National
Historic Park

Bridgeport

276

PENNSYLVANIA

King of Prussia

Conshoho

476

Pennsylvania Tnpk.

76

202

76

Radnor

Villanova

30

Devon

Paoli

Bryn Mawr

30

Haverford
Ardmore

Newtown Square

476

West Chester Pike

3

320

1

Upper
Darby

322

West
Chester

Springfield

13

100

252

202

Media

322

Swarthmore

52

Wallingford

100

Chadds
Ford

BRANDYWINE

1

Longwood
Gardens

322

52

Chester

100

VALLEY

202

Delaware River

DELAWARE

95

Bridgeport

495

Penns
Grove

295

322

Wilmington

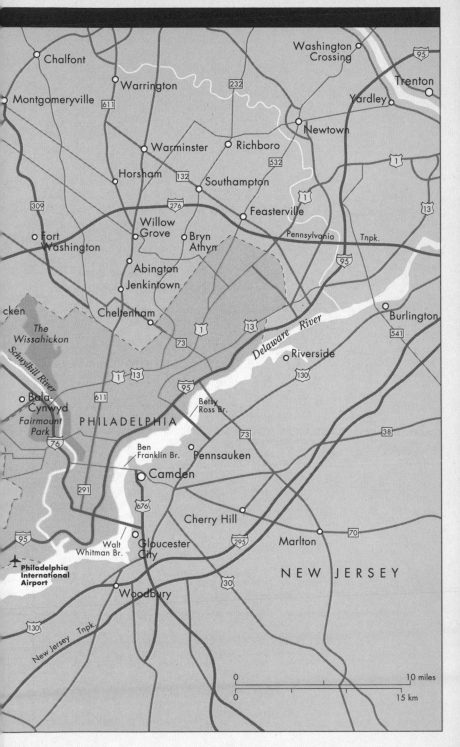

Philadelphia

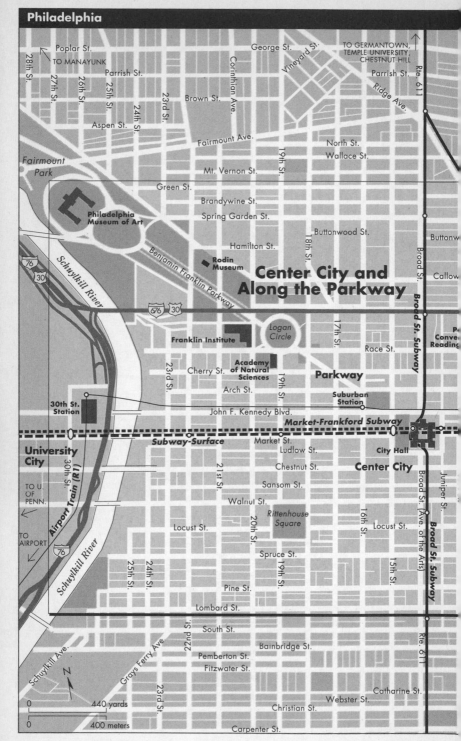

28th St.

Poplar St.
TO MANAYUNK

27th St.
26th St.
25th St.
24th St.
23rd St.

Parrish St.

Brown St.

Corinthian Ave.

George St.

Vineyard St.

TO GERMANTOWN,
TEMPLE UNIVERSITY,
CHESTNUT HILL

Rte. 611

Parrish St.

Ridge Ave.

Aspen St.

Fairmount Ave.

North St.
Wallace St.

Fairmount Park

Mt. Vernon St.

Green St.

Brandywine St.

Spring Garden St.

Buttonwood St.

19th St.

18th St.

Broad St.

Buttonw

Callow

Philadelphia Museum of Art

Hamilton St.

Rodin Museum

Center City and Along the Parkway

76
30

Schuylkill River

Benjamin Franklin Parkway

76 30

Logan Circle

17th St.

Franklin Institute

Academy of Natural Sciences

Race St.

Broad St. Subway

P.
Conve
Reading

23rd St.

Cherry St.

19th St.

Parkway

Arch St.

Suburban Station

30th St. Station

John F. Kennedy Blvd.

Market-Frankford Subway

Subway-Surface

Market St.

Ludlow St.

City Hall

University City

30th St.

Airport Train (R1)

21st St.

Chestnut St.

Sansom St.

20th St.

Walnut St.

Rittenhouse Square

Center City

16th St.

Broad St. (Ave. of the Arts)

Juniper St.

Broad St. Subway

TO U. OF PENN.

TO AIRPORT

76

Locust St.

Locust St.

15th St.

Schuylkill River

Spruce St.

19th St.

25th St.
24th St.

Pine St.

Lombard St.

Schuylkill Ave.

N

22nd St.

South St.

Grays Ferry Ave.

Pemberton St.
Fitzwater St.

Bainbridge St.

Rte. 611

23rd St.

Catharine St.

0   440 yards

Webster St.

0   400 meters

Christian St.

Carpenter St.

SMART TRAVEL TIPS A TO Z

Basic Information on Traveling in Philadelphia and the Pennsylvania Dutch Country, Savvy Tips to Make Your Trip a Breeze, and Companies and Organizations to Contact

A

AIR TRAVEL

MAJOR AIRLINE OR LOW-COST CARRIER?

Most people choose a flight based on price. Yet there are other issues to consider. Major airlines offer the greatest number of departures; smaller airlines—including regional, low-cost and no-frills airlines— usually have a more limited number of flights daily. Major airlines have frequent-flyer partners, which allow you to credit mileage earned on one airline to your account with another. Low-cost airlines offer a definite price advantage and fewer restrictions, such as advance-purchase requirements. Safety-wise, low-cost carriers as a group have a good history, but **check the safety record before booking**; call the Federal Aviation Administration's Consumer Hotline (☞ Airline Complaints, *below*).

➤ MAJOR AIRLINES: **American** (☎ 800/433–7300). **Continental** (☎ 800/231–0856). **Delta** (☎ 800/241–4141). **Northwest** (☎ 800/225–2525). **TWA** (☎ 800/892–4141). **United** (☎ 800/241–6522). **US Airways** (☎ 800/428–4322).

➤ SMALLER AIRLINES: **Midwest Express** (☎ 800/452–2022).

➤ FROM THE U.K.: Only **British Airways** (☎ 0345/222–111) serves Philadelphia directly. Other carriers include **American** (☎ 0345/789–789), via Boston; **United** (☎ 0800/888–555), via New York; and **Virgin Atlantic** (☎ 01293/747–747), via Washington, D.C. or New York.

GET THE LOWEST FARE

The least expensive airfares to Philadelphia are priced for round-trip travel. Major airlines usually require that you **book in advance and buy the ticket within 24 hours,** and you may have to **stay over a Saturday night.** It's smart to **call a number of airlines, and when you are quoted a good price, book it on the spot**—the same fare may not be available on the same flight the next day. Airlines generally allow you to change your return date for a fee of $25–$50. If you don't use your ticket, you can apply the cost toward the purchase of a new ticket, again for a small charge. However, most low-fare tickets are nonrefundable. To get the lowest airfare, **check different routings.** If your destination or home city has more than one gateway, compare prices to and from different airports. Also price less expensive off-peak flights.

To save money on flights from the United Kingdom and back, **look into an APEX or Super-PEX ticket.** APEX tickets must be booked in advance and have certain restrictions. Super-PEX tickets can be purchased at the airport on the day of departure— subject to availability.

DON'T STOP UNLESS YOU MUST

When you book, **look for nonstop flights** and **remember that "direct" flights stop at least once.** Try to **avoid connecting flights,** which require a change of plane. Two airlines may jointly operate a connecting flight, so ask if your airline operates every segment—your preferred carrier may fly you only part of the way.

USE AN AGENT

Travel agents, especially those who specialize in finding the lowest fares (☞ Discounts & Deals, *below*), can be especially helpful when booking a plane ticket. When you're quoted a price, **ask your agent if the price is likely to get any lower.** Good agents know the seasonal fluctuations of airfares and can usually anticipate a sale or fare war. However, waiting can be risky: The fare could go *up* as seats become scarce, and you may wait so long that your preferred flight sells out. A wait-and-see strategy works best if your plans are flexible, but if you must arrive and depart on certain dates, don't delay.

Airlines routinely overbook planes, knowing that not everyone with a ticket will show up, but sometimes everyone does. When that happens, airlines ask for volunteers to give up their seats. In return, these volunteers usually get a certificate for a free flight and are rebooked on the next flight out. If there are not enough volunteers, the airline must choose who will be denied boarding. The first to get bumped are passengers who checked in late and those flying on discounted tickets, **so get to the gate and check in as early as possible,** especially during peak periods.

Always **bring a photo ID to the airport.** You may be asked to show it before you are allowed to check in.

ENJOY THE FLIGHT

For better service, **fly smaller or regional carriers,** which often have higher passenger-satisfaction ratings. Sometimes you'll find leather seats, more legroom, and better food.

For more legroom, **request an emergency-aisle seat;** don't however, sit in the row in front of the emergency aisle or in front of a bulkhead, where seats may not recline.

If you don't like airline food, **ask for special meals when booking.** These can be vegetarian, low-cholesterol, or kosher, for example.

COMPLAIN IF NECESSARY

If your baggage goes astray or your flight goes awry, complain right away. Most carriers require that you file a claim immediately.

➤ AIRLINE COMPLAINTS: U.S. Department of Transportation **Aviation Consumer Protection Division** (✉ C-75, Room 4107, Washington, DC 20590, ☎ 202/366–2220). **Federal Aviation Administration (FAA) Consumer Hotline** (☎ 800/322–7873).

AIRPORTS & TRANSFERS

The major gateway to Philadelphia is **Philadelphia International Airport,** 8

mi from downtown in the southwest part of the city.

➤ AIRPORT INFORMATION: **Philadelphia International Airport** (✉ 8900 Essington Ave., off I–95, ☎ 215/937–6937 for operator or 215/937–6800 for general information).

TRANSFERS

Allow at least a half hour, more during rush hour, for the 8-mi trip between the airport and Center City. By car the airport is accessible via I–95 south or I–76 east.

Taxis at the airport are plentiful but expensive—about $20 plus tip. "Limos" (vans, not stretch limousines) cost about $10 per person, but service is less frequent, and most limos stop only at certain hotels and downtown points.

SEPTA (Southeastern Pennsylvania Transportation Authority) runs the Airport Rail Line R1, which leaves the airport every 30 minutes from 6:10 AM to 12:10 AM. The trip to Center City takes about 20 minutes and costs $5. For $1 more you can transfer to any train in the regional rail system. Trains serve the 30th Street, Suburban, Market East, and North Broad stations.

➤ BY LIMOUSINE: Among the companies are **Carey Limousine Philadelphia** (☎ 610/595–2800) and **Limelight Limousine** (☎ 215/342–5557).

➤ BY TRAIN: For schedules and other information, call the **Airport Information Desk** (☎ 215/937–6800)) or **SEPTA** (☎ 215/580–7800).

B

BUS TRAVEL

TO & FROM PHILADELPHIA

Greyhound Lines operates long-haul service out of the terminal at 10th and Filbert streets, just north of the Market East commuter rail station. Peter Pan/Trailways has service to and from Baltimore, Washington, D.C., and New York from the same terminal. NJ Transit stops at the Greyhound terminal and offers service between Philadelphia and Atlantic City and other New Jersey destinations

➤ BUS COMPANIES: **Greyhound Lines** (☎ 215/931–4075 or 800/231–

2222). **NJ Transit** (☎ 215/569–3752). **Peter Pan Trailways** (☎ 800/343–9999).

WITHIN PHILADELPHIA

Buses make up the bulk of the SEPTA system, with 110 routes extending throughout the city and into the suburbs. Bus 76, called the "Ben FrankLine," connects the zoo in West Fairmount Park with Penn's Landing at the Delaware River, stopping at major sights along the way including the Pennsylvania Convention Center and the art museum. Route 76 costs 50¢ and operates daily from around 9 to 6; it runs later on Wednesday evening, when the Philadelphia Museum of Art stays open longer.

The distinctive purple minibuses you'll see around Center City are SEPTA's newest convenience line for visitors, the PHILLY PHLASH. The loop runs from Logan Circle on the Benjamin Franklin Parkway through Center City to Penn's Landing. Since a ride on the PHLASH costs $1.50 for a one-way ticket, **consider the handy all-day, unlimited-ride pass available for $3.** These buses run daily from 10 AM to midnight in the summer, 10 to 6 September 15–May 14. There is service every 10 minutes.

The base fare for subways, trolleys, and buses is $1.60, paid with exact change or a token. Transfers cost 40¢. Senior citizens (with valid ID) ride free during off-peak hours and holidays. Tokens sell for $1.15 and can be purchased in packages of 2, 5, or 10 from cashiers along the Broad Street subway and Market–Frankford lines and in many downtown stores (including some Rite Aid pharmacies).

If you plan to travel extensively within Center City, it's a good idea to **get a SEPTA pass.** The Day Pass costs $5 and is good for 24 hours of unlimited use on all SEPTA vehicles within the city, plus one trip on any regional rail line including the Airport Express train. A weekly transit pass costs $17.50. Tokens and transit passes are good on buses and subways but not on commuter rail lines.

You can purchase tokens and transit passes in the SEPTA sales offices in the concourse below the northwest corner of 15th and Market streets; in the Market East station (⊠ 8th and Market Sts.); and in 30th Street Station (⊠ 30th and Market Sts.). They are also sold at the Philadelphia Visitors Center (⊠ 16th St. and John F. Kennedy Blvd.).

Though SEPTA's new automated answering system has cut down on your phone wait, **be prepared for a busy signal and a long time on hold.**

➤ SCHEDULES AND INFORMATION: **SEPTA** (☎ 215/580–7800). To have a schedule mailed to you, call SEPTA (☎ 215/580–7777).

C

CAMERAS, CAMCORDERS, & COMPUTERS

Always **keep your film, tape, or computer disks out of the sun.** Carry extra batteries and **be prepared to turn on your camera, camcorder, or laptop** to prove to security personnel that the device is real. Always **ask for hand inspection of film,** which becomes clouded after successive exposure to airport X-ray machines, and **keep videotapes and computer disks away from metal detectors.**

➤ PHOTO HELP: Kodak Information Center (☎ 800/242–2424). *Kodak Guide to Shooting Great Travel Pictures,* in bookstores or from Fodor's Travel Publications (☎ 800/533–6478; $16.50 plus $4 shipping).

CAR RENTAL

Rates in Philadelphia begin at $35 a day and $176 a week for an economy car with air-conditioning, an automatic transmission, and unlimited mileage. This does not include tax on car rentals, which is 7%.

➤ MAJOR AGENCIES: **Alamo** (☎ 800/327–9633, 0800/272–2000 in U.K.). **Avis** (☎ 800/331–1212, 800/879–2847 in Canada). **Budget** (☎ 800/527–0700, 0800/181181 in U.K.). **Dollar** (☎ 800/800–4000; 0990/565656 in U.K., where it is known as Eurodollar). **Hertz** (☎ 800/654–3131, 800/263–0600 in Canada, 0345/555888 in U.K.). **National InterRent** (☎ 800/227–7368; 01345/222525 in U.K., where it is known as Europcar InterRent).

CUT COSTS

To get the best deal, **book through a travel agent who is willing to shop**

around. When pricing cars, **ask about the location of the rental lot.** Some off-airport locations offer lower rates, and their lots are only minutes from the terminal via complimentary shuttle. You also may want to **price local car-rental companies,** whose rates may be lower still, although their service and maintenance may not be as good as those of a name-brand agency. Remember to ask about required deposits, cancellation penalties, and drop-off charges if you're planning to pick up the car in one city and leave it in another.

Also **ask your travel agent about a company's customer-service record.** How has it responded to late plane arrivals and vehicle mishaps? Are there often lines at the rental counter, and if you're traveling during a holiday period, does a confirmed reservation guarantee you a car?

NEED INSURANCE?

When driving a rented car, you are generally responsible for any damage to or loss of the vehicle. You also are liable for any property damage or personal injury you may cause while driving. Before you rent, **see what coverage you already have** under the terms of your personal auto-insurance policy and credit cards.

For about $14 a day, rental companies sell protection, known as a collision- or loss-damage waiver (CDW or LDW), which eliminates your liability for damage to the car; it's always optional and should never be automatically added to your bill.

In most states you don't need CDW if you have personal auto insurance or other liability insurance. However, **make sure you have enough coverage to pay for the car.** If you do not have auto insurance or an umbrella policy that covers damage to third parties, purchasing CDW or LDW is highly recommended.

BEWARE SURCHARGES

Before you pick up a car in one city and leave it in another, **ask about drop-off charges or one-way service fees,** which can be substantial. Note, too, that some rental agencies charge extra if you return the car before the time specified on your contract. To avoid a hefty refueling fee, **fill the** tank just before you turn in the car, but be aware that gas stations near the rental outlet may overcharge.

MEET THE REQUIREMENTS

In the United States you must be 21 to rent a car, and rates may be higher if you're under 25. You'll pay extra for child seats (about $3 per day), which are compulsory for children under five, and for additional drivers (about $2 per day). In order to pick up a car, residents of the United Kingdom will need a reservation voucher, a passport, a U.K. driver's license, and a travel policy that covers each driver.

CHILDREN & TRAVEL

CHILDREN IN PHILADELPHIA

Be sure to plan ahead and **involve your youngsters** as you outline your trip. When packing, include things to keep them busy en route. On sightseeing days try to schedule activities of interest to your children. If you rent a car, don't forget to **arrange for a car seat** when you reserve.

➤ BABY-SITTING: **Rocking Horse Child-Care Center** (✉ 6th and Walnut Sts., Curtis Center, Suite 25 LL, 19106, ☎ 215/592–8257) offers part- and full-time care for children ages six weeks to 10 years.

HOTELS

Most hotels in Philadelphia allow children under a certain age to stay in their parents' room at no extra charge, but others will charge extra; be sure to **ask about the cutoff age for children's discounts.**

FLYING

As a general rule, infants under two not occupying a seat fly free. If your children are two or older, **ask about children's airfares.**

In general, the adult baggage allowance applies to children paying half or more of the adult fare.

According to the FAA, it's a good idea to use safety seats aloft for children weighing less than 40 pounds. Airlines, however, can set their own policies: U.S. carriers allow FAA-approved models but usually require that you buy a ticket, even if your child would otherwise ride free, since the seats must be strapped into regular seats. Airline rules vary regarding their use, so it's important to **check your airline's policy about using safety seats during takeoff and landing.** Safety seats cannot obstruct any other passengers in the row, so get an appropriate seat assignment early.

When making your reservation, **request children's meals or a freestanding bassinet** if you need them; the latter is available only to those seated at the bulkhead, where there's enough legroom. Remember, however, that bulkhead seats may not have their own overhead bins, and there's no storage space in front of you.

GROUP TRAVEL

If you're planning to take your kids on a tour, look for companies that specialize in family travel.

➤ FAMILY-FRIENDLY TOUR OPERATORS: **Grandtravel** (✉ 6900 Wisconsin Ave., Suite 706, Chevy Chase, MD 20815, ☎ 301/986–0790 or 800/247–7651) for people traveling with grandchildren ages 7–17. **Families Welcome!** (✉ 92 N. Main St., Ashland, OR 97520, ☎ 541/482–6121 or 800/326–0724, FAX 541/482–0660).

CONSULATES

➤ U.K.: The **British Consulate** (✉ 226 Walnut St., 19106, ☎ 215/925–0118) is an honorary one with limited powers, but it can refer British travelers to other sources of assistance.

CONSUMER PROTECTION

Whenever possible, **pay with a major credit card** so you can cancel payment if there's a problem, provided that you have documentation. This is a good practice whether you're buying travel arrangements before your trip or shopping at your destination.

If you're doing business with a particular company for the first time, **contact your local Better Business Bureau** and **the attorney general's offices** in your state and the company's home state, as well. Have any complaints been filed?

Finally, if you're buying a package or tour, always **consider travel insurance** that includes default coverage (☞ Insurance, *below*).

➤ LOCAL BBBs: **Better Business Bureau of Philadelphia** (✉ 1930 Chestnut St., Box 2297, 19103, ☎ 215/985–9313). **Council of Better Business Bureaus** (✉ 4200 Wilson Blvd., Suite 800, Arlington, VA 22203, ☎ 703/276–0100, FAX 703/525–8277).

CUSTOMS & DUTIES

ENTERING THE U.S.

Visitors age 21 and over may import the following into the United States: 200 cigarettes or 50 cigars or 2 kilograms of tobacco, 1 liter of alcohol, and gifts worth $100. Prohibited items include meat products, seeds, plants, and fruits.

ENTERING CANADA

If you've been out of Canada for at least seven days, you may bring in C$500 worth of goods duty-free. If you've been away for fewer than seven days but more than 48 hours, the duty-free allowance drops to C$200; if your trip lasts 24–48 hours, the allowance is C$50. You may not pool allowances with family members. Goods claimed under the C$500 exemption may follow you by mail; those claimed under the lesser exemptions must accompany you.

Alcohol and tobacco products may be included in the seven-day and 48-hour exemptions but not in the 24-hour exemption. If you meet the age requirements of the province or territory through which you reenter Canada, you may bring in, duty-free, 1.14 liters (40 imperial ounces) of wine or liquor *or* 24 12-ounce cans or bottles of beer or ale. If you are 16 or older, you may bring in, duty-free, 200 cigarettes and 50 cigars; these items must accompany you.

You may send an unlimited number of gifts worth up to C$60 each duty-free to Canada. Label the package UNSOLICITED GIFT—VALUE UNDER $60. Alcohol and tobacco are excluded.

➤ INFORMATION: **Revenue Canada** (✉ 2265 St. Laurent Blvd. S, Ottawa, Ontario K1G 4K3, ☎ 613/993–0534, ☎ 800/461–9999 in Canada).

ENTERING THE U.K.

From countries outside the European Union (EU), including the United States, you may import, duty-free, 200 cigarettes or 50 cigars; 1 liter of spirits or 2 liters of fortified or sparkling wine or liqueurs; 2 liters of still table wine; 60 milliliters of perfume; 250 milliliters of toilet water; plus £136 worth of other goods, including gifts and souvenirs.

➤ INFORMATION: **HM Customs and Excise** (✉ Dorset House, Stamford St., London SE1 9NG, ☎ 0171/202–4227).

D

DISABILITIES & ACCESSIBILITY

TIPS & HINTS

When discussing accessibility with an operator or reservationist, **ask hard questions.** Are there any stairs, inside *or* out? Are there grab bars next to the toilet *and* in the shower/tub? How wide is the doorway to the room? To the bathroom? For the most extensive facilities meeting the latest legal specifications, **opt for newer accommodations,** which are more likely to have been designed with access in mind. Older buildings or ships may offer more limited facilities. Be sure to **discuss your needs before booking.**

➤ COMPLAINTS: **Disability Rights Section** (✉ U.S. Department of Justice, Box 66738, Washington, DC 20035-6738, ☎ 202/514–0301 or 800/514–0301, FAX 202/307–1198, TTY 202/514–0383 or 800/514–0383) for general complaints. **Aviation Consumer Protection Division** (☞ Air Travel, *above*) for airline-related problems. **Civil Rights Office** (✉ U.S. Department of Transportation, Departmental Office of Civil Rights, S-30, 400 7th St. SW, Room 10215, Washington, DC 20590, ☎ 202/366–4648) for problems with surface transportation.

TRAVEL AGENCIES & TOUR OPERATORS

The Americans with Disabilities Act requires that travel firms serve the needs of all travelers. That said, you should note that some agencies and operators specialize in making travel arrangements for individuals and groups with disabilities.

➤ TRAVELERS WITH MOBILITY PROBLEMS: **Access Adventures** (✉ 206 Chestnut Ridge Rd., Rochester, NY 14624, ☎ 716/889–9096), run by a former physical-rehabilitation counselor. **Hinsdale Travel Service** (✉ 201 E. Ogden Ave., Suite 100, Hinsdale, IL 60521, ☎ 630/325–1335), a travel agency that benefits from the advice of wheelchair traveler Janice Perkins. **Wheelchair Journeys** (✉ 16979 Redmond Way, Redmond, WA 98052, ☎ 206/885–2210 or 800/313–4751), for general travel arrangements.

➤ TRAVELERS WITH DEVELOPMENTAL DISABILITIES: **Sprout** (✉ 893 Amsterdam Ave., New York, NY 10025, ☎ 212/222–9575 or 888/222–9575, FAX 212/222–9768).

DISCOUNTS & DEALS

Be a smart shopper and **compare all your options before making a choice.** A plane ticket bought with a promotional coupon may not be cheaper than the least expensive fare from a discount ticket agency. For high-price travel purchases, such as packages or tours, keep in mind that what you get is just as important as what you save. Just because something is cheap doesn't mean it's a bargain.

LOOK IN YOUR WALLET

When you use your credit card to make travel purchases, you may get free travel-accident insurance, collision-damage insurance, and medical or legal assistance, depending on the card and the bank that issued it. American Express, MasterCard, and Visa provide one or more of these services, so **get a copy of your credit card's travel-benefits policy.** If you are a member of the American Automobile Association (AAA) or an oil-company-sponsored road-assistance plan, always **ask hotel or car-rental reservationists about auto-club discounts.** Some clubs offer additional discounts on tours, cruises, or admission to attractions. And don't forget that auto-club membership entitles you to free maps and trip-planning services.

DIAL FOR DOLLARS

To save money, **look into 1-800 discount reservations services,** which use their buying power to get a better price on hotels, airline tickets, even car rentals. When booking a room, always **call the hotel's local toll-free number** (if one is available) rather than the central reservations number—you'll often get a better price.

Always ask about special packages or corporate rates.

➤ AIRLINE TICKETS: ☎ 800/FLY–4–LESS. ☎ 800/FLY–ASAP.

➤ HOTEL ROOMS: **Accommodations Express** (☎ 800/444–7666). **Central Reservation Service (CRS)** (☎ 800/548–3311).

SAVE ON COMBOS

Packages and guided tours can both save you money, but don't confuse the two. When you buy a package, your travel remains independent, just as though you had planned and booked the trip yourself. Fly/drive packages, which combine airfare and car rental, are often a good deal. In cities **ask the local visitor center about hotel packages.** These often include tickets to major museum exhibits and other special events and some extra benefits. Philadelphia has been offering an increasing number of these in the past few years.

JOIN A CLUB?

Many companies sell discounts in the form of travel clubs and coupon books, but these cost money. You must use participating advertisers to get a deal, and only after you recoup the initial membership cost or book price do you begin to save. If you plan to use the club or coupons frequently, you may save considerably. Before signing up, **find out what discounts you get for free.**

➤ DISCOUNT CLUBS: **Entertainment Travel Editions** (✉ 2125 Butterfield Rd., Troy, MI 48084, ☎ 800/445–4137; $23–$48, depending on destination). **Great American Traveler** (✉ Box 27965, Salt Lake City, UT 84127, ☎ 800/548–2812; $49.95 per year). **Moment's Notice Discount Travel Club** (✉ 7301 New Utrecht Ave., Brooklyn, NY 11204, ☎ 718/234–6295; $25 per year). **Privilege Card International** (✉ 237 E. Front St., Youngstown, OH 44503, ☎ 330/746–5211 or 800/236–9732; $74.95 per year). **Sears's Mature Outlook** (✉ Box 9390, Des Moines, IA 50306, ☎ 800/336–6330; $14.95 per year). **Travelers Advantage** (✉ CUC Travel Service, 3033 S. Parker Rd., Suite 1000, Aurora, CO 80014, ☎ 800/548–1116 or 800/648–4037; $49 per year, single or family). **Worldwide**

Discount Travel Club (✉ 1674 Meridian Ave., Miami Beach, FL 33139, ☎ 305/534–2082; $50 per year family, $40 single).

DRIVING

Getting to and around Philadelphia by car is often difficult and at rush hour can be a nightmare. The main east–west freeway through the city, the Schuylkill Expressway (I–76), is often tied up for miles.

The main north–south highway through Philadelphia is the Delaware Expressway (I–95). To reach Center City heading southbound on I–95, take the Vine Street exit.

From the west the Pennsylvania Turnpike begins at the Ohio border and intersects the Schuylkill Expressway (I–76) at Valley Forge. The Schuylkill Expressway has several exits in Center City. The Northeast Extension of the turnpike, newly renamed I–476, runs from Scranton to Plymouth Meeting, north of Philadelphia. From the east the New Jersey Turnpike and I–295 access U.S. 30, which enters the city via the Benjamin Franklin Bridge, or New Jersey Route 42 and the Walt Whitman Bridge into South Philadelphia.

With the exception of a few wide streets (notably the Benjamin Franklin Parkway, Broad Street, Vine Street, and part of Market Street), streets in Center City are narrow and one-way. Parking in Center City can be tough. A spot at a parking meter, if you're lucky enough to find one, costs 25¢ per 15 minutes. Parking garages are plentiful, especially around Independence Park, City Hall, and the Pennsylvania Convention Center, but can charge up to $1.50 per 15 minutes and up to $20 or so for the day. Fortunately the city is compact, and you can easily **get around downtown on foot or by bus after you park your car.**

E

EMERGENCIES

Police, fire, and **ambulance,** ☎ 911.

➤ HOSPITALS: Near the historic area: **Pennsylvania Hospital** (✉ 8th and Spruce Sts., ☎ 215/829–3000 for information or ☎ 215/829–3358 for emergency room). Near City Hall:

Hahnemann (✉ Broad and Vine Sts., ☎ 215/762–7000 for general information or ☎ 215/448–7963) for emergency room). Near Rittenhouse Square: **Graduate Hospital** (✉ 1800 Lombard St., ☎ 215/893–2000 for general information or ☎ 215/893–2350 for emergency room).

➤ LATE-NIGHT PHARMACIES: **CVS Pharmacy** (✉ 10th and Reed Sts., ☎ 215/465–2130) is the 24-hour pharmacy closest to downtown, in South Philadelphia, 10 minutes by car. Downtown, **Corson's Pharmacy** (✉ 15th and Spruce Sts., ☎ 215/735–1386) is open 9 AM–9:45 PM Monday through Friday, 9–5 Saturday, and 9–2 Sunday. **Medical Tower Pharmacy** (✉ 255 S. 17th St., ☎ 215/545–3525) is open weekdays 8:30–7 and Saturday 8:30–4.

F

FERRY TRAVEL

The RiverLink Ferry, a seasonal (March–November) passenger ferry between Philadelphia and Camden, site of the New Jersey Aquarium, has hourly departures from Penn's Landing on the hour, weekdays 10–5, weekends 10–9, with extended hours for Penn's Landing and Blockbuster-Sony Entertainment Centre concerts. The cost is $5 round-trip.

➤ FERRY SERVICE: RiverLink Ferry (✉ Penn's Landing near Walnut St., ☎ 215/925–LINK).

G

GAY & LESBIAN TRAVEL

➤ GAY- AND LESBIAN-FRIENDLY TRAVEL AGENCIES: **Advance Damron** (✉ 1 Greenway Plaza, Suite 800, Houston, TX 77046, ☎ 713/850–1140 or 800/695–0880, FAX 713/888–1010). **Club Travel** (✉ 8739 Santa Monica Blvd., West Hollywood, CA 90069, ☎ 310/358–2200 or 800/429–8747, FAX 310/358–2222). **Islanders/Kennedy Travel** (✉ 183 W. 10th St., New York, NY 10014, ☎ 212/242–3222 or 800/988–1181, FAX 212/929–8530). **Now Voyager** (✉ 4406 18th St., San Francisco, CA 94114, ☎ 415/626–1169 or 800/255–6951, FAX 415/626–8626). **Yellowbrick Road** (✉ 1500 W. Balmoral Ave., Chicago, IL 60640, ☎ 773/561–1800 or 800/642–2488, FAX 773/561–4497).

Skylink Women's Travel (✉ 3577 Moorland Ave., Santa Rosa, CA 95407, ☎ 707/585–8355 or 800/225–5759, FAX 707/584–5637), serving lesbian travelers.

I

INSURANCE

Travel insurance is the best way to **protect yourself against financial loss.** The most useful policies are trip-cancellation-and-interruption, default, medical, and comprehensive insurance. Without insurance you will lose all or most of your money if you cancel your trip, regardless of the reason. It's essential that you **buy trip-cancellation-and-interruption insurance,** particularly if your airline ticket, cruise, or package tour is nonrefundable and cannot be changed. When considering how much coverage you need, look for a policy that will cover the cost of your trip plus the nondiscounted price of a one-way airline ticket, should you need to return home early. Also **consider default or bankruptcy insurance,** which protects you against a supplier's failure to deliver.

Citizens of the United Kingdom can buy an annual travel-insurance policy valid for most vacations during the year in which it's purchased. If you are pregnant or have a preexisting medical condition, make sure you're covered. According to the Association of British Insurers, a trade association representing 450 insurance companies, it's wise to buy extra medical coverage when you visit the United States.

If you have purchased an expensive vacation, comprehensive insurance is a must. **Look for comprehensive policies that include trip-delay insurance,** which will protect you in the event that weather problems cause you to miss your flight, tour, or cruise. A few insurers sell waivers for preexisting medical conditions. Companies that offer both features include Access America, Carefree Travel, Travel Insured International, and Travel Guard (☞ *below*).

Always **buy travel insurance directly from the insurance company**; if you buy it from a travel agency or tour operator that goes out of business, you probably will not be covered for the agency's or operator's default, a major risk. Before you make any purchase, **review your existing health and home-owner's policies** to find out whether they cover expenses incurred while traveling.

➤ TRAVEL INSURERS: In the U.S., **Access America** (⊠ 6600 W. Broad St., Richmond, VA 23230, ☎ 804/285–3300 or 800/284–8300), **Carefree Travel Insurance** (⊠ Box 9366, 100 Garden City Plaza, Garden City, NY 11530, ☎ 516/294–0220 or 800/323–3149), **Near Travel Services** (⊠ Box 1339, Calumet City, IL 60409, ☎ 708/868–6700 or 800/654–6700), **Travel Guard International** (⊠ 1145 Clark St., Stevens Point, WI 54481, ☎ 715/345–0505 or 800/826–1300), **Travel Insured International** (⊠ Box 280568, East Hartford, CT 06128-0568, ☎ 860/528–7663 or 800/243–3174), **Travelex Insurance Services** (⊠ 11717 Burt St., Suite 202, Omaha, NE 68154-1500, ☎ 402/445–8637 or 800/228–9792, FAX 800/867–9531), **Wallach & Company** (⊠ 107 W. Federal St., Box 480, Middleburg, VA 20118, ☎ 540/687–3166 or 800/237–6615). In Canada, **Mutual of Omaha** (⊠ Travel Division, 500 University Ave., Toronto, Ontario M5G 1V8, ☎ 416/598–4083, 800/268–8825 in Canada). In the U.K., **Association of British Insurers** (⊠ 51 Gresham St., London EC2V 7HQ, ☎ 0171/600–3333).

L
LODGING

APARTMENT & VILLA RENTALS

If you want a home base that's roomy enough for a family and comes with cooking facilities, **consider a furnished rental.** These can save you money; however, some rentals are luxury properties, economical only when your party is large. Home-exchange directories list rentals (often second homes owned by prospective house swappers), and some services search for a house or apartment for you and handle the paperwork. Some send an illustrated catalog; others send photographs only of specific properties, sometimes at a charge. Up-front registration fees may apply.

➤ RENTAL AGENTS: **Property Rentals International** (⊠ 1008 Mansfield

Crossing Rd., Richmond, VA 23236, ☎ 804/378–6054 or 800/220–3332, FAX 804/379–2073). **Rent-a-Home International** (⊠ 7200 34th Ave. NW, Seattle, WA 98117, ☎ 206/789–9377 or 800/488–7368, FAX 206/789–9379). **Hideaways International** (⊠ 767 Islington St., Portsmouth, NH 03801, ☎ 603/430–4433 or 800/843–4433, FAX 603/430–4444) is a travel club whose members arrange rentals among themselves; yearly membership is $99.

HOME EXCHANGES

If you would like to exchange your home for someone else's, **join a home-exchange organization,** which will send you its updated listings of available exchanges for a year and will include your own listing in at least one of them. Making the arrangements is up to you.

➤ EXCHANGE CLUBS: **HomeLink International** (⊠ Box 650, Key West, FL 33041, ☎ 305/294–7766 or 800/638–3841, FAX 305/294–1148) charges $83 per year.

M
MONEY

ATMS

Before leaving home, **make sure your credit cards have been programmed for ATM use.**

➤ ATM LOCATIONS: **Cirrus** (☎ 800/424–7787). **Plus** (☎ 800/843–7587).

P
PACKING FOR PHILADELPHIA

Portage and luggage trolleys are hard to find, so **pack light.** Philadelphia is a fairly casual city, although men will need a jacket and tie in some of the better restaurants. Jeans and sneakers or other casual clothing are fine for sightseeing. You'll need a heavy coat for winter, which can be cold and snowy. Summers are hot and humid, but you'll need a shawl or jacket for air-conditioned restaurants. Many areas are best explored on foot, so **bring good walking shoes.**

Bring an extra pair of eyeglasses or contact lenses in your carry-on luggage, and if you have a health problem, **pack enough medication** to last the entire trip. It's important that you

don't put prescription drugs or valuables in luggage to be checked: It might go astray.

LUGGAGE

In general you are entitled to check two bags on flights within the United States. A third piece may be brought on board, but it must fit easily under the seat in front of you or in the overhead compartment.

If you are flying between two foreign destinations, note that baggage allowances may be determined not by piece but by weight—generally 88 pounds (40 kilograms) in first class, 66 pounds (30 kilograms) in business class, and 44 pounds (20 kilograms) in economy. If your flight between two cities abroad *connects* with your transatlantic or transpacific flight, the piece method still applies.

Airline liability for baggage is limited to $1,250 per person on flights within the United States. On international flights it amounts to $9.07 per pound or $20 per kilogram for checked baggage (roughly $640 per 70-pound bag) and $400 per passenger for unchecked baggage. Insurance for losses exceeding these amounts can be bought from the airline at check-in for about $10 per $1,000 of coverage; note that this coverage excludes a rather extensive list of items, which are shown on your airline ticket.

Before departure, **itemize your bags' contents** and their worth and label the bags with your name, address, and phone number. (If you use your home address, cover it so that potential thieves can't see it readily.) Inside each bag **pack a copy of your itinerary.** At check-in **make sure each bag is correctly tagged** with the destination airport's three-letter code. If your bags arrive damaged or fail to arrive, file a written report with the airline before leaving the airport.

PASSPORTS & VISAS

CANADIANS

A passport is not required to enter the United States.

U.K. CITIZENS

British citizens need a valid passport to enter the United States. If you are staying for fewer than 90 days on vacation, with a return or onward ticket, you probably will not need a visa. However, you will need to fill out the Visa Waiver Form, 1-94W, supplied by the airline.

➤ INFORMATION: **London Passport Office** (☎ 0990/21010) for fees and documentation requirements and to request an emergency passport. **U.S. Embassy Visa Information Line** (☎ 01891/200–290) for U.S. visa information; calls cost 49p per minute or 39p per minute cheap rate. **U.S. Embassy Visa Branch** (✉ 5 Upper Grosvenor St., London W1A 2JB) for U.S. visa information; send a self-addressed, stamped envelope. Write the **U.S. Consulate General** (✉ Queen's House, Queen St., Belfast BTI 6EO) if you live in Northern Ireland.

R

RADIO STATIONS

➤ AM: **KYW 1060**, news and weather. **WCZN 1590**, country.

➤ FM: **WXPN 88.5** and **WHYY 90.1**, National Public Radio. **WMMR 93.3**, album rock.

S

SAFETY

As in many other major cities, sections of Philadelphia range from posh old-money enclaves to inner-city slums. Center City and the major tourist destinations are safe during the day. After dark exercise caution in the neighborhoods ringing downtown. You can **ask hotel personnel or the Philadelphia Visitors Center about the safety of places** you're interested in visiting. As you would in any city, **keep your car locked and watch your possessions carefully.** Remember to **remove items from your car.**

Subway crime has diminished in recent years. During the day cars are crowded and safe. However, platforms and cars can be relatively empty in the late evening hours. SEPTA train travelers should **avoid North Philadelphia Station**, which is in an economically depressed neighborhood. Instead of waiting for a subway or train in off hours, **take a cab late at night.**

SENIOR-CITIZEN TRAVEL

To qualify for age-related discounts, **mention your senior-citizen status up front** when booking hotel reservations (not when checking out) and before you're seated in restaurants (not when paying the bill). Note that discounts may be limited to certain menus, days, or hours. When renting a car, **ask about promotional car-rental discounts,** which can be cheaper than senior-citizen rates.

Seniors should avail themselves of an enormous array of discounts. From cut-rate Amtrak tickets to free rides on SEPTA buses, from numerous hotel discount rates to free admissions at attractions, from 10% senior discounts at various restaurants to flat-rate programs at leading car-rental companies, Philly promises its senior-citizen visitors will leave the city richer in more ways than one. For a complete list on all the discount options, **ask for the "Seniors on the Go" booklet,** available from the Philadelphia Convention and Visitors Bureau (☞ Visitor Information, *below*).

➤ EDUCATIONAL TRAVEL PROGRAMS: Elderhostel (✉ 75 Federal St., 3rd floor, Boston, MA 02110, ☎ 617/426–8056).

SIGHTSEEING

Following are some sightseeing options for Philadelphia. For information about special tours in the Brandywine Valley, Bucks County, and Lancaster County, *see* the A to Z sections at the end of Chapters 8, 9, and 10.

CARRIAGE RIDES

Numerous horse-drawn carriages wend their way through the narrow streets of the historic area. Tours last anywhere from 15 minutes to an hour and cost from $15 to $60. Carriages line up on Chestnut and 5th streets near Independence Hall and at Head House Square, 2nd Street between Pine and Lombard streets, from about 10 AM to 2 AM. You can reserve a carriage and be picked up anywhere downtown. Carriages operate year-round, except when the temperature is below 20°F or above 94°F.

➤ CARRIAGE OPERATORS: **Ben Franklin Carriages** (☎ 215/923–8516),

Philadelphia Carriage Company (☎ 215/922–6840), **'76 Carriage Company** (☎ 215/923–8516), and **Society Hill Carriage Company** (☎ 215/627–6128).

MULTILINGUAL TOURS

➤ TOUR COMPANY: **Centipede Tours** (☎ 215/735–3123) can supply German-, French-, Spanish-, Russian-, Chinese-, Japanese-, Swedish-, Finnish-, Danish-, or Italian-speaking guides for all parts of Philadelphia.

ORIENTATION TOURS

Two companies offer narrated tours in buses designed to resemble Victorian-style trolleys. With both companies, the fare is an all-day pass, allowing unlimited on/offs. Board at any stop including the Philadelphia Visitors Center, the Pennsylvania Convention Center, and the Liberty Bell.

The Philadelphia Trolley Works tour takes about 90 minutes and costs $10. The tour makes 15 stops on a route covering the historic area, the Benjamin Franklin Parkway, the Avenue of the Arts (✉ S. Broad St.), and Penn's Landing.

American Trolley Tours offers free pickup at major hotels as well as historic sites, the Pennsylvania Convention Center and the Visitors Centers. Tours run every 45 minutes between 9 and 3:45 and take approximately two hours; the cost is $14.

Gray Line Tours gives a three-hour bus tour of the city focusing on the historic and cultural areas, plus tours of Valley Forge, Bucks County, and Rittenhousetown. Most tours cost $16 and leave from 30th Street Station twice daily.

➤ TOUR COMPANIES: **American Trolley Tours** (☎ 215/333–2119); **Gray Line Tours** (☎ 215/569–3666); **Philadelphia Trolley Works** (☎ 215/923–8522).

RIVER CRUISES

The *Spirit of Philadelphia* runs lunch and dinner cruises along the Delaware River. This three-deck ship leaves Penn's Landing at Lombard Circle and Columbus Boulevard for lunch, dinner, and moonlight cruises. Dinner cruises include a band and singing waitstaff, while both moonlight and

Saturday afternoon "Philly Jam" cruises have a bar, band, and dancing.

Liberty Belle Cruises, aboard a new 600-passenger Mississippi paddle-wheel riverboat, offer lunch, dinner, and Sunday brunch cruises with a banjo player, sing-alongs, and a buffet. Board at Penn's Landing (✉ Columbus Blvd. at Lombard Circle).

➤ CRUISE BOATS: *Liberty Belle* Cruises (☎ 215/629–1131); *Spirit of Philadelphia* (☎ 215/923–1419).

SPECIAL-INTEREST TOURS

➤ ARCHITECTURE: **Foundation for Architecture** (☎ 215/569–3187) offers the "Hidden River Tour: A View of the Schuylkill," and several other Schuylkill River boat tours on some Saturdays and Sundays.

➤ ITALIAN MARKET: **Italian Market Tours** (☎ 215/334–6008) gives an afternoon's introduction to America's oldest outdoor ethnic market. The route includes cheese, meat and pastry shops, as well as sites ranging from the Mario Lanza Museum to the street where Sylvester Stallone's character in *Rocky* lived.

WALKING TOURS

➤ TOUR COMPANIES: **Audio Walk and Tour** (☎ 215/925–1234) from the Norman Rockwell Museum (✉ 6th and Sansom Sts.) offers go-at-your-own-pace tours of historic Philadelphia with cassette players and an accompanying map. **Centipede Tours** (☎ 215/735–3123) offers a candle-light stroll through Society Hill led by guides in Colonial dress. Tours begin at the Thomas Bond House (✉ 129 S. 2nd St.) Friday and Saturday at 6:30 PM, May–October. **Foundation for Architecture** (☞ Special-Interest Tours, *above*) tours focus on architecture but also touch on history. Area tours include Chestnut Hill, Manayunk, and Spruce Hill. Theme tours include Art Deco, skyscrapers, the University of Pennsylvania campus, and Judaic architecture and influence. Most tours begin weekends at 2 and occasionally on Wednesday at 6.

STUDENTS

To save money, **look into deals available through student-oriented travel agencies.** To qualify you'll need a bona fide student ID card. Members

of international student groups are also eligible.

➤ STUDENT IDs AND SERVICES: **Council on International Educational Exchange** (✉ CIEE, 205 E. 42nd St., 14th floor, New York, NY 10017, ☎ 212/822–2600 or 888/268–6245, FAX 212/822–2699), for mail orders only, in the United States. **Travel Cuts** (✉ 187 College St., Toronto, Ontario M5T 1P7, ☎ 416/979–2406 or 800/667–2887) in Canada.

➤ HOSTELING: **Hostelling International–American Youth Hostels** (✉ 733 15th St. NW, Suite 840, Washington, DC 20005, ☎ 202/783–6161, FAX 202/783–6171). **Hostelling International–Canada** (✉ 400–205 Catherine St., Ottawa, Ontario K2P 1C3, ☎ 613/237–7884, FAX 613/237–7868). **Youth Hostel Association of England and Wales** (✉ Trevelyan House, 8 St. Stephen's Hill, St. Albans, Hertfordshire AL1 2DY, ☎ 01727/855215 or 01727/845047, FAX 01727/844126). Membership in the U.S., $25; in Canada, C$26.75; in the U.K., £9.30).

➤ STUDENT TOURS: **Contiki Holidays** (✉ 300 Plaza Alicante, Suite 900, Garden Grove, CA 92840, ☎ 714/740–0808 or 800/266–8454, FAX 714/740–2034).

SUBWAY TRAVEL

The Broad Street Subway runs from Fern Rock station in the northern part of the city to Pattison Avenue and the sports complex (CoreStates Center and Veterans Stadium) in South Philadelphia. The Market–Frankford line runs across the city from the western suburb of Upper Darby to Frankford in the northeast. Both lines shut down from midnight to 5 AM, during which time "Night Owl" buses operate along the same routes.

➤ SCHEDULES AND INFORMATION: **SEPTA** (☎ 215/580–7800; ☞ Bus Travel, *above*).

T

TAXES

SALES

The main sales tax in Pennsylvania is 7%; this also applies to restaurant meals. Various other taxes—including a liquor tax—apply. There is no sales tax on clothing.

HOTEL

Besides the room rate, you pay a 13% hotel tax (7% state, 6% city).

TAXIS

Cabs cost $1.80 at the flag throw and then $1.80–$2.30 per mile. They are plentiful during the day downtown—especially along Broad Street and near hotels and train stations. At night and outside Center City, taxis are scarce. You can call for a cab, but they frequently show up late and occasionally never arrive. Be persistent: Calling back if the cab is late will often yield results.

➤ CAB COMPANIES: **Olde City Taxi** ☎ 215/338–0838). **Quaker City Cab** (☎ 215/728–8000). **Yellow Cab** (☎ 215/922–8400).

TELEPHONES

CALLING HOME

AT&T, MCI, and Sprint long-distance services make calling home relatively convenient and let you avoid hotel surcharges. Typically you dial an 800 number in the United States.

➤ TO OBTAIN ACCESS CODES: **AT&T USADirect** (☎ 800/874–4000). **MCI Call USA** (☎ 800/444–4444). **Sprint Express** (☎ 800/793–1153).

TOUR OPERATORS

Buying a prepackaged tour or independent vacation can make your trip less expensive and more hassle-free. Because everything is prearranged, you'll spend less time planning. Operators that handle several hundred thousand travelers per year can use their purchasing power to give you a good price. Their high volume may also indicate financial stability. But some small companies provide more personalized service; because they tend to specialize, they may be more knowledgeable about a given area.

A GOOD DEAL?

The more your package or tour includes, the better you can predict the ultimate cost of your vacation. Make sure you know exactly what is covered, and **beware of hidden costs.** Are taxes, tips, and service charges included? Transfers and baggage handling? Entertainment and excursions? These can add up.

If the package or tour you are considering is priced lower than in your wildest dreams, **be skeptical.** Also, **make sure your travel agent knows the accommodations** and other services. Ask about the hotel's location, room size, beds, and whether it has a pool, room service, or programs for children, if you care about these. Has your agent been there in person or sent others you can contact?

BUYER BEWARE

Each year consumers are stranded or lose their money when tour operators—even very large ones with excellent reputations—go out of business. So **check out the operator.** Find out how long the company has been in business and ask several agents about its reputation. **Don't book unless the firm has a consumer-protection program.**

Members of the National Tour Association and United States Tour Operators Association are required to set aside funds to cover your payments and travel arrangements in case the company defaults. Nonmembers may carry insurance instead. Look for the details, and for the name of an underwriter with a solid reputation, in the operator's brochure. Note: When it comes to tour operators, **don't trust escrow accounts.** Although the Department of Transportation watches over charter-flight operators, no regulatory body prevents tours operators from raiding the till. You may want to protect yourself by buying travel insurance that includes a tour-operator default provision. For more information, *see* Consumer Protection, *above*.

It's also a good idea to choose a company that participates in the American Society of Travel Agent's Tour Operator Program (TOP). This gives you a forum if there are any disputes between you and your tour operator; ASTA will act as mediator.

➤ TOUR-OPERATOR RECOMMENDATIONS: **National Tour Association** (✉ NTA, 546 E. Main St., Lexington, KY 40508, ☎ 606/226–4444 or 800/755–8687). **United States Tour Operators Association** (✉ USTOA, 342 Madison Ave., Suite 1522, New

York, NY 10173, ☎ 212/599–6599,
FAX 212/599–6744). **American Society
of Travel Agents** (☞ *below*).

USING AN AGENT

Travel agents are excellent resources.
In fact, large operators accept book-
ings made only through travel agents.
But it's a good idea to **collect
brochures from several agencies,**
because some agents' suggestions may
be influenced by relationships with
tour and package firms that reward
them for volume sales. If you have a
special interest, **find an agent with
expertise in that area;** ASTA (☞
Travel Agencies, *below*) has a data-
base of specialists worldwide. Do
some homework on your own, too:
Local tourism boards can provide
information about lesser-known and
small-niche operators, some of which
may sell only direct.

SINGLE TRAVELERS

Prices for packages and tours are
usually quoted per person, based on
two sharing a room. If traveling solo,
you may be required to pay the full
double-occupancy rate. Some operators eliminate this surcharge if you
agree to be matched with a roommate
of the same sex, even if one is not
found by departure time.

GROUP TOURS

Among companies that sell tours to
Philadelphia, the following are nationally known, have a proven reputation, and offer plenty of options.
The classifications used below repre-
sent different price categories. You'll
probably encounter these terms when
talking to a travel agent or tour
operator. The key difference is usually
in accommodations, which run from
budget to better, and better to better-
yet to best. Escorted tours of Philadelphia typically include a tour of Amish
country and the sights of Bucks
County.

➤ DELUXE: **Globus** (✉ 5301 S. Federal Circle, Littleton, CO 80123–
2980, ☎ 303/797–2800 or 800/221–
0090, FAX 303/347–2080). **Tauck
Tours** (✉ Box 5027, 276 Post Rd. W,
Westport, CT 06881–5027, ☎ 203/
226–6911 or 800/468–2825, FAX
203/221–6828).

➤ FIRST-CLASS: **Collette Tours** (✉ 162
Middle St., Pawtucket, RI 02860, ☎

401/728–3805 or 800/832–4656, FAX
401/728–1380).

➤ BUDGET: **Cosmos** (☞ Globus, *above*).

PACKAGES

Like group tours, independent vacation packages are available from
major tour operators and airlines.
The companies listed below offer
packages in a broad price range.

➤ AIR/HOTEL: **American Airlines Fly
AAway Vacations** (☎ 800/321–
2121). **Delta Dream Vacations** (☎
800/872–7786).

➤ HOTEL ONLY: **SuperCities** (✉ 139
Main St., Cambridge, MA 02142, ☎
800/333–1234).

➤ CUSTOM PACKAGES: **Amtrak's Great
American Vacations** (☎ 800/321–
8684).

➤ FROM THE U.K.: **British Airways
Holidays** (✉ Astral Towers, Betts
Way, London Rd., Crawley, West
Sussex RH10 2XA, ☎ 01293/723–
121). **Cosmos Holidays** (✉ Ground
Floor, Dale House, Tiviot Dale,
Stockport, Cheshire SK1 1TB, ☎
0161/480–5799). **Jetsave** (✉ Sussex
House, London Rd., East Grinstead,
West Sussex RH19 1LD, ☎ 01342/
312–033). **Kuoni Travel** (✉ Kuoni
House, Dorking, Surrey RH5 4AZ,
☎ 01306/742–222). **Premier Holi-
days** (✉ Premier Travel Centre,
Westbrook, Milton Rd., Cambridge
CB4 1YG, ☎ 01223/516–688).

THEME TRIPS

For additional theme trips, *see* Chapter 10.

➤ AMISH LIFE: **Lang's Great Escapes**
(✉ Box 117386, Dept. STI,
Burlingame, CA 94011, ☎ 415/343–
9705, FAX 415/343–9044) has trips
that foster personal interaction with
the Amish, such as sharing a meal
with an Amish family or riding in a
horse-drawn buggy. Trips may include a visit to Longwood Gardens or
Valley Forge.

➤ SPORTS: **Dan Chavez's Sports
Empire** (✉ Box 6169, Lakewood, CA
90714, ☎ 310/809–6930 or 800/
255–5258) has packages that include
hotel accommodations, air transportation, and tickets to see the
baseball Phillies, football Eagles, and
other local Philadelphia teams.

TRAIN TRAVEL

Philadelphia's 30th Street Station (✉ 30th and Market Sts.) is a major stop on Amtrak's Northeast Corridor line. You can **travel by train between Philadelphia and New York City on the cheap** by taking the SEPTA commuter line R7 to Trenton, New Jersey, and transferring to a NJ Transit commuter line to Manhattan. Ask for the excursion rate. The trip takes an extra 30 minutes, but costs about $12, versus Amtrak's $36. Amtrak also serves Philadelphia from points west, including Harrisburg, Pittsburgh, and Chicago.

At the 30th Street Station you can connect with SEPTA commuter trains to two downtown stations—Suburban Station, at 16th Street and John F. Kennedy Boulevard (near major hotels), and Market East Station, at 10th and Market streets (near the historic district)—and to outlying areas.

➤ SCHEDULES AND INFORMATION: **30th Street Station** (☎ 215/222–7820). **SEPTA** (☎ 215/580–7800). **Amtrak** (☎ 215/824–1600 or 800/872–7245).

WITHIN PHILADELPHIA

Philadelphia's fine network of commuter trains, operated by SEPTA (☞ Bus Travel, *above*), serves both the city and the suburbs. The famous Main Line, a cluster of affluent suburbs, got its start—and its name—from the Pennsylvania Railroad route that ran westward from Center City.

All trains serve 30th Street Station (✉ 30th and Market Sts.), where they connect to Amtrak trains, Suburban Station (✉ 16th St. and John F. Kennedy Blvd., across from the Visitors Center), and Market East Station (✉ 10th and Market Sts.), beneath the Gallery at Market East shopping complex. Fares, which vary according to route and time of travel, range from $2.50 to $5 one-way. These trains are your best bet for reaching Germantown, Chestnut Hill, Merion (site of the Barnes Foundation), and other suburbs.

PATCO (Port Authority Transit Corporation) High Speed Line trains run underground from 16th and Locust streets to Lindenwold, New Jersey. Trains stop at 13th and Locust, 9th and Locust, and 8th and Market streets, then continue across the Benjamin Franklin Bridge to Camden. It's one way to get to the New Jersey State Aquarium or the Blockbuster-Sony Entertainment Centre; NJ Transit has a shuttle bus from the Broadway stop to the aquarium on weekends and to the center during performances. Fares run 75¢ to $1.60. Sit in the very front seat for a great view going across the bridge.

➤ SCHEDULES AND INFORMATION: **PATCO** (☎ 215/922–4600). **SEPTA** (☎ 215/580–7800).

TRAVEL AGENCIES

A good travel agent puts your needs first. Look for an agency that has been in business at least five years, emphasizes customer service, and has someone on staff who specializes in your destination. In addition, **make sure the agency belongs to the American Society of Travel Agents** (ASTA). If your travel agency is also acting as your tour operator, *see* Tour Operators, *above*.

➤ LOCAL AGENT REFERRALS: **American Society of Travel Agents** (✉ ASTA, 1101 King St., Suite 200, Alexandria, VA 22314, ☎ 800/965–2782 24 hr hot line, FAX 703/684–8319). **Alliance of Canadian Travel Associations** (✉ Suite 201, 1729 Bank St., Ottawa, Ontario K1V 7Z5, ☎ 613/521–0474, FAX 613/521–0805). **Association of British Travel Agents** (✉ 55–57 Newman St., London W1P 4AH, ☎ 0171/637–2444, FAX 0171/637–0713).

TRAVEL GEAR

Travel catalogs specialize in useful items, such as compact alarm clocks and travel irons, that can **save space when packing.**

➤ MAIL-ORDER CATALOGS: **Magellan's** (☎ 800/962–4943, FAX 805/568–5406). **Orvis Travel** (☎ 800/541–3541, FAX 540/343–7053). **TravelSmith** (☎ 800/950–1600, FAX 800/950–1656).

TROLLEYS

Philadelphia once had an extensive trolley network, and nostalgia buffs can still ride on two SEPTA (☞ Bus

Travel, *above*) lines in some of the few remaining Presidential Conference Committee cars, popular in the 1940s. The "Welcome Line" runs a short downtown loop, with some cars continuing out to the zoo in West Fairmount Park. The "Chestnut Hill Trolley" operates on Saturday and Sunday along Germantown Avenue in the northwest section of the city. For privately run trolleys, *see* Orientation Tours *in* Sightseeing, *above*.

U
U.S. GOVERNMENT

The U.S. government can be an excellent source of inexpensive travel information. When planning your trip, **find out what government materials are available.**

➤ PAMPHLETS: **Consumer Information Center** (✉ Consumer Information Catalogue, Pueblo, CO 81009, ☎ 719/948–3334) for a free catalog that includes travel titles.

VISITOR INFORMATION

For general information before you go, call the Convention and Visitors Bureau, Independence National Historical Park, and state tourism office. When you get there, stop by the Philadelphia Visitors Center, just one block from City Hall, and the Independence National Historical Park visitor center. If you are planning to make side trips from Philadelphia or are traveling on to Bucks County or Lancaster County, you should also *see* Visitor Information *in* the A to Z sections of Chapters 8, 9, and 10.

➤ CITY: **Philadelphia Convention and Visitors Bureau** (✉ 1515 Market St., Suite 2020, 19102, ☎ 215/636–3300 or 800/537–7676, FAX 215/636–

3327). **Philadelphia Visitors Center** (✉ 16th Street and John F. Kennedy Blvd., ☎ 215/636–1666).

➤ NATIONAL PARKS: **Independence National Historical Park** (✉ Visitor Center, 3rd and Chestnut Sts., ☎ 215/597–8974 or 215/597–1785 TTY; 215/597–8974 for a recorded message; mailing address is ✉ 313 Walnut St., 19106.

➤ STATE: **Pennsylvania Office of Travel and Tourism** (✉ Forum Bldg., Room 404, Harrisburg 17120, ☎ 717/787–5453 or 800/847–4872 for brochures).

➤ IN THE U.K.: **Pennsylvania Tourism Office** (✉ Suite 302, 11–15 Betterton St., Covent Garden, London WC2H 9BP, ☎ 0171/470–8801, FAX 0171/470–8810).

W
WHEN TO GO

Like other northern American cities, Philadelphia can be hot and humid in the summer and cold in winter (winter snowfall averages 21 inches). However, any time is right to enjoy the special pleasures offered throughout the year. *See* Festivals and Seasonal Events *in* Chapter 1 for the city's special-events calendar. The period around July 4th is particularly festive; there are special activities in the historic area throughout the summer.

CLIMATE

The following are average daily maximum and minimum temperatures for Philadelphia.

➤ FORECASTS: **Weather Channel Connection** (☎ 900/932–8437), 95¢ per minute from a Touch-Tone phone.

CLIMATE IN PHILADELPHIA

Jan.	40F	4C	May	72F	22C	Sept.	76F	24C
	27	- 3		54	12		61	16
Feb.	41F	5C	June	81F	27C	Oct.	67F	19C
	27	- 3		63	17		50	10
Mar.	49F	9C	July	85F	29C	Nov.	54F	12C
	34	- 1		68	20		40	- 4
Apr.	61F	16C	Aug.	83F	28C	Dec.	43F	6C
	43	6		67	19		31	- 1

1 Destination: Philadelphia and the Pennsylvania Dutch Country

YO, PHILADELPHIA!

YO, WORLD! Which is not a mere "Hello," but a run-them-all-together salutation of "Hithere," "Howareya," and "Have-a-good-day."

Philadelphians claim credit for "Yo" as a greeting, although they concede it wasn't in vogue when Quaker William Penn founded Philadelphia or when the city's most distinguished citizen, Benjamin Franklin, prowled the streets in pensive solitude. Instead, a muscle-bound movie hero may be the source of its popularity.

In the movie *Rocky,* Philadelphians shout "Yo, Rocky!" as the underdog boxer jogs over some of the city's cobbled streets, through the open-air Italian Market, up the Benjamin Franklin Parkway (America's "Champs-Elysées"), and up the expansive steps of the Philadelphia Museum of Art. Reaching the top, he raises his arms in a "V" in sweet anticipation of victory.

Today many people try to imitate Rocky's dash up the 99 steps of this sandstone-color Greco-Roman building before entering to browse through its fabled art treasures. That incongruity is only one of the many examples of Philadelphia's audacious uniqueness.

Philadelphia is a fountainhead of superlatives cherished by both historians and tourists: the world's largest city-owned park, Fairmount Park; the oldest art school in America, the Pennsylvania Academy of the Fine Arts; the first U.S. medical school to admit women, Women's Medical College of Pennsylvania (now part of Allegheny University); the oldest natural science museum, the Academy of Natural Sciences; the oldest U.S. opera house still in use, the Academy of Music; the first library in America to circulate books, the Library Company of Philadelphia, founded by Benjamin Franklin; the world's largest sculpture atop a building, the statue of William Penn atop City Hall; the oldest black newspaper in America, the *Philadelphia Tribune;* the oldest African Methodist Episcopal church, Mother Bethel A.M.E.; and the nation's oldest street of continuous occupation, Elfreth's

Alley, a narrow one-block street of 33 Colonial homes. All of these buildings still breathe architectural vitality. Or as that popular song cheerfully promises, "Everything old is new again."

But if love is a many-splendored thing, the name, Philadelphia, is a many-storied legend.

The "Philadelphia Lawyer," long a symbol of legal genius was probably invented when a gout-ravaged, white-haired Philadelphian, Andrew Hamilton, successfully defended Peter Zenger in the nation's first libel case in 1735. The plaintiff was New York governor William Cosby (no relation, of course, to a famous and cherished Philadelphia son, Bill Cosby).

The Philadelphia Story amused theater goers with its inside peek at upper-class eccentricities. *The Philadelphia Negro,* by W. E. B. DuBois, set a standard for sociological research. Philadelphia Cream Cheese enhances hors d'oeuvres (although the name alone doesn't claim to titillate taste buds). And Philadelphians still yearn to make the world forget W. C. Fields's suggested impudence for his epitaph: "On the whole I'd rather be in Philadelphia."

Classical music lovers around the world pay homage to the Philadelphia Orchestra for its buoyant interpretations of Tchaikovsky. During winter the orchestra delights its fans in the chandeliered splendor of the Academy of Music, a building modeled after La Scala Opera House. When summer comes, the orchestra moves to Fairmount Park's outdoor Mann Center for the Performing Arts, where music lovers can lie on blankets under the stars and soar with the classics.

Musical diversity is a Philadelphia tradition. Jazz still reflects the swinging sassiness of three Philadelphia jazz greats, Dizzy Gillespie, Stan Getz, and John Coltrane. Popular music went through a golden period when South Philadelphia's "Golden Boys"—Frankie Avalon, Fabian, Jimmy Darren, and Bobby Rydell—seduced a whole generation into swooning to their love songs. "Philly Sounds" still transform contemporary music, with Teddy Pendergrass, the O'Jays, the Stylistics, and the irrepressible Patti LaBelle, who can blow a hole in your soul every time she belts out a tune. If Americans have "danced by the light of the moon," they owe that terpsichorean pleasure to a Philadelphian. South Philadelphian Chubby Checker popularized the "Twist"—and America's sacroiliacs have never been the same since.

The Philadelphia metropolitan area also has an amazing array of institutions of higher education, including a University for the Arts. *Parade* magazine nominated Philadelphia's Central High School as one of the nation's 12 best high schools. The city wins high marks nationally as a center for medical training and research, with six medical schools as well as veterinary medicine, pharmacy, and podiatry schools.

Given this explosive creativity, it's easy to understand why no city has nurtured the arts more lovingly. Visitors can share that affection when they visit the majestic Free Library with its Parthenon-like facade, the famed Rodin Museum, and the Museum of American Art of the Pennsylvania Academy of the Fine Arts, a spectacular urban maharajah's palace.

But this "Athens of America" has also encouraged commerce to be an equally dominant force. Four of the city's most distinctive buildings are the oval-front Philadelphia Merchant's Exchange (1832), which majestically adjoins a cobblestoned street; the huge glass-paned dome that capacious Memorial Hall wears like a Victorian dowager's tiara; Independence Blue Cross's blue-glass-tinted headquarters at 1901 Market Street; and the stately City Hall, an exquisite example of Second French Empire style.

Visitors to the nation's capital may have noticed City Hall's architectural twin, the Executive Office Building, across the street from the White House. Ironically, this City Hall also became an excuse for resisting progress. An unspoken rule decreed that no building could be constructed higher than City Hall, with its statue of William Penn on top. Eventually, Philadelphia's plow-resisting mentality succumbed to American ingenuity. Today Liberty Place, the Mellon Bank Center, and other skyscrapers have virtually doubled the height of the city's skyline.

In wintertime Philadelphians follow convention. They lunch indoors. But when summer arrives, they lunch in their ubiquitous park. Fairmount Park winds through the city, an urban oasis from smoke-clogged, noisy traffic jams. You can relax in its verdant serenity with noon-day picnics, softball tournaments, and family barbecues. The Schuylkill River meanders through the park and attracts a daily stream of neighborhood anglers and rowers from the city's 13 rowing clubs.

Because Quaker William Penn founded Philadelphia, Quakers quickly dominated the city's early political and commercial life. The Quaker City influence has diminished, but the memory lingers. Today the nation's most enduring exercise in multiethnicity flavors the city's political and social life.

Although all of the city's founding fathers were WASPs, Philadelphia soon opened its arms to the world's "tired . . . huddled masses, yearning to be free." Successive waves of immigrants swarmed into Philadelphia as they did into New York City. Mention the name of a neighborhood, and Philadelphians will candidly identify its ethnic abundance: Italian South Philadelphia, black North Philadelphia, Irish Olney, Jewish Northeast, Puerto Rican Hunting Park, Chestnut Hill WASPs, Center City Chinatown, Vietnamese West Philadelphia, Polish Port Richmond, and Ukrainian Nicetown. Each enclave's lifestyles and restaurants exalt its ethnic heritage.

AT THE SAME TIME, the city's peoplescape is changing. Recently arrived yuppies are gentrifying black and Puerto Rican low-income neighborhoods within walking distance of Center City office buildings and the art museum. The relentless survival of ethnic neighborhoods, however, unfrocks a won't-lie-down-and-die spirit behind the city's name.

William Penn chose the name "Philadelphia" (Greek for "brotherly love"). He hoped it would fill expectations for his "Holy Experiment"—"you shall be governed by laws of your own making, and live a free, and if you will, a sober and industrious people." Since 1682 Philadelphia has diligently met all of those goals, even if the great journalist Lincoln Steffens dubbed it in 1903 "the worst-governed city in the country."

But Philadelphians have been forced to cope with the reality that their "City of Brotherly Love" is no more brotherly—nor even sisterly—than any other American city. Philadelphia has endured its share of white-black confrontations, other interethnic battles (early settlers roaming the streets, beating up Germans and Quakers), and electoral decisions decided solely on race.

When the controversial and colorful former top cop Frank L. Rizzo held the office of mayor in the 1970s, the Italian-American community provided his staunchest electoral base. When the city's first black mayor, W. Wilson Goode, made a more perverse kind of history by approving the bombing of a neighborhood in 1985, black voters supported his reelection with 98% of their vote, even though an entire city block of black homes was incinerated and 11 blacks (including five children) were killed.

Every city should enjoy an interlude of greatness. Between 1949 and 1962 Richardson Dilworth and Joseph Clark dominated the city's politics, and "for one brief, shining moment," Philadelphia seemed like Camelot. Although the "Dilworth-Clark Renaissance" lasted only 13 years, it set a standard by which Philadelphia is still judged. These men dared to envision a people who would owe a higher loyalty to their city than to their neighborhoods.

TODAY THE CITY is riding high under the second term of Mayor Ed Rendell, a popular, energetic, aggressive leader who has good connections in Washington. He is given much of the credit for the revitalization of Center City, specifically the Avenue of the Arts and the Delaware waterfront development. In general he has made the city more inviting with better lighting and a greater police presence.

Philadelphia's neighborhoods have triumphed because they are more than houses on a street. They are daily celebrations of life, where families still sit on the marble steps of sentrylike row houses and gossip as the sun sets. They lounge in their bu-colic backyards behind 12-room fieldstone houses, attend religious services in Colonial-period churches, or just hang out on the street corner. "Yo, Angelo, your mother's lookin' for ya. Dinner's ready," is a refrain you might hear.

A *Washington Post* feature installed Philadelphia in the culinary Hall of Fame with this observation of stunning authority: "There are four kinds of cuisine, Italian, French, Chinese, and Philadelphia." Not only will the truth set you free, it will emancipate your taste buds. Cheese steaks (as Philadelphian as the Liberty Bell), barbecued ribs (that will remind Southerners of home), hoagies (subs or hero sandwiches), pepper pot soup, Jewish deli corned beef, and Philadelphia's ubiquitous mustard-smeared pretzels cover the city's foodscape like a midwinter blizzard.

For food shopping, either the Reading Terminal Market, in a cavernous railroad shed, with its Amish farmers and Asian proprietors, or the outdoor Italian Market, with barrel-by-carton sidewalk displays of fruits, vegetables, and exotic foods offer great money-saving values.

And then there's South Street, a one-thoroughfare adventure that combines the fascinations of New York's Greenwich Village and San Francisco's Ghirardelli Square. As former Philadelphia *Daily News* writer Kathy Sheehan summed it up: "South Street must be the only street in America where, in one trip, you can do your laundry, watch live Jello-O wrestling, and buy a bridal gown, used books, natural foods, crazy hats, a mattress and box spring, wind-up toys, toilet paper, a VCR, key chains with condoms, Central American art, a box of wood screws, fresh flowers, used clothing, a fountain pen, window shades, water ice, margaritas, mint juleps, rolling papers, healing crystals, and Halloween masks."

Manayunk, today the city's hottest neighborhood, draws a different crowd than South Street—ladies who lunch, upscale suburban couples who like to browse after they dine, singles who frequent the lively bars. The restaurants, galleries and clothing stores of this old mill town are decidedly trendy. You'll find a cigar café, lots of cappuccino, and a Nicole Miller boutique.

Along the east bank of the Schuylkill River, boathouses are contoured by strings of white lights that brighten the dark night. It's a year-round festival of lights.

As the seasons change, so do the sports teams. Philadelphia's Eagles, the Flyers, the Phillies, and the 76ers are supported by fanatically loyal fans. How fanatic? "Philadelphia fans will boo Santa Claus," a national news magazine once groused.

O N NEW YEAR'S DAY, while Americans are recovering from night-before revelry and blearily watching football bowl games, energetic Philadelphians strut into the national limelight with the Mummers, gaudily plummeted string bands. After kicking up their frisky heels in an all-day parade of skits and dances, they dissolve into all-night neighborhood revelries.

But with all of Philadelphia's festive enticements, *caveat peregrinator* (let the tourist beware). As with any big city, Philadelphia does have a crime problem, although the efficiency of the PAVies (Parking Authority Vultures) might lead you to believe that illegal parking is the city's most serious offense.

PAVies will ticket your car if you pause one minute on a street to buy a hot dog or pick up a package. If you're parked in a no-stopping zone, your car stands a good chance of being towed. Unsuspecting tourists have filled the columns of letters-to-the-editor with tales of horror because they erroneously assumed the Philadelphia Parking Authority fanatics would exercise a reciprocal civility respected in their hometowns. In Philadelphia, PAVies don't. Beware of these ticket-writing zealots.

Yo, America!

Check out your "Cradle of Liberty" with its Independence Hall, Liberty Bell, Philadelphia Museum of Art, cheese steaks, Reading Terminal Market, ethnic neighborhoods, vibrant waterfront, cobbled streets, hoagies, Center City boutiques, theaters, buoyant classical music, jazz nightclubs, and the neighborhood streets teeming with life.

As the rock groups at two simultaneous Live Aid concerts in London and Philadel-phia sang, "We are the world, we are the children." In Philadelphia we are the neighborhoods, we are the people—just like all of America.

— Chuck Stone

A former editor of the *Philadelphia Daily News*, Chuck Stone is currently a professor at the School of Journalism and Mass Communication of the University of North Carolina, Chapel Hill.

NEW AND NOTEWORTHY

If you can measure a city's vitality by the number of new construction and renovation projects and the amount of money sunk into them, then Philadelphia is flying high. There are new sports and entertainment venues, a bus with wings, and lovely homes for Picassos—and penguins.

Today the city is marketing its historical attractions, museums, and hotels with inviting packages so effectively that *USA Today* recently cited it as the nation's leader in cultural tourism. Tickets to the 1996 Cézanne show at the **Philadelphia Museum of Art** were so scarce that the only way to get in was with a hotel/ticket package. Expect a similar situation during the museum's Delacroix retrospective in late 1998 (the Philadelphia Visitors Center has information about packages).

The **Pennsylvania Convention Center,** which opened in 1994, has increased convention business and tourism to such an extent that by mid-1997 proposals were on the table for 14 new Center City hotels. Only time will tell which ones materialize. The convention center has a new grand entrance on Market Street, now that the century-old Italian Renaissance–style Reading Terminal Headhouse (where passengers once waited for trains) has been overhauled.

The **Philadelphia International Airport,** which used to give arriving visitors a bad first impression of the city, has completed a $1 billion capital improvement program that includes a new terminal, expansion of existing terminals, and upgraded runways. Artworks have been installed, and a Marriott Hotel was built adjacent to Terminal B.

New to Center City are the bright purple **PHLASH—Downtown Loop** shuttle buses with blue wings. The comfortable, inexpensive buses make frequent and continuous loops around the city, linking the waterfront area to the Ben Franklin Parkway. They run on clean-burning compressed natural gas.

Penguins are splashing down by the riverside since the **New Jersey State Aquarium** opened its outdoor penguin exhibit. Nearby in Camden is the **Blockbuster-Sony Music Entertainment Centre,** an indoor/outdoor amphitheater that hosts top name concerts and theatrical performances. The venue has gotten rave reviews from concert goers and is accessible from Penn's Landing by the RiverLink Ferry. On the Philadelphia side of the river at Penn's Landing, the *Moshulu* has set anchor. The world's oldest and largest four-masted sailing ship, it returned to the Delaware River after a $6 million restoration. Three decks, with authentic Art Nouveau design, are open to the public as a restaurant and entertainment facility.

Development of the **Avenue of the Arts** along north and south Broad Street has already produced two new venues—the Arts Bank and the Wilma Theater, bedecked in neon. Future plans include renovation of the Academy of Music and a new performance center for the Philadelphia Orchestra. In Merion you'll find Albert C. Barnes's renovated French Renaissance–style mansion, home of the **Barnes Foundation.** The museum, which houses his breathtaking collection of Impressionist and Postimpressionist paintings (including Picassos, Cézannes, and van Goghs) has been engaged in a heated lawsuit with neighbors to determine how many days the museum can be open; call before you visit.

Good news for shopping and sports enthusiasts: Renovations and an expansion at **The Plaza & The Court** in King of Prussia are complete, making it the second-largest retail mall in the nation. Newest stores include Nordstrom and Neiman Marcus. In Center City, **Lord & Taylor** has opened in the former John Wanamaker store; happily, the famous eagle and the nine-story grand court with its pipe organ can still be seen in all their glory. In South Philadelphia, the state-of-the-art **CoreStates Center** debuted as the home of the Flyers

hockey team and the 76ers basketball team; it's also used for entertainment and special events.

The multiyear effort to upgrade utility systems in some of the **Independence National Historical Park**'s buildings will soon be completed. But until fall 1998 Congress Hall will be closed to the public. Independence Hall remains open to visitors, but its West Wing and its second floor have been closed, and the furniture in the Assembly Room has been removed to protect it during construction.

WHAT'S WHERE

Back in the 18th century William Penn laid out his new city of Philadelphia as though it were a huge chessboard. Charles Dickens lamented in 1842 that "it is a handsome city but distractingly regular: After walking about it for an hour or two, I felt that I would have given the world for a crooked street," but today many people readily give thanks to ol' Billy Penn. The center of the city is intersected by two main thoroughfares: Broad Street (the city's spinal column, which runs north to south), and Market Street (which runs east to west). Where Broad and Market meet (neatly dividing the city center into four segments), you'll find City Hall, Philadelphia's center of gravity.

What makes Philadelphia different from other urban centers around the world? Simply stated, this sprawling cosmopolis has the feel of a friendly small town. Actually, several small towns, as Philly is a city of distinct neighborhoods, each with its own personality, rhythm, and lore. Here's a quick overview of the city's main districts plus some of the other destinations covered in this guide.

Benjamin Franklin Parkway

From City Hall the Benjamin Franklin Parkway stretches northwest to a Greco-Roman temple on a hill—the Philadelphia Museum of Art. The parkway is the city's Champs-Elysées, a grand boulevard designed by French architects and alive with flowers, trees, and fountains. Along the way are many of the city's grandest buildings and finest cultural institutions: the Academy of Natural Sciences, the Franklin

Institute, and the Rodin Museum. Don't forget to check out the great paintings of Thomas Eakins at the Philadelphia Museum of Art. If Philadelphia's soul could be said to have been captured in a single image, it would likely be Eakins's *Concert Singer,* a portrait of Weda Cook, a friend of Walt Whitman.

Center City

As a cultural palimpsest, Philadelphia has many pasts, but if you're interested in its present and future, head for Center City. This is Philly's business district, anchored by Oz-like skyscrapers and solidly Victorian City Hall, crowned by the enormous statue of William Penn. From Chinatown to Rittenhouse Square, Center City is crammed with sights. A sample? How about the Academy of Music; that leviathan horn of plenty, the Reading Terminal Market; the spanking new Pennsylvania Convention Center; Thomas Jefferson University (its gallery holds Philly's greatest painting, Thomas Eakins's *Gross Clinic*); and for those with itchy credit cards, the Shops at Liberty Place. In broad local usage, Center City refers to the entire area between the Delaware and Schuylkill rivers (east and west boundaries) and Vine Street and South Street (north and south)—an area that would be synonymous with downtown in another city—but here it refers specifically to the business district around City Hall and Market Street.

Fairmount Park

When in need of elbow room, Philadelphians head for Fairmount Park, whose 8,500 acres make it the largest landscaped city park in the world. Deemed by many Philly dwellers to be their own backyard, Fairmount beckons with a wide range of pleasures. Joggers, walkers, and bicyclists consider it prime territory. Along Kelly Drive are the Victorian houses of Boathouse Row, headquarters of the rowing clubs that make up what's called the "Schuylkill Navy." The Mann Center for the Performing Arts hosts open-air concerts in the summer. Children flock to the Philadelphia Zoo, America's oldest. Many people are also drawn to the centuries-old houses that dot the park, including Mt. Pleasant, Strawberry Mansion, and Lemon Hill. Here you can also find the noted Greek Revival Fairmount Waterworks. The Wissahickon, in the northern section of the park, beckons the adventurous with miles of paths through the gorge carved by Wissahickon Creek.

Germantown and Chestnut Hill

When Germantown, an area north of Center City, was settled by Germans fleeing economic and religious turmoil, it was way out in the country, linked to the city 6 mi away by a dirt road. Before long, the Germans' modest homes and farms were interspersed with the grand homes of affluent Philadelphians who hoped to escape the city's summer heat. They escaped the heat but not the British, who occupied the town and deployed troops from here during the Battle of Germantown. Today Germantown is an integrated neighborhood prized for its large old homes; several of the historic houses that line Germantown Avenue are open for tours. Over the years, development continued along the avenue, farther from the city, culminating in Chestnut Hill, today one of Philadelphia's prettiest neighborhoods.

The Historic District

No matter how you first approach Philadelphia, all things start at Independence National Historical Park. As the birthplace of the country, "America's most historic square mile" was the arena across which the nation strode to its national identity and independence. One can't list the historical highlights because *everything* is a highlight. Independence Hall—where the Declaration of Independence was approved and the U.S. Constitution adopted—Congress Hall, Old City Hall, Carpenters' Hall, Franklin Court, Declaration House, and, of course, the Liberty Bell Pavilion are just some of the attractions. If seeing these sights doesn't bring out the gee-whiz patriotism in your nine-year-old, nothing will.

Manayunk

This old mill town, wedged between the Schuylkill River and some very steep hills 7 mi northwest of Center City, was once crucial to Philadelphia's industrial fortune; it became part of the city in 1854. Today it's bringing in dollars with its restaurants and boutiques. In the 10 years since Manayunk was designated a historic district, it has become the city's hottest neighborhood. More than a half mile of stores stretch along Main Street, while behind it are remnants of the

Schuylkill Navigational Canal that originally brought life to this area.

Old City

Long considered one of Society Hill's poorer neighbors and known as a melting pot for immigrants, Old City is associated with three historic monuments: Christ Church, Elfreth's Alley, and the Betsy Ross House. Landmarked by its gleaming white spire, Christ Church is a gem of English Palladian architecture (its central window was the model for the one in Independence Hall). A few blocks north you'll find Elfreth's Alley, the most beautifully preserved street in the city— by some magical flick of a Wellsian time machine, you feel transported back to the 18th century here. To find the Betsy Ross House, look for the 13 stars and the 13 stripes flying from a second-story window of 239 Arch Street, a splendid example of a Colonial Philadelphia house. Today the area is also known for its chic art galleries, cafés, and restaurants, and rehabbed houses and residential lofts. The presence of theater and dance companies, art workshops, and design firms adds to the neighborhood's renewed vitality as a cultural, shopping, and dining district.

Penn's Landing

Ever since William Penn sailed up the Delaware into Dock Creek, Philadelphia's waterfront has been a vibrant part of the city's life. Once home to sailing ships and counting houses and still one of the world's largest freshwater ports, Penn's Landing today has become a 37-acre-long riverside park, home to the Independence Seaport Museum, the Great Plaza—where an open-air stage hosts concerts all summer long— and a flotilla of ship museums: the USS *Becuna,* the USS *Olympia,* and the *Gazela of Philadelphia.* A ferry link to the New Jersey State Aquarium and the Block-buster-Sony Music Entertainment Center has helped revitalize part of Camden's waterfront.

Rittenhouse Square

Like a grande dame, Rittenhouse Square is never in a hurry. The prettiest of Philadelphia's public squares, it beckons frazzled city dwellers to slow down and find balm among its blades. Today the park is the heart of upper-crust Philly. Christopher Morley, the humorist and author of *Kitty Foyle,* was alluding to a district like Rit-tenhouse Square when he described Philadelphia as being "at the confluence of the Drexel and Biddle families." Swank hotels and modern office buildings now intrude, but the trappings of onetime grandeur remain on view in its Victorian town houses. Many treasures are tucked away here, including the Curtis Institute of Music and the Rosenbach Museum and Library, home to 130,000 manuscripts, including James Joyce's *Ulysses.*

Society Hill

Society Hill is Philadelphia as it has been for more than 200 years. Old chimney pots, hidden courtyards, ornate door knockers, and cobblestone streets: Untouched by neon lights, Society Hill basks in its own patina. Although many houses are "trinity" abodes—one room to a floor—others are numbered among America's Federal-style showplaces, including the Physick House and the Powel House. Sit outside them for a while and watch the people go by—and not just those of the 20th century: Guides in Colonial dress sometimes lead candlelight strolls through the district.

Southwark

Chiseled in stone on the facade of an old Southwark building are the words: ON THIS SITE IN 1879, NOTHING HAPPENED! Today a great deal is happening in this district, which stretches from Front to 6th streets and from South to Washington avenues. The renovation generation has helped make the Queen Village area a winner in the revival-of-the-fittest contest among Philly's neighborhoods. As a result, rents here are catching up to nearby Society Hill. Although Southwark has never been as renowned as its neighbor, it offers some of the most charming streets in the city, such as Hancock and Queen. For real Philly flash, check out the Mummers Museum, on Washington Avenue.

South Philadelphia

Yes, this is the neighborhood that gave the world Rocky Balboa, as well as Bobby Rydell, Frankie Avalon, Fabian, and Pat's cheese steaks. The city's "Little Italy" can sometimes seem more Naples than Philly— just take in the five-block outdoor Italian Market, where piles of peppers and mountains of mozzarella make your taste buds sit up and beg. You can satisfy your cravings in any number of eateries here, many of them simple neighborhood spots.

University City

Once known as the "Athens of America," Philadelphia boasts an astonishing concentration of colleges and universities, nearly unrivaled in the country. Two of the larger institutions, the University of Pennsylvania and Drexel University, are in an area dubbed University City in West Philadelphia. Here, too, is the University Museum, containing one of the world's finest archaeology and anthropology collections. City buses travel along Walnut Street from Society Hill to University City; 34th and Walnut streets is the stop for Penn. On the southwest corner is the Institute of Contemporary Art, with its innovative exhibitions. Take Locust Walk to explore this Ivy League campus; ivy really does cling to the buildings.

Side Trips: From Brandywine to Valley Forge

Think of the Brandywine Valley, and the paintings of Andrew Wyeth come to mind: stone or clapboard farmhouses, forests that could tell a story or two, meadows with getaway space and privacy. The valley's palette is quintessentially Wyeth, too—russet, fieldstone gray, shades of amber. A journey through this valley can make for a restful experience. From Chadds Ford, the heart of Wyeth Country, head south to discover the splendid homes and estates of the du Ponts: Winterthur, Nemours, and Longwood Gardens. Nearby, Valley Forge, the site of George Washington's heroic 1777–78 encampment, awaits. For some retail shopping therapy, don't forget to check out Reading, the "outlet capital of the world."

Bucks County

Long a vacation spot for New Yorkers as well as for Philadelphians, Bucks County is a day-tripper's delight, filled with historic sites, artists' colonies, nature preserves, old fieldstone inns, and country-chic restaurants. Once hailed as "The Genius Belt" and home to such luminaries as Dorothy Parker, James Michener, and Oscar Hammerstein II, the region is packed with attractions: New Hope and Lahaska offer delightful shopping and antiquing; Doylestown has Fonthill, a millionaire's do-it-yourself castle right out of the Brothers Grimm; and the Delaware Canal towpath runs through countryside that conjures up England's Cotswolds.

Lancaster County, Hershey, and Gettysbury

An hour's drive from Philadelphia will take you to Lancaster County and the Pennsylvania Dutch Country, an area known for delicious foods and stunning farmlands. The folks responsible are the "Plain People," who still use horse-drawn buggies and dress simply and unfussily, as their families have dressed for centuries. Around the hub of Lancaster you can tour farmers' markets (shoofly pie should be at the top of your take-home goody list) or replicas of Amish villages, or you can stop in at the oldest pretzel bakery in the country and twist your own pretzel. Shoppers will find antiques, crafts, and outlet stores in the area, too. For dessert head west to Hershey, the only town in the world that has streetlights shaped like foil-wrapped Hershey Kisses. About 55 mi from Lancaster is Gettysburg, where the greatest artillery battle on this continent was fought in July 1863—and later immortalized through the words of Lincoln's Gettysburg Address.

PLEASURES AND PASTIMES

The Spirit of 1776

Many Americans think they know something about the birthplace of the nation: Benjamin Franklin, Thomas Jefferson's drafting of the Declaration of Independence, the sayings of Poor Richard, the signing of the Constitution. Still, these grade school facts and figures do little to prepare you for the actual Philadelphia experience. To walk through "America's most historic square mile"—Independence National Historical Park—is a tour that exercises not only the feet but the spirit. Who can fail to be moved by the words PROCLAIM LIBERTY THRO' ALL THE LAND," inscribed on America's best-loved relic, the Liberty Bell?

The story begins in 1753, when the Provincial Assembly, meeting at Independence Hall, notified the British Parliament of its refusal to "make laws by direction." The meeting of the Second Continental Congress in 1775 then lighted the fuse for the American Revolution. The spirit of 1776 found its fullest expression as Congress acted on Richard Henry Lee's famous Resolution for Independence. Today, Independence National Historical Park continues to embody America's noblest ideals.

Oh, Dem Golden Slippers

Buttoned-up Philadelphia explodes in a tidal wave of sequins, feathers, riotous sound, and pageantry every New Year's Day: the Mummers Parade. For this day of sudden liberation, the City of Brotherly Love dons "dem Golden Slippers" and cakewalks up Broad Street in a parade that outglitters Las Vegas. This little shindig, initially brought from England, had its American beginnings early in the 19th century, when gaily costumed groups rang doorbells, seeking donations after reciting rhymes intended to explain their strange garb. Add in Philly's heritage of minstrel shows and vaudeville, and you wind up with today's 12 nonstop hours of song, dance, and costumed splendor. If you're not in town for this phenomenon, you can still catch its flavor at the Mummers Museum; the Mummers also stage a summer parade around July 4, during the city's Welcome America! celebration.

Philly Fare

Philadelphia has finally managed to beat those cordon bleus. For decades gourmet groupies wrote the city off as a lackluster dining center. How things have changed! In 1994 Philly was named the best restaurant city in the nation, according to the *Condé Nast Traveler*'s readers' poll. The soufflé continued to rise with the opening of the Striped Bass, hailed by *Esquire* as Restaurant of the Year. And the béarnaise never curdles at Le Bec-Fin, which some epicureans cite as the greatest temple of French gastronomy in America. Today the city holds stellar Italian and Chinese restaurants as well as notable seafood and steak houses, not to mention a wide variety of ethnic eateries. Quintessential Philly dining spots include the City Tavern—called by John Adams "the most genteel tavern in America," Reading Terminal Market, and Pat's King of Steaks. Pat's aficionados claim that nothing is more delicious than a cheese steak—served with onions, spitting fat, and drizzled with real melt-in-your-mouth provolone.

The Emerald City

Envisioned by William Penn as a "greene countrie towne," Philadelphia is famous as a city with a green thumb. It counts its trees as avidly as a miser counts gold and now claims more than 2 million—maples, elms, oaks, beeches, and poplars—scattered among city squares, parks, streets, and innumerable backyards. The city's main "garden" is Fairmount Park, the largest municipal park in the world. For Philly at its flower-spangled best, check out some of the great Society Hill house gardens. Continuing evidence that Philly is "the city with the country heart" is the annual Philadelphia Flower Show—the largest indoor horticultural event in the world—held every March at the Pennsylvania Convention Center. Events throughout the city celebrate Flower Show Week. Around the area other gardens beckon, whether it's the Morris Arboretum, in the city's northwest corner; manicured Longwood Gardens, in Kennett Square; or the springtime splendors of Winterthur, near Wilmington, Delaware.

Artistically Speaking

Artistically, Philadelphia has always been fertile aesthetic territory. From the innovative, probing realism of such 19th-century masters as Thomas Eakins and Robert Henri to famous collectors like the McIlhennys and the Arensbergs—among the first Americans to collect Monets, Matisses, and Duchampses—Philadelphia has always played off the contrast between its traditionally staid origins and a lively interest in the new. Nowhere is this more evident than at the Barnes Foundation, with a collection of 175 Renoirs alone in its Merion mansion. Out in the Brandywine Valley, the Brandywine River Museum showcases the art of native son Andrew Wyeth and his famous family. Thanks to the Philadelphia Art Alliance, the Painted Bride Art Center, the Institute of Contemporary Art, and the Museum of American Art at the Pennsylvania Academy of the Fine Arts, the city's art scene remains as spirited as ever. The performing arts rival the fine arts, with the Avenue of the Arts development on Broad Street serving as a new focus for venues as diverse as the Academy of Music (home of the Philadelphia Orchestra), the Wilma Theater, and the Philadelphia Arts Bank, among others.

Sportsmania

Philadelphia is one of the only three cities on the East Coast with four professional sports teams—the Phillies (baseball), the Eagles (football), the 76ers (basketball), and the Flyers (hockey)—teams that claim devoted fans. But there's another sport at which Philadelphians are expert: spectating. Forget about just passing the popcorn; be prepared to throw snowballs at Santa Claus! Visiting teams say they've never seen anything like the behavior of Philly's sports fans, whose hijinks make events at the CoreStates Center and Veterans Stadium shake, rattle, and roll.

GREAT ITINERARIES

You could easily spend two weeks exploring Philadelphia, but if you're here for just a short period, you need to plan carefully so you don't miss the must-see sights. The following suggested itineraries will help you structure your visit efficiently. See the neighborhood exploring tours in Chapter 2 for more information about individual sights. For itineraries that cover Bucks County and Lancaster County, *see* Chapters 9 *and* 10.

If You Have 2 Days

Begin your first day with an exploration of the city's historic district. Sign up at the Independence National Historical Park **Visitor Center** for a walking tour hosted by a National Park Service guide; try a go-at-your-own-pace tour offered by Audio Walk and Tour; or take a walk on your own. For lunch, proceed to the **Reading Terminal Market,** where dozens of ethnic food stands await. After lunch walk about a mile east on Arch Street (or take a bus on Market Street) to Old City; **Christ Church,** the **Betsy Ross House,** and **Elfreth's Alley** are all in close proximity. The galleries and cafés in the area may tempt you to take a short break from your pursuit of history. In the late afternoon head back to Independence Hall for a **horse-drawn carriage ride.**

Spend the morning of Day 2 exploring the **Philadelphia Museum of Art,** on Benjamin Franklin Parkway, followed by lunch in the museum's lovely dining room.

Afterward, depending on your interests and the day of the week, you could head to Merion by bus or car to see the **Barnes Foundation**'s world-renowned collection of Impressionist paintings. You could also walk to **Eastern State Penitentiary** for a hard-hat tour of a historic (now-closed) prison or to the **Franklin Institute Science Museum.** While there, be sure to catch the current Omniverse Theater film. At night, visit a waterfront club or restaurant or pick a place with your favorite kind of food.

If You Have 4 Days

Follow the two-day itinerary described above, with one exception: Instead of having lunch at the Reading Terminal Market on Day 1, dine at the restored **City Tavern** in the historic district, where the authentically costumed waitstaff serves food of the Colonial period (make reservations in advance). Or if time is limited, grab a sandwich at the **Bourse** before heading to the **Old City** sights. Start Day 3 in Center City with a ride to the top of **City Hall** for a pigeon's-eye view of the city. Next, head across the street to the **Masonic Temple** for a surreal tour through time—and architectural history—led by a Mason. Art lovers may prefer a visit to the **Museum of American Art at the Pennsylvania Academy of the Fine Arts,** two blocks north of City Hall at Broad and Cherry streets. Eat lunch at the **Reading Terminal Market,** where you can sample the real Philadelphia "cuisine"—cheese steaks, soft pretzels, and Bassett's ice cream—or something else from the dozens of food stalls. In the afternoon visit **Penn's Landing,** where you can check out the **Independence Seaport Museum** and/or take the ferry across the river to the **New Jersey State Aquarium.** At sunset have a drink on the deck of the **Moshulu,** which is docked on the Delaware River.

On Day 4 leave the city behind for a day trip by car to the Brandywine Valley. Your first stop will be the **Brandywine River Museum,** in Chadds Ford, which showcases the art of Andrew Wyeth and his family, as well as works by other area painters and illustrators. Next, head south to **Winterthur** and feast your eyes on Henry Francis du Pont's extraordinary collection of American decorative art in an equally extraordinary mansion. Spend the balance of your day strolling through **Longwood Gardens,** in Kennett Square, which is in bloom even in winter. If it's a Tuesday, Thursday, or Saturday in summer, stay for dinner and the fountain light show.

If You Have 6 Days

Follow the first three days of the four-day itinerary outlined above. Begin Day 4 by exploring either **Society Hill** or the **Rittenhouse Square** area. Then take a bus west on Walnut Street to the **University Museum of Archaeology and Anthropology,** in University City. You can have lunch at the museum or on campus. In the afternoon head back to Center City to the **Philadelphia Visitors Center,** at 16th Street and John F. Kennedy Boulevard, to pick up the Philadelphia Trolley Works' narrated tour of **Fairmount Park;** or you can see a few park sites on your own. Afterward, head out by car or by the SEPTA R6 train to **Manayunk,** where you can have dinner in one of the restaurants lining Main Street; many stores here are open late, too.

On Day 5 head out of the city by car, this time to **Valley Forge National Historical Park,** where you can hike or picnic after you've taken the self-guided auto tour of General Washington's winter encampment. If you like to shop, spend the afternoon at **The Plaza & The Court,** in nearby King of Prussia. Or head back toward the city to take in the **Barnes Foundation,** the **Eastern State Penitentiary,** or the **Franklin Institute**—whichever ones you didn't see on Day 2.

Another option for Day 5 is to stay in the city and explore **Southwark** and **South Philadelphia.** Follow up a visit to the **Mummers Museum** with a strut along 9th Street, site of the outdoor **Italian Market.** You can pick up the makings for a great picnic or duck into one of the restaurants here for lunch. In the afternoon visit the museums you missed on Day 2. Check the local papers for an evening activity—perhaps a sporting event at the South Philadelphia stadiums, a show in Center City, or live music at a jazz club.

For Day 6, head to the **Brandywine Valley,** described in Day 4 of the four-day itinerary above.

FODOR'S CHOICE

No two people will agree on what makes a perfect vacation, but it's fun and helpful to know what others think. We hope you'll have a chance to experience some of Fodor's Choices yourself while visiting Philadelphia and the Pennsylvania Dutch Country. For detailed information about each, refer to the appropriate chapters in this guidebook.

Quintessential Philadelphia

★ **A walk across the Benjamin Franklin Bridge.** From dawn to dusk you can jog, walk, or bicycle the 1.8-mi span. The metal walkway 150 ft over the Delaware River gives you a terrific view of the waterfront.

★ **Boathouse Row illuminated at night.** Every night the dozen or so houses lining the Schuylkill River just beyond the Philadelphia Museum of Art are outlined by hundreds of tiny white lights. There's a magical feel to the way they shimmer and reflect in the river. Views are best from the West River Drive.

★ **The city's weeklong Fourth of July celebration.** Philadelphia throws itself a spectacular birthday party each year— the Welcome America! festival—with several nights of fireworks, an illuminated boat parade, outdoor concerts with superstar talent, and the awarding of the Philadelphia Liberty Medal to world leaders like Nelson Mandela and Shimon Peres.

★ **A walking tour of Independence National Historical Park.** Even if you're not a history buff, we predict a few quivers. Start at the Visitor Center and follow the red-brick road past a dozen stirring sites, including Independence Hall and the Liberty Bell.

★ **A run up the steps of the Philadelphia Museum of Art, followed by a visit inside.** If you saw Sylvester Stallone do it in the *Rocky* movies, you *will* have the urge to run up the steps. Go ahead, indulge! Then, unlike Rocky, *go inside*—wander through the 200 galleries and discover one of the world's great collections of art.

★ **Lunch on a park bench in Rittenhouse Square.** With majestic elms, Victorian statues, and playing children, Philadelphia's toniest downtown park seems to have sprung from the brush of Mary Cassatt.

★ **An afternoon at the Barnes Foundation.** In this Merion mansion is one of the world's finest collections of Impressionist and post-Impressionist art, eccentrically hung floor to ceiling between household tools, antique door latches, and folk art. Sixty-five works by Matisse, 66 by Cézanne, and 175 by Renoir are just part of the bounty.

After Hours

★ **Delaware River waterfront.** You can club-hop by river taxi to more than a dozen nightspots along the water near the Ben Franklin Bridge.

★ **First Fridays.** On the first Friday of each month from 5 to 9, the chic galleries of Old City open their doors to browsers and buyers alike with receptions and exhibit openings. The area is great for dining and strolling, too.

★ **Manayunk.** This old mill neighborhood has been transformed into a mecca for upscale diners and shoppers who want to see and be seen on trendy Main Street.

★ **A Philadelphia Orchestra concert at the Academy of Music.** Even if you didn't plan ahead, you can often get last-minute tickets for performances in the nosebleed section, four stories above the pit—for only $7. The sound is still lush, and from this vantage point the chandelier is breathtaking (there are afternoon concerts, too).

★ **South Street.** From fine restaurants to tattoo parlors, from art galleries to condom boutiques, South Street—from Front to 7th streets—is, as the song, says "the hippest place in town."

★ **Zanzibar Blue.** The hottest *and* the coolest jazz room in town, with the best local and national talent.

Lodging

★ **Four Seasons.** Philly's swankiest hotel has the best restaurants, service, and—if you get a room overlooking the fountains in Logan Circle—the most romantic views. $$$$

★ **The Rittenhouse.** You'll be pampered at this small luxury hotel that makes the best of its setting on tony Rittenhouse Square. $$$$

★ **Omni Hotel at Independence Park.** This posh charmer in the Historic District has a pleasantly intimate feeling. $$$–$$$$

★ **Ritz-Carlton.** Art on display and abundant luxurious touches enhance the feeling of complete comfort. $$$–$$$$

★ **Penn's View Inn.** Urban charm and a fine Italian restaurant distinguish this Old City inn. $$–$$$

Dining

★ **Le Bec-Fin.** *Formidable!* As the most prestigious and expensive restaurant in town, the Bec has become internationally renowned for its impeccable service, elegant decor, and the soufflés *tous parfums* of owner-chef Georges Perrier. You can also check out the exuberant new, less pricey ($$–$$$) Brasserie Perrier up the street. $$$$

★ **Jake's.** Fine contemporary crafts decorate a stellar eatery in Manayunk; try the scallops if you want to taste perfection. $$$–$$$$

★ **Striped Bass Restaurant and Bar.** At this chic see-and-be-seen spot, the food (all seafood) is delicious, and so is the stunning setting in a former brokerage house. Striped Bass took the town by storm a few years ago and continues to serve up surprises. $$$–$$$$

★ **Tony Clark's.** Smart decor and open kitchens are matched with the veteran chef's imaginative entrées and superb desserts. $$$–$$$$

★ **Rangoon.** Wonderful curries and ginger-seasoned lentil fritters are some of the discoveries at the city's only Burmese restaurant. $–$$

★ **Salumeria.** One of Reading Terminal Market's treasures takes the hoagie to new heights with such extra touches as roasted pimientos and artichoke hearts. $

Brandywine Valley

★ **Longwood Gardens.** The number-one attraction in the Brandywine Valley has more than 1,000 acres of flowers, trees, color, and beauty, 365 days a year.

★ **Brandywine River Museum.** A converted 19th-century gristmill on the banks of the Brandywine is the showcase for the art of three generations of the Wyeth family.

★ **Winterthur Museum and Gardens.** The most glamorous attic in the world, Henry Francis du Pont's nine-story mansion is filled with an unrivaled collection of American decorative arts from 1640–1860. The gardens are particularly lovely in spring.

Bucks County

★ **Fonthill.** The astonishing storybook castle-home of Henry Chapman Mercer in Doylestown has an air of magic and fantasy whenever you visit. The walls and ceilings are lined with Arts and Crafts–style tiles from Mercer's Moravian Pottery and Tile Works.

★ **Tubing on the Delaware.** For a summer delight travel down the Delaware River in an inner tube or a canoe rented from Bucks County River Country Canoe and Tube.

★ **Exploring along River Road.** Drive north out of New Hope (Route 32) along the Delaware River towpath, past old stone farmhouses, 18th-century mills, and lush rolling hills.

Lancaster County

★ **Visit a farmers' market.** For the best "sweets and sours" and chowchow, head for the Central Market in downtown Lancaster or the Green Dragon Farmers Market and Auction, in Ephrata.

★ **Exploring Amish Country.** To see the Amish farms and roadside stands, drive along the back-country roads between Routes 23 and 340 or take a leisurely ride to Paradise aboard the old-fashioned steam train of the Strasburg Railroad.

★ **Eat family style.** Try one of the all-you-can-eat restaurants like Good and Plenty or Plain and Fancy Farm. There's no menu—they'll bring you all the Pennsylvania Dutch food you can eat.

FESTIVALS AND SEASONAL EVENTS

For exact dates and other information about the following events, contact the **Philadelphia Visitors Center** (☞ Visitor Information *in* The Gold Guide).

WINTER

➤ FIRST WEEKEND IN DEC.: During **Elfreth's Alley Christmas Open House** (✉ Elfreth's Alley, between Front, 2nd, Arch, and Race Sts., ☎ 215/574–0560), the community opens its homes to the public for tours.

➤ DEC.: **Christmas Tours of Historic Houses** (☎ 215/684–7922) take visitors around historic Fairmount Park and Germantown houses decorated with Christmas finery.

➤ DEC.: *The Nutcracker* (✉ Academy of Music, Broad and Locust Sts., ☎ 215/893–1999), the Pennsylvania Ballet's production of the Tchaikovsky classic, is a Philadelphia Yuletide tradition.

➤ DEC. 25: **Washington Crossing the Delaware** (✉ Washington Crossing Historic Park, Washington Crossing, ☎ 215/493–4076) is reenacted with four 40-ft replicas of Durham boats. On Christmas Day 1776 George Washington and his troops took the Hessian camp at Trenton by surprise.

➤ DEC. 31–JAN. 1: **Neighbors in the New Year** (✉ Columbus Blvd. and Chestnut St., ☎ 215/636–1666) is a New Year's Eve celebration with fireworks set to music over the Delaware River at Penn's Landing.

➤ JAN. 1: The **Mummers Parade** (☎ 215/636–1666) is an all-day event during which some 30,000 sequined and feathered paraders—members of string bands, "fancies," comics, and fancy brigades—march north on Broad Street to City Hall.

➤ JAN.: The **Philadelphia Boat Show** (✉ Pennsylvania Convention Center, 12th and Arch Sts., ☎ 610/449–9910) displays more than 500 boats.

➤ FEB.: **Black History Month** includes exhibits, lectures, and music at the Afro-American Historical and Cultural Museum (✉ 701 Arch St., ☎ 215/574–0380), plus related events around the city.

➤ LATE FEB.: **Comcast U.S. Indoor Tennis Championships** (✉ CoreStates Center, 1 CoreStates Complex, Broad St. and Pattison Ave., ☎ 215/336–3600) attracts many of the world's top male tennis pros.

SPRING

➤ FEB.–MAY: **Chinese New Year** (✉ Chinese Cultural Center, 125 N. 10th St., ☎ 215/923–6767) celebrations include 10-course banquets from Tuesday through Sunday nights beginning at 6:30.

➤ MAR.: The **St. Patrick's Day Parade** (☎ 215/636–1666) brings the wearing of the green to Benjamin Franklin Parkway.

➤ MAR.: The **Philadelphia Flower Show** (✉ Pennsylvania Convention Center, 12th and Arch Sts., ☎ 215/988–8800), the nation's largest indoor flower show, has acres of exhibits and creative themed displays. Flower Show Week includes for additional events around the city.

➤ MAR.: **QVC's The Book and the Cook** (☎ 215/636–1666) teams the city's best chefs and the world's top cookbook authors in a weeklong event held in 60 restaurants. Festivities include wine tastings, market tours, and food sampling. It ends with the Book and the Cook Fair, at the Pennsylvania Convention Center.

➤ MAR.–JUNE: The **American Music Theater Festival** (☎ 215/893–1579) presents opera, musical comedy, children's programs, and experimental works at theaters around the city.

➤ APR.: The **Philadelphia Antiques Show** (✉ 103rd Engineers Armory, 33rd St. above Market St., ☎ 215/387–3500) offers museum-quality antiques, lectures, and appraisals.

➤ APR.: The **Easter Promenade** (✉ 8th and South Sts., ☎ 215/636–1666) is a parade down South Street with music, entertainment, celebrities, and a fashion contest.

➤ MID-APR.: **Historic Houses in Flower** (☎ 215/

684–7922) combines the elegance of 18th-century furniture with the beauty and color of spring floral designs when florists decorate seven Fairmount Park houses.

➤ LATE APR.: **Penn Relays** (✉ Franklin Field, 33rd and Spruce Sts., ☎ 215/ 898–6154) is one of the world's oldest and largest amateur track meets.

➤ LATE APR.: **St. Walpurgis Night Festival** (✉ American-Swedish Historical Museum, 1900 Pattison Ave., ☎ 215/389– 1776), the traditional Swedish welcome to spring, has food, song, dance, and bonfires.

➤ LATE APR.–MAY: **Philadelphia Open House** (☎ 215/928–1188) is a three-week period when selected private homes, gardens, and historic buildings in neighborhoods around the city— including Society Hill, Germantown, and the Main Line—open their doors to the public.

➤ EARLY MAY: International House's **Philadelphia Festival of World Cinema** (☎ 800/969– 7392) presents more than 100 features, documentaries, and short films from more than 30 countries at venues throughout the city during the first two weeks of May.

➤ MAY: The **Dad Vail Regatta** (☎ 215/248– 2600) is the largest collegiate rowing event in the country. Up to 500 shells from more than 100 colleges race on a 2,000-meter course on the Schuylkill River in Fairmount Park.

➤ THIRD WEEK IN MAY: For more than 80 years, the **Rittenhouse Square**

Flower Market (✉ 18th and Walnut Sts., ☎ 215/ 271–7149) has held this two-day sale of plants, flowers, and food, including the traditional candy lemon stick.

➤ MEMORIAL DAY WEEK-END: **Jam on the River** (✉ Great Plaza at Penn's Landing, ☎ 215/636– 1666) is Philadelphia's kickoff to summer, showcasing Cajun, blues, gospel, jazz, pop, and R&B music, in an event geared to families.

➤ LATE MAY–EARLY JUNE: The **Devon Horse Show and Country Fair** (✉ Devon Fairgrounds, U.S. 30, ☎ 610/964–0550), first held in 1896, is a nine-day event in which top riders compete for more than $200,000 in prize money.

SUMMER

➤ LATE MAY–AUG.: Longwood Garden's **Summer Festival of Fountains** (✉ Rte. 1, Kennett Square, ☎ 610/388– 1000) includes fountain displays during the day and fountain light shows set to music several nights a week, usually Tuesday, Thursday, and Saturday.

➤ JUNE: The **Rittenhouse Square Fine Arts Annual** (✉ Rittenhouse Sq., 18th and Walnut Sts., ☎ 215/ 634–5060), America's oldest (1931) and largest outdoor juried art show, exhibits paintings and sculpture by more than 100 Delaware Valley artists.

➤ FIRST WEEKEND IN JUNE: **Elfreth's Alley Fete Days**

(✉ Elfreth's Alley, between Front, 2nd, Arch, and Race Sts., ☎ 215/ 574–0560) is the time for open houses on America's oldest continuously occupied street, along with food and fife-and-drum music.

➤ JUNE: The **Mellon PSFS Jazz Festival** (☎ 610/ 667–3559) presents music from local talent to the top names in jazz in a weeklong series of concerts (many free) at locations around town.

➤ JUNE: The **CoreStates U.S. Pro Cycling Championship** (☎ 215/636– 1666), the country's premier bicycle race, attracts the world's top cyclists to its 156-mi course, including the grueling Manayunk Wall. A two-week celebration leads up to the event.

➤ JUNE–SEPT.: At the **Head House Crafts Fair** (✉ 2nd and Pine Sts., ☎ 215/ 790–0782), more than 30 artisans exhibit jewelry, stained glass, leather, and quilts on summer weekends, noon–11 Saturday and noon–6 Sunday.

➤ LAST WEEKEND IN JUNE: The **Manayunk Annual Arts Fest** (✉ Main St., ☎ 215/790–0782) lines this neighborhood's main drag with more than 200 artists from all over the country displaying arts and crafts.

➤ LATE JUNE–EARLY JULY: The **Kutztown Pennsylvania German Festival** (☎ 610/375–4085 or 800/ 963–8824) is an annual celebration of Pennsylvania Dutch culture, with local foods, quilting, folklore seminars, and children's activities.

➤ JUNE–JULY: The **Philadelphia Orchestra's**

Summer Season (✉ Mann Center for the Performing Arts, 52nd St. and Parkside Ave., ☎ 215/878–7707 or 215/567–0707) showcases noted guest conductors and soloists in outdoor concerts.

➤ JULY: The **Sunoco Welcome America! Festival** (☎ 215/636–1666) celebrates the nation's birth with more than a week of parades (including the Mummers), hot-air-balloon races, a drum-and-bugle competition, Independence Day ceremonies at Independence Hall, and the Old City Outdoor Restaurant Festival. It culminates in fireworks on July 4.

➤ SUNDAY BEFORE JULY 14: The Eastern State Penitentiary (✉ 22nd St. and Fairmount Ave., ☎ 215/236–3300) reenacts the storming of the Bastille at a **Bastille Day Celebration,** which includes an appearance by Marie Antoinette.

➤ AUG.–MID-OCT.: The **Pennsylvania Renaissance Faire** (✉ Mt. Hope Estate and Winery, Lancaster County, ☎ 717/665–7021) is a re-creation of Elizabethan England, with 11 stages and the largest jousting area outside Europe. There are magicians, storytellers, and performers; craftspeople demonstrating ancient arts; and food of the period.

➤ LATE AUG.: The **Philadelphia Folk Festival** (✉ Old Pool Farm, Schwenksville, ☎ 215/242–0150), America's oldest (1962) continuous folk festival, lasts three days. Performers range from the relatively new to

folk superstars. There's also food, folk dancing, and sing-alongs. Many "folkies" camp out on the grounds.

➤ LABOR DAY WEEKEND: The **YO! Philadelphia Festival** (✉ Great Plaza at Penn's Landing, ☎ 215/636–1666) celebrates Philly style with games, children's activities, ethnic foods, and live music— oldies and contemporary—that originated in the city.

➤ LABOR DAY WEEKEND: The big **Long's Park Art & Craft Festival** (☎ 717/295–7054) in Lancaster offers three days of fine shopping and seasonal festivities.

AUTUMN

➤ SEPT.: The **Philadelphia Distance Run** (☎ 610/293–0786) is the country's premier half-marathon, with more than 7,000 runners completing a 13-mi course through downtown and along the Schuylkill River.

➤ SEPT.: **Super Sunday** (✉ Benjamin Franklin Pkwy., ☎ 215/665–1050) is Philadelphia's largest block party, with food, entertainment, rides, games, 400 exhibit booths, and as many as 250,000 guests.

➤ LATE SEPT.: The **Von Steuben Day Parade** (☎ 215/636–1666), along Benjamin Franklin Parkway, honors the Prussian general who trained the

Continental soldiers at Valley Forge.

➤ OCT.: The **Pulaski Day Parade** (☎ 215/636–1666) marches up Broad Street; the Polish-American Congress honors this hero of the Revolutionary War, the Polish general known as the "father of the American cavalry."

➤ SECOND MON. IN OCT.: The **Columbus Day Parade** (☎ 215/636–1666) includes both a parade on South Broad Street and a festival at Marconi Plaza.

➤ OCT.: **Candlelight Tours of the Edgar Allan Poe National Historic Site** (✉ 532 N. 7th St., ☎ 215/597–8780) celebrate Halloween and Poe with "ghostly" weekend walks through the house.

➤ EARLY NOV.: The **Philadelphia Craft Show** (✉ Pennsylvania Convention Center, 12th and Arch Sts., ☎ 215/636–1666) is four days of exhibits by 100 top national craftspeople.

➤ NOV.: The **Philadelphia Marathon** (☎ 215/686–3645) draws several thousand runners for the 26-mi race along the Schuylkill River.

➤ NOV. OR DEC.: The **Dog Show** (✉ Pennsylvania Convention Center, 12th and Arch Sts., ☎ 215/947–1677), sponsored by the Kennel Club of Philadelphia, includes 2,500 entries.

➤ LATE NOV.: The **Thanksgiving Day Parade** (✉ Benjamin Franklin Pkwy., ☎ 215/636–1666) has thousands of marchers, floats, and local personalities.

2 Exploring Philadelphia

As the city that gave us the Declaration of Independence and the Twist, William Penn's principles of peace and purity and the soft pretzel, Philadelphia can be both significant and lighthearted. It delivers all the art and cultural treasures you'd expect from the nation's fifth-largest city (and more), plus more chapters of American history than you'll find anywhere else—packaged in an appealingly quirky town with a friendly feel.

By Rathe Miller
and Joyce
Eisenberg

Updated by
Joyce
Eisenberg

N THE WHOLE I'D RATHER BE IN PHILADELPHIA."
W. C. Fields may have been joking when he
wrote his epitaph, but if he were here today, he
would eat his words. They no longer roll up the sidewalks at night in
Philadelphia. An entertainment boom, a restaurant renaissance, and a
cultural revival have helped transform the city. For the past decade there
has been a new optimistic mood, aggressive civic leadership, and national recognition of what the locals have long known: Philadelphia
can be a very pleasant place to live—a city with an impressive past and
a fascinating future. Indeed, *Fortune* magazine ranked it as the "third-
best region to live and work in." For many observers, Philadelphia really
is the only civilized big city in America.

FROM BENJAMIN FRANKLIN TO GRACE KELLY

Philadelphia is a place of contrasts: Grace Kelly and Rocky Balboa; Le
Bec-Fin—perhaps the nation's finest French haute cuisine restaurant—
and the fast-food heaven of Pat's King of Steaks; Independence Hall
and the Mario Lanza Museum; 18th-century national icons with 21st-
century-style skyscrapers soaring above them. The world-renowned
Philadelphia Orchestra performs at the Academy of Music, a dignified,
opulent opera house on Broad Street. Along the same street 25,000 Mummers dressed in outrageous sequins and feathers pluck their banjos and
strut their stuff to the strains of "Oh, Dem Golden Slippers" on New
Year's Day. City residents include descendants of the staid Quaker founding fathers, the self-possessed socialites of the Main Line (remember
Katharine Hepburn and Cary Grant in *The Philadelphia Story*?), and
the unrestrained sports fans, who are as vocal as they are loyal. Together all these people make for a wonderful mix.

Historically speaking, Philadelphia is a city of superlatives: the world's
largest municipal park, the best public collection of art in the United
States, the widest variety of urban architecture in America, and according
to some experts, the greatest concentration of institutions of higher learning in the country.

A CITY OF NEIGHBORHOODS

In addition, Philadelphia is known as a city of neighborhoods (109 by
one count). Shoppers haggle over the price of tomatoes in South Philly's
Italian Market; families picnic in the parks of Germantown; street vendors hawk soft pretzels in Logan; and all over town kids play street
games such as stickball, stoopball, wireball, and chink. It's a city of
neighborhood loyalty: Ask a native where he's from and he'll tell you:
Fairmount, Fishtown, or Frankford, rather than Philadelphia. The
city's population is less transient than in other large cities; people who
are born here generally remain, and many who leave home to study
or work eventually return. Although the population is close to 2 million, residents are intricately connected; on any given day, a Philadelphian is likely to encounter someone with whom he grew up. The
"it's-a-small-world" syndrome makes people feel like they belong.

THE PHILADELPHIA STORY

William Penn founded the city in 1682 and chose to name it Philadelphia—Greek for "brotherly love"—after an ancient Syrian city, site of
one of the earliest and most venerated Christian churches. Penn's
Quakers settled on a tract of land he described as his "greene countrie towne." After the Quakers, the next wave of immigrants to arrive
were Anglicans and Presbyterians (who had a running conflict with the
"stiff Quakers" and their distaste for music and dancing). The new residents forged traditions that remain strong in parts of Philadelphia today:

united families, comfortable houses, handsome furniture, and good education. From these early years came the attitude Mark Twain summed up as: "In Boston, they ask: 'What does he know?' In New York, 'How much does he make?' In Philadelphia, 'Who were his parents?' "

The city became the queen of the English-speaking New World from the late 1600s to the early 1800s. In the latter half of the 1700s Philadelphia was the largest city in the colonies, a great and glorious place. So, when the delegates from the colonies wanted to meet in a centrally located, thriving city, they chose Philadelphia. They convened the First Continental Congress in 1774 at Carpenters' Hall. The rest, as they say, is history. It is here that the Declaration of Independence was written and adopted, the Constitution was framed, the capital of the United States was established, the Liberty Bell was rung, the nation's flag was sewn by Betsy Ross (though scholars debate this), and George Washington served most of his presidency.

GETTING YOUR BEARINGS

Today you will find Philadelphia's compact 2-square-mi downtown (William Penn's original city) nestled between the Delaware and the Schuylkill (pronounced *skoo*-kull) rivers. Thanks to Penn's grid system of streets—laid out in 1681—the downtown area is a breeze to navigate. The traditional heart of the city is Broad and Market streets (Penn's Center Square), where City Hall now stands. Market Street divides the city north and south; 130 South 15th Street, for example, is in the second block south of Market. North–south streets are numbered, starting with Front (1st) Street, at the Delaware River, and increasing to the west. Broad Street is the equivalent of 14th Street. The diagonal Benjamin Franklin Parkway breaks the rigid grid pattern by leading from City Hall out of Center City into Fairmount Park, which straddles the Schuylkill River and the Wissahickon Creek for 10 mi.

Although Philadelphia is the fifth-largest city in the nation, it maintains a small-town feel. It's a cosmopolitan, exciting, but not overwhelming city, a town that's easy to explore on foot yet big enough to keep surprising even those most familiar with it.

AROUND INDEPENDENCE HALL

The Most Historic Square Mile in America

Whether this is your first day or your only day in Philadelphia, it should be savored in the city area that comprises Independence National Historical Park. Philadelphia was the birthplace of the United States, the home of the country's first government, and nowhere is the spirit of those miraculous early days—the boldness of conceiving a brand-new nation—more palpable than along the cobbled streets of the city's most historic district.

In the late 1940s, before civic-minded citizens banded together to save the area and before the National Park Service stepped in, Independence Hall was crowded with factories and run-down warehouses. Then the city, state, and federal government took interest. Some buildings were restored, others reconstructed on their original sites, with several attractions built for the 1976 Bicentennial celebration. Today the park covers 42 acres and holds close to 40 buildings. Urban renewal in Independence Mall plaza and in Washington Square East (Society Hill) ensure that Independence Hall will never again keep unsightly company. The city's most historic area is now also one of its loveliest.

The best time to visit Independence National Historic Park is on America's birthday; expect crowds, though. Here, in America's birthplace, the city throws a 10-day party with parades (including the Mummers and an illuminated boat procession), a drum-and-bugle competition, outdoor concerts, elaborate fireworks, and the awarding of the prestigious Philadelphia Liberty Medal. If you visit anytime during the summer, there are plays, musicals, parades, and more; town criers dressed in 18th-century garb perform short vignettes about life in Colonial America. The town criers dispense maps and schedules of their performances. For information on the entertainment schedule, call Historic Philadelphia, Inc. (☎ 800/76–HISTORY).

The Independence National Historical Park Visitor Center, Independence Hall and the Liberty Bell Pavilion are open year-round from 9 to 5. Hours can vary in the other park buildings, especially in the winter months. In summer, hours are often extended. The park visitor center's 24-hour hot line (☎ 215/597–8974 or 215/597–1785 TTY) will give you current hours plus a schedule of park programs. Except as noted, all attractions run by Independence National Historical Park are free.

You can easily explore the park on your own; in each building there's a knowledgeable park ranger available to answer all your questions. On spring weekends and during the summer, the rangers lead a variety of walking tours; some are specifically for families. In the winter there are talks—"What Was It Like to Be a Soldier During the Revolution," at the New Hall Military Museum; "A Brush with History," in which children are detectives and art experts, in the Second Bank's Portrait Gallery. Inquire about these in the morning at the information desk of the visitor center.

If you are planning a trip here in 1998, take note: The park's Utilities Improvement Project, a multiyear effort to upgrade the utility systems of many park buildings, is slated to continue until fall 1998. Until then Congress Hall, on Independence Square, will be closed to the public. Independence Hall remains open to visitors, but its West Wing and its second floor have been closed, and the furniture in the Assembly Room has been removed to protect it during construction.

Numbers in the text correspond to numbers in the margin and on the Historic Area and Penn's Landing map.

A Good Walk

This is a walk back in time that will immerse you in Colonial history. The best place to orient yourself is at the Independence National Historical Park **Visitor Center** ① on 3rd and Chestnut streets. Directly across 3rd Street is the **First Bank of the United States** ②, a handsome example of Federal architecture. A redbrick path alongside manicured lawns and ancient oaks and maples leads to the first group of historic buildings, Carpenters' Court; **Carpenters' Hall** ③, with its displays of 18th-century tools, is on your left. On your right is **Pemberton House,** now a bookstore and gift shop. Behind the bookstore is the **New Hall Military Museum** ④; it contains a variety of weapons and uniforms. Leave Carpenters' Court and continue west on the redbrick path across 4th Street to the Parthenon look-alike, the **Second Bank of the United States** ⑤, with its portrait gallery of Colonial Americans. Its entrance is on Chestnut Street. As you continue west on that redbrick path, which now runs along cobblestoned Library Street, you'll see on your right **Library Hall** ⑥, a reconstruction of the first public library in the United States. Crossing 5th Street, you arrive at **Independence Square**; the first building on your right is **Philosophical Hall,** home of the country's oldest learned society. Just behind it is **Old City Hall** ⑦, home of the U.S. Supreme Court from 1791 to 1800. Tours of **Independence Hall** ⑧, where the Declaration of Independence was signed, begin in the courtyard alongside Old City Hall. Just past Independence Hall, on the corner of 6th and Chestnut streets is **Congress Hall** ⑨, with the restored chambers of the U. S. Congress.

Walk back through the square to 6th and Sansom streets to the **Norman Rockwell Museum** ⑩, housed in the Curtis Publishing Building; you can see many of the artist's magazine covers and other works. Then head north on 6th Street (here dubbed Independence Mall West). Just past Chestnut Street, head diagonally into the mall. One block up is Philadelphia's best-known symbol, the **Liberty Bell** ⑪. Head west on the walkway between Market and Chestnut streets under the Rohm and Haas Building. You'll pass the sculpture-fountain *Milkweed Pod.* Installed in 1959, it was one of the first examples of Philadelphia's law requiring public buildings to spend 1% of construction costs for art. The walkway will lead you to 7th Street. Directly in front of you is the **Balch Institute for Ethnic Studies** ⑫, with its library and exhibits on immigration and ethnicity. To your immediate left is the **Atwater Kent Museum** ⑬, which chronicles the city's history. Next to the Balch Institute is the reconstructed **Declaration House** ⑭, where Thomas Jefferson wrote his rough draft of the Declaration of Independence. If you have time to see just one other site (and particularly if you have children in tow), make it **Franklin Court** ⑮. To get there, turn right (east) on Market to Number 316. After seeing the Colonial-era print shop and post office, head into the courtyard to the underground museum that celebrates the achievements of Benjamin Franklin. Continue through the courtyard to Chestnut, turn left (east), and you'll be back at the visitor center.

If you have more time and energy, continue east on Chestnut Street. Just opposite the grand U.S. Customs House, you'll find the **Trading Post,** home to a small museum and store run by the United American Indians of the Delaware Valley. Turn right (south) on 2nd Street. Halfway down the block is **Welcome Park** ⑯, marking the spot where William Penn once lived. Follow Walnut Street a half block west to see the **Philadelphia Merchant's Exchange,** the city's commercial center for part of the 19th century. On the corner of 3rd and Walnut streets is the lavishly furnished **Bishop White House** ⑰, which stands in direct contrast to the simply furnished **Todd House** ⑱, home of Dolley Madison, at the corner of 4th and Walnut streets. Alongside Todd House is a lovingly maintained 18th-century garden.

TIMING

If you've put on your walking shoes and are good at negotiating the cobblestones, you can wander through this compact area in about 90 minutes. But the city's atmospheric historic district is its top attraction and warrants a slower pace. Budget a full day here. An early start lets you factor in the park visitor center's daily schedule of special events and reserve tickets for the Todd and Bishop White house tours. It also might decrease your chances of having to wait in line at Independence Hall. Allow about one hour there (with the wait) and another hour each at Franklin Court and the Todd and Bishop White houses. Allow 30 minutes each at Declaration House and the visitor center, where it's a good idea to see the film *Independence* before you set out.

Sights to See

⑬ **Atwater Kent Museum.** Founded in 1938 and housed in an elegant 1826 Greek Revival building designed by John Haviland, this museum portrays Philadelphia history from the beginning to the present day, with an emphasis on manufacturing and popular culture. It was founded by Atwater Kent, a wealthy inventor, radio magnate, and manufacturer.

The collections, best for history buffs, include exhibits on municipal services such as police, fire, water, and gas; shipbuilding; model streets and railroads; and maps showing the city's development. One gallery, *The City Beneath Our Feet,* has changing exhibits culled from the thousands of artifacts uncovered during 20th-century excavations. ⊠ *15 S. 7th St.,* ☎ *215/922–3031.* ☞ *$3, free Sun. until noon.* ⊘ *Wed.– Mon. 10–4.*

⑫ **Balch Institute for Ethnic Studies.** More a research center than a museum, the Balch Institute has a 60,000-volume library on immigration history and ethnicity that is open to the public several days a week. *Discovering America: The Peopling of Pennsylvania* is an exhibition tracing the diversity of the ethnic groups in the state, from Native Americans and Europeans to newer arrivals from Asia and other countries. Changing exhibitions examine contemporary issues of ethnic and racial identity. ⊠ *18 S. 7th St.,* ☎ *215/925–8090.* ☞ *$2.* ⊘ *Exhibitions, Mon.–Sat. 10–4; library, Tues., Thurs., and Sat. 10–4.*

⑰ **Bishop White House.** Built in 1786, this restored upper-class house gives you a look at Colonial and Federal elegance. It was the home of Bishop William White, rector of Christ Church, first Episcopal bishop of Pennsylvania, and spiritual leader of Philadelphia for 60 years. White, who founded the Episcopal church after the break with England, was chaplain to the Continental Congress and entertained many of the country's first families, including Washington and Franklin. The second-floor study contains much of the bishop's own library. Unlike most houses of the period, the bishop's house had an early form of flush toilet. The house tour is not recommended for small children (they get bored). ⊠ *309 Walnut St.,* ☎ *215/597–8974.* ☞ *$2; purchase tickets at the visitor center for one of the daily 1-hr tours that include the Todd House and the Bishop White House.* ⊘ *Daily 9:30–4:30.*

❸ **Carpenters' Hall.** This handsome patterned red-and-black brick building dating from 1770 was the headquarters of the Carpenters' Company, a guild founded to support carpenters, who were both builders and architects in this era, and to aid their families. In September 1774 the First Continental Congress convened here and addressed a declaration of rights and grievances to King George III. Today re-creations of Colonial settings include original Windsor chairs and candle sconces and displays of 18th-century carpentry tools. The building is still owned and operated by the Carpenters' Company. ⊠ *320 Chestnut St.,* ☎ *215/597–8974.* ☞ *Free.* ⊘ *Jan.-Feb., Wed.–Sun. 10–4; Mar.– Dec., Tues.–Sun. 10–4.*

❾ **Congress Hall.** Formerly the Philadelphia County Courthouse, Congress Hall was the meeting place of the U.S. Congress from 1790 to 1800—one of the most important decades in our nation's history. Here the Bill of Rights was added to the Constitution; Alexander Hamilton's proposals for a mint and a national bank were enacted; and Vermont, Kentucky, and Tennessee became the first new states after the original colonies. On the first floor is the House of Representatives, where President John Adams was inaugurated in 1797. On the second floor is the Senate chamber, where in 1793 George Washington was inaugurated for his second term. Both chambers have been authentically restored. ⊠ *6th and Chestnut Sts.,* ☎ *215/597–8974.* ☞ *Free.* ⊘ *Daily 9–5. Closed until fall 1998 due to the park's Utilities Improvement Project.*

⑭ **Declaration House.** In a second-floor room that he had rented from bricklayer Jacob Graff, Thomas Jefferson drafted the Declaration of Independence here in June 1776. The home was reconstructed for the

24

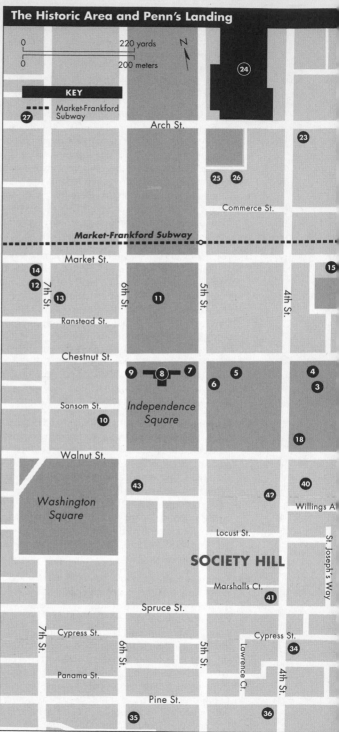

The Historic Area and Penn's Landing

0   220 yards
0   200 meters

N

KEY

Market-Frankford Subway

Arch St.

Commerce St.

Market-Frankford Subway

Market St.

7th St.

6th St.

5th St.

4th St.

Ranstead St.

Chestnut St.

Sansom St.

Independence Square

Walnut St.

Washington Square

Willings A

Locust St.

SOCIETY HILL

Marshalls Ct.

St. Joseph's Way

Spruce St.

7th St.

Cypress St.

6th St.

5th St.

Lawrence Ct.

Cypress St.

4th St.

Panama St.

Pine St.

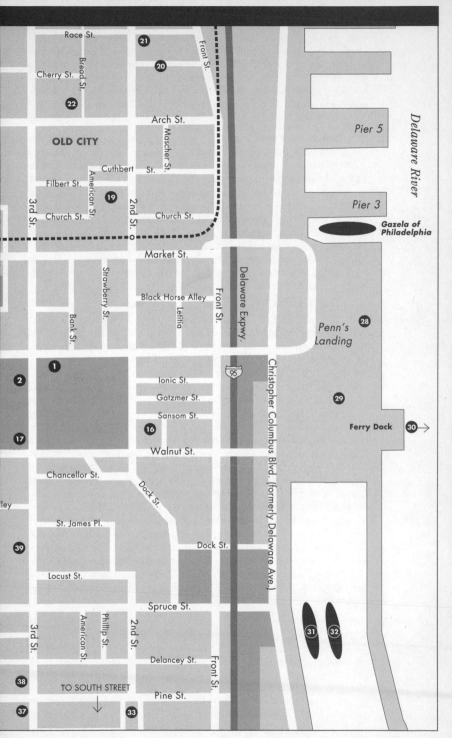

Race St.

㉑

⑳

Cherry St.

Bread St.

㉒

Arch St.

OLD CITY

Cuthbert

Mascher St.

St.

Filbert St.

American St.

⑲

3rd St.

2nd St.

Church St.

Church St.

Market St.

Strawberry St.

Black Horse Alley

Bank St.

Letitia

Front St.

Delaware Expwy.

Pier 5

Delaware River

Pier 3

Gazela of Philadelphia

Penn's Landing

㉘

❶

❷

⑰

Ionic St.

Gatzmer St.

Sansom St.

⑯

Walnut St.

95

㉙

Ferry Dock

㉚→

Chancellor St.

Dock St.

...ley

St. James Pl.

Christopher Columbus Blvd. (formerly Delaware Ave.)

㊴

Dock St.

Locust St.

Spruce St.

American St.

Phillip St.

2nd St.

㉛ ㉜

3rd St.

Delancey St.

Front St.

㊳

TO SOUTH STREET
↓

Pine St.

㊲

㉝

Bicentennial celebration; the bedroom and parlor in which Jefferson lived that summer were re-created with period furnishings. The first floor has a Jefferson exhibition and a seven-minute film, *The Extraordinary Citizen*. The display on the Declaration of Independence shows some of the changes Jefferson made while writing it. You can see Jefferson's original version—which would have abolished slavery had the passage not been stricken by the committee that included Benjamin Franklin and John Adams. ⊠ *7th and Market Sts.,* ☎ *215/597–8974.* ⬚ *Free.* ⊙ *Daily 9–5.*

② **First Bank of the United States.** A fine example of Federal architecture, the oldest bank building in the country was headquarters of the government's bank from 1797 to 1811. It was an imposing structure in its day, designed to exemplify strength, dignity, and security. Head first to the right, to the north side of the structure, to find a beautiful wrought-iron gateway topped by an eagle. Pass through it into the courtyard, and you magically step out of modern-day Philadelphia and into Colonial America. Before you do so, check out the bank's beautiful pediment. Executed in 1797 by Clodius F. Legrand and Sons, its cornucopia, oak branch, and American eagle are carved from mahogany—it's amazing to see that this late-18th century masterpiece has withstood acid rain better than the bank's marble pillars. ⊠ *120 S. 3rd St.* ⊙ *Interior closed to public.*

⌚ **⑮** **Franklin Court.** In 1763, at the age of 57, Franklin built his first permanent home in Philadelphia, in a courtyard off Market Street. This underground museum on the site of the house is an imaginative tribute to a Renaissance man. In the courtyard adjacent to the museum, architect Robert Ventura erected a steel skeleton of Franklin's former home. You can peek through "windows" into cutaways to see wall foundations, outdoor privy wells, and other parts of his home that were uncovered during excavations. Within the museum the accomplishments of the statesman, diplomat, scientist, inventor, printer, and author are brought to life. Dial-a-quote to hear his thoughts or pick up a telephone and listen to what his contemporaries really thought of him. There is also an informative 20-minute film on Franklin's life. At the Market Street side are several houses, now exhibition halls, that Franklin had rented in addition to his main home. In one, visitors can see how Franklin fireproofed the building: His interest in fireproofing led him to experiment with kite flying and lightning (remember the delightful rendition of those experiments in Disney's animated cartoon *Ben and Me?*). Here, too, you'll find a restoration of a Colonial-era print shop and a post office. Don't forget to get a letter hand-stamped with a "B. FREE FRANKLIN cancellation. ⊠ *314–322 Market St., or enter from Chestnut St. walkway,* ☎ *215/597–2760.* ⬚ *Free.* ⊙ *Daily, fall–winter 10–5; summer–Sept. 10–6; spring 9–5.*

★ **⑧** **Independence Hall.** Try to get a place at the head of the hordes of schoolchildren who've come to see one of our nation's greatest gems, the birthplace of the United States. America's most historic building was constructed in 1732 as the Pennsylvania State House. What happened here between 1775 and 1787 changed the course of American history—and the name of the building to Independence Hall. The delegates to the Second Continental Congress met in the hall's Assembly Room in May 1776, united in anger over the blood that had been shed when British troops fired on citizens in Concord. In this same room George Washington was appointed commander in chief of the Continental Army, Thomas Jefferson's eloquent Declaration of Independence was signed, and later the Constitution of the United States was adopted. Here the first foreign minister to visit the United States was welcomed, the news of Cornwallis's defeat was announced, signaling the end of the Revolutionary War, and John Adams and Abraham Lincoln lay in state. The memories this building holds linger in the collection of polished muskets, the silver inkstand used by delegates to sign the Declaration of Independence, and the "Rising Sun" chair in which George Washington sat. (After the Constitution was adopted, Benjamin Franklin said about the sun carving on the chair, "I have the happiness to know that it is a rising and not a setting sun.") On the second floor you'll find the 100-ft Long Room, the site of many of the fledgling nation's most important banquets, receptions, balls, and suppers.

In the **East Wing**—attached to Independence Hall by a short colonnade—you can embark on free tours that start every 15 to 20 minutes and last 35 minutes. The **West Wing** of Independence Hall contains a book store and gift shop. Admission is first come, first served. (Note that from early May to Labor Day, you may wait from 15 minutes to an hour for the Independence Hall Tour.)

In front of Independence Hall, next to the statue of George Washington, note the plaques marking the spot where Abraham Lincoln stood on February 22, 1861, and a few steps away where John F. Kennedy delivered an address on July 4, 1962. Each year on July 4, the Philadelphia Liberty Medal is presented to a world leader: In 1996 Mayor Ed Rendell lauded the Mideast peace efforts by presenting the medal to former Israeli prime minister Shimon Peres and King Hussein of Jordan. The site was chosen as the backdrop for the Presidential Summit on America's Future, held in spring 1997, attended by Clinton and past former presidents Bush and Ford. With Independence Hall in front of you and the Liberty Bell behind you, this is a place to stand for a moment and soak up a sense of history. ⊠ *Chestnut St. between 5th and 6th Sts.,* ☎ *215/597–8974.* ☐ *Free.* ☉ *Daily 9–5; due to the park's Utilities Improvement Project, Independence Hall's West Wing and 2nd floor will be closed to the public until fall 1998; in addition, furniture in the Assembly Room has been removed to protect it during construction.*

Independence Square. On July 8, 1776, the Declaration of Independence was first read here in public. Although the square is not as imposing today, you can imagine the impact this setting had on the colonists. ⊠ *Bounded by Walnut and Chestnut Sts. and 5th and 6th Sts.*

★ ⑪ **Liberty Bell.** The bell fulfilled the biblical words of its inscription when it rang to "proclaim liberty throughout all the land unto all the inhabitants thereof," beckoning Philadelphians to the State House yard to hear the first reading of the Declaration of Independence. Ordered in 1751 and originally cast in England, the bell cracked during testing and was recast in Philadelphia by Pass and Stow two years later. To keep it from falling into British hands during the Revolution—they would have melted it down for ammunition—the bell was spirited away by horse and wagon to Allentown, 60 mi to the north. The bell is the subject of much legend; one story says it cracked when tolled at the funeral of Chief Justice John Marshall in 1835. Actually, the bell cracked slowly over a period of years. It was repaired but cracked again in 1846 and was then forever silenced. It was called the State House Bell until the 1830s, when a group of abolitionists adopted it as a symbol of freedom and renamed it the Liberty Bell.

After being housed in Independence Hall for more than 200 years, the bell was moved to a glass-enclosed pavilion for the Bicentennial, in 1976. This modern home is an incongruous setting for such a historic object, but it does display the bell 24 hours a day. While the building is open, rangers and volunteers tell the story. After hours you can press a button on the outside walls to hear a recorded account of the bell's history. ⊠ *Market St. between 5th and 6th Sts.,* ☎ *215/597–8974.* ⌨ *Free.* ⊙ *Daily 9–5.*

NEED A   Enter the **Bourse** (⊠ 5th Street across from the Liberty Bell Pavilion, ☎
BREAK?   215/625–0300) and you're in another century. The sky-lighted Great Hall, with its Corinthian columns, marble, wrought-iron stairways, and Victorian gingerbread details, has been magnificently restored. Built in 1895 as a stock exchange, it now houses shops and a food court, where you can grab a cup of cappuccino or a Philly cheese steak.

6 **Library Hall.** This 20th-century building is a reconstruction of Franklin's Library Company of Philadelphia (☞ Rittenhouse Square, *below*), the first public library in the colonies. Home of the library of the American Philosophical Society, one of the country's leading institutions for the study of science, it is basically a research facility for scholars. Its vaults contain such treasures as a copy of the Declaration of Independence handwritten by Thomas Jefferson, William Penn's 1701 Charter of Privileges, and journals from the Lewis and Clark expedition of 1803–06. The library's collection also includes first editions of Newton's *Principia Mathematica,* Franklin's *Experiments and Observations,* and Darwin's *On the Origin of Species.* In the lobby there are fascinating changing exhibitions open to the public; *Wedgwood Portrait Medallions* was a recent one. ⊠ *105 S. 5th St.,* ☎ *215/440–3400.* ⌨ *Free.* ⊙ *Weekdays 9–4:45.*

4 **New Hall Military Museum.** On display in this reconstructed 1790 building that briefly served as headquarters for the U.S. Department of War are Revolutionary War uniforms, medals, and authentic weapons, including powder horns, swords, and a 1763 flintlock musket. Dioramas depict highlights of the Revolutionary War; the building also houses a Marine Corps memorial. ⊠ *Chestnut St. east of 4th St.,* ☎ *215/597–8974.* ⌨ *Free.* ⊙ *Daily 9–5.*

10 **Norman Rockwell Museum.** The Curtis Publishing Company Building, where Rockwell delivered his paintings to the editors of the *Saturday Evening Post,* now has the world's largest collection of the artist's works. Displays include all 324 Rockwell *Post* cover illustrations; lithographs, prints, collotypes, and sketches; and a replica of his studio in Stockbridge, Massachusetts. A 10-minute video illustrates Rockwell's life. The lobby of the Curtis Building, incidentally, has a great treasure: a 15-by-50-ft glass mosaic mural, *The Dream Garden,* based on a Maxfield Parrish painting. It was executed by the Louis C. Tiffany Studios in 1916. With 260 colors of opalescent hand-fired glass, it is perhaps the finest Tiffany mural in the world. ⊠ *60l Walnut St., lower level,* ☎ *215/922–4345.* ⌨ *$2.* ⊙ *Mon.–Sat. 10–4, Sun. 11–4.*

7 **Old City Hall.** Independence Hall is flanked by Congress Hall to the west and Old City Hall to the east: three distinctive Federal-style buildings erected to house the city's growing government. But when Philadelphia became the nation's capital in 1790, the just-completed city hall was lent to the federal government. It housed the U.S. Supreme Court from 1791 to 1800; John Jay was the Chief Justice. Later, the boxlike building with a peaked roof and cupola was used as the city hall. Today you can find out about the early days of the federal judiciary here. ⊠ *5th and Chestnut Sts.,* ☎ *215/597–8974.* ⌨ *Free.* ⊙ *Daily 9–5.*

Pemberton House. The former Army–Navy Museum now serves as "America's National Parks" store offering books, videos, and souvenirs, plus Civil War, Revolutionary War, and Constitution memorabilia. ⊠ *316 Chestnut St.,* ☎ *215/597–8019.* ⊙ *Daily 9–5.*

Philadelphia Merchant's Exchange. Designed by the well-known Philadelphia architect William Strickland and built in 1832, this impressive Greek Revival structure served as the city's commercial center for 50 years. It was both the stock exchange and a place where merchants met to trade goods. In the tower a watchman scanned the Delaware River and notified merchants of arriving ships. The exchange stands behind Dock Street, a cobblestone thoroughfare closed to traffic. It is not open to the public. ⊠ *3rd and Walnut Sts.*

Philosophical Hall. This is the headquarters of the American Philosophical Society, founded by Benjamin Franklin in 1743 to promote "useful knowledge." The members of the oldest learned society in America have included Washington, Jefferson, Lafayette, Emerson, Darwin, Edison, Churchill, and Einstein. Erected between 1785 and 1789 in what has been called a "restrained Federal style" (designed, probably, to complement, not outshine, adjacent Independence Hall), Philosophical Hall is brick with marble trim and has a handsome arched entrance. The society's library is across the street in Library Hall (☞ *above*). ⊠ *104 S. 5th St.,* ☎ *215/440–3400.* ⊙ *Closed to the public except by appointment.*

❺ Second Bank of the United States. When Second Bank President Nicholas Biddle held a design competition for a new building, he required all architects to use the Greek style. Built in 1824, the bank, with its Doric columns, was based on the design of the Parthenon and helped establish the popularity of Greek Revival architecture in the United States. The interior banking hall, though, was Roman, with a dramatic, barrel-vaulted ceiling. Housed here are portraits of prominent Colonial Americans by noted artists such as Charles Willson Peale, William Rush, and Gilbert Stuart. Don't miss Peale's portrait of Jefferson: It's the only one that shows him with red hair. The permanent exhibition, *Portraits of the Capital City,* has a life-size wooden statue of George Washington by William Rush; a mural of Philadelphia in the 1830s by John A. Woodside Jr.; and the only known likeness of William Floyd, a lesser-known signer of the Declaration of Independence. ⊠ *420 Chestnut St.,* ☎ *215/597–8974.* ▣ *$2.* ⊙ *Daily 9–5.*

⓲ Todd House. Built in 1775, Todd House has been restored to its 1790s appearance, when its best-known resident, Dolley Payne Todd, lived here. She lost her husband, the Quaker lawyer John Todd, to the yellow fever epidemic of 1793. Dolley later married James Madison, who became the fourth president. Her time as a hostess in the White House was quite a contrast to her years in this simple home. There's an 18th-century garden next to Todd House. ⊠ *4th and Walnut Sts.,* ☎ *215/ 597–8974.* ▣ *$2; purchase tickets at the visitor center for one of the daily 1-hr tours that include the Todd House and the Bishop White House.* ⊙ *Daily 9:30–4:30.*

Trading Post. Just when your mind is crammed with Colonial history, drop in here, the headquarters of the United American Indians of the Delaware Valley. The small museum is a reminder that long before— 10,000 years before—Charles II granted William Penn this land, it was home to some 15,000 Native Americans. Besides the museum and gift shop, the building serves as a gathering place for urban Native Americans. ⊠ *225 Chestnut St.,* ☎ *215/574–9020.* ⊙ *Daily 9–5.*

NEED A
BREAK?   The **Custom House Cafe** (⊠ 103 S. 2nd St., ☎ 215/627–0654) serves a great cup of coffee, along with cold drinks, sandwiches, muffins, and

bagels. If you want to get an early start sightseeing, you can stop by
here first; the café opens weekdays at 7, weekends at 9.

❶ Visitor Center. The center is staffed by park rangers who answer questions and distribute maps and brochures on Independence National Historical Park and other sites in the historic area. Before you set off on
a walking tour, acquaint yourself with this period of American history
by watching the founding fathers come to life in the 30-minute movie
Independence. The center's main attraction is *Promise of Permanency,*
a video-computer exhibition that gives you an opportunity to delib-
erate on key constitutional cases; it was installed to mark the Constitution's 200th birthday. A city information desk is inside the center,
as is an excellent bookstore, where you can stock up on books, videos,
brochures, prints, and wall hangings about historic figures and events.
You can buy a reproduction of a 1787 map of Philadelphia or copies
of the Declaration and the Constitution on parchmentlike paper. The
most popular items are the tiny Liberty Bell reproductions. The bell
atop the visitor center's tower, cast at the same foundry as the Liberty
Bell, was a Bicentennial birthday gift from Queen Elizabeth II.

To see two of the city's famous historic homes—the Bishop White House,
where the wealthy first Episcopal bishop of Pennsylvania lived, and
the modest home of Quaker John Todd, from whence Todd's widow,
Dolley Payne, emerged to become the first lady of President James Madison—you'll need to stop at the information desk to purchase a ticket
($2) and reserve a spot on one of the hour-long tours. ⊠ *3rd and Chest-
nut Sts.,* ☏ *215/597–8974.* ☉ *Daily 9–5.*

⓰ Welcome Park. The park is the site of the slate-roof house where
William Penn lived briefly and where he granted the Charter of Privileges in 1701. (The *Welcome* was the ship that transported Penn to
America.) Written by Penn, the Charter of Privileges served as Pennsylvania's constitutional framework until 1776; the Liberty Bell was
commissioned to commemorate the charter's 50th anniversary. In the
park, on a 60-ft-long map of Penn's Philadelphia carved in the pave-
ment, sits a scale model of the Penn statue that sits atop City Hall. The
wall surrounding the park displays a time line of his life, with information about his philosophy and quotations from his writings. The
City Tavern, across the street, marks the site where George Washington once dined. It is still open for historically correct lunches and din-
ners (☞ Chapter 3). ⊠ *2nd St. just north of Walnut St.*

OLD CITY
Living "North of Market"

In Colonial days, the rich folks in residential Society Hill spoke in hushed
tones of those who lived "north of Market," for this area, between Front
and 5th streets and Chestnut and Vine streets, was the city's commercial area for industry and wholesale distributors, filled with wharves
and warehouses and taverns. Interspersed were the modest homes of
the craftsmen and artisans who resided here. Old City (as it became
known some 40 years ago, to distinguish it from the national park area)
is aptly named; it is one of the city's oldest and most historic neighborhoods, home to Elfreth's Alley, the Betsy Ross House, and Christ
Church, where Washington and Adams came (across the tracks!) to
worship at services. There's evidence of the Quaker presence here too,
in the Arch Street Meeting House.

This area has been dubbed Philadelphia's SoHo. Many cast-iron building facades remain, though the old warehouses, with telltale names exposing their original use, like the Sugar Refinery and the Hoopskirt Factory, now house well-lighted loft apartments popular with artists and architects. There are small theaters—the Painted Bride, the Arden Theatre Company—and numerous art galleries. Many good restaurants have opened in the neighborhood, adding to its appeal. The Old City Arts Association hosts a festive, popular event the first Friday of each month (known, appropriately enough, as First Friday), when the galleries throw open their doors during evening hours.

Numbers in the text correspond to numbers in the margin and on the Historic Area and Penn's Landing map.

A Good Walk

A walk through Old City begins at 2nd and Market streets, location of the impressive **Christ Church** ⑲, attended by George and Martha Washington, among other notables. Continuing north on 2nd Street for a block and passing Arch Street, you'll come to a tiny Colonial street on the right, **Elfreth's Alley** ⑳; two houses are open to the public. Head back to 2nd Street, turn right (north), and a few footsteps will take you to the **Fireman's Hall Museum** ㉑, with exhibits on the history of fire fighting. If you then follow 2nd Street back to Arch and turn right (west), you'll find the most popular residence in Philadelphia, the **Betsy Ross House** ㉒.

A bit farther along, between 321 and 323 Arch Street, you can peer into the gated **Loxley Court** and its 18th-century houses and then cross the street to the Society of Friends' **Arch Street Meeting House** ㉓. Just ahead one block is the **Christ Church Burial Ground,** final resting place for Ben Franklin and other signers of the Declaration of Independence. Across 5th Street is the **Free Quaker Meeting House,** built for Friends who had been disowned by their pacifist meetings for participating in the Revolutionary War. Diagonally across Arch Street stands the **United States Mint** ㉔, where you can watch coins being made. If you're up for an adventure—and a hearty 1¾-mi walk (each way)—you could cross the Benjamin Franklin Bridge. The walkway entrance is about two blocks north of the Mint, on 5th Street. Otherwise, turn left (south) on 5th Street, cross Arch Street, and walk until you find a redbrick courtyard, entrance to the modern building that houses both the **National Museum of American Jewish History** ㉕ and **Mikveh Israel** ㉖, the oldest Jewish congregation in Philadelphia. Walking two blocks west on Arch Street to 7th Street brings you to the **Afro-American Historical and Cultural Museum** ㉗, with displays that illuminate the black experience through the centuries. At this point you might want to choose between Poe and toes—follow 7th Street (on foot or by bus) five blocks north to the residence and exhibits at the Edgar Allan Poe National Historical Site or walk one block north and one block west to 8th and Race streets to peruse the collection of footwear at the **Shoe Museum** (call ahead for an appointment).

TIMING
If possible, set aside four to five hours on a Sunday for your visit to Old City. You could attend the 9 AM service at Christ Church, as George and Martha Washington did, and then join the 10:30 Quaker meeting at the Arch Street Friends Meeting House, where William Penn worshiped. Try to avoid scheduling a Monday visit, when two of the top sights—the Betsy Ross House and Elfreth's Alley—are closed. On a weekday it's worth your while to see the coin-making operation at the Mint. If you detour to the Poe House, allow another two hours.

You can take this walk in any kind of weather and at any time of year since the neighborhood is a small one.

㉗ **Afro-American Historical and Cultural Museum.** Permanent and changing exhibits are dedicated to the history, fine art, artifacts, crafts, and culture of African-Americans in the United States—with a focus on Philadelphia and Pennsylvania. Recent exhibitions have showcased African-American female sculptors and sports in Philadelphia. Every year the museum presents a jazz series. The museum's gift shop offers the area's widest selection of books on black culture, history, fiction, poetry, and drama, along with African textiles and sculpture and African-American jewelry, prints, and tiles. Opened in the Bicentennial year of 1976, this is the first museum of its kind funded and built by a city. ⊠ *701 Arch St.,* ☎ *215/574–0380.* ⊡ *$6.* ⊙ *Tues.–Sat. 10– 5, Sun. noon–6.*

㉓ **Arch Street Meeting House.** Constructed in 1804 for the Philadelphia Yearly Meeting of the Society of Friends, this building of simple lines is still used for that purpose, as well as for biweekly services. The largest Friends meeting house in the world, it was built to hold 3,000 people. When a contemporary architect measured the space, he determined that each of those folks would have only 18 inches to sit in. Today the meeting house can accommodate about 800 20th-century-size behinds! A small museum in the church presents a series of dioramas and a 14-minute slide show depicting the life and accomplishments of William Penn, who gave the land on which the meeting house sits to the Society of Friends. Quaker guides give tours year-round. ⊠ *4th and Arch Sts.,* ☎ *215/627–2667.* ⊡ *$1 minimum donation requested.* ⊙ *Mon.– Sat. 10–4; services Thurs. at 10 and Sun. at 10:30.*

OFF THE
BEATEN PATH

BENJAMIN FRANKLIN BRIDGE – When the bridge opened in 1926, its 1,750-ft main span made it the longest suspension bridge in the world. Paul Cret, architect of the Rodin Museum, was the designer. After a new blue paint job and a lighting system that shows off its contours, the bridge is more beautiful than ever. You can get the best view of riverfront Philadelphia by walking or bicycling across the smooth, resurfaced walkway. Cars, trucks, and trains zoom past, and brisk winds make your face tingle as you cross the Delaware River, 150 ft below. Start the 1¾-mi walk from either the Philadelphia side, two blocks north of the U.S. Mint, or the Camden, New Jersey, side. Only the south walkway is open, but that's the best view anyway. ⊠ *5th and Vine Sts.,* ☎ *215/ 925-8780.* ⊡ *Free.* ⊙ *Daily 6 AM–around 7 PM (earlier in winter).*

★ ☾ **㉒** **Betsy Ross House.** It's easy to find this little brick house with the gabled roof: Just look for the 13-star flag displayed from its second-floor window. Whether Betsy Ross—who worked in her family's flag making and upholstery business—actually lived here and whether she really made the first Stars and Stripes is debatable. Nonetheless, the house, built about 1760, is a splendid example of a Colonial Philadelphia home and is fun to visit. Owned and maintained by the city of Philadelphia, the eight-room house is crammed with artifacts such as a family Bible and Betsy Ross's chest of drawers and reading glasses. The small rooms are furnished with period pieces to reflect the life of this hardworking Quaker (who died at the age of 84, outliving three husbands). You may have to wait in line here, as this is one of the city's most popular tourist attractions. The house, with its winding narrow stairs, is not accessible to people with disabilities. Alongside the house is brick-paved Atwater Kent Park, with a fountain, benches, and the graves of Betsy Ross and her third husband, John Claypoole. ⊠ *239 Arch St.,* ☎ *215/627–5343.* ⊡ *Free.* ⊙ *Tues.–Sun. 10–5.*

NEED A
BREAK? **Mulberry Market** (✉ 236 Arch St., ☎ 215/592–8022) is a great little
market stocked floor to ceiling with goodies, from freshly baked breads
and steaming coffee to deli sandwiches and cereal. You can pick up
anything you might need for a picnic or to stock your hotel room. The
small restaurant in the rear is open daily from 7 AM to 10 or 11 PM.

❶ Christ Church. The Anglicans of the Church of England built a wooden
church on this site in 1697. When they outgrew it, they erected a new
church, the most sumptuous in the colonies, modeled on the work of
famed English architect Sir Christopher Wren. The symmetrical, classical facade with arched windows, completed in 1754, is a fine example of Georgian architecture; the church is one of the city's treasures.
The congregation included 15 signers of the Declaration of Independence. The bells and the soaring 196-ft steeple, the tallest in the
colonies, were financed by lotteries run by Benjamin Franklin. Brass
plaques mark the pews of George and Martha Washington, John and
Abigail Adams, Betsy Ross, and others. Two blocks west of the church
is ☞ **Christ Church Burial Ground.** ✉ *2nd St. north of Market St.,* ☎
215/922–1695. ☉ *Mar.–Dec., Mon.–Sat. 9–5, Sun. 1–5; Jan.–Feb.,
Wed.–Sat. 9–5, Sun. 1–5; services Sun. 9 and 11, Wed. noon.*

Christ Church Burial Ground. Weathered gravestones fill the resting place
of five signers of the Declaration and other Colonial patriots. The best-
known is Benjamin Franklin; he lies alongside his wife, Deborah, and
their son, Francis, who died at age four. According to local legend, throw-
ing a penny onto Franklin's grave will bring you good luck. Although
visitors can no longer walk through the cemetery, you can toss your
penny from outside the iron gate. ✉ *5th and Arch Sts.,* ☎ *215/922–
1695.*

OFF THE
BEATEN PATH **EDGAR ALLAN POE NATIONAL HISTORIC SITE** – Poe lived here, in the only
one of his Philadelphia residences still standing, from 1843 to 1844.
During that time some of his best-known short stories were published:
"The Telltale Heart," "The Black Cat," and "The Gold Bug." You can tour
the 19th-century three-story brick house; to evoke the spirit of Poe, the
National Park Service deliberately keeps the three-story brick house
empty. An adjoining house has exhibits on Poe and his family, his work
habits, and his literary contemporaries; there is also an eight-minute film
and a small Poe library and reading room. A statue of a raven helps set
the mood, too. Special programs include "March Is Poetry Month" tours
and popular "ghostly" tours in October (reservations required). The site,
easily reached from the Afro-American Historical and Cultural Museum,
is five blocks north of Market Street. SEPTA Bus 47 travels on 7th Street
to Spring Garden Street, where you should disembark. ✉ *532 N. 7th
St.,* ☎ *215/597–8780.* ▣ *Free.* ☉ *June–Oct., daily 9–5; Nov.–May,
Wed.–Sun. 9–5.*

★ **❷ Elfreth's Alley.** The alley, the oldest continuously occupied residential
street in America, dates to 1702. Much of Colonial Philadelphia re-
sembled this area, with its cobblestone streets and narrow two- or three-
story brick houses. These were modest row homes, most built for rent,
lived in by craftsmen, such as cabinetmakers, silversmiths, pewterers,
and their families. They also housed captains and others who made
their living in the city's busy shipping industry. The earliest houses (two
stories) have pent eaves; taller houses, built after the Revolution, show
the influence of the Federal style. The Elfreth's Alley Association has
restored Numbers 124 and 126; the latter is a Colonial dressmaker's
home, with authentic furnishings and a Colonial kitchen. On the first
weekend in June residents celebrate Fete Days, when about 25 of the

30 homes are open to the public for tours hosted by guides in Colonial garb. On the first weekend in December homeowners again welcome visitors for Christmas tours. The rest of the year only Numbers 124 and 126 are open. ⊠ *Front and 2nd Sts. between Arch and Race Sts.,* ☎ *215/574–0560.* 🖭 *$2 for Nos. 124 and 126.* ☉ *Jan.–Feb., Sat. 10–4, Sun. noon–4; Mar.–Dec., Tues.–Sat. 10–4, Sun. noon–4.*

☙ ㉑ **Fireman's Hall Museum.** This museum, housed in an authentic 1876 firehouse, traces the history of fire fighting, from the volunteer company founded in Philadelphia by Benjamin Franklin in 1736 to the professional departments of the 20th century. The collection includes early hand- and horse-drawn fire engines, such as an 1815 hand pumper and a 1907 three-horse Metropolitan steamer; fire marks (18th-century building signs marking them as insured for fire); uniforms; and other memorabilia. ⊠ *147 N. 2nd St.,* ☎ *215/923–1438.* 🖭 *Free.* ☉ *Tues.–Sat. 9–5.*

Free Quaker Meeting House. A small museum here is dedicated to the history of the Free "Fighting" Quakers, a group that broke away from the Society of Friends to take up arms against the British during the Revolutionary War. The building was designed as a place of worship by Samuel Wetherill, one of the original leaders of the group, after they were disowned by their pacifist brothers. Among the 100 members were Betsy Ross (then Elizabeth Griscom) and Thomas Mifflin, a signer of the Constitution. After the Free Quaker group dissolved (many left to become Episcopalian), the building was used as a school, library, and warehouse. The meeting house, built in the Quaker plain style with a brick front and gable roof, has been carefully restored. ⊠ *500 Arch St.,* ☎ *215/923–6777.* 🖭 *Free.* ☉ *Memorial Day–Labor Day, Tues.–Sat. 10–4; Sun. 12–4.*

Loxley Court. One of the restored 18th-century houses in this lovely court was once home to Benjamin Loxley, a carpenter who worked on Independence Hall. The court's claim to fame, according to its residents, is as the spot where Benjamin Franklin flew his kite in his experiment with lightning; the key tied to it was the key to Loxley's front door. ⊠ *321–323 Arch St.*

㉖ **Mikveh Israel.** Nathan Levy, a Colonial merchant whose ship, the *Myrtilla,* brought the Liberty Bell to America, helped found this congregation in 1740, making it the oldest in Philadelphia and the second oldest in the United States. The original synagogue was at 3rd and Cherry streets; the congregation's current space (1976) is in the Sephardic style and occupies the same building as the ☞ **National Museum of American Jewish History.** The synagogue's cemetery (about eight blocks away, outside Old City) was established in 1738. Levy acquired the land from William Penn as a family burial ground; it was later expanded to accommodate the Jewish community. Buried there are Haym Salomon, a financier of the American Revolution, and Rebecca Gratz, the inspiration for the character Rebecca in Sir Walter Scott's novel *Ivanhoe.* ⊠ *Synagogue: 44 N. 4th St.,* ☎ *215/922–5446.* ☉ *Mon.–Thurs. 9:30–5, Fri. 9:30–3, Sun. noon–5. Services Fri. evening and Sat. 9 AM. To arrange a tour, call the National Museum of American Jewish History,* ☎ *215/923–3811.* ⊠ *Cemetery: Spruce St. between 8th and 9th Sts.,* ☎ *215/922–5446.* ☉ *Guide present in summer, weekdays 10–4; Sept.–June, visiting arrangements made through synagogue office.*

㉕ **National Museum of American Jewish History.** Established in 1976, the museum is the only one in the nation dedicated exclusively to collecting, preserving, and interpreting artifacts pertaining to the American

Jewish experience. It presents exhibits and programs exploring not only Jewish life in general but also issues of American ethnic identity, history, art, and culture. In the fall of 1998 a new permanent exhibition, *Creating American Jews*, will interpret the shaping of American Jewish cultural identity over 300 years. The museum shares a building with ☞ **Mikveh Israel.** ⊠ *55 N. 5th St.,* ☎ *215/923–3811.* ⊠ *$2.50.* ☉ *Mon.–Thurs. 10–5, Fri. 10–3, Sun. noon–5.*

Shoe Museum. Housed on the sixth floor of the Pennsylvania College of Podiatric Medicine, this unusual museum displays 500 pairs of "Footwear Through the Ages." The collection includes burial sandals from ancient Egypt, Eskimo snowshoes, Moroccan two-heeled shoes, and shoes used in the foot binding of Chinese women. Celebrity items include basketball player Julius Erving's huge sneakers, Joe Frazier's boxing shoes, Lucille Ball's pink silk sandals, and shoes belonging to past presidents and four first ladies. ⊠ *8th and Race Sts.,* ☎ *215/625–5243.* ☉ *Tours by appointment only, usually Wed. and Fri.*

㉔ United States Mint. The first U.S. mint was built in Philadelphia at 16th and Spring Garden streets in 1792, when the Bank of North America adopted dollars and cents instead of shillings and pence as standard currency; the current mint was built in 1971. On the self-guided tour, you can see blank disks being melted, cast, and pressed into coins, which are then inspected, counted, and bagged. The visitors' gallery has an exhibition of medals from the nation's wars, including the Medal of Honor, the Purple Heart, and the Bronze Star. Seven beautiful Tiffany glass tile mosaics depict coin making in ancient Rome. A shop in the lobby sells special coins and medals—in mint condition. Note that no camera or video equipment is allowed. ⊠ *5th and Arch Sts.,* ☎ *215/597–7350.* ⊠ *Free.* ☉ *Sept.–Apr., weekdays 9–4:30; May–June, Mon.–Sat. 9–4:30; July–Aug., daily 9–4:30. Coinage machinery operates weekdays only.*

SOCIETY HILL AND PENN'S LANDING
Enduring Grace and the Waterfront City

In the 18th century Society Hill was—as it still is today—Philadelphia's showplace. A gem of a preserved district, it is easily the city's most photogenic neighborhood, filled with hidden courtyards, delightful decorative touches like chimney pots and brass door knockers, wrought-iron foot scrapers, and other remnants from the days of horse-drawn carriages and muddy, unpaved streets. Here time has not quite stopped but meanders down the cobblestone streets, whiling away the hours.

A trove of Colonial- and Federal-style brick row houses and narrow streets, Society Hill stretches from the Delaware River to 6th Street, south of Independence National Historical Park. Those homes built before 1750 in the Colonial style generally have 2½ stories and a dormer window jutting out of a steep roof. The less heavy, more graceful houses built after the Revolution were often in the Federal style, popularized in England in the 1790s.

Here lived the "World's People," wealthier Anglicans who arrived after William Penn and loved music and dancing—pursuits the Quakers shunned when they set up their enclave in Old City, north of Market Street, in a less desirable commercial area. The "Society" in the neighborhood's moniker refers, however, to the Free Society of Traders, a group of business investors who settled here on William Penn's advice.

Today many homes in this area have been lovingly restored by modern pioneers who began moving into the area 30 years ago and rescued Society Hill from becoming a slum. Inspired urban renewal efforts have since transformed vast empty factory spaces into airy lofts; new town houses were carefully designed to blend in with the old. Colonial houses have been rehabbed, and picturesque city corners rediscovered. As a result, Society Hill is not just a showcase for historic churches and mansions but a living, breathing neighborhood.

Before setting out to explore Society Hill, you may want to tour Philadelphia's nearby waterfront, with attractions that include a seaport museum, historic marine vessels, and an aquarium. Those who don't wish to enjoy this waterside detour should jump ahead in the following walk to Head House Square.

Numbers in the text correspond to numbers in the margin and on the Historic Area and Penn's Landing map.

A Good Walk

Begin your waterfront visit at **Penn's Landing** ㉘. with its riverfront plaza, museum, and restaurants. To get there, cross Chestnut Street at Front Street and walk through the park, which deposits you at the top of the Great Plaza. Descend the steps and walk one block to your right to see the centerpiece of Penn's Landing, the **Independence Seaport Museum** ㉙; interactive exhibits, nautical artifacts, and ships add to the fun. From March through November, right in front of the museum you can catch the "ferry to the fishies": The RiverLink Ferry crosses the Delaware River to Camden, New Jersey, in about 10 minutes, leaving you a few steps from the **New Jersey State Aquarium** ㉚.

On your return you'll see the tall masts of the 1883 fishing ship *Gazela of Philadelphia,* docked next to the museum—when it's in port. A five-minute stroll south along the river brings you to two historic ships well worth a visit. Descend the steep metal ladder into the **USS *Becuna*** ㉛. Arise from the depths of this submarine and cross the gangplank for a decidedly different shipboard experience on Commodore Dewey's flagship, the **USS *Olympia*** ㉜. If you have a car, before you head to Society Hill you could take a detour to visit Fort Mifflin and the John Heinz National Wildlife Refuge at Tinicum, both near the airport.

Your next stop is Society Hill. Backtrack half a block north on Columbus Boulevard to cobblestone Dock Street and turn left—right will land you in the Delaware River! Just ahead are the Society Hill Towers, three high-rise apartment buildings designed in the early '60s by I. M. Pei. These, along with the Society Hill Townhouses at 3rd and Locust streets, were the winning entries in a design competition for housing that would symbolize the renewal of Society Hill. At the dead end turn left. You'll be walking along 38th Parallel Street; in the park to your left is Philadelphia's Vietnam Veterans Memorial. Turn right (west) on Spruce Street and left (south) on 2nd Street to Delancey Street. On summer weekends you may want to continue a few blocks farther on 2nd Street to **Head House Square** ㉝, a Colonial marketplace that hosts a crafts and fine arts fair. Just one block ahead is South Street, with its funky shops, bookstores, restaurants, and bars. Otherwise, walk west along Delancey Street, lined with some of the city's prized Colonial homes.

On your right at 4th Street is the freestanding **Physick House** ㉞, with its superb Federal and Empire furnishings. In the next few blocks, you'll see three of the city's historic churches. Follow 4th Street half a block south to Pine Street and turn right (west) toward 6th Street. Between Pine and Lombard streets, on what has been christened Richard Allen

Avenue, is **Mother Bethel African Methodist Episcopal Church** ㉟. Head east on Pine Street; on your right, just before 4th Street, is **Old Pine Street Presbyterian Church** ㊱. This, and **St. Peter's Episcopal Church** ㊲, which dominates most of the next block, were designed by Robert Smith. St. Peter's slim belfry tower is six stories high, topped by a wooden steeple. On the northwest corner of 3rd and Pine streets is the **Thaddeus Kosciuszko National Memorial** ㊳, honoring the Polish general who fought in the Revolution.

Turn left (north) on Third Street. Within a few blocks, you'll come across the brownstones of **Bouvier's Row** (Nos. 258–262), once owned by Jacqueline Kennedy Onassis's ancestors. Just a few doors up is the brick Georgian **Powel House** ㊴, filled with fine 18th-century furniture. Continue north on 3rd Street to Willings Alley (just opposite the former Old St. Paul's Church). Turn left and then right into the courtyard of **Old St. Joseph's Church** ㊵, the city's first Catholic church. Walk up the alley to 4th Street and then a half block south to **Old St. Mary's Church** ㊶, another early Catholic church. Following 4th Street back north brings you to the nation's oldest fire-insurance company, the **Philadelphia Contributionship for the Insurance of Houses from Loss by Fire** ㊷. Turn left on Walnut Street to 6th Street, and you'll come upon tree-shaded **Washington Square,** one of the five in Penn's original city plan. On the east side of the square is the **Athenaeum** ㊸ research library and gallery. If you have an interest in medicine, walk two blocks south and two more west to Pennsylvania Hospital, the nation's oldest.

TIMING

You could easily spend a whole day here, with the bulk of your time allotted to Penn's Landing. If your kids are in tow, you'll want to allow an hour and a half for the Independence Seaport Museum and its historic boats and another two to three hours for the ferry ride and visit to the aquarium. You'll need about one hour to walk through Society Hill, more if you tour the Powel and Physick houses. If walking is your main interest, save this excursion for a warm day, because it can be quite windy along the waterfront. In winter you can ice-skate at the RiverRink. The prime time for this walk? A summer Sunday, when the Great Plaza at Penn's Landing bustles with festivals and Head House Square turns into an open-air fine arts and crafts market.

Sights to See

㊸ **Athenaeum.** Housed in a national landmark Italianate brownstone dating from the mid-1800s and designed by John Notman, the Athenaeum of Philadelphia is a research library specializing in architectural history and design. Its American Architecture Collection has close to a million items. Founded in 1814, the library also contains significant materials on the French in America and on early American travel, exploration, and transportation. Besides books, the Athenaeum houses notable paintings, period furniture, and changing exhibits in the gallery. ⊠ *219 S. 6th St.,* ☎ *215/925–2688.* ⊠ *Free.* ☺ *Gallery: Mon.–Tues. and Thurs.–Fri. 9–5, Wed. noon–8; tours and research by appointment only.*

Bouvier's Row. Three of the Victorian brownstones on a stretch of 3rd Street near Spruce Street, often called Bouvier's Row, were once owned by the late Jacqueline Kennedy Onassis's ancestors. Michel Bouvier, her great-great-grandfather—the first of the family to come from France— and many of his descendants lie in the family vault at Old St. Mary's Church, a few blocks away on 4th Street. ⊠ *258–262 S. 3rd St.*

FORT MIFFLIN – Because of its Quaker origins, Philadelphia had no defenses until 1772, when the British began building Fort Mifflin. It was completed in 1776 by Revolutionary forces under General Washington. In a 40-day battle in 1777, 300 Continental defenders held off British forces long enough for Washington's troops to flee to Valley Forge. The fort was almost totally destroyed but was rebuilt in 1798 from plans by French architect Pierre Charles L'Enfant, who also designed the plan for Washington, D.C. In use until 1962, the fort has served as a prisoner-of-war camp, an artillery battalion, and a munitions dump. Within this 49-acre National Historic Landmark, you can see cannons and carriages, officers' quarters, soldiers' barracks (which contain an exhibition called *Defense of the Delaware*), an artillery shed, a blacksmith shop, a bomb shelter, and a museum. Special events include Civil War Garrison Days in October and a reenactment of the siege of Fort Mifflin held in November. From Penn's Landing you can easily hop on I-95 to reach the fort; call for directions. ⊠ *Island Rd. and Hog Island Rd., on the Delaware River near Philadelphia International Airport,* ☎ *215/685–4192.* 🖼 *$4.* ☉ *Apr.–Nov., Wed.–Sun. 10–4; tours at 11, 1, and 3.*

Gazela of Philadelphia. Built in 1883 and formerly named *Gazela Primeiro*, this 177-ft square-rigger is the last of a Portuguese fleet of cod-fishing ships. Still in use as late as 1969, it is the oldest and largest wooden square-rigger still sailing. As the Port of Philadelphia's ambassador of goodwill, the *Gazela* sails up and down the Atlantic Coast to participate in harbor festivals and celebrations. It is also a school ship and a museum. An all-volunteer crew of 35 works all winter on ship maintenance; in summer they set sail. ⊠ *Penn's Landing at Market St.,* ☎ *215/923–9030.* ☉ *Call ahead; tours can be arranged when the ship is in port.*

㉝ **Head House Square.** This open-air Colonial marketplace, extending from Pine Street to Lombard Street, is a reminder of how people used to shop on market days. It was first established as New Market in 1745. George Washington was among the people who came here to buy butter, eggs, meat, fish, herbs, and vegetables. The Head House, a boxy building with a cupola and weathervane, was built in 1803 as the office and home of the market master, who tested the quality of the goods. Today, on weekends from June through September, the square is home to a crafts and fine arts fair with more than 100 Delaware Valley artists. It bustles until 11 on Saturday nights; on Sunday from 1 to 3 there are free children's workshops. ⊠ *2nd and Pine Sts.,* ☎ *215/790–0782.*

Ready for milk and cookies? **Koffmeyers** can deliver on the latter. The store is famous for their all-natural old-fashioned cookies. Try the chocolate chip and macadamia nut cookie or a Head House Square—a vanilla brownie filled with chocolate and walnuts. ⊠ *Head House Sq. at 2nd and Lombard Sts.,* ☎ *215/922–0717.*

★ ☾ ㉙ **Independence Seaport Museum.** This bigger, better incarnation of the old Philadelphia Maritime Museum houses many nautical artifacts, figureheads, and ship models, but now the emphasis is on interactive exhibits that convey just what the river has meant to Philadelphia's fortunes over the years. You can climb in the gray, cold wooden bunks used in steerage, unload cargo from giant container ships with a miniature crane, weld and rivet a ship's hull, or even hop in a scull and row along the Schuylkill. Enter the museum by passing under the three-story replica of the Benjamin Franklin Bridge. ⊠ *211 S. Columbus Blvd., at*

Walnut St., ☏ 215/925−5439. ▱ $5 museum only; $7.50 museum and ☞ USS Olympia *and ☞ USS* Becuna. ☉ *Daily 10−5.*

OFF THE
BEATEN PATH

JOHN HEINZ NATIONAL WILDLIFE REFUGE AT TINICUM − More than 280 species of ducks, herons, egrets, geese, gallinules, and other birds have been spotted at this environmental center. Resident earthbound animals include turtles, foxes, muskrats, deer, raccoons, weasels, and snakes. Facilities in this 1,200-acre freshwater tidal marsh, the largest remaining in Pennsylvania (it used to be 6,000 acres), include 8 mi of foot trails, an observation blind, an observation deck, boardwalks through the wet areas, and a canoe launch into the 4½-mi stretch of Darby Creek that runs through the preserve (the best way to see it). Bird-watchers can prepare for their visit by calling 215/567−BIRD for recent sightings. The refuge is convenient to I-95, which you can pick up from Penn's Landing. Call for directions. ✉ *86th St. and Lindbergh Blvd.,* ☏ *215/365− 3118.* ▱ *Free.* ☉ *Daily 8−sunset; visitor center daily 9−4.*

㉟ **Mother Bethel African Methodist Episcopal Church.** Society Hill holds a notable landmark in the history of African-Americans in the city. In 1787, Richard Allen led fellow blacks who left St. George's Methodist Church as a protest against the segregated worship. Allen, a lay minister and former slave who had bought his freedom from the Chew family of Germantown, purchased this site in 1791. It is believed to be the country's oldest parcel of land continuously owned by African-Americans. When the African Methodist Episcopal Church was formed in 1816, Allen was its first bishop. The current church, the fourth on the site, is an example of the 19th-century Romanesque Revival style, with broad arches and a square corner tower, opalescent stained-glass windows, and stunning woodwork. The earlier church buildings were the site of a school where Allen taught slaves to read and also a stop on the Underground Railroad. Allen's tomb and a small museum are on the lower level. ✉ *419 Richard Allen Ave., 6th St. between Pine and Lombard Sts.,* ☏ *215/925−0616.* ▱ *Free.* ☉ *Museum and guided tours, Tues.−Sat. 10−2.*

㉚ **New Jersey State Aquarium.** This marvel across the Delaware in Camden opened in 1992, and 6,000 fish now call it home. Ocean Base Atlantic has a 760,000-gallon open ocean tank (the country's second largest), with sharks, stingrays, sea turtles, 1,400 fish, and a diver who can answer your questions via a "scubaphone." The latest exhibition—*WOW! Weird? Or Wonderful?*—showcases 400 of the world's freakiest fish. There are daily seal shows, dive demonstrations, and even the chance to pet a shark. You can drive here or take the ferry from Penn's Landing. *Aquarium:* ✉ *S. Riverside Dr., Camden, NJ,* ☏ *609/ 365−3300.* ▱ *$10.95.* ☉ *Mid-Mar.−mid-Sept., daily 9:30−5:30; mid-Sept.−mid-Mar., daily 10−5.* ✉ *RiverLink Ferry: Penn's Landing near Walnut St.,* ☏ *215/925−LINK.* ▱ *$5 round-trip.* ☉ *Mar.−Nov.; departs from Penn's Landing every hour on the hour, daily 10−5; departs from New Jersey every hour on the ½ hour, daily 10:30−5:30. Extended hours for Penn's Landing events and Blockbuster-Sony Entertainment Centre concerts.*

㊱ **Old Pine Street Presbyterian Church.** Designed by Robert Smith in 1768 as a simple brick Georgian-style building, Old Pine is the only remaining Colonial Presbyterian church and churchyard in Philadelphia. Badly damaged by British troops during the Revolution, it served as a hospital and then a stable. In the mid-19th century, its exterior had a Greek Revival facelift that included Corinthian columns. In the 1980s, the interior walls and ceiling were stenciled with thistle and wave motifs, a reminder of its true name—Third, Scots, and Mariners Presbyterian Church, which documented the congregation's mergers. It is beautifully restored and painted in soft shades of periwinkle and yellow. In the churchyard are the graves of 100 Hessian soldiers from the Revolution—and of Eugene Ormandy, former conductor of the Philadelphia Orchestra. ⊠ *412 Pine St.,* ☎ *215/925–8051.* 🎫 *Free.* ☉ *Mon.– Sat. 9–3.*

㊵ Old St. Joseph's Church. In 1733, a tiny chapel was established by Jesuits for Philadelphia's 11 Catholic families. It was the first place in the English-speaking world where Catholic mass could be legally celebrated, under William's Penn 1701 Charter of Privileges, which guaranteed religious freedom. But freedom didn't come easy; on one occasion Quakers had to patrol St. Joseph's to prevent a Protestant mob from disrupting the service. The present church, built in 1839, is the third on this site. The late 19th-century stained-glass windows are notable. ⊠ *321 Willings Alley,* ☎ *215/923–1733.* ☉ *Daily 11–4; from 2 to 4, stop at the rectory for admittance.*

㊶ Old St. Mary's Church. The city's second-oldest Catholic church, circa 1763, became its first cathedral when the archdiocese was formed in 1808. A Gothic-style facade was added in 1880; the interior was redone in 1979. The stained-glass windows, a ceiling mural of St. Mary, and brass chandeliers that hung in the Founders Room of Independence Hall until 1967 are highlights. Commodore John Barry, a Revolutionary War naval hero, and other famous Philadelphians are buried in the small churchyard. ⊠ *252 S. 4th St.,* ☎ *215/923–7930.* ☉ *Mon.–Sat. 9–4:45, Sun. 9–1 (for services).*

㉘ Penn's Landing. The spot where William Penn stepped ashore in 1682 is the hub of a 37-acre park that stretches from Market Street south to Lombard Street. The development of this area—an ambitious effort to reclaim the Delaware River waterfront—began back in 1967. Today a dozen clubs and restaurants line the waterfront; future plans include condominiums, offices, hotels, and more recreation areas and restaurants. In warm weather, the **Great Plaza** at Penn's Landing—an outdoor amphitheater—is the scene of the annual Riverblues and Jambalaya Jam festivals, as well as jazz and big band concerts, ethnic festivals, children's events and more. In winter (from the Friday after Thanksgiving to March 10), you can ice-skate outdoors at the **Blue Cross River-Rink,** next to the Great Plaza. The ☞ **Independence Seaport Museum** is here, too. Walk along the waterfront, and you'll see scores of pleasure boats moored at the marina and cargo ships chugging up and down the Delaware. Philadelphia's harbor, which includes docking facilities in New Jersey and Delaware, is one of the world's largest freshwater ports. ⊠ *On the Delaware River from Market St. to Lombard St.,* ☎ *215/923–4992.*

OFF THE
BEATEN PATH
    PENNSYLVANIA HOSPITAL – Inside the fine 18th-century original buildings of the oldest hospital in the United States are the nation's first medical library and first surgical amphitheater (an 1804 innovation, with a skylight). Dr. Thomas Bond thought of the idea of a community hospital to improve care for the poor and enrolled Franklin in his vision. The Pennsylvania Assembly agreed to put up £2,000 if those interested in a hospital could do the same: It took Franklin only a month and a half to raise the money. The hospital also has a portrait gallery, early medical instruments, art objects, and a rare-book library with items dating from 1762. The artwork includes the Benjamin West painting *Christ Healing the Sick in the Temple.* Today Pennsylvania Hospital is a full-service modern medical center four blocks southwest of the ☞ **Athenaeum.** Pick up a

copy of "Pennsylvania Hospital: A Walking Tour" in the marketing department on the second floor of the Pine Building. ⊠ *8th and Spruce Sts.,* ☎ *215/829–3971.* ⊠ *Free.* ⊙ *Weekdays 8:30–5; call to arrange a guided group tour.*

㊷ Philadelphia Contributionship for the Insurance of Houses from Loss by Fire. The Contributionship, the nation's oldest fire insurance company, was founded by Benjamin Franklin in 1752; the present Greek Revival building with fluted marble Corinthian columns dates from 1836 and has some magnificently elegant salons (particularly the boardroom, where a seating plan on the wall lists Benjamin Franklin as the first incumbent of seat Number One). The architect, Thomas U. Walter, was also responsible for the dome and House and Senate wings of the U.S. Capitol in Washington, D.C. This is still an active business, but there is a small museum open to the public. ⊠ *212 S. 4th St.,* ☎ *215/627–1752.* ⊠ *Free.* ⊙ *Weekdays 10–3.*

★ **㉞ Physick House.** Built in 1786, the only freestanding house in Society Hill (you will have noticed the famous Philadelphia row houses by now) is also one of the most beautiful homes in America, with elegantly restored interiors and some of the finest Federal and Empire furniture in Philadelphia. Touches of Napoléon's France are everywhere: the golden bee motif woven into upholstery, the magenta-hued Aubusson rug (the emperor's favorite color), and stools in the style of Pompeii, the Roman city rediscovered at the time of the house's construction. Upstairs in the parlor, note the inkstand that still retains Benjamin Franklin's fingerprints. The house's most famous owner was Philip Syng Physick, a leading physician in the days before anesthesia and known as the "Father of American Surgery." His most celebrated patient was Chief Justice John Marshall. The garden planted on three sides of the house is filled with plants common in the 19th century: Complete with an Etruscan sarcophagus, a natural grotto, and antique cannon, it is considered by some to be the city's loveliest. ⊠ *321 S. 4th St.,* ☎ *215/ 925–7866.* ⊠ *$3.* ⊙ *Thurs.–Sat., guided tours at 11, noon, 1, and 2.*

★ **㊴ Powel House.** The 1765 brick Georgian house purchased by Samuel Powel in 1769 remains one of the most elegant homes in Philadelphia. Powel— the "Patriot Mayor"—was the last mayor of Philadelphia under the Crown and the first in the new republic. The lavish home, once a wreck slated for demolition, is furnished with important pieces of 18th-century Philadelphia furniture. The front hall is embellished with a mahogany staircase from Santo Domingo, and there is a signed Gilbert Stuart portrait in the parlor. In the second-floor ballroom, Mrs. Powel—the city's hostess-with-the-mostest—served floating islands and whipped syllabubs to distinguished guests (including Adams, Franklin, and Lafayette) on Nanking china that was a gift from George and Martha Washington. Today the ballroom can be rented for parties and special events, and high tea and a tour can be had by special arrangement. ⊠ *244 S. 3rd St.,* ☎ *215/627–0364.* ⊠ *$3.* ⊙ *Thurs.–Sat. noon–5, Sun. 1–5; other times by appointment.*

★ **㊲ St. Peter's Episcopal Church.** Founded by members of Christ Church (☞ *Old City, above*) who were living in newly settled Society Hill, St. Peter's has been in continuous use since its first service on September 4, 1761. William White (Bishop White), rector of Christ Church, also served in that role at St. Peter's until his death in 1836. The brick Palladian-style building was designed by Scottish architect Robert Smith, who was also responsible for Carpenters' Hall and the steeple on Christ Church. William Strickland's simple steeple, a Philadelphia landmark, was added in 1042. Notable features include the grand Palladian window on the chancel wall, high-backed box pews that were raised off the floor to eliminate drafts, and the unusual arrangement of altar and pulpit at either end of the main aisle. The design has been called "restrained," but what is palpable on a visit is the silence and grace of the stark white interior. In the churchyard lie Commodore John Hazelwood, a Revolutionary War hero, painter Charles Willson Peale, and seven Native American chiefs who died of smallpox on a visit to Philadelphia in 1793. ⊠ *313 Pine St.,* ☏ *215/925–5968.* ☉ *Weekdays 9–4, Sat. 11–3, Sun. 1–3. A guide is on hand Sat. and Sun. to answer questions; tours can be arranged by calling ahead on weekdays.*

㊳ Thaddeus Kosciuszko National Memorial. A Polish general who later became a national hero in his homeland, Kosciuszko came to the United States in 1776 to help fight in the Revolution; he distinguished himself as one of the first foreign volunteers in the war. The plain three-story brick house, built around 1776, has a portrait gallery; you can also view a six-minute film (in English and Polish) that portrays the general's activities during the Revolution. ⊠ *301 Pine St.,* ☏ *215/597–8974.* ▣ *Free.* ☉ *June–Oct., daily 9–5; Nov.–May, Wed.–Sun. 9–5.*

㊱ USS Becuna. You can tour this 318-ft-long "guppy class" submarine, which was commissioned in 1944 and conducted search-and-destroy missions in the South Pacific. The guides—all World War II submarine vets—tell amazing stories of what life was like for a crew of 88 men, at sea for months at a time, in these claustrophobic quarters. Then you can step through the narrow walkways, climb the ladders, and glimpse the torpedoes in their firing chambers. Kids will love it, but it's fascinating for adults, too. ⊠ *Penn's Landing at Spruce St.,* ☏ *215/922–5439.* ▣ *$7.50; must be purchased at* ☞ *Independence Seaport Museum, except in summer, when there is a booth outside ship; ticket also includes admission to seaport museum and* ☞ USS *Olympia.* ☉ *Daily 10–5.*

㊲ USS Olympia. Commodore George Dewey's flagship at the Battle of Manila in the Spanish-American War is the only remaining ship from that war. Dewey entered Manila Harbor after midnight on May 1, 1898. At 5:40 AM, he told his captain, "You may fire when ready, Gridley," and the battle began. By 12:30 the Americans had destroyed the entire Spanish fleet. The *Olympia* was the last ship of the "New Navy" of the 1880s and 1890s, the beginning of the era of steel ships. You can tour the entire restored ship, including the officers' staterooms, engine room, galley, gun batteries, pilothouse, and conning tower. ⊠ *Penn's Landing at Spruce St.,* ☏ *215/922–5439.* ▣ *$7.50; must be purchased at* ☞ *Independence Seaport Museum, except in summer, when there is a booth outside ship; ticket also includes admission to seaport museum and* ☞ USS *Becuna.* ☉ *Daily 10–5.*

Washington Square. Said to resemble a London square, this leafy area has been through numerous incarnations since it was set aside by William Penn. From 1705 until after the Revolution, the square was lined on three sides by houses and on the fourth by the Walnut Street Prison. The latter was home to Robert Morris, who went to debtors' prison after he helped finance the Revolution. The square served as a burial ground for victims of the 1793 yellow fever epidemic and for British and American soldiers who perished during the Revolution. By the 1840s the square had gained prestige as the center of the city's most fashionable neighborhood. It later became the city's publishing center. Today the grand buildings surrounding the square are mostly inhabited by businesses. Washington Square holds a Tomb of the Unknown Soldier, erected to the memory of unknown Revolutionary War soldiers. ⊠ *Between 6th and 7th Sts. and Walnut and Locust Sts.*

CENTER CITY
City Hall and Environs

For a grand introduction to the heart of the downtown area, climb the few steps to the plaza in front of the Municipal Services Building at 15th Street and John F. Kennedy Boulevard to get a great overview of the city. You'll feel surrounded by Philadelphia—City Hall, the PSFS Building, the art museum, the new skyscrapers at Liberty Place, Oldenburg's *Clothespin* statue, and more spread out around you.

There's a story behind this skyline. It begins with Philadelphia's historic City Hall, which reaches to 40 stories and was the tallest structure in the metropolis until 1987. No law prohibited taller buildings, but the tradition sprang from a gentleman's agreement not to build higher. In May 1984, when a developer proposed building two office towers that would break the 491-ft barrier, it became evident how much Philadelphians cared about their city—and how entrenched this tradition was: The proposal provoked a public outcry. The traditionalists contended the height limitation had made Philadelphia a city of human scale, given its streets and public places, and showed respect for tradition. The opposing camp thought that a dramatic new skyline would shatter the city's conservative image and encourage economic growth. After painstaking debate the go-ahead was granted. In short order, the midtown area became the hub of the city's commercial center, Market Street west of City Hall became a district of high-rise office buildings, and the area became a symbol of the city's ongoing transformation from a dying industrial town to a center for service industries. Here, too, are a number of museums, the excellent Reading Terminal Market and the convention center, and Chinatown.

Numbers in the text correspond to numbers in the margin and on the Center City and Along the Parkway map.

A Good Walk

Ask most locals where "downtown" or "Center City" is, and you'll find they agree that Victorian **City Hall** ① is at its heart. Take the elevator up to the tower for an incomparable bird's-eye view of the city. Leave City Hall by the north exit and cross John F. Kennedy Boulevard to the **Masonic Temple** ②, with its ornate interiors and collection of Masonic items. Two blocks north on Broad Street, at Cherry Street in a striking Victorian Gothic building, is the **Museum of American Art of the Pennsylvania Academy of the Fine Arts** ③, filled with paintings by such artists as Winslow Homer and Andrew Wyeth. Head west on Cherry Street one block to 15th Street, turn left, and walk south three blocks to Market Street. This walk will take you from the classics to the avant-garde: Claes Oldenburg's 45-ft-high, 10-ton steel **Clothespin.** (From here you can take public transportation to a few of the city's more distant sites—the Insectarium, the American-Swedish Historical Museum, and Bartram's Garden.)

Two blocks west of the sculpture are **Liberty Place One and Two** ④; the food court between them makes a great stop for lunch. Exit the building at 16th and Chestnut; three blocks east at 13th Street is **Lord & Taylor** ⑤, formerly the John Wanamaker store, famous for its eagle and its nine-story grand court. Walk over to Market Street, turn right, and go one block to 12th Street. Here is the **Philadelphia Saving Fund Society (PSFS) Building,** an early (1930) skyscraper. On the same block, SEPTA's headquarters holds the new **Transit Museum.** Two blocks block north on 12th Street is the **Reading Terminal Market** ⑥, filled with vendors of all kinds of food. Across Arch Street is the **Pennsyl-**

44

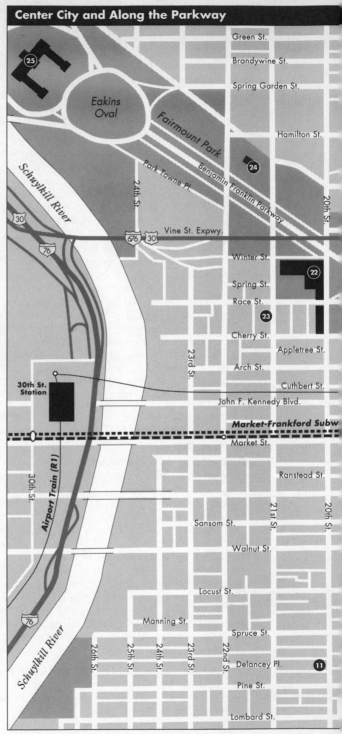

Center City and Along the Parkway

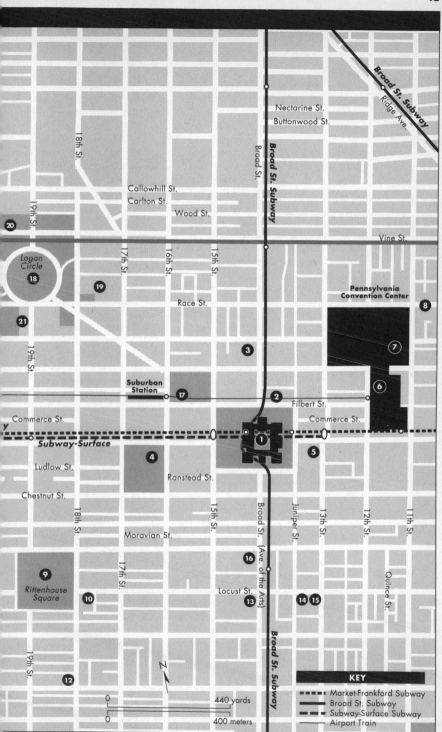

Nectarine St.
Buttonwood St.
Ridge Ave.
Broad St. Subway
18th St.
Callowhill St.
Carlton St.
Wood St.
19th St.
Broad St.
Vine St.
Logan Circle
17th St.
16th St.
15th St.
Race St.
Pennsylvania Convention Center
19th St.
Suburban Station
Filbert St.
Commerce St.
Commerce St.
Subway-Surface
Ludlow St.
Ranstead St.
Chestnut St.
18th St.
Moravian St.
15th St.
Broad St. (Ave. of the Arts)
Juniper St.
13th St.
12th St.
11th St.
17th St.
Rittenhouse Square
Locust St.
Quince St.
19th St.
Broad St. Subway

440 yards
400 meters

KEY
Market-Frankford Subway
Broad St. Subway
Subway-Surface Subway
Airport Train

vania Convention Center ⑦, which houses a terrific collection of contemporary art. Walking two blocks east on Arch Street brings you to the 40-ft-tall Chinese Friendship Gate, the unofficial entrance to the restaurants and stores of **Chinatown** ⑧.

TIMING

To get a feel for the city at work and its people, save this walk for a weekday, when the streets are bustling (on weekends the area can be quite deserted). Besides, the City Hall Observation Tower is open weekdays only, and both the Reading Terminal Market and the Masonic Temple, two don't-miss spots, are closed Sunday. You could complete this walk in 45 minutes, but if you want to sightsee, reserve about half a day, with an hour each at the Masonic Temple, City Hall Tower, and the Museum of American Art. If you get an early start, you can finish with lunch at the Reading Terminal Market.

Sights to See

OFF THE
BEATEN PATH

AMERICAN-SWEDISH HISTORICAL MUSEUM – The Swedes settled the Delaware Valley in the mid-1600s before William Penn, but few traces remain other than Gloria Dei (Old Swedes') Church (☞ Southwark and South Philadelphia, *below*) and this museum. Modeled after a 17th-century Swedish manor house, the museum has 14 galleries that trace the history of Swedes in the United States. The John Ericsson Room honors the designer of the Civil War ironclad ship the *Monitor,* and the Jenny Lind Room contains memorabilia from the Swedish Nightingale's American tour of 1848 to 1851. Other rooms display handmade costumed Swedish peasant dolls, crafts, paintings, and drawings. You can pick up the subway just below the *Clothespin* sculpture, at 15th and Market streets. ✉ *1900 Pattison Ave.,* ☎ *215/389-1776. Take Broad St. subway south to Pattison Ave. Cross Broad St., walk 5 blocks west through park to museum.* ☜ *$5.* ☉ *Tues.-Fri. 10-4, weekends noon-4.*

BARTRAM'S GARDEN – This 44-acre oasis is tucked into a heavily industrialized and depressed corner of southwest Philadelphia. Begun in 1728 by John Bartram, America's oldest surviving botanical garden has remained relatively unchanged while the surrounding areas have altered dramatically. With stone columns and carvings by Bartram himself, the 18th-century farmhouse on the grounds reflects his peculiar vision of classical and Colonial architecture. The self-trained Bartram became botanist to King George III, traveling throughout the colonies and returning with many unusual species. He corresponded and exchanged plants with botanists around the world. The house is a National Historic Landmark, and the trails extending to the Schuylkill River are part of the National Recreation Trails System. You can get the subway in front of the *Clothespin,* at 15th and Market streets. Note that you can get a map to tour the gardens only when the house is open. ✉ *54th St. and Lindbergh Blvd.,* ☎ *215/729-5281. 20-min ride on Trolley 36 from 15th and Market Sts., then right to the entrance.* ☜ *$3 for house tour; garden free.* ☉ *Garden, daily dawn to dusk; house May-Oct., Wed.-Sun. noon-4; Nov.-Apr., Wed.-Fri. noon-4.*

BRYN ATHYN CATHEDRAL – At one of the most beautiful spots in the Philadelphia area is a spectacular cathedral built in 12th-century Romanesque and 14th-century Gothic styles. Atop a hill overlooking the Pennypack Valley, the cathedral is the Episcopal seat of the Church of the New Jerusalem, a sect based on the writings of the Swedish scientist and mystic Emanuel Swedenborg. The main patrons of the church are descendants of John Pitcairn, an industrialist who made his fortune in paint and plate glass. Construction of the cathedral began in 1914 and went on for decades. It was built according to the medieval guild system: All materials—wood, metal, glass, stone—were brought to crafts-people at the site, and everything was fashioned by hand. The stained glass includes two colors, striated ruby and cobalt blue, found nowhere else in the Americas. Also on the hill is the former home of Raymond and Mildred Pitcairn, **Glencarin** (☎ 215/947–9919; call for appoint-ment), a neo-Romanesque building that's now a museum. From Broad Street in Center City, go north on Broad Street to Route 611, right on County Line Road, and south on Route 232 to the second traffic light; the cathedral will be on your right. ⊠ *Rte. 232, Huntingdon Pike at Cathedral Rd., Bryn Athyn, 15 mi north of Center City, ☎ 215/947–0266.* ⊡ *Free.* ⊙ *Daily 1–4 for 30–min tours (sometimes preempted by special events); visitors also welcome at services Sun. 9:30 and 11.*

❽ Chinatown. Centered on 10th and Race streets just two blocks north of Market Street, Chinatown serves as the residential and commercial hub of the Chinese community. Along with more than 50 restaurants, Chinatown has grocery stores, souvenir and gift shops, martial arts stu-dios, a fortune cookie store, bilingual street signs, and red-and-green pagoda-style telephone booths.

One striking Chinatown site is the **Chinese Friendship Gate,** straddling 10th Street at Arch Street. This intricate and colorful 40-ft-tall arch—the largest authentic Chinese gate outside China—was created by Chi-nese artisans, who brought their own tools and construction materials. The citizens of Tianjin, Philadelphia's sister city in China, donated the building materials, including the ornamental tile.

From February to May you can celebrate Chinese New Year with a 10-course banquet at the **Chinese Cultural Center** (⊠ 125 N. 10th St., ☎ 215/923–6767). The center occupies an 1831 building of the Peking Mandarin-palace style. ⊠ *9th to 11th Sts., Arch to Vine Sts.*

★ ❶ City Hall. Topped by a 37-ft bronze statue of William Penn, City Hall was Philadelphia's tallest building until 1987. With 642 rooms, it is the largest city hall in the country and the tallest masonry-bearing build-ing in the world: No steel structure supports it. Designed by architect John McArthur Jr., it took 30 years to build (from 1871 to 1900) and cost taxpayers more than $23 million to construct what has been called a "Victorian wedding cake of Renaissance styles." Placed about the facade are hundreds of statues by Alexander Milne Calder, who also designed the statue of William Penn at the top (Calder's son and grandson were artists, too; ☞ Logan Circle *in* The Benjamin Franklin Parkway, *below*). Calder's 27-ton cast iron statue of Penn is the largest single piece of sculpture on any building in the world.

Not only the geographic center of Penn's original city plan, City Hall is also the center of municipal and state government. Start at the north-east corner and ascend one flight to the mayor's ornate reception room (Room 202) and the recently restored Conversation Hall (Room 201). Many of the magnificent interiors—splendidly decorated with ma-hogany paneling, gold-leaf ceilings, and marble pillars—are patterned after the Second Empire salons of part of the Louvre in Paris. Take look, too, at the Supreme Court of Pennsylvania (municipal court se sions are open to the public) and the city council chambers (Room 4(you can attend these often heated meetings, held each Thursday m ing at 10.

To top off your visit, take the elevator from the 7th floor up the to the observation deck at the foot of Billy Penn's statue for panoramic view of the city and surroundings. The elevator h six people per trip and runs every 15 minutes; the least crowded time is early morning. ⊠ *Broad and Market Sts. (tour office: East Portal, Room 121),* ☎ *215/686–1776 or 215/686–2840 for tour information.* 🎫 *Free; donations appreciated.* ⊙ *Tower: weekdays 9:30–4:15; 90-min. tour including tower: weekdays at 12:30.*

NEED A
BREAK?   Grab a pita sandwich and a fresh fruit cup from one of the **sidewalk vendors** along 15th Street around Market Street and munch and relax in Dilworth Plaza (on the west apron of City Hall) or John F. Kennedy Plaza (⊠ 15th St. and John F. Kennedy Blvd.).

Clothespin. Claes Oldenburg's 45-ft-high, 10-ton steel sculpture stands in front of the Center Square Building. Lauded by some and scorned by others, this pop art piece contrasts with the traditional statuary so common in Philadelphia. ⊠ *15th and Market Sts.*

OFF THE
BEATEN PATH   **INSECTARIUM –** Even if you hate bugs, you'll love this ugly, yet beautiful collection of 1,500 different creepy crawlers—tarantulas, giant centipedes, scorpions, assassin bugs, butterflies, and metallic beetles that look like pieces of gold jewelry. About half the insects are mounted; the rest are alive. Don't forget to check out the amazing bug gift shop. It's easier to drive here than to take public transportation; call the museum for directions, though you can pick up the subway in front of the *Clothespin.* ⊠ *8046 Frankford Ave., Northeast Philadelphia,* ☎ *215/338–3000. By public transit: From 15th and Market St. station take the Market-Frankford subway to end (Bridge St.); transfer to SEPTA Bus 66 to Welsh Rd.* 🎫 *$4.* ⊙ *Mon.–Sat. 10–4.*

❹ Liberty Place One and Two. One Liberty Place is the 945-ft, 63-story office building designed by Helmut Jahn that propelled Philadelphia into the "ultra-high" skyscraper era. Built in 1987 at a cost of $225 million, it became the tallest structure in Philadelphia. The art deco–style structure, vaguely reminiscent of New York's Chrysler Building, is visible from almost everywhere in the city. In 1990 the adjacent 58-story tower, **Two Liberty Place** opened, with the Ritz-Carlton Hotel. Zeidler Roberts designed this second building. ⊠ *One Liberty Place, 1650 Market St.;* ⊠ *Two Liberty Place, 1601 Chestnut St.*

NEED A
BREAK?   The **Shops at Liberty Place** (⊠ 1625 Chestnut St., between Liberty One and Liberty Two, ☎ 215/851-9055) houses a large international food court on the second level, above the upscale boutiques. You'll find anything from salad to sushi to those familiar Philly cheese steaks.

❺ Lord & Taylor. This building, the former John Wanamaker department store, is almost as prominent a Philadelphia landmark as the Liberty Bell. Wanamaker began with a clothing store in 1861 and became one of America's most innovative and prominent retailers. The massive building, which occupies a city block with grace, was designed by the noted Chicago firm of D. H. Burnham and Company. Its focal point is the nine-story grand court with its 30,000-pipe organ—the largest ever built—and a 2,500-pound statue of an eagle, both remnants of the 1904 Louisiana Purchase Exposition in St. Louis. "Meet me at the Eagle" was a popular way for Philadelphians to arrange a rendezvous. Philadelphians were dismayed to hear this city institution was up for sale and relieved to find out that the new owners promised to keep the eagle and continue the famous Christmas sound-and-light show and the organ performances. ⊠ *13th and Market Sts.,* ☎ *215/241–9000.* ⊙ *Mon., Tues., Thurs.–Sat. 10–7; Wed. 10–8; Sun. noon–5.*

★ **②** **Masonic Temple.** The temple is one of the city's architectural jewels, but like the order that built it, it remains a hidden treasure even to many Philadelphians. Historically, freemasons were skilled stoneworkers of the Middle Ages who possessed secret signs and passwords. Their worldwide fraternal order—the Free and Accepted Masons—included men in the building trades, plus many honorary members; it prospered in Philadelphia during Colonial times. Brother James Windrim designed this elaborate temple as a home for the Grand Lodge of Free and Accepted Masons of Pennsylvania. The trowel used here at the laying of the cornerstone in 1868, while 10,000 brothers looked on, was the same one that Brother George Washington used to set the cornerstone of the U.S. Capitol. The temple's ornate interior consists of seven lavishly decorated lodge halls built to exemplify specific styles of architecture: Corinthian, Ionic, Italian Renaissance, Norman, Gothic, Oriental, and Egyptian. The Egyptian room, with its accurate hieroglyphics, is the most famous. The Temple also houses an interesting museum of Masonic treasures, including Benjamin Franklin's printing of the first book on Freemasonry published in America and Brother George Washington's Masonic Apron, which was embroidered by Madame Lafayette, wife of the famous marquis. ✉ *1 N. Broad St.,* ☎ *215/988–1917.* ✉ *Free.* ☉ *45-min. tours Sept.–June, weekdays 10, 11, 1, 2, and 3; Sat. 10 and 11; July–Aug., weekdays 10, 11, 1, 2, and 3.*

★ **③** **Museum of American Art of the Pennsylvania Academy of the Fine Arts.** This High Victorian Gothic structure is a work of art in itself. Designed in 1876 by the noted, and sometimes eccentric, Philadelphia architects Frank Furness and George Hewitt, the multicolor stone-and-brick exterior is an extravagant blend of columns, friezes, and Richardsonian Romanesque and Moorish flourishes. The interior is just as lush, with rich hues of red, yellow, and blue and an impressive staircase. Inside, the oldest art institution in the United States (founded 1804) displays a collection that ranges from the Peale family, Gilbert Stuart, Benjamin West, and Winslow Homer to Andrew Wyeth and Red Grooms. The academy faculty has included Thomas Sully, Thomas Eakins, and Charles Willson Peale. The permanent collection is supplemented by constantly changing exhibitions of sculpture, paintings, and mixed-media artwork. The art school's classes are now held a block away at 1301 Cherry Street. ✉ *118 N. Broad St., at Cherry St.,* ☎ *215/972–7600.* ✉ *$5.95; free Sun. 3–5.* ☉ *Mon.–Sat. 10–5, Sun. 11–5.*

❼ **Pennsylvania Convention Center.** Opened in June 1993 with galas, parties, and Vice President Al Gore cutting the ribbon, the convention center is helping to rejuvenate Philadelphia's economy and instigate a hotel boom. It's big: With 313,000 square ft, the area of the main exhibition hall equals seven football fields. And it's beautiful: The 1.9 million square ft of space are punctuated by the largest permanent collection of contemporary art in a building of its kind. Many city and state artists are represented in the niches, nooks, and galleries built to house their multimedia works. You can sneak a peek at the architectural highlight of the building—the magnificently restored Victorian Reading Terminal train shed—by crossing over the sky bridge from the third floor of the Philadelphia Marriott next door. The train shed was transformed into the convention center's four-story-high Grand Hall, ballroom, and meeting rooms. Now underway is a renovation of the Reading Terminal Headhouse to make it the grand entrance to the convention center (at 12th and Market streets) ✉ *1101 Arch St.,* ☎ *215/418–* ✉ *Free.* ☉ *45-min tours Tues. and Thurs. by reservation.*

Philadelphia Saving Fund Society (PSFS) Building. Built in 193 of the city's first skyscrapers, this still modern-looking stru influential in the design of other American buildings. The creation of architects George Howe and William Lescaze, it was the first International-style skyscraper in this country. Pay special attention to the enormous escalators and the main banking floor, two striking contrasts to the utilitarian approach of architecture today. This floor is now part of the Mellon PFSF Bank; if you have banking needs, here's a place to take care of them and see an interesting sight at the same time. ⊠ *12 S. 12th St.,* ☎ *215/928–2000.* ☉ *Mon.–Wed. 8–4, Thurs.–Fri. 8–6.*

★ ❻ **Reading Terminal Market.** The market is nothing short of a historical treasure and a food heaven to Philadelphians and visitors alike. One floor beneath the former Reading Railroad's 1891 train shed, the sprawling market has more than 80 food stalls and other shops. Some stalls change daily, offering items from hooked rugs and handmade jewelry to South American and African crafts. Here, amid the local color, you can sample Bassett's ice cream, Philadelphia's best; down a cheese steak, a bowl of snapper soup, or a soft pretzel; or nibble Greek, Mexican, and Indian specialties. From Wednesday through Saturday the Amish from Lancaster County cart in their goodies, including Lebanon bologna, shoofly pie, and scrapple. Many stalls have their own counters with seating; there's also a central eating area. If you want to cook, you can buy a large variety of fresh food from fruit and vegetable stands, butchers, fish stores, and Pennsylvania Dutch markets. The entire building is a National Historic Landmark, and the train shed is a National Engineering Landmark. ⊠ *12th and Filbert Sts.,* ☎ *215/922– 2317.* ☉ *Mon.–Sat. 8–6.*

Transit Museum. This recently opened museum, in the new headquarters of the Southeastern Pennsylvania Transportation Authority (SEPTA), showcases the history and development of public transportation in the region and its impact on social, political, and economic life. On display is a 1947 Presidents Conference Committee trolley, along with transit memorabilia and photographs. ⊠ *Concourse level, 1234 Market St.,* ☎ *215/580–7168.* 🎟 *Free.* ☉ *Mon.–Sat. 10–5.*

RITTENHOUSE SQUARE
Living the Good Life

Rittenhouse Square, at 18th and Walnuts streets, has long been one of the city's swankiest addresses. The square's entrances, plaza, pool, and fountains were designed in 1913 by Paul Cret, one of the people responsible for the Benjamin Franklin Parkway. The square was named in honor of one of the city's 18th-century stars: David Rittenhouse, president of the American Philosophical Society and a professor of astronomy at the University of Pennsylvania. The first house facing the square was erected in 1840, soon to be followed by other grand mansions. Almost all the private homes are now gone, replaced by hotels and apartments and cultural institutions. The former home of banker George Childs Drexel was transformed into the Curtis Institute, alma mater of Leonard Bernstein and Gian Carlo Menotti. The former Samuel Price Wetherill mansion is now the Philadelphia Art Alliance, sponsor of exhibitions, drama, dance, and literary events.

The area south and west of the square is still largely residential and lovely, with cupolas and balconies, hitching posts and stained-glass windows. You can also find some small shops and two fine museum/library collections tucked in—the Civil War Museum and the Rosenbach Museum. In the heart of the city there are green places, too. Peek in the streets behind these homes or through their wrought-iron gates, and you'll see beautiful gardens. On Delancey Place, blocks alternate narrow and wide. The wide blocks had the homes of the wealthy, while the smaller ones held dwellings for servants or stables (today these carriage houses are prized real estate). When he saw 18th Street and Delancey Place, author R. F. Delderfield, author of *God Is an Englishman,* said, "I never thought I'd see anything like this in America. It is like Dickensian London." Today the good life continues in Rittenhouse Square. Annual events include the Rittenhouse Square Flower Market and the Fine Arts Annual, an outdoor juried art show.

Numbers in the text correspond to numbers in the margin and on the Center City and Along the Parkway map.

A Good Walk

The lovely residential area around **Rittenhouse Square** ⑨ is dotted with small museums. A walk through this neighborhood logically begins at the square itself, on Walnut Street between 18th and 19th streets. East of the square are the Barclay Hotel (closed for renovation at press time), celebrated for decades as the most fashionable hotel in the city; the Philadelphia Art Alliance (⊠ 251 S. 18th St.), housed in an 1890s mansion with galleries open to the public; and the **Curtis Institute of Music** ⑩, which offers concerts to the public. West of the square you'll find a branch of the Free Library of Philadelphia, the Rittenhouse Hotel, and the Church of the Holy Trinity, presided over in the mid-19th century by Reverend Phillips Brooks, who achieved renown as the lyricist of "O Little Town of Bethlehem."

Leave the square on its south side and continue south on 19th Street to **Delancey Place,** then turn right and take a look at this urban residential showcase with its grand houses. The 2000 block of Delancey wins the prize: At Number 2010 is the **Rosenbach Museum and Library** ⑪, a local treasure, with paintings, manuscripts, and rare books. Heading east a block south of Delancey, you'll find the **Civil War Library and Museum** ⑫, at 18th and Pine streets. Back at Rittenhouse Square, an elegant tea time can be had in the tearoom at the Rittenhouse Hotel.

From Rittenhouse Square walk east on Locust Street four blocks to the **Academy of Music** ⑬, home of the Philadelphia Orchestra. Cross Broad Street and continue east; within the first block you come across two renowned collections, the **Library Company of Philadelphia** ⑭ and the **Historical Society of Pennsylvania** ⑮. Double back to Broad Street, which has been dubbed the **Avenue of the Arts.** As you walk along the west side of Broad between Spruce and Walnut streets (a block south and north of Locust), notice the more than 30 plaques in the sidewalk honoring some of those who contributed to Philadelphia's cultural history. Where else could Frankie Avalon and Dizzy Gillespie rub shoulders with Anna Moffo and Eugene Ormandy? A block north of the venerable Academy of Music is another grande dame of South Broad Street, the former Bellevue Stratford Hotel, now the **Park Hyatt Philadelphia the Bellevue** ⑯. As you continue up Broad Street, you'll pass a French Renaissance–style building, the **Union League of Philadelphia.**

TIMING
This is one of the city's loveliest neighborhoods for strolling. Two would allow you enough time to wander through the Ritt Square area and visit the Rosenbach Museum and Library before 2:45). If you start midday, you could conclude with tea at the Rittenhouse.

Sights to See

⑬ Academy of Music. Home of the Philadelphia Orchestra, the academy attracts not only music lovers and students but also many members of Philadelphia's elite. Completed in 1857, the building has a modest exterior; the builders ran out of money and couldn't put marble facing on the brick, as they had intended. It hides a lavish, neo-Baroque interior modeled after Milan's La Scala opera house, with gilt, carvings, murals on the ceiling, and a huge Victorian crystal chandelier. Friday-afternoon orchestra concerts are legendary for their audience of "Main Line matrons" from the wealthy suburbs. Tickets are available at the box office; if you're willing to wait in line and sit in the cramped amphitheater four levels above the stage, you can take advantage of one of the music world's great bargains—the $7 "nosebleed" seats. The academy is also home to the Opera Company of Philadelphia and the Luciano Pavarotti International Voice Competition and the site of the Pennsylvania Ballet's Christmas production of *The Nutcracker*. Tours are occasionally given on Tuesday at 2 by reservation (☎ 215/893–1935). ⊠ *Broad and Locust Sts.,* ☎ *215/893–1999 for box office.*

NEED A BREAK? Hot cocoa and s'mores? Espresso and biscotti? A martini and a chocolate layer cake brushed with Chambord liqueur and topped with fresh raspberries? Your choices are many at the fashionable, funky **Xando** (⊠ 235 S. 15th St., ☎ 215/893–9696).

Avenue of the Arts. "Let us entertain you" could be the theme of the major cultural development plan that is transforming North and South Broad Street into a world-class cultural destination (☞ Chapter 6 for more information about some of these venues). New performance spaces are being built, old ones are being refurbished, and south Broad Street has been spruced up with landscaping, cast-iron lighting fixtures, and decorative sidewalk paving. Joining the Merriam Theater and the University of the Arts on South Broad Street are three new venues: the Wilma Theater, a 300-seat theater for this innovative company at Broad and Spruce Sts.; a cabaret-style theater and classrooms for the Philadelphia Clef Club, a group dedicated solely to jazz; and the intimate Philadelphia Arts Bank at the University of the Arts. Ground has been broken for the Regional Performing Arts Center, with a 2,500-seat concert hall and an adaptable theater that will be home to six companies, including the Philadelphia Orchestra and the Pennsylvania Ballet. The Academy of Music, the current venue for those organizations, will be overhauled so it can host large-scale Broadway shows and contemporary music concerts. On North Broad Street, the Museum of American Art of the Pennsylvania Academy of the Fine Arts has completed structural renovations, while the Freedom Theatre, the state's oldest African-American theater, is in the midst of building a new auditorium in their majestic Italianate mansion. The Apollo of Temple, Temple University's multipurpose convocation and recreation complex, is set to open by early 1998.

⑫ Civil War Library and Museum. This is one of the country's premier collections of Civil War memorabilia pertaining to the Union. Artifacts include two life masks of Abraham Lincoln, dress uniforms and swords that belonged to generals Grant and Meade, plus many other weapons, uniforms, and personal effects of Civil War officers and enlisted men. The library has more than 12,000 volumes about the war. ⊠ *1805 Pine St.,* ☎ *215/735–8196.* ☜ *$5.* ☉ *Wed.–Sun. 11–4:30.*

Curtis Institute of Music. Graduates of this tuition-free school for outstanding students include Leonard Bernstein, Samuel Barber, Ned Rorem, and Anna Moffo. You may recognize the exterior of the Curtis Institute from the Eddie Murphy movie *Trading Places*. The school occupies four former private homes; the main building is in the mansion that belonged to George W. Childs Drexel. Built in 1893 by the distinguished Boston firm of Peabody and Stearns, it is notable for Romanesque and Renaissance architectural details. Free student and faculty concerts are given from October through May at 8, usually on Monday, Wednesday, and Friday evenings; their recital hot line lists events. ✉ *1726 Locust St.*, ☎ *215/893–5261 for hot line.*

Delancey Place. This fine residential area southwest of Rittenhouse Square was once the address of Pearl S. Buck (✉ 2019 Delancey Pl.) and Rudolf Serkin. At one corner (✉ 320 S. 18th St.) there is an interesting old sea captain's house. At Number 2010 is the ☞ **Rosenbach Museum and Library.** Cypress Street, just north of Delancey Place, and Panama Street (especially the 1900 block, one block south of Delancey) are two of the many intimate streets lined with trees and town houses characteristic of the area.

OFF THE
BEATEN PATH

THE GROSS CLINIC – Most art historians would put Thomas Eakins's magnificent medical painting *The Gross Clinic* (1875) on the list of top 10 American paintings; you can view it in the alumni hall of Thomas Jefferson University, a medical school. Eakins depicts Dr. Samuel D. Gross, Jefferson's celebrated surgeon and teacher, presiding over an operation for osteomyelitis in an amphitheater under a skylighted roof. His assistants are removing the bone, while the patient's mother stands off to the side. It's a dramatic piece: in size (96 by 78 inches), contrast (the light streaming into the murky room), and in subject matter. The alumni hall is three blocks east of the Historical Society of Pennsylvania; request entry at the information desk. ✉ *Jefferson Alumni Hall, 1020 Locust St.*, ☎ *215/955–6000.* 🎟 *Free.* 🕐 *Mon.–Sat. 10–4, Sun. 12–4.*

⑮ Historical Society of Pennsylvania. More than a half-million books and 14 million manuscripts, the largest privately owned manuscript collection in the United States, are housed here. Founded in 1824 for the purpose of "elucidating the history of the state," the society has expanded its scope to cover the original 13 colonies. Notable items from the collection include the Penn family archives, President Buchanan's papers, a printer's proof of the Declaration of Independence, and the first draft of the Constitution. The staff in the genealogical library will help you trace your roots. ✉ *1300 Locust St.*, ☎ *215/732–6200.* 🎟 *$5 for use of library.* 🕐 *Tues. and Thurs.–Sat. 10–5, Wed. 1–9.*

⑭ Library Company of Philadelphia. Founded in 1731, this is one of the oldest cultural institutions in the United States and the only major Colonial American library that has survived virtually intact, despite having moved from building to building. You can stop by and read the rare books, although nothing circulates. Ben Franklin and his Junto, a group of people who read and then discussed philosophical and political issues, started the Library Company; they also founded the American Philosophical Society. From 1774 to 1800 it functioned as the de facto Library of Congress, and until the late 19th century it was the city library. The membership has included 10 signers of the Declaration of Independence, among them Robert Morris, Benjamin Rush and Thomas McKean. The 400,000-volume collection includes 200 rare books. Among the first editions—many acquired when they first published—are Melville's *Moby-Dick* and Whitman's *Leaves of Grass.* The library is particularly rich in Americana up to 1880, history to 1915, the history of science, and women's history. Locust St., ☎ 215/546–3181. 🎟 *Free.* 🕐 *Weekdays 9–4:4*

⑯ Park Hyatt Philadelphia at the Bellevue. Though its name has been changed many times, this building will always be "the Bellevue" to Philadelphians. It's had an important role in city life, much like the heroine of a long-running soap opera. The epitome of the opulent hotels characteristic of the early 1900s, the Bellevue Stratford was the city's leading hotel for decades. It closed in 1976 after the first outbreak of Legionnaires' disease, which spread through the building's air-conditioning system during an American Legion convention. Reopened as the Fairmont several years later, it failed to regain its luster and closed again in 1986. When renovations were completed in 1989, this magnificent building debuted as home to a number of upscale shops (the Shops at the Bellevue), restaurants, and a food court, as well as the luxurious Hotel Atop the Bellevue. The hotel has once again been renamed, though its character seems to have remained the same (☞ Chapter 4). ⊠ *Broad and Walnut Sts.,* ☎ *215/893–1776.*

❾ Rittenhouse Square. Once grazing ground for cows and sheep, Philadelphia's most elegant square is reminiscent of a Parisian park. Another of William Penn's original five city squares, the park was named in 1825 to honor David Rittenhouse, 18th-century astronomer, clock maker, and the first director of the United States Mint. Many of Philadelphia's movers, shakers, and celebrities have lived here. Extra paths were made for Dr. William White, a leader in beautifying the square, so he could walk directly from his home to the exclusive Rittenhouse Club across the square and lunch with the likes of Henry James. Until 1950 town houses bordered the square, but they have now been replaced on three sides by swank apartment buildings and hotels. Some great houses remain, including the celebrated former residence of Henry P. McIlhenny (on the southwest corner), once home to one of the world's great art collections, now on view at the Philadelphia Museum of Art. If you want to join the office workers who have lunch-hour picnics in the park, you'll find scores of restaurants and sandwich shops along Walnut, Sansom, and Chestnut streets east of the square. ⊠ *Walnut St. between 18th and 19th Sts.*

NEED A BREAK?   The **Mary Cassatt Tearoom** in the Rittenhouse (⊠ 210 W. Rittenhouse Sq., ☎ 215/546–9000) serves an elegant afternoon tea accompanied by tiny tea sandwiches and a tower of pastries from 2 to 5. In warm weather you can dine alfresco in the hotel's cloistered garden.

★ ⑪ Rosenbach Museum and Library. This 1863 three-floor town house is furnished with Persian rugs and 18th-century British, French, and American antiques (plus an entire living room that once belonged to poet Marianne Moore), but the real treasures are the artworks, books, and manuscripts here. Amassed by Philadelphia collectors Philip H. and A. S. W. Rosenbach, the collection includes paintings by Canaletto, Sully, and Lawrence; drawings by Daumier, Fragonard, and Blake; book illustrations ranging from medieval illuminations to the works of Maurice Sendak; the only known copy of the first edition of Benjamin Franklin's *Poor Richard's Almanack;* and the library's most famous treasure—the original manuscript of James Joyce's *Ulysses.* The library has more than 300,000 manuscripts and 30,000 rare books. ⊠ *2010 Delancey Pl.,* ☎ *215/732–1600.* ☜ *$5.* ☉ *Sept.–July, Tues.–Sun. 11– 4. Guided 1-hr tour as visitors arrive; last tour at 2:45.*

Union League of Philadelphia. An elegant double staircase sweeps from Broad Street up to the entrance of this French Renaissance–style building; within lies a bastion of Philadelphia conservatism. The Union League is a private social club founded during the Civil War to support the Union—in a big way. They contributed $100,000, then a huge sum. ⊠ *140 S. Broad St.* ⊙ *Closed to the public.*

THE BENJAMIN FRANKLIN PARKWAY
Museums and Marvels

The Benjamin Franklin Parkway is the city's Champs-Elysées, home to many great cultural institutions. Alive with colorful flowers, flags, and fountains, this 250-ft-wide boulevard stretches northwest from the John F. Kennedy Plaza to the Kelly (East) and West River drives. It is crowned by a Greco-Roman temple on a hilltop—the Philadelphia Museum of Art. French architects Jacques Greber and Paul Cret designed the parkway in the 1920s. Today a distinguished assemblage of museums, institutions, hotels, and apartment buildings line the road, competing with each other in grandeur.

Here you'll find the Free Library of Philadelphia and the Family Court, housed in buildings whose designs are both copied from the palaces on Paris's Place de la Concorde. The newest addition is the Four Seasons Hotel, on the south side of Logan Circle, though its dignified design has made it look like a local institution since the day it opened. A grand processional route, the parkway occasionally lets down its hair as the route for city parades and the site of many festivals and events, including the Thanksgiving and Columbus Day parades, Super Sunday, and the CoreStates U.S. Pro Cycling championship (☞ Festivals and Seasonal Events *in* Chapter 1).

Numbers in the text correspond to numbers in the margin and on the Center City and Along the Parkway map.

A Good Walk
Begin at John F. Kennedy Plaza, on the west side of City Hall. On the corner of 16th Street, in what looks like a UFO, is the **Philadelphia Visitors Center** ⑰, full of helpful maps and information. (If you'd prefer not to walk the length of the Benjamin Franklin Parkway, you could pick up one of Philadelphia Trolley Works' trolley buses here; the 90-minute narrated tour of the city includes stops at the parkway museums. Or you could board SEPTA Bus 44 to Merion, home of the Barnes Foundation, with its Impressionist and Postimpressionist paintings.) From the plaza walk northwest on the parkway about four blocks to **Logan Circle** ⑱ and its lovely fountain sculpture. Next visit the Italian Renaissance–style **Cathedral of Saints Peter and Paul** ⑲, at 18th Street.

Walking counterclockwise around Logan Circle, you'll see twin marble Greek Revival buildings off to your right. The nearer of the two is the city's Family Court; the other is the **Free Library of Philadelphia** ⑳. Cross Logan Circle to see the dinosaur exhibition and more at the **Academy of Natural Sciences** ㉑. From the academy walk west o Race Street to 20th Street and tour the hands-on exhibits at the **Frank Institute Science Museum** ㉒. If it's a warm day, head outside to the **ence Park,** a play-and-learn area just behind the museum on Street. If you have children under the age of seven, don't miss teractive displays at the **Please Touch Museum** ㉓, just a half bloc on 21st Street. If your kids are older and if you and they a the macabre, it's worth walking a few blocks south to see th Museum's amazing collection of skulls and specimens.

Head back to the north side of the parkway and walk n your right is the Youth Study Center (a detention cente offenders) with two striking tableaux depicting families. At the next corner, guarded by a bronze cast of the famous sculpture *The Thinker,* is the **Rodin Museum** ㉔. Just ahead, atop Faire Mount, the plateau at the end of Franklin Parkway, is the **Philadelphia Museum of Art** ㉕, with its world-class collections. Before you see the beauty at the art museum, you could choose to tour the "beast." Half a mile north on 21st Street, Eastern State Penitentiary is the unrestored building of what was once an influential prison and is now one of the city's newest attractions. From there, following Fairmount Avenue west toward the higher numbers is the quickest route back to the art museum.

TIMING

The parkway is at its most colorful in spring, when the trees and flowers are in bloom. It's a long 10-block walk from the Philadelphia Visitors Center to the Art Museum, so if the day's too hot or too cold, hail a taxi. Leave early in morning and plan to spend an entire day—and possibly the evening—in this area. On Wednesday you can cap off your day of culture with dinner and entertainment at the Philadelphia Museum of Art's special evening program. If it's a Friday or Saturday, save the Franklin Institute for mid-afternoon, head out to dinner in the neighborhood, and return for a film on the giant screen of the Omniverse Theater, followed by a rock-and-roll laser light show in Fels Planetarium (the last show is at midnight). How much time you spend at each museum depends on your interests; be aware that the art museum and the Rodin Museum are closed on Monday.

Sights to See

㉑ **Academy of Natural Sciences.** The world-famous dioramas of animals from around the world displayed in their natural habitats give this natural history museum an old-fashioned charm; the latest discoveries give it drawing power. The most popular attraction is *Discovering Dinosaurs,* with reconstructed skeletons of a tyrannosaurus rex and a dinosaur dig in which kids can search for fossils. This is the first museum to display the latest paleontological find—the giganotosaurus, who is reputed to be bigger and fiercer than T. rex. In a new permanent exhibition, live tropical butterflies flutter all around you in a tropical rain forest setting. *Outside In* is a minimuseum where children can handle fossils, dinosaur teeth, and live animals such as snakes, lizards, and a tarantula. If you're keeping track of Philadelphia firsts, note that the academy, America's first museum of natural history, was founded in 1812; the present building dates from 1868. ⊠ *19th St. and Benjamin Franklin Pkwy.,* ☎ *215/299–1020.* ⌑ *$6.75.* ⊙ *Weekdays 10–4:30, weekends 10–5.*

OFF THE
BEATEN PATH

BARNES FOUNDATION – It used to be pretty much a secret that one of the world's greatest collections of Impressionist and Postimpressionist art—175 Renoirs, 66 Cézannes (including his *Card Players*), 65 Matisses, plus masterpieces by van Gogh, Degas, Picasso, and others—was on view in the little town of Merion, 8 mi west of Center City. That was the way Albert C. Barnes wanted it. The son of a Philadelphia butcher who made millions by inventing Argyrol (used to treat eye inflammations), Barnes considered art an educational tool, and until a 1961 court order the collection was open only to students of the educational institution he had chartered. Now that the trustees of Lincoln University have taken over, Barnes's public-be-damned attitude is a thing of the past. Thanks to a spectacularly successful worldwide tour of the collection (which allowed the trustees to renovate Barnes's French Renaissance–style mansion), the secret is out. The Gauguins, Tintorettos, and Degases are displayed as they have always been: wallpapered floor to ceiling and cheek by jowl with household tools, Amish chests, and New

Mexican folk icons (a Matisse and an antique door latch shared similar aesthetics, according to Barnes). A bus right outside the ☞ **Philadelphia Visitors Center** will take you to these treasures. ⊠ *300 Latches La., Merion,* ☎ *610/667–0290.* ⌑ *$5.* ⊙ *Thurs. 12:30–5, Fri.–Sun. 9:30–5; call to check hours before you go. SEPTA Bus 44 runs from 15th St. and Kennedy Blvd. to Old Lancaster Rd. and Latches La., ½ block from the museum.*

⑲ Cathedral of Saints Peter and Paul. This is the basilica of the archdiocese of Philadelphia and the spiritual center for the Philadelphia area's 1.4 million Roman Catholics. Topped by a huge copper dome, it was built between 1846 and 1864 in the Italian Renaissance style. Many of the interior decorations were done by Constantino Brumidi, who painted the dome of the U.S. Capitol. Six Philadelphia bishops and archbishops are buried beneath the altar. ⊠ *18th and Race Sts.,* ☎ *215/561–1313.* ⊙ *Daily 7–3.*

OFF THE BEATEN PATH

EASTERN STATE PENITENTIARY – Built by John Haviland in 1829, Eastern State was the most expensive building in America; it influenced penal design around the world and was the model for some 300 prisons from China to South America. The massive hulk was built with 30-ft-high, 12-ft-wide walls, a hub-and-spoke floor plan, and a revolutionary and controversial concept: to reform prisoners through solitary confinement, in accordance with the Quaker belief that if prisoners had light from heaven (in their private exercise yard), the word of God (the Bible), and honest work, they would reflect and repent. Charles Dickens came to American in 1842 to see Niagara Falls and Eastern State; he became its most famous detractor, insisting that solitary confinement was cruel. Before it closed in 1971, the prison was home to Al Capone, Willie Sutton, and Pep the Dog, who killed the cat of a governor's wife. The guides on the hourly tours of the unrestored structure (visitors must wear hard hats) tell terrific anecdotes and take you on a visit to Death Row. The penitentiary, just a half mile north of the Rodin Museum, hosts changing art exhibitions, Haunted House tours around Halloween, and a Bastille Day celebration the Sunday before July 14, with a reenactment of the storming of the Bastille. ⊠ *22nd St. and Fairmount Ave.,* ☎ *215/236–3300.* ⌑ *$7.* ⊙ *Early May–Memorial Day and Labor Day–Oct., weekends 10–6; Memorial Day–Labor Day, Thurs.–Sun. 10–6.*

★ ☙ ㉒ Franklin Institute Science Museum. Founded to honor Benjamin Franklin, the institute is a science museum that is as clever as its namesake, thanks to an abundance of dazzling hands-on exhibits. To make the best use of your time, study the floor plan before you begin exploring. You can sit in the cockpit of a T-33 jet trainer, trace the route of a corpuscle through the world's largest artificial heart (15,000 times life size), and ride to nowhere on a 350-ton Baldwin steam locomotive. The many exhibits cover energy, motion, sound, physics, astronomy, aviation, ships, mechanics, electricity, time, and other scientific subjects. You'll also find a working weather station and the world's largest pinball machine. The **Fels Planetarium** has shows about the stars, space exploration, comets, and other phenomena, plus laser light shows to rock-and-roll favorite on Friday and Saturday nights (the last show's at midnight). The **Ma⸱ dell Center** includes the Cyberzone computer lab with 20 comput⸱ linked to the Web; Material Matters, a chemistry lesson; and an C niverse Theater, with a 79-ft domed screen and a 56-speaker high⸱ sound system. One don't-miss: the 30-ft statue of Benjamin Fra⸱ ⊠ *20th St. and Benjamin Franklin Pkwy.,* ☎ *215/448–1200 o 448–1388 for laser show hot line.* ⌑ *Ticket packages range fror to $14.50.* ⊙ *Franklin Institute Science Museum: Mon.–Sat.*

Sun. 9:30–6. Mandell Center and Omniverse Theater: Mon.–Thurs. 9:30–5, Fri.–Sat. 9:30–9, Sun. 9:30–6.

㉓ Free Library of Philadelphia. Philadelphia calls its vast public library system the "Fabulous Freebie." Founded in 1891, the central library has more than 1 million volumes. With its grand entrance hall, sweeping marble staircase, 30-ft ceilings, enormous reading rooms with long tables, and spiral staircases leading to balconies, this Greek Revival building looks the way libraries should. With more than 12,000 musical scores, the Edwin S. Fleisher Collection is the largest of its kind in the world. Tormented by a tune whose name you can't recall? Hum it to one of the Music Room's librarians, and he or she will track it down. The Department of Social Science and History has nearly 100,000 charts, maps, and guidebooks. The Newspaper Room stocks papers (back issues are on microfilm) from all major U.S. and foreign cities, some dating all the way to Colonial times. The Rare Book Room is a beautiful suite housing first editions of Dickens, ancient Sumerian clay tablets, illuminated medieval manuscripts, and more modern manuscripts, including Poe's *Murders in the Rue Morgue* and "The Raven."

With 100,000 books for kids from preschool to eighth grade, the Children's Department houses the city's largest collection of children's books in a made-for-kids setting. Historical collections include copies of the Hardy Boys and Nancy Drew series, over which adults wax nostalgic. The foreign-language collection has children's books in more than 50 languages. The department also sponsors story hours and film festivals. ⊠ *19th St. and Benjamin Franklin Pkwy.,* ☎ *215/686–5322.* ⊙ *Nov.–Apr., Mon.–Wed. 9–9, Thurs.–Fri. 9–6, Sat. 9–5, Sun. 1–5; May–Oct., Mon.–Wed. 9–9, Thurs.–Fri. 9–6, Sat. 9–5; tours of Rare Book Room weekdays at 11.*

....

NEED A BREAK?   The rooftop cafeteria of the **Free Library** (⊠ 19th St. and Benjamin Franklin Pkwy., ☎ 215/686–5322) provides inexpensive meals at indoor umbrellaed tables weekdays from 9 to 4:30.

....

㉓ Logan Circle. One of William Penn's five squares, Logan Circle was originally a burying ground and the site of a public execution by hanging in 1823. It found a fate better than death, though. In 1825 the square was named for James Logan, Penn's secretary; it later became a circle and is now one of the city's treasures. The focal point of Logan Circle is the **Swann Fountain** of 1920, designed by Alexander Stirling Calder, son of Alexander Milne Calder, who created the William Penn statue atop City Hall. (In the nearby ☞ **Philadelphia Museum of Art** you'll find many works by a third generation of the family, noted modern sculptor Alexander Calder, the mobile- and stabile maker.) The main figures in the fountain symbolize Philadelphia's three leading waterways: the Delaware and Schuylkill rivers and Wissahickon Creek. Around Logan Circle are some examples of Philadelphia's magnificent collection of outdoor art, including *General Galusha Pennypacker,* the Shakespeare Memorial (*Hamlet and the Fool,* by Alexander Stirling Calder), and *Jesus Breaking Bread.*

....

FF THE ᴀTEN PATH   **MUTTER MUSEUM** – Skulls, antique microscopes, and a cancerous tumor removed from President Grover Cleveland's mouth in 1893 form just part of the unusual medical collection in the Mutter Museum, in the College of Physicians of Philadelphia, a few blocks south of the Please Touch Museum. The museum has hundreds of anatomical and pathological specimens, medical instruments, and organs removed from patients, including a piece of John Wilkes Booth's neck tissue. The collection contains 139 skulls; items that belonged to Marie Curie, Louis Pasteur, and Joseph Lister; and a 7'6" skeleton, the tallest on public exhibition in the United States. ⊠ *19 S. 22nd St.,* ☎ *215/563-3737.* ◪ *$8.* ⊘ *Mon.–Sat. 10–4.*

★ **Philadelphia Museum of Art.** The city's premier cultural attraction is one of the country's leading museums. Actually, one of the greatest treasures of the museum is the building itself. Constructed in 1928 of Minnesota dolomite, it's modeled after ancient Greek temples but on a grander scale. Covering 10 acres, it has 200 galleries and a collection of more than 300,000 works. You can enter the museum from the front or the rear; we recommend the front, where you can run up the 99 steps made famous in the movie *Rocky* (Rocky ran up only 72). From the expansive terrace look up to the pediment on your right, at a group of 13 glazed multicolor statues of classical gods. After passing Jacques Lipchitz's statue *Prometheus Strangling the Vulture,* climb the last flight of steps; before entering the museum, turn around to savor the impressive view down the parkway.

Once inside, you'll see the grand staircase and Saint-Gaudens's statue of *Diana;* she formerly graced New York's old Madison Square Garden. The museum has several outstanding permanent collections: The John G. Johnson Collection covers Western art from the Renaissance to the 19th century; the Arensberg and A. E. Gallatin collections contain modern and contemporary works by artists such as Brancusi, Braque, Matisse, and Picasso. Famous paintings from among these collections include Van Eyck's *St. Francis Receiving the Stigmata,* Rubens's *Prometheus Bound,* Benjamin West's *Benjamin Franklin Drawing Electricity from the Sky,* van Gogh's *Sunflowers,* Cézanne's *The Large Bathers,* and Picasso's *Three Musicians.* A recent arrival was the personal collection of Henry P. McIlhenny: It contains world-famous paintings by Ingres and van Gogh, along with Toulouse-Lautrec's incomparable *Bal at the Moulin-Rouge.*

The enigmatic Marcel Duchamp, whose varied creations influenced many 20th-century artists, is a specialty of the house; the museum has the world's most extensive collection of his works, including the world-famous *Nude Descending a Staircase* and *The Bride Stripped Bare by Her Bachelors, Even.* Among the American art worth seeking out is a fine selection of the works by 19th-century Philadelphia artist Thomas Eakins, including *The Concert Singer* and some notable portraits. The most spectacular "objects" in the museum are entire structures and great rooms moved lock, stock, and barrel from around the world: a 12th-century French cloister, a 16th-century Indian temple hall, a 16th-century Japanese Buddhist temple, a 17th-century Chinese palace hall, and a Japanese ceremonial teahouse. Among the other collections: costumes, Early American furniture, and Amish and Shaker crafts. An unusual touch—and one that children especially like—is the Kienbusch Collection of Arms and Armor.

Pick up a map of the museum at either of the two entrances and wander on your own, or you can select from a variety of guided tours. You'll have at least one or two special exhibits to choose from, too. Every Wednesday evening throughout the year, the museum throws a theme party including music, entertainment, films, tours, lectures, storytelling, demonstrations, poetry readings, food, and drink. The muse⁀ has a cafeteria and a restaurant. ⊠ *26th St. and Benjamin Fran⁀ Pkwy.,* ☎ *215/763–8100 or 215/684–7500 for 24-hr taped mes⁀* ◪ *$7; free Sun. 10–1.* ⊘ *Tues.–Sun. 10–5, special programs evening until 8:45.*

⓱ **Philadelphia Visitors Center.** Here you can get maps, brochures about the city and surroundings, lists of restaurants and hotels, and information about current events. You can also pick up the Philadelphia Trolley Works trolley, the PHLASH downtown loop bus, or SEPTA's Bus 76, which takes you to the parkway museums and the zoo. Volunteers and staff members are on hand to answer your questions. What are the most common questions they hear? Where's the Liberty Bell? Where's Independence Hall? Where's the nearest bathroom? In the gift shop you can buy a Philadelphia T-shirt, a Liberty Bell necktie, or a bumper sticker showing an inscribed tombstone: "I'd rather be in Philadelphia." ⊠ *16th St. and John F. Kennedy Blvd.,* ☎ *215/636–1666.* ☉ *Fall–winter, daily 9–5, summer, 9–6.*

🍼 ㉓ **Please Touch Museum.** The first U.S. museum designed specifically for children age seven and younger, the Please Touch Museum is recognized as one of the nation's top children's museums. The exhibits are interactive: SuperMarket Science has a child-size television studio, a supermarket, a kitchen, and a lab where kids can shop, cook, and experiment. An oversize exhibition on author Maurice Sendak lets kids really get into his *Where the Wild Things Are* and *In the Night Kitchen.* Other exhibits explore art and various forms of transportation, as well as growing up. ⊠ *210 N. 21st St.,* ☎ *215/963–0667.* ☎ *$6.95.* ☉ *Sept.–June, daily 9–4:30; July–Aug., daily 9–6.*

★ ㉔ **Rodin Museum.** Considered a jewel of a museum, this 20th-century building designed by French architects Jacques Greber and Paul Cret houses the best collection outside France of sculptor Auguste Rodin's work. You'll pass through Rodin's *Gates of Hell*—a 21-ft-high sculpture with more than 100 human and animal figures—into an exhibition hall where the sculptor's masterworks are made even more striking by the use of light and shadow. Here are the French master's *The Kiss, The Burghers of Calais,* and *Eternal Springtime.* A small room is devoted to one of Rodin's most famous sitters, the French novelist Balzac. Photographs by Edward Steichen showing Rodin at work round out the collection. ⊠ *22nd St. and Benjamin Franklin Pkwy.,* ☎ *215/586–6026.* ☎ *$3 donation requested.* ☉ *Tues.–Sun. 10–5.*

🍼 **Science Park.** A cooperative venture between the Franklin Institute and the Please Touch Museum, sponsored by CoreStates, the park presents interactive displays in an outdoor setting—which means children get a chance to run around and play while they learn. Swings demonstrate the laws of gravity and energy, golf illustrates physics in motion, and a high-wire bike displays principles of balance and energy. ⊠ *21st St. between Winter and Race Sts.* ☎ *Free with admission to the Franklin Institute or the Please Touch Museum.* ☉ *First Sat. in May–last Sun. in Oct., daily 9:30–4:30.*

FAIRMOUNT PARK
The Emerald City

Stretching from the edge of downtown to the city's northwest corner, Fairmount Park is the largest landscaped city park in the world. With more than 8,500 acres and 2 million trees (someone claims to have counted), the park winds along the banks of the Schuylkill River—which divides it into west and east sections—and through parts of the city. Quite a few city dwellers consider the park their backyard. On weekends the 4-mi stretch along Kelly Drive is crowded with joggers, bicycling moms and dads with children strapped into kiddie seats atop the back wheel, hand-holding senior citizens out for some fresh air, collegiate crew teams sculling along the river, and budding artists trying to capture the sylvan magic just as Thomas Eakins once did.

Fairmount Park encompasses beautiful natural areas—woodlands, meadows, rolling hills, two scenic waterways, and a forested 5½-mi gorge. It also contains tennis courts, ball fields, playgrounds, trails, exercise courses, several celebrated cultural institutions, and some beautiful and historic Early American country houses open to visitors. Philadelphia has more works of outdoor art than any other city in North America, and more than 200 of these works—including statues by Frederic Remington, Jacques Lipchitz, and Auguste Rodin—are scattered throughout Fairmount Park. Some sections of the park that border depressed urban neighborhoods are neglected, but it's especially well-maintained along the Schuylkill.

The park was established in 1812 when the city purchased 5 acres behind Faire Mount, the hill upon which the Philadelphia Museum of Art now stands, for waterworks and public gardens. Through private bequests and public purchases (which continue today), it grew to its present size and stature.

The following tour highlights many of the park's treasures. You can tour by car, starting near the Philadelphia Museum of Art. Signs help point the way, and the historic houses have free parking. Before you set out, call Park House Information (☎ 215/684–7922) to find out which historic houses are open that day and what special events are planned. Another option is to take the narrated tour offered by Philadelphia Trolley Works (board it at the Philadelphia Visitors Center, Philadelphia Museum of Art, or the Park Houses). The trolley bus visits many of these sites, and you can get on and off all day (☞ Sightseeing *in* the Gold Guide).

Numbers in the text correspond to numbers in the margin and on the Fairmount Park map.

A Good Drive

Your visit can start where the park began, at **Faire Mount** ①. If it's a nice day, you could begin this outing with a short walk before you set off by car. Park behind the art museum and walk down the stairs. To your right is the museum's Azalea Garden, designed in the English romantic style. Straight ahead, overlooking the Schuylkill River, is the **Fairmount Waterworks** ②, an elegant group of Greek Revival buildings. A few steps north of the Waterworks you'll see the Victorian structures of **Boathouse Row** ③; watch for rowers on the river here, too. Walking north along Kelly Drive, alongside the river, you soon reach the **Ellen Phillips Samuel Memorial Sculpture Garden** ④, with works by 16 artists.

Now's the time to walk back to your car for a driving tour of East Fairmount Park. Follow Kelly Drive to the end of Boathouse Row; turn right up the hill to a Federal-style country house, **Lemon Hill** ⑤. Head back to Kelly Drive, turn right, pass through the rock archway, and turn right again at the equestrian statue of Ulysses S. Grant. The first left takes you to **Mt. Pleasant** ⑥, an Georgian mansion. Continue along the road that runs to the right of the house (as you face it) past Rockland, a handsome Federal house that's currently closed. At the dead end turn left onto Reservoir Drive. You'll pass the redbrick Georgian-style Ormiston, also closed. Take the next left, Randolph Drive, to another Georgian house, **Laurel Hill** ⑦, on Edgely Drive, which become Dauphin Street. Just about 10 ft before reaching 33rd Street, turn le on Strawberry Mansion Drive, and you're at **Woodford** ⑧, which h an interesting collection of household goods. A quarter mile northw

62

Fairmount Park

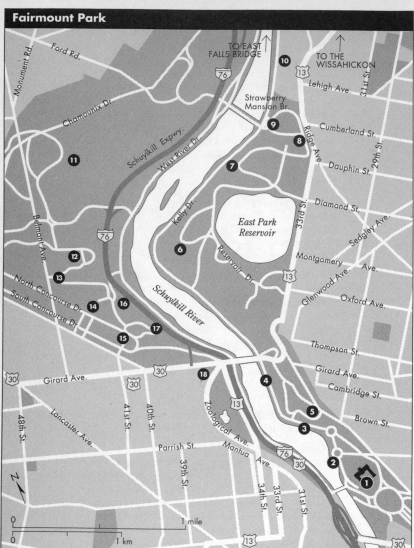

Belmont Plateau, **11**
Boathouse Row, **3**
Cedar Grove, **16**
Ellen Phillips Samuel Memorial Sculpture Garden, **4**
Faire Mount, **1**
Fairmount Water-works, **2**
Horticulture Center, **12**
Japanese House, **13**
Laurel Hill, **7**

Laurel Hill Cemetery, **10**
Lemon Hill, **5**
Memorial Hall, **14**
Mt. Pleasant, **6**
Philadelphia Zoo, **18**
Smith Civil War Memorial, **15**
Strawberry Mansion, **9**
Sweetbriar, **17**
Woodford, **8**

of Woodford stands the house that gave its name to the nearby section of Philadelphia, **Strawberry Mansion** ⑨. It has furniture from three periods of its history. Drive back up the driveway, turn left, and follow the narrow road as it winds right to the light. Turn left onto Ridge Avenue to lovely, historic **Laurel Hill Cemetery** ⑩; the entrance gate sits between eight Greek columns.

You'll have to drive for about 10 minutes to reach West Fairmount Park, now that the Strawberry Mansion bridge over the river is closed. Continue down Ridge Avenue (through East Falls), past Midvale Avenue. Turn left on Calumet Street (just past the Mobil station), cross the East Falls Bridge, and turn left onto West River Drive. Go almost a mile and make the first right turn (onto a diagonal road leading uphill). Turn right (left would take you over the closed bridge). Looping through the park, you'll reach Chamounix Drive, a long straightaway. Turn left and then left again on Belmont Mansion Drive for a fine view from **Belmont Plateau** ⑪. Follow Belmont Mansion Drive down the hill. Where it forks, stay to the left, cross Montgomery Drive, and bear left to reach the **Horticulture Center** ⑫ with its greenhouse and garden. Loop all the way around the Horticulture Center to visit the serene **Japanese House** ⑬ and its waterfall and gardens.

Drive back around the Horticulture Center and continue through the gates to Montgomery Drive. Turn left and then left again at the first light (Belmont Avenue). Turn left again on North Concourse Drive. On your left is **Memorial Hall** ⑭, a building from the 1876 Centennial Exposition. The two towers just ahead are part of the **Smith Civil War Memorial** ⑮. Turn left just past them to see furniture from over the centuries at **Cedar Grove** ⑯. Just south of Cedar Grove, atop a hill sloping down to the Schuylkill, is a Federal mansion, **Sweetbriar** ⑰. Continue past the house, make the first left, and turn left again at the stop sign onto Lansdowne Drive. Follow the signs straight ahead to the **Philadelphia Zoo** ⑱. If you enjoy hiking, you could continue on to the Wissahickon, in the northwest section of Fairmount Park.

TIMING

Any time but winter is a fine time to explore the great outdoors in Fairmount Park. In spring the cherry blossoms rival those along the Potomac; in fall the changing leaves are a match for New England's. In winter you can explore the indoors, on Christmas tours of the historic houses. If you leave the driving to the Philadelphia Trolley Works, your narrated tour will take just 40 minutes. If you drive, after you've explored Kelly Drive on foot, you'll need about two hours. Add another 20–30 minutes for each historic house you tour. Because each property keeps its own quirky schedule, it's hard to choose one day that's best for seeing the interiors, although a summer Saturday is your best bet. Animal lovers can spend half a day at the Philadelphia Zoo.

Sights to See

⑪ **Belmont Plateau.** Literally the high point of your park tour, Belmont Plateau's main attraction is the view from 243 ft above river level. In front of you lie the park, the Schuylkill River winding down to the Philadelphia Museum of Art, and—4 mi away—the Philadelphia skyline. ✉ *Belmont Mansion Dr., West Fairmount Park.*

③ **Boathouse Row.** These architecturally varied 19th-century buildings— in Victorian Gothic, Gothic Revival, and Italianate styles—are home to the rowing clubs that make up the "Schuylkill Navy," an association of boating clubs organized in 1858. The view of the houses from the west side of the river is splendid—especially at night, when they' outlined with hundreds of small lights. ⊠ *Kelly Dr., East Fairmount Park*.

⑯ Cedar Grove. Five styles of furniture—Jacobean, William and Mary, Queen Anne, Chippendale, and Federal—reflect the accumulations of five generations of the Paschall-Morris family. The house stood in Frankford, in northeastearn Philadelphia, for 180 years before being moved to this location in 1927. ⊠ *Lansdowne Dr. off N. Concourse Dr., West Fairmount Park,* ☎ *215/763–8100, ext. 4013.* ▦ *$2.50.* ☉ *Tues.–Sun. 10–5.*

❹ Ellen Phillips Samuel Memorial Sculpture Garden. Bronze and granite statues by 16 artists stand in a series of tableaux and groupings on riverside terraces. Portraying American themes and traits, they include *The Quaker,* by Harry Rosen; *Birth of a Nation,* by Henry Kreis; and *Spirit of Enterprise,* by Jacques Lipchitz. ⊠ *Kelly Dr., East Fairmount Park*.

❶ Faire Mount. This is now the site of the Philadelphia Museum of Art (☞ A Good Walk *in* Museums and Marvels, *above*). In 1812 a reservoir was built here to distribute water throughout the city.

★ **❷ Fairmount Waterworks.** Designed by Frederick Graff, this National Historic Engineering Landmark was the first steam-pumping station of its kind in the country. This notable assemblage of Greek Revival buildings—one of the city's most beautiful sights—is undergoing extensive renovation. ⊠ *Along the Schuylkill River,* ☎ *215/685–4908.* ▦ *Free.* ☉ *Tours June–mid-Oct., weekends 1–3.*

⑫ Horticulture Center. Within the Horticulture Center's 22 wooded acres are a butterfly garden, a greenhouse where plants and flowers used on city property are grown, and a pavilion in the trees for bird-watching from the woodland canopy. Don't miss the whimsical *Seaweed Girl* fountain in the display house. The center stands on the site of the 1876 Centennial Exposition's Horticultural Hall ⊠ *N. Horticultural Dr., West Fairmount Park,* ☎ *215/685–0096.* ▦ *Free.* ☉ *Daily 9–3.*

⑬ Japanese House. A reconstructed 16th-century house and garden built in Japan, this house was exhibited temporarily at the Museum of Modern Art in New York, then reassembled here in 1958. The architectural setting and the waterfall, gardens, Japanese trees, and pond make a serene contrast to the busy city. The house is called Shofu-So, which means "pine breeze villa." ⊠ *Lansdowne Dr. east of Belmont Ave., West Fairmount Park,* ☎ *215/878–5097.* ▦ *$2.50.* ☉ *May–Labor Day., Tues.–Sun. 11–4; Sept.–Oct., weekends 11–4.*

❼ Laurel Hill. This Georgian house built around 1767 on a laurel-covered hill overlooking the Schuylkill River once belonged to Dr. Philip Syng Physick (also owner of Society Hill's Physick House; ☞ Society Hill and Penn's Landing, *above*). On some Sunday evenings during the summer, Women for Greater Philadelphia sponsors candlelight chamber music concerts here. ⊠ *E. Edgely Dr., East Fairmount Park,* ☎ *215/235–1776.* ▦ *$1.50.* ☉ *Wed.–Fri. 10–5.*

⑩ Laurel Hill Cemetery. John Notman, architect of the Athenaeum and many other noted local buildings, designed Laurel Hill in 1836. The cemetery is an important example of an early rural burial ground and the first cemetery in America designed by an architect. Its rolling hills overlooking the Schuylkill River, its rare trees, and its monuments and mausoleums sculpted by greats such as Notman, Alexander Milne Calder, Alexander Stirling Calder, William Strickland, and Thomas U. Walter made it a popular picnic spot in the 19th century; today it's a great place for a stroll. Those buried in this 99-acre necropolis include prominent Philadelphians and Declaration of Independence signers. Burials still take place here. ⊠ *3822 Ridge Ave.,* ☎ *215/228–8200.* ☉ *Tues.– Sat. 9:30–1:30. Friends of Laurel Hill Cemetery arranges tours (*☎ *215/ 228–8817).*

❺ Lemon Hill. This beautiful example of a Federal-style country house was built in 1800 on a 350-acre farm. Its most distinctive features are its oval-shaped parlors with concave doors and the entrance hall's checkerboard floor of Valley Forge marble. ⊠ *Poplar Dr., East Fairmount Park,* ☎ *215/232–4337.* ▨ *$1.50.* ☉ *July–mid-Dec., Wed.–Sun. 10–4; Apr.– June, by appointment; call ahead as hrs may vary.*

⑭ Memorial Hall. Architect Hermann J. Schwarzmann's grand stone building with a glass dome and Palladian windows served as an art museum during the Philadelphia Centennial Exposition, a celebration of the nation's 100th birthday. Close to 10 million people attended the exposition to see the novel exhibits of machinery, produce, and art sent by foreign countries. The hall, a notable example of beaux arts architecture, influenced the design of many American and European museums and government buildings. The only major building remaining from the event, it is sometimes open for viewing of a 20-by-40-ft model of the fair. ⊠ *N. Concourse Dr., West Fairmount Park.*

❻ Mt. Pleasant. John Adams called this Georgian mansion "the most elegant seat in Pennsylvania." Built in 1761 by Captain John Macpherson, a pirate, the house was later purchased by Revolutionary War traitor Benedict Arnold. ⊠ *Mt. Pleasant Dr., East Fairmount Park,* ☎ *215/ 763–8100, ext. 4014.* ▨ *$2.50.* ☉ *Tues.–Sun. 10–5.*

★ ☙ **⑱ Philadelphia Zoo.** Opened in 1874, America's first zoo is home to more than 1,700 animals representing six continents. Most romp in naturalistic habitats that allow you to get close enough to hear them breathe. At each exhibit an old-fashioned Talking Storybook provides narration when activated by an elephant-shape key. Main attractions include the zoo's two rare white lions; Carnivore Kingdom, where meat eaters prowl just inches away; the Rare Animal House, with naked mole rats; terrific bird and reptile houses; and the African Plains, stomping ground of giraffes and zebras. A tragic fire in 1995 wiped out many of the primates in the *World of Primates* exhibition; a new exhibition is scheduled to open in 1999. In the George D. Widener Memorial Treehouse, children can climb inside a four-story tree, hatch from an egg, and ride a dinosaur. The Children's Zoo has pony rides and a barnyard-animal petting area. Set in a lovely 42-acre Victorian garden, the zoo has trees dating from the 18th century. There's a monorail in season. ⊠ *34th St. and Girard Ave., West Fairmount Park,* ☎ *215/243– 1100.* ▨ *$8.50; additional charge for Treehouse.* ☉ *Mar.–Nov., weekdays 9:30–4:45, weekends 9:30–5:45; Dec.–Feb., daily 10–4.*

⑮ Smith Civil War Memorial. Built from 1897 to 1912 with funds donated by wealthy foundry owner Richard Smith, the memorial honors Pennsylvania heroes of the Civil War. Among those immortalized in bronze are Generals Meade and Hancock—and Smith himself. At the base of each tower is a curved wall with a bench. If you sit at one end and listen to a person whispering at the other end, you'll understand why they're called the Whispering Benches. Unfortunately, the litter around the site reflects its location near an economically struggling neighborhood. ⊠ *N. Concourse Dr., West Fairmount Park.*

❾ Strawberry Mansion. The largest mansion in Fairmount Park has furniture from the three main phases of its history: Federal, Regency, and Empire. In the parlor is a collection of rare Tucker porcelain; the attic holds fine antique dolls. ✉ *Near 33rd and Dauphin Sts., East Fairmount Park,* ☎ *215/228–8364.* ☑ *$1.50.* ⊘ *Tues.–Sun. 10–4.*

⑰ Sweetbriar. Built in 1797, this three-story Federal mansion was the park's first year-round residence, built by Samuel and Jean Breck to escape the yellow fever epidemic that ravaged the city. ✉ *Lansdowne Dr. off N. Concourse Dr., West Fairmount Park,* ☎ *215/222–1333.* ☑ *$1.50.* ⊘ *July–mid-Dec., Wed.–Sun. 10–4; mid-Dec.–June, by appointment.*

OFF THE
BEATEN PATH

THE WISSAHICKON – In the northwestern section of Fairmount Park is a gorge carved out by the Wissahickon Creek—5½ mi of towering trees, cliffs, trails, and animals. Of the Philadelphia areas that William Penn encountered, the Wissahickon has changed the least. You can easily visualize the Leni-Lenape who lived here and gave the creek its name. Many inns once stood along the banks of the Wissahickon; only two remain. One is now a police station; the other is the **Valley Green Inn** (✉ Springfield Ave. and Wissahickon Creek, ☎ 215/247–1730), built in 1850. It is nestled in one of the loveliest parts of the Wissahickon gorge. You can sit on a bench alongside the creek, look at the stone bridge reflected in the water, and savor the tranquillity of this spot.

Forbidden Drive, a dirt-and-gravel pathway along the west side of the creek, is a haunt of joggers, bikers, horseback riders, fishermen, and nature lovers. There are foot trails along both sides of the creek and interesting statues along the route. Walking less than a half mile south of the inn brings you to Devil's Pool, Shakespeare Rock (with a quotation carved on its face), and Hermit's Cave, where German mystic Johannes Kelpius and his followers came in 1694 to await the millennium. A visit to Historic RittenhouseTown, America's first paper mill, requires a 3-mi hike south. To the north of the inn are Indian Rock and a covered bridge (built around 1855), the last still standing within the boundaries of a major American city.

You'll need a car to get here: To reach Valley Green Inn from downtown, take the Schuylkill Expressway west to the Lincoln Drive–Wissahickon Park exit (Exit 32). Follow Lincoln Drive to Allen's Lane, then turn right. At Germantown Avenue turn left, go about a mile, turn left at Springfield Avenue, and follow it to the end. A map of the Wissahickon showing all the trails and sites can be purchased for $5 at the inn's snack-booth window, open daily from 10 to 6.

⑧ Woodford. The Naomi Wood collection of household goods, including furniture, unusual clocks, and English delftware, can be seen in this fine Georgian mansion built about 1756. ✉ *Near 33rd and Dauphin Sts., East Fairmount Park,* ☎ *215/229–6115.* ☑ *$1.50.* ⊘ *Tues.–Sun. 10–4.*

SOUTHWARK AND SOUTH PHILADELPHIA

Strutting South of South

Two of the city's most interesting neighborhoods lie south of South Street—Southwark and South Philadelphia. Southwark, stretching from Front to 6th Street and from South Street to Washington Avenue, was the center of the commercial and ship-building activity that made Philadelphia the biggest port in the colonies and in the young United States. One of the oldest sections of the city, Southwark was already settled by the Swedes when the English arrived; the Swedish influence shows in street names like Swanson, Christian, and Queen.

Directly south of Society Hill, Southwark is neither as glamorous nor as historically renowned as its neighbor. Chiseled in stone on one facade are these words: ON THIS SITE IN 1879, NOTHING HAPPENED! But like Society Hill, Southwark's Queen Village neighborhood has been gentrified by young professionals; the restoration attracted chic restaurants and interesting shops.

Through the years South Philadelphia has absorbed boatloads of immigrants—European Jews, Italians, and most recently, Asians. The city's Little Italy, it is a huge area of identical row houses with gleaming white marble steps, stretching south and west of Southwark. At the heart of the neighborhood, along 9th Street, is the outdoor Italian Market, packed with vendors hawking crabs and octopus, eggplants and tomatoes. From butcher shop windows hang skinned animals; cheese shops are crammed with barrels of olives. Sylvester Stallone walked along 9th Street in the films *Rocky* and *Rocky II,* and almost every campaigning president has visited the market on his swing through Philadelphia. It's a great photo op for them—and for you.

Although there are chic eateries in South Philadelphia, the majority of the neighborhood restaurants are not fancy (decor such as red-checked vinyl tablecloths and plastic grapes hanging from plastic vines is not uncommon), but the food can be terrific and—more importantly—authentic. You'll wonder if Mama is in the kitchen preparing a southern Italian specialty just for you. This is the neighborhood that gave the world Mario Lanza, Bobby Rydell, Frankie Avalon, and Fabian, and some area restaurants proudly display gold records earned by these neighborhood celebrities. Plenty of locals and visitors alike head for South Philly's competing culinary shrines, Pat's King of Steaks and Geno's, both at the corner of 9th Street and Passyunk Avenue. One of their cheese steaks makes a perfect prelude to an evening spent at the city's sports complexes, at the southern end of South Philadelphia.

A Good Walk

A leisurely stroll through Southwark and neighboring South Philadelphia is a fun day's outing. From Bainbridge Street, proceed south (right turn) on 2nd Street, which old-timers call Two Street. The homes along these streets are the oldest in the city, dating from the mid-1700s. Even when their construction dates are not chiseled on the facades, the settling bricks above the overhangs, the crooked windows, and the shutters that don't hang straight all attest to their vintage. Turn east (left) on Catharine Street and then south (right) on Hancock Street, one of the most charming streets in the city. The tiny clapboard houses at Numbers 813 and 815 were built by a shipwright and are the last of their type. Detour onto Queen Street to see the old firehouse with gas lamps at Number 117. It has been beautifully converted to a single-family home.

Continue down Hancock to Christian Street; go east (left) about one block (under the I–95 overpass) to Swanson Street. Here is **Gloria Dei,** the oldest church in Pennsylvania. Return to 2nd Street by way of Christian Street and walk south (left turn), past a neighborhood landmark, the Shot Tower, where lead shot was made during the War of 1812. At Washington Avenue is the **Mummers Museum,** where you can get a feeling for this local institution. From the museum walk west on Washington Avenue to 9th Street and then proceed north to the five-block-long open-air **Italian Market.** At Christian Street walk east to 5th Street, half a block north to Queen Street, and then east again to the **Mario Lanza Museum,** with memorabilia and photos of the singer. Following 4th Street north will bring you back to South Street.

TIMING

It's best to visit this neighborhood Tuesday through Saturday, because the Italian Market and the Mummers Museum are closed Sunday and Monday (the Italian Market *is* open Sunday morning, though). Start early—the Italian Market winds down by midafternoon—and allow three to four hours.

Sights to See

Gloria Dei. One of the few remnants of the Swedes who settled Pennsylvania before William Penn, Gloria Dei (Old Swedes') Church was organized in 1642. Built in 1698, the church has numerous intriguing religious artifacts, such as a 1608 Bible once owned by Sweden's Queen Christina. The carvings on the lectern and balcony were salvaged from the congregation's first church, which was destroyed by fire. Models of two of the ships that transported the first Swedish settlers hang from the ceiling—right in the center of the church. Grouped around the church are the parish hall, the caretaker's house, the rectory, and the guild house. The church sits in the center of its graveyard; it forms a picture that is pleasing in its toylike simplicity and tranquillity. ⊠ *916 Swanson St., near Christian St. and Columbus Blvd.,* ☎ *215/389–1513.* ⊒ *Free.* ☉ *Daily 9–5, but call first.*

Italian Market. It's more Naples than Philadelphia: Vendors crowd the sidewalks and spill out onto the streets; live crabs and caged chickens wait for the kill; picture-perfect produce is piled high. The market dates back 125 years to its Italian immigrant founders. You'll find imported and domestic products, kitchenware, fresh pastas, cheeses, spices, meats, fruits and vegetables, and dry goods. ⊠ *9th St. between Washington Ave. and Christian St.,* ☎ *215/922–5557.* ☉ *Tues.–Sat., 9:30–late afternoon; Sun. 9:30–12:30.*

| NEED A BREAK? | For authentic Italian rum cake, cheese- or custard-filled cannoli, or double-chocolate biscotti and a cup of coffee, try **Litto's Bakery Caffe** (⊠ 910 Christian St., ☎ 215/627-7037), a bakery and restaurant in the Italian Market. |

Mario Lanza Museum. In this museum devoted to the famous tenor and Hollywood star (1921–59), you'll find thousands of photos, memorabilia, videocassette showings of Lanza's films, and souvenirs for sale. Lanza was supposedly moving a piano into the Academy of Music when he seized the opportunity to sing from its stage—and was first discovered. Lanza's birthplace, at 634 Christian Street, is a few blocks away. ⊠ *In the Settlement Music School, 416 Queen St.,* ☎ *215/468–3623.* ☉ *Sept.–June, Mon.–Sat. 10–3; July–Aug., weekdays 10–3.*

☣ **Mummers Museum.** Even if you aren't in Philadelphia on New Year's Day, you can still experience this unique local institution and phenomenon. Famous for extravagant sequin-and-feather costumes and string bands, the Mummers spend the year preparing for an all-day parade up Broad Street on January 1. The museum has costumes, photos of parades, and audiovisual displays of Mummerabilia. You can push buttons to compose your own Mummers medley, with banjos, saxophones, and xylophones, and you can dance the Mummers strut to the strains of "Oh, Dem Golden Slippers." A 45-inch screen shows filmed highlights of past parades.

Early English settlers brought to the colonies their Christmastime custom of dressing in costume and performing pantomimes—the name Mummers derives from *mum,* meaning "to be silent." In Philadelphia, families would host costume parties on New Year's Day; on January 1, 1876, the first individual groups paraded informally through the city.

In case you want to see the world.

At American Express, we're here to make your journey a smooth one. So we have over 1,700 travel service locations in over 120 countries ready to help. What else would you expect from the world's largest travel agency?

do more

AMERICAN EXPRESS

http://www.americanexpress.com/travel

Travel

In case you want to be welcomed there.

We're here to see that you're always welcomed at establishments everywhere. That's why millions of people carry the American Express® Card – for peace of mind, confidence, and security, around the world or just around the corner.

do more

Cards

In case you're running low.

We're here to help with more than 118,000 Express Cash locations around the world. In order to enroll, just call American Express before you start your vacation.

do more

And just in case.

We're here with American Express® Travelers Cheques and Cheques *for Two*® They're the safest way to carry money on your vacation and the surest way to get a refund, practically anywhere, anytime.
Another way we help you...

do more ®

AMERICAN
EXPRESS

Travelers
Cheques

The parade caught on, and by 1901 the city officially sanctioned the parade and 42 Mummers clubs strutted for cash prizes.

In recent years the Mummers have staged a summer Mummers Parade around July 4 (during the city's Welcome America! celebration); in late February they present the "Show of Shows" at the Spectrum. The latter is a chance to hear the original 16 string bands perform indoors. The museum presents free outdoor concerts (weather permitting) on most Tuesday evenings 8–10 from May to September. ⊠ *1100 S. 2nd St., at Washington Ave.,* ☎ *215/336–3050.* ⊠ *$2.50.* ☉ *Tues.–Sat. 9:30–5, Sun. noon–5.*

UNIVERSITY CITY

University City is the portion of West Philadelphia that includes the campuses of the University of Pennsylvania, Drexel University, and the Philadelphia College of Pharmacy and Science. It also has the University City Science Center (a leading think tank), the Annenberg Center performing arts complex, a large and impressive collection of Victorian houses, and a variety of moderately priced restaurants, movie theaters, stores, and lively bars catering to more than 32,000 students and other residents. It stretches from the Schuylkill River west to 44th Street and from the river north to Powelton Avenue.

This area was once the city's flourishing western suburbs, where wealthy Philadelphians built grand estates and established summer villages. It officially became part of the city in 1854. Twenty years later the University of Pennsylvania moved its campus here from the center of the city. The university moved into many of the historic homes, while others were adopted by fraternities. There are still many privately owned, architecturally exciting properties, particularly on Locust, Spruce and Pine streets. The university is also renovating and reshaping its campus, with plans that include building a new hotel at Walnut Street and 36th Street. Penn's Information Center is at 34th and Walnut streets (☎ 215/898–1000).

A Good Walk

This walk through University City is chiefly a stroll around and through the Ivy League campus of the University of Pennsylvania, where ivy really does cling to many buildings. Begin at the University's **Institute of Contemporary Art,** at 36th and Sansom streets. Walk east (right turn) on Sansom Street to 34th Street and turn right (south). At 220 South 34th Street is the historic Furness Building, which houses the **Arthur Ross Gallery** and the **Fisher Fine Arts Library.** Continue to Spruce Street and turn left after one block to explore the treasures of the **University Museum of Archaeology and Anthropology,** which holds everything from mummies to Mayan artifacts. Just across the street you see Franklin Field, the university's football stadium. Following 33rd Street north back to Walnut Street brings you to the Moore School of Engineering, home of the post–World War II era **ENIAC,** the world's first all-electronic general-purpose digital computer.

You can enter the heart of the University of Pennsylvania campus, Locust Walk, at 34th and Walnut streets. You're now at the edge of College Green (Blanche Levy Park), the crossroads of the campus. You'll see a statue of Benjamin Franklin, who founded the university in 1740, in the middle of the green. To your right, the huge Van Pelt Library stretches from 34th Street to 36th Street. In front of it is Claes Oldenburg's *Broken Button.* To your left is College Hall, an administration building said to be the inspiration for the scary Addams House in cartoonist Charles Addams's work. Just west of 36th Street, the Annenberg School of Communications and the Annenberg Center (☞ The Arts *in* Chapter 5) are to the right; the famed Wharton School of Economics, to the left. As you pass the intersection of 37th Street, say hello to the statue of Ben Franklin sitting on a bench. A footbridge takes you over 38th Street (turn around for a good view of Center City) to Superblock, three high-rise student dormitories. Locust Walk ends at 40th Street with the dental school and a row of stores and restaurants.

Follow Locust Walk back to 37th Street and walk south (right) to Spruce Street. The Gothic sprawl ahead of you is the Quad, the university's first dorm buildings. Designed by Cope and Stewardson in 1895, the Quad became the prototype of the collegiate Gothic style prevalent in campuses coast to coast. These dormitory buildings—awash with gargoyles and gables—easily conjure up the England of everyone's dreams. South of the Quad on Hamilton Walk, you're smack back in the 20th century, thanks to Louis Kahn's Alfred Newton Richards Medical Research Laboratories building, an award-winning masterpiece of this important architect. Kahn, a brilliant teacher and architectural theorist, did not leave many completed buildings.

TIMING

University City is at its best when college is in session; it's the students rushing to classes who give this area its flavor. Allow half an hour each in the Arthur Ross Gallery and the Institute of Contemporary Art, two hours in the University Museum, and an hour exploring the campus. If your time is limited, skip all but the University Museum, a don't-miss treasure for the archaeologically inclined.

Sights to See

Arthur Ross Gallery. Penn's official art gallery showcases treasures from the university's collections and traveling exhibitions, like the recent *Treasures of Asian Art, Sculpture, and Ceramics from the Mr. and Mrs. John D. Rockefeller III Collection.* The gallery shares a historic landmark building, designed by Frank Furness, with the ☞ **Fisher Fine Arts Library.** ⊠ *220 S. 34th St.,* ☎ *215/898–2083.* ▨ *Free.* ☉ *Tues.–Fri. 10–5, weekends noon–5.*

ENIAC. Here's a chance for computer aficionados to see the place where the computer age dawned. During World War II engineers at the Moore School of Engineering at the University of Pennsylvania undertook a secret project to develop the world's first all-electronic, large-scale general-purpose digital computer. They called it ENIAC, an acronym for electronic numerical integrator and calculator. The largest electronic machine in the world, it weighed 30 tons and contained 18,000 vacuum tubes—one of which burned out every few seconds when ENIAC was first built. Although most of ENIAC is now in the Smithsonian Institution, a small portion is still on view at the Moore School. Photos and informative signs tell ENIAC's story. ⊠ *Moore School of Electrical Engineering, 200 S. 33rd St., enter on 33rd St. just below Walnut St.,* ☎ *215/898–4706 or 215/898–2492.* ▨ *Free.* ☉ *By appointment only.*

Fisher Fine Arts Library. One of finest examples remaining of the work of Philadelphia architect Frank Furness, this was the most innovative library building in the country when it was completed in 1890. It was the first library to separate the reading room and the stacks. Peek into the catalog room, dominated by a huge fireplace, and the reading room, with study alcoves lit from the lead-glass windows above. The unusual exterior stirred controversy when it was built: Note the terracotta panels, short heavy columns, and gargoyles on the north end. ⊠ *220 S. 34th St.,* ☎ *215/898–8325.* ▨ *Free.* ☉ *During the academic* *year, weekdays 8:30 AM–11 PM, Sat. noon–8, Sun. noon–11; in summer, Mon.-Thurs. 8:30–7, Fri. 8:30–5.*

Institute of Contemporary Art. This museum, part of the University of Pennsylvania, has established a reputation for identifying promising artists and exhibiting them at a critical point in their careers. Among the artists who have had shows at ICA and later gone on to international prominence are Andy Warhol, Robert Mapplethorpe, and Laurie Anderson. ⊠ *118 S. 36th St., at Sansom St., ☎ 215/898–7108. ⊠ $3. ⊘ Wed. and Fri.–Sun. 10–5, Thurs. 10–7.*

NEED A BREAK?	From morning till night you can fill up at **Le Bus** (⊠ 3402 Sansom St., ☎ 215/387–3800), a cafeteria-style restaurant known for its terrific freshly baked breads.

★ ☾ **University Museum of Archaeology and Anthropology.** Indiana Jones, look out! Rare treasures from the deepest jungles and most ancient tombs make this one of the finest archaeological/anthropological museums in the world. The collection of more than a million objects, gathered largely during worldwide expeditions by University of Pennsylvania scholars, includes a 12-ton sphinx from Egypt, a crystal ball once owned by China's Dowager Empress, the world's oldest writing—Sumerian cuneiform clay tablets—and the 4,500-year-old golden jewels from the royal tombs of the kingdom of Ur. The museum has a superb collection of Chinese monumental (large-scale) art and more than 400 artifacts in its *Ancient Greek World* exhibition. Kids run to *The Egyptian Mummy: Secrets and Science* and to *Living in Balance: The Universe of the Hopi, Zuni, Navajo and Apache.* There are two gift shops and a café, too. ⊠ *33rd and Spruce Sts., ☎ 215/898–4000. ⊠ $5 suggested donation. ⊘ Sept.–May, Tues.–Sat. 10–4:30, Sun. 1–5; Memorial Day to Labor Day, Tues.–Sat. 10–4:30.*

GERMANTOWN AND CHESTNUT HILL

About 6 mi northwest of Center City is Germantown, which has been an integrated, progressive community since 13 German Quaker and Mennonite families settled here in 1683 and soon welcomed English, French, and other Europeans seeking religious freedom. Germantown has a tradition of free thinking—the first written protest against slavery came from its residents. Today it houses a wealth of still-occupied and exceptionally well-preserved architectural masterpieces.

The Germantown area is rich in history. It was the site of Philadelphia's first gristmill (1683) and America's first paper mill (1690). The American colonies' first English-language Bible was printed here (1743). By the time of the Revolution, Germantown had become an industrial town. In 1777 Colonial troops under George Washington attacked part of the British force here and fought the Battle of Germantown in various skirmishes. After the Revolutionary War Germantown became a rural retreat for wealthy city residents who wanted to escape summer heat and disease. The Deshler-Morris House was the summer White House where President Washington and his family resided in 1793 and 1794, when the yellow fever epidemic drove them from the city.

Farther northwest is Chestnut Hill. Although it's part of the city, Chestnut Hill is more like the classy suburbs of the Main Line. When Germantown's second railroad, the Chestnut Hill Line, began operation west of Germantown Avenue in 1884, it spurred the development of Chestnut Hill. Beyond cobblestoned Germantown Avenue, lined with restaurants, galleries and boutiques, you'll find lovely examples of the

Colonial Revival and Queen Anne style houses. The Woodmere Art Museum is in this neighborhood. For tours and information, contact the Chestnut Hill Business Association (⌧ 8426 Germantown Ave., ☎ 215/247–6696).

The best way to tour the area is by car. From Center City follow Kelly Drive to Midvale Avenue and turn right. Follow Midvale up the hill to Conrad Street and turn right, then make a left on Queen Lane, which ends at Grumblethorpe house. You can also reach Germantown from Center City via SEPTA Bus 23; pick it up at 11th and Market streets and get off at Queen Lane.

A Good Drive

You can follow Germantown Avenue from lower Germantown north to Chestnut Hill. Many homes you'll see were built when Germantown Avenue was a dirt road; today it's lined with cobblestones. At Queen Lane is John Wister's **Grumblethorpe,** built from stones quarried on the property. A few blocks north on Germantown Avenue is Market Square, a park that was once the site of a prison and its stocks and a focal point for trade. Facing Market Square on your left is the **Deshler-Morris House,** with fine antiques and lovely gardens; diagonally across the square in a row of beautifully restored redbrick buildings is the **Germantown Historical Society,** which offers a good introduction to the houses in the area. Drive north a half mile farther to the delightful Quaker-style **Wyck** house, at the corner of Germantown Avenue and Walnut Lane.

Just before Pastorius Street is the tiny, historic Germantown Mennonite Church. On this site in 1708 the Mennonites established their first church in the New World. The little log church was replaced in 1770 by the current building. Turn left on Tulpehocken Street; at Number 200 West is the Victorian Gothic **Ebenezer Maxwell House.** Continue north on Germantown Avenue past the Johnson House (⌧ 6306 Germantown Ave.), once a tannery, later a station on the Underground Railway. At Number 6401 is **Cliveden,** an elaborate house set at the end of a long, graceful driveway. Across the street is **Upsala,** a Federal-style Johnson family home (this family also owned the Johnson House).

Adjacent to Germantown is the residential community of Mount Airy, and farther north, at the "top" of Germantown Avenue, is **Chestnut Hill.** The town's tony shopping district runs from Number 7900 to 8700. Half a mile north at Number 9201 is the **Woodmere Art Museum,** with works from the 19th and 20th centuries. From here, if it's a nice day, you could detour to the landscaped Morris Arboretum or the natural setting of the Schuylkill Center for Environmental Education.

TIMING

Each historic house has its own schedule, so it's difficult to coordinate your visit to include all the sights. However, you could catch five homes open on a Thursday afternoon and four on Saturday or Sunday afternoon. You could then head to Chestnut Hill for dinner. Avoid this trip in winter, when most of the homes are closed.

Sights to See

★ **Cliveden.** Built in 1763 by Benjamin Chew, Germantown's most elaborate country house was occupied by the British during the Revolution. On October 4, 1777, Washington's unsuccessful attempt to dislodge the British resulted in his defeat at the Battle of Germantown. You can still see bullet marks on the outside walls. Today a museum, Cliveden occupies a 6-acre plot, with outbuildings and a barn converted into offices and a gift shop. It remained in the Chew family until 1972, when it was donated to the National Trust for Historic Preservation.

⊠ *6401 Germantown Ave.,* ☎ *215/848–1777.* ▩ *$6.* ☉ *Apr.–Dec., Thurs.–Sun. noon–4.*

Deshler-Morris House. This is where President Washington lived in 1793–94, making it the seat of government of the new republic for a short time. Beautiful antiques accent the rooms, and, as one of the many Germantown houses built flush with the road, it has enchanting side and back gardens. ⊠ *5442 Germantown Ave.,* ☎ *215/596–1748.* ▩ *$1.* ☉ *Apr.–Nov., Tues.–Sat. 1–4.*

Ebenezer Maxwell Mansion. Philadelphia's only mid-19th-century house-museum is a Victorian Gothic extravaganza of elongated windows, arches, and a three-story tower that is the incarnation of an old haunted house. ⊠ *200 W. Tulpehocken St.,* ☎ *215/438–1861.* ▩ *$4.* ☉ *Apr.–mid-Dec., Fri.–Sun. 1–4.*

Germantown Historical Society. Home to a historical and genealogical library and a museum showcasing collections of industrial and decorative arts, the society serves as an orientation point for visiting all the Germantown houses. ⊠ *5501 Germantown Ave.,* ☎ *215/844–0514.* ▩ *$3.* ☉ *Tues. and Thurs. 10–4, Sun. 1–5.*

Grumblethorpe. Built by John Wister in 1744, this Georgian house is one of Germantown's leading examples of early 18th-century architecture. ⊠ *5267 Germantown Ave.,* ☎ *215/843–4820.* ▩ *$3.* ☉ *Apr.–mid-Dec., Tues., Thurs., and Sun. 1–4.*

OFF THE
BEATEN PATH

MORRIS ARBORETUM – In the very northwest corner of the city, near the Woodmere Art Museum in Chestnut Hill, you'll find 166 acres of romantic landscaped seclusion. Morris Arboretum of the University of Pennsylvania is an eclectic retreat with a formal rose garden, English garden, Japanese garden, meadows, and woodlands. Begun in 1887 by siblings John and Lydia Morris and bequeathed to the university in 1932, the arboretum typifies Victorian-era garden design, with winding paths, a hidden grotto, tropical ferns, and natural woodland. It has 3,500 trees and shrubs from around the world, including one of the finest collections of Asian plants outside Asia. ⊠ *Hillcrest Ave. between Germantown and Stenton Aves.,* ☎ *215/247-5777. Chestnut Hill East or West commuter trains stop ½ mi away; Bus L stops at corner of Hillcrest and Germantown Aves.* ▩ *$4.* ☉ *Apr.-Oct., daily 10–5; Nov.-Mar., daily 10–4; guided tours weekends at 2.*

SCHUYKILL CENTER FOR ENVIRONMENTAL EDUCATION – This sanctuary consists of more than 500 acres of wildflowers, ferns, and thickets; ponds, streams, and woodlands; 6 mi of winding trails; and the 8-acre Pine Plantation. You may spot deer, hawks, Canada geese, red foxes, and other animals. Hands-on exhibits in the Discovery Museum explain the flora and fauna you see outside. There are nature programs on weekends. The bookstore and gift shop follow the nature theme. ⊠ *8480 Hagy's Mill Rd., Roxborough,* ☎ *215/482-7300. Bus 27 stops at Ridge Pike and Port Royal Ave. 1 mi away.* ▩ *$5.* ☉ *Sept.-July, Mon.-Sat. 8:30–5, Sun. 1–5; Aug., Mon.-Sat. 8:30–5.*

Upsala. One of Germantown's best examples of Federal-style architecture, Upsala was built about 1755. The Johnsons, who owned the house, were a well-to-do family of tanners. Continental troops set up their cannons on Upsala's front lawn and shelled the British at ☞ **Cliveden.** ⊠ *6430 Germantown Ave.,* ☎ *215/842–1798.* ▩ *$3.* ☉ *Apr.–mid-Dec., Thurs. and Sat. 1–4.*

Woodmere Art Museum. American and European art from the 19th and 20th centuries is displayed here in a fine collection of paintings, prints, tapestries, sculptures, porcelains, ivories and Japanese rugs. There's also a focus on works by Philadelphia artists. ⊠ *9201 Germantown Ave.,* ☎ *215/247–0476.* ⊐ *$3.* ⊙ *Tues.–Sat. 10–5, Sun. 1–5.*

The British presence can still be felt in this area at **Best of British** (⊠ 8513 Germantown Ave., ☎ 215/242–8848), a cute Chestnut Hill tearoom where you can have tea with clotted cream—or lunch. And since this is America, you can have your afternoon tea beginning at 10:30 in the morning.

Wyck. One of the most charming of Quaker-style houses, Wyck has an old pump, barn, carriage house and idyllic gardens. The house remained the property of the same Quaker family from 1736 to 1973. Known as the oldest house in Germantown, Wyck was used as a British field hospital after the Battle of Germantown. ⊠ *6026 Germantown Ave.,* ☎ *215/848–1690.* ⊐ *$5.* ⊙ *Apr.–mid-Dec., Tues., Thurs., and Sat. 1–4; other times by appointment only.*

MANAYUNK
Where We Go to Drink—and Eat and Shop

Manayunk, 7 mi northwest of Center City along the Schuylkill River, was a prosperous mill town in the 19th century, during the years when Philadelphia was the nation's leading industrial city. Today, in its rebirth as a trendy dining and shopping district, few hints remain of its former life, although the Main Street Historic District still retains sections of the Schuylkill Navigation Canal, along which barges once transported goods to and from the textile mills.

When the Manayunk section of that canal was developed in 1819, it made the river passable and the town viable. Not long after water power became available, the first mill was built along the banks of the Schuylkill. Originally called Flat Rock, for the rock formations in this section of the river, the town was rechristened Manayunk, a Leni-Lenape word that translates as "where we go to drink." By the 1850s Manayunk was the Manchester of the United States, home to a number of Philadelphia's 185 cotton mills, which provided raw material for the region's thriving paper and textile industries. It was incorporated as part of Philadelphia in 1854. Italian, Polish, Irish, and German immigrants settled here to work in the mills; they built row houses in the steep hills overlooking the river.

During the Civil War the mills were able to switch from cotton to wool textiles to produce blankets for the troops. When they closed because of competition with cheaper labor in southern mills, the town's fortunes declined. The sagging commercial district lined with abandoned warehouses didn't spruce itself up until 1984, when the neighborhood was designated a historic district and business owners saw a golden opportunity. Good fortune struck again in 1986, when the CoreStates U.S. Pro Cycling championship picked Philadelphia as its home and included Manayunk's steep hills (now dubbed the "Wall") on its route.

Manayunk has replaced South Street as the "hippest street in town." More than 30 restaurants compete for attention with alfresco dining, creative menus, and valet parking. Most of the 80-some stores are one-of-a-kind; among them are art galleries, antiques shops, and clothing boutiques (Nicole Miller has a store here). The half-mile stretch of shopping keeps stretching farther east as more and more businesses want a Main Street address. On the weekends you'll be strolling with hundreds of visitors—and fighting with them for parking spaces, although more parking is promised.

Manayunk has filled its calendar with popular special events: The Main Street Stroll is a Victorian street festival with a costume parade and carnival games. It's held the first Friday night in June, an exciting kickoff to the CoreStates U.S. Pro Cycling championship on Sunday. The last weekend in June the Manayunk Arts Festival lines Main Street with artists from around the country and with curbside food stands offering samples from area restaurants.

A Good Walk

Manayunk is just 7 mi from Center City. You can take the SEPTA R6 (Norristown) train from Market East, Suburban Station, or 30th Street Station downtown to the Manayunk station (on Cresson Street) and walk downhill to Main Street. To drive, follow I–76 west (the Schuylkill Expressway) to the Belmont Avenue exit. Turn right across the bridge and then right again onto Main Street. Begin your Main Street stroll at Green Lane. Follow Main Street east (you're actually walking southeast) on the south side of the street for about a half mile; the Farmers' Market, open year-round Wednesday through Sunday, marks the end of the shopping area. You'll pass some reminders of the town's former calling: Ma Jolie (⊠ 4340 Main St.) is housed in a historic bank building dating back to about 1912; the River Cafe (⊠ 4100 Main St.) occupies an old mill (behind is a riverfront deck); and the Farmers' Market set up shop in a former knitting mill. A right turn on Lock Street, just before the market, brings you to the towpath of the Manayunk Canal, built between 1817 and 1823 and rehabbed in 1979. You can walk along a path for a few blocks before doubling back to the market. Make the return trip on the north side of Main Street. Many of the cross streets have interesting shops on their first block. At any point along the way you could walk a few blocks uphill to get a sense of the neighborhood's residential character.

TIMING
Manayunk is a stay-up-late, sleep-in-in-the-morning place, and to enjoy it, you should do the same. Your best bet is to put aside a weekend evening to explore Main Street. You could set out in the late afternoon, explore the town, have a leisurely dinner, and still have plenty of time to shop. Many stores stay open until 9 or 10 on Friday and Saturday nights. If you do come on a weekday, note that most stores don't open until noon.

3 Dining

Once known mainly for hoagies and snapper soup, Philadelphia has extended its culinary range to embrace the world. French food set the pace for years, but these chefs now share honors with stars from Italy and China; distinctive ethnic eateries and excellent seafood and steak houses round out the dining scene. Although revamped banks and brokerage houses hold some pricey dazzlers, simpler treasures abound, including Reading Terminal Market and the Italian eateries of South Philadelphia.

By Barbara
Ann Rosenberg

WHETHER YOU WANT TO DINE at a fine French restaurant, sample innovative American food in a sophisticated setting, or just grab a quick (but sublime) bite for lunch, you'll discover a welcome abundance of choices here. The restaurant renaissance that put Philadelphia on the national culinary map began in the 1970s, largely a result of the influx of a new group of restaurateurs with ideas for radical change. Some started a sweeping trend by incorporating Asian and other exotic flavors into otherwise familiar dishes. Others incorporated their own personal visions to augment the city's formerly predictable and rather dreary repertoire of restaurant foodstuffs. An outstanding chef with exquisite credentials—Georges Perrier—came to the city, eventually opening his own fine dining venue, Le Bec-Fin, which was then, and is now, the most expensive in the city. The number of restaurants and the range of their cuisines have continued to explode until Philadelphia dining options are now truly international in scope.

Over the years the city's restaurants have become more sophisticated in every way, including their incorporation of striking architectural details to augment the excitement of the food. Just a few years ago, a new all-fish restaurant, Striped Bass, put a daring spin on the concept of what dining interiors should look like by moving into a handsomely renovated brokerage house. Others restaurants followed, metamorphosing turn-of-the-century banks into trendy dining locations or building contemporary space designed for smashing visual impact.

There are also more modest ethnic restaurants of nearly every persuasion, from Vietnamese to Jamaican. Steak houses abound, both top-of-the-line and more modestly priced establishments. And hotel dining is enjoying a real departure from its previously less-than-stellar reputation. Philadelphia hotels now claim some of the best chefs in the business, including some with national reputations. Italian food in Philadelphia has its own connotation, ranging from South Philadelphia home style to restaurants that rate among the most elegant in the city.

No rundown of Philadelphia's dining scene would be complete without mention of national celebrity chef Susanna Foo, who revolutionized Chinese food to include many of her own dishes, blending ingredients from other cultures without detracting from the essential purity of her basic cuisine. Her establishment is one of many on Rittenhouse Row (formerly Restaurant Row), the stretch of Walnut Street from Broad through 17th streets that holds some of the city's most elegant eateries, including Le Bec-Fin, Il Portico, and Circa.

Then there is Manayunk, the working-class city neighborhood transformed in the past few years into a trendy, upscale destination drawing beautiful people (and even mere mortals) to eat, to shop, and to see and be seen. In Old City, too, many exciting new eateries have opened. And this doesn't even begin to consider the other, somewhat unusual Philadelphia specialties that residents feel a bona fide passion for. Some of these local favorites have produced a number of long-standing rivalries for the title "the best of the best." Hoagies (Italian sandwiches) and cheese steaks fall into this category.

Bear in mind that Philadelphia is becoming a well-attended convention city, and so it's always wise to make reservations ahead and to reconfirm when you get to town, particularly for the most popular restaurants. (Le Bec-Fin is generally booked several *months* ahead for Saturday night). In general, you should tip 15% of the check, depending on the service.

In the listings, reservations are noted only when they're essential or when they are not accepted. Unless otherwise indicated, restaurants are open daily for lunch and dinner. Most of Philadelphia's restaurants can be classified as casual, but not, with the exception of inexpensive spots or the University City area, of the jeans and sneakers variety. Smart casual wear usually works except in the top hotel dining rooms and the most expensive places, where women will feel more comfortable in some version of basic black and men in ties and jackets. Dress is mentioned in reviews only when men are required to wear a jacket or a jacket and tie.

DISTRICT BY DISTRICT

A neighborhood reference is provided along with the street address of each restaurant. Many of Philadelphia's fine restaurants are concentrated in the downtown area known locally as Center City, bounded by the Schuylkill and Delaware rivers, Vine Street to the north, and South Street to the south. To make finding restaurants easier, this large area has been subdivided geographically. Center City is used to describe the midtown area bounded roughly by the Schuylkill River to the west, 6th Street to the east, South Street to the south, and Vine Street to the north. Within this area is Chinatown, which lies between 9th and 11th streets and Vine and Arch streets. The neighborhood identified as the Historic Area in addresses takes in the eastern part of Center City, including the area around Independence National Historical Park, with Old City to the north and Society Hill to the south. The boundaries of this area are 6th Street to the west, the Delaware River to the East, Vine Street to the north, and Bainbridge Street to the south.

Also included are a number of restaurants on or near the Benjamin Franklin Parkway, which leads diagonally from John F. Kennedy Plaza past Logan Circle and the Philadelphia Museum of Art to Kelly and West River drives. University City, west of the Schuylkill River around the University of Pennsylvania and Drexel University, has a number of restaurants. South Philadelphia lies south of Bainbridge Street; included here are a few places in Queen Village and Southwark. Manayunk, 7 mi northwest of Center City along the Schuylkill, has some outstanding places to dine. A restaurant along City Line Avenue and a few suburban spots are listed; other suburban restaurants are mentioned in Chapter 8.

A good source for reasonably up-to-the-minute dining information is *Philadelphia,* a monthly magazine with restaurant listings. There are also a couple of weekly local papers that have restaurant reviews and numerous listings. These are available free in metal sidewalk dispensers on nearly every Center City street corner.

CATEGORY	COST*
$$$$	over $45
$$$	$35–$45
$$	$20–$35
$	under $20

*per person excluding drinks, service, and 7% sales tax

Brunch

In Philadelphia, as in other cities, many restaurants have latched on to the habit of serving copious amounts of food as a high point after a harried workweek. Several of the city's top-notch hotels have outstanding (and expensive) brunches that are virtual extravaganzas (☞ Chapter 4 for the addresses and telephone numbers of these hotels).

There are also plenty of more laid-back, casual places to enjoy socializing with a not-so-early Sunday coffee in hand.

The Wyndham Franklin Plaza has **Between Friends,** a new entrant into the fray, with a jazz- and champagne-embellished buffet brunch. **The Dining Room** at the Ritz-Carlton has a sumptuous brunch, with a caviar station of several kinds and colors of high-quality, classy fish eggs. At the **Four Seasons** the price is determined by the cost of the served-at-the table entrée, although the rest of the meal is an all-you-can-stuff buffet of delicacies. **Treetops** at the Rittenhouse hotel has an à la carte brunch in a lovely setting overlooking the elms of Rittenhouse Square.

Bridget Foy's Second Street Grill (✉ 200 South St., ☎ 215/922–1813) has a make-your-own-Bloody-Mary station as part of the fun. The old-timey, funky **Knave of Hearts** (✉ 230 South St., ☎ 215/922–3956) gives you the flavor of South Street. On a casual note, **Le Bus** (✉ 4266 Main St., ☎ 215/487–2663), in Manayunk, is a favorite for omelets and other innovative egg preparations, with all the wonderful breads this supercasual, friendly place is known for. It's a mob scene, so go early. **Meiji En** (✉ Pier 19 at Callowhill St., ☎ 215/592–7100), an otherwise Japanese restaurant with stupendous river views, has a reasonably priced, eye-popping buffet of bagels, waffles, and all the accoutrements from smoked salmon to fruit (and even some sushi) in a huge, bright room. A jazz duo or trio adds the finishing touch. A jazz brunch at **Zanzibar Blue** (✉ 200 S. Broad St., ☎ 215/732–5200) includes really good jazz along with eggs and other creditable food in a downstairs location at the Bellevue Building.

American

$$$$
★
× **Fountain Restaurant.** Dining at the Fountain is a glamorous and cosmopolitan experience, blending pleasant, polished service with elegance of appointments. The peak of the experience, however, is unquestionably the food. Chef Jean-Marie Lacroix and his staff are constantly experimenting to create culinary excitement that changes with the seasons. Among the favorites are fingerling potatoes lyonnaise with caviar cream; pot-au-feu of rabbit and artichokes; and sautéed venison medallions swaddled in homemade pasta. There are equally delicious healthy menu choices. The restaurant is tucked away off the lavish but understated lobby of the Four Seasons hotel—a culinary oasis for travelers and a favorite dining location for locals, as well. ✉ *1 Logan Sq., Benjamin Franklin Pkwy.,* ☎ *215/963–1500. Reservations essential. AE, D, DC, MC, V.*

$$$–$$$$
× **The Garden.** This quintessential Philadelphia town house-turned-restaurant manages to convey the impression of France as you walk through the elegantly subtle hallway into the bar or directly into the somewhat formal yet welcoming dining room. The restaurant takes its name from the charming back garden that has service in appropriate weather on a canopied deck or at umbrella-covered tables in the lower garden. Among owner-chef Kathleen Mulhern's specialties is exquisitely fresh grilled Dover sole equal to any served on the other side of the pond. Desserts are all homemade, including white chocolate mousse. Two *cruvinets* (devices for keeping opened bottles of wine fresh) dispense glasses of selected red and white wines from an outstanding wine list. ✉ *1617 Spruce St., Center City,* ☎ *215/546–4455. AE, DC, MC, V. Closed Sun.; Sat. in July and Aug.*

$$$–$$$$
★
× **Jake's.** Owner-chef Bruce Cooper (his wife is Jake) has garnered a reputation for food that is innovative but somehow classic rather than quirky. The place has recently undergone a face-lift yet still displays

Dining

Assagi, **50**

Azalea, **66**

Between Friends, **34**

Bookbinder's Seafood House, **26**

Brasserie Perrier, **31**

Bridget Foy's Second Street Grill, **59**

Café Republic, **18**

Chanterelles, **46**

Chart House, **63**

Ciboulette, **22**

Circa, **28**

City Tavern, **65**

Corned Beef Academy, **30**

Dardanelles, **67**

Deux Cheminées, **45**

DiLullo Centro, **23**

The Dining Room, **33**

Dock Street Brewery & Restaurant, **9**

Fez Moroccan Cuisine, **57**

Fountain Restaurant, **7**

Friday, Saturday, Sunday, **17**

The Garden, **20**

Genji, **10, 19**

Hikaru, **2, 15, 62**

Il Portico, **25**

Jake's, **3**

Jamaican Jerk Hut, **21**

Joy Tsin Lau, **40**

Knave of Hearts, **58**

La Veranda, **72**

Le Bec-Fin, **29**

Le Bus, **4**

Lee How Fook, **37**

The Marker, **35**

Meiji En, **73**

Melrose Diner, **47**

Monte Carlo Living Room, **61**

Morton's of Chicago, **8**

Museum Restaurant, **6**

Nicholas Nickolas, **16**

Ocean Harbor, **38**

Old Original Bookbinder's, **64**

Outback Steakhouse, **36, 71**

Overtures, **55**

Palm, **22**

Pamplona, **44**

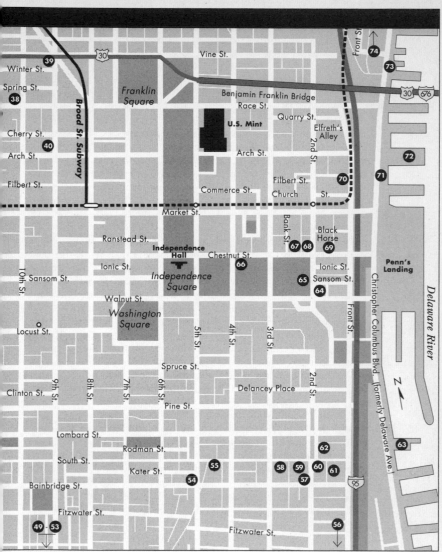

the hottest in contemporary crafts, many from local art galleries that punctuate trendy Manayunk. Cooper has a particular affinity for scallops and transforms them into dishes that range from simple to complex—always tender, sweet, and perfectly cooked. This is one of the places that helped Manayunk achieve its reputation as a dining mecca. ✉ *4365 Main St., Manayunk,* ☎ *215/483–0444. AE, DC, MC, V.*

$$$–$$$$ ✕ **Tony Clark's.** A new stunner of a restaurant! The chef/owner, a 12-
★ year veteran of the exalted kitchen at the Four Seasons, brought to his new Avenue of the Arts venue a raft of ideas. Smart contemporary decor punctuated by a magnificent floral display provides the setting for the exciting food to come, including *crépinette* (sausage) of lamb with creamed salsify and quail with grits. Open kitchens subtly screened from the dining room allow the curious to watch the chefs at work. The pastry kitchen is especially fascinating and delivers equally intriguing desserts, such as a chocolate and candied walnut gâteau with orange-caramel sauce. There is a busy bar and a downstairs caviar, champagne, and meet-and-greet "club." ✉ *121 S. Broad St., Center City,* ☎ *215/ 772–9238. Reservations essential. AE, D, MC, V.*

$$–$$$$ ✕ **Chart House.** Most people come here for the atmosphere rather than the more ordinary food. The Penn's Landing location of this national chain has dramatic Delaware River views; the nautical theme includes ultramodern paintings, sculptures, and striking architecture, with a waterfall that descends from the lobby to the lounge. The dining area and lounge seat 250 yet have a measure of intimacy lacking in many other large restaurants. For appetizers try the oysters Rockefeller or the extensive salad bar. All fish, including salmon, swordfish, and mahimahi, is flown in from its home ports fresh daily and served grilled or baked. Mud pie, the house dessert, is an ultrarich concoction of coffee ice cream with a chocolate wafer crust topped with fudge, fresh whipped cream, and almonds. ✉ *555 S. Columbus Blvd., Historic Area,* ☎ *215/625– 8383. AE, D, DC, MC, V.*

$$–$$$$ ✕ **Nicholas Nickolas.** The most recent of a limited string of large, distinctive restaurants that extend from Hawaii through Chicago and Boca Raton has brought its extensive menu of straightforward food to a handsome, well-appointed location in the Rittenhouse hotel. As evidence of the management's concern for guest comfort, some tables even have adjustable controls for the overhead light fixtures. The solicitous, thoroughly professional waitstaff delivers huge portions of well-prepared food—steaks, chops, lobster—to diners who enjoy quality but aren't searching for innovative style. Hawaiian and other immaculately fresh fish comes in daily. The crab cake appetizer suffices as a meal for smaller appetites. ✉ *210 W. Rittenhouse Sq., Center City,* ☎ *215/546–8440. AE, D, DC, MC, V.*

$$–$$$ ✕ **Azalea.** The views from the large windows of the gracious dining room of the Omni Hotel are lovely, overlooking Independence National Historical Park and the classic Second Bank of the United States. The food, however, is quite another matter—20th century all the way, using local products to create world-class dishes such as seared Atlantic salmon with shiitake mushrooms. Add to this the comfortable, neutral banquettes and the zebra-fabric-upholstered chairs, and you have a memorable setting for a delightful lunch or dinner, convenient to the city's historic monuments and the nightlife action of lower Chestnut Street. ✉ *4th and Chestnut Sts., Historic Area,* ☎ *215/931–4270. AE, DC, MC, V.*

$$–$$$ ✕ **Brasserie Perrier.** To fulfill his dream of a "less informal place where
★ people can go to eat well and have a good time" (presumably without breaking the bank), Georges Perrier of Le Bec-Fin (☞ *below*) opened this large, exuberant, Americanized version of a brasserie, complete with a lively bar, striking modern-deco ambience, and a delightful

menu of highly personal, contemporary food such as a halibut with potato ravioli and olive *jus*, and *brik* (flaky pastry) of salmon with bok choy and lime sauce. Chef Francesco Martorella also prepares four- and five-course tasting menus of his choice of foods (after consultation with the customer). This is, unquestionably, the most happening place in town—cheap by no means, but people concede they get their money's worth. ⊠ *1619 Walnut St., Center City,* ☎ *215/568–3000. AE, DC, MC, V. No lunch Sat.*

$$–$$$ ✕ **Circa.** Yet another lapsed bank with soaring arched ceilings, this restaurant by day and blend of restaurant-cum-club at night is firmly entrenched. The food is as bright and lively as the people who flock here for reasonably priced meals on Rittenhouse Row, where so many heavy-hitter restaurants rattle their pots. You walk into an atmosphere punctuated by flickering votive candles; the greeter's station is a church pulpit, and pews do duty as benches in the bar. The lower floor, open only for dinner, includes the original bank vault, where you can indulge in fanciful yet hearty dishes. The chef has a particular penchant for global cuisine made with anything from seafood to buffalo. ⊠ *1518 Walnut St., Center City,* ☎ *215/545–6800. AE, D, MC, V.*

$$–$$$ ✕ **City Tavern.** A recent, authentic re-creation of the City Tavern has resulted in an ambience that lets you time-travel to the 18th century. The atmosphere suggests that founding fathers such as John Adams, George Washington, Thomas Jefferson, and the rest of the gang *might* have supped here. In 1994, under the supervision of the National Park Service, international consultant/restaurateur Walter Staib refurbished this spot to the exact specifications of the original 1773 tavern. The food is prepared from period recipes —from West Indies pepper pot soup to Martha Washington's turkey stew—and served on china with authentic Colonial patterns by waiters in period dress. Fresh fruit cobblers come in pewter dishes. Wash the food down with a tankard of 1774 ale made from a recipe created especially for the restaurant or with a wine from the extensive list. There is live harpsichord music on Friday and Saturday nights. ⊠ *138 S. 2nd St., Center City,* ☎ *215/ 413–1443. AE, D, DC, MC, V.*

$$–$$$ ✕ **The Marker.** This restaurant in the Adam's Mark hotel has become increasingly popular as its menu has developed a more adventurous style under the tutelage of creative chef Vincent Alberici. Popular items include jumbo lump crab cakes with smoked red-pepper butter; herb-and-mustard-crusted domestic rack of lamb carved table-side; and a flaky raspberry napoleon for dessert. The Library, a cozy room with a fireplace and built-in bookshelves, is a favorite seating choice, but there are two other larger, somewhat more formal locations as well. ⊠ *City Line Ave. and Monument Rd., City Line Ave. area,* ☎ *215/ 581–5000. AE, D, DC, MC, V.*

$$–$$$ ✕ **Rococo.** Another new architectural stunner, this restaurant makes its home in the former turn-of-the-century Corn Exchange Bank. Executive chef Albert Paris and his sidekick Mustapha Rouissiya each brought their individual style of cooking to what has become an instant hit. The lively front bar gives way to a handsome, large, rather noisy dining room that extends up a flight of steps to an area for smokers. Sesame-crusted rare tuna and roast duck are high points of the menu, and many regulars make their meal out of a succession of appetizers. ⊠ *123 Chestnut St., Historic Area,* ☎ *215/629–1100. AE, D, DC, MC, V.*

$$ ✕ **Friday, Saturday, Sunday.** This small neighborhood restaurant—once considered innovative but now predictable—looks pretty much the way it did when it opened 20 years ago and still attracts a mostly neighborhood clientele. Fabrics are draped from the ceiling; mirrors and pin lights line the walls. Classical and jazz music plays in the background,

helping to mask the conversations from the cheek-by-jowl tables. The printed menu is augmented by a blackboard listing the daily specials. Many local favorites echo back to when this place *was* only open the three days a week mentioned in its name. Popular entrées include duck, salmon, and striped bass. Dessert favorites are crème brûlée and coconut cream pie. ⊠ *261 S. 21st St., Center City,* ☎ *215/546–4232. AE, D, DC, MC, V.*

$$ ✕ **Museum Restaurant.** After years of dreary, disappointing food, the venerable Philadelphia Museum of Art has finally hit on a workable formula for giving its visitors an opportunity to feed their bodies while nourishing their souls: It hired nationally renowned Restaurant Associates, which in turn brought in a fine chef and a professional, pleasant waitstaff. Now the restaurant serves a more-than-contented group of eaters at lunch, as well as Wednesday-night dinner and Sunday brunch. When the weather is amenable, there's a rather remarkable cold buffet of grilled vegetables and overstuffed sandwiches presented under a large tent on a terrace with a glorious view of the city. ⊠ *26th St. and Benjamin Franklin Pkwy.,* ☎ *215/763–8100. AE, DC, MC, V. Closed Mon. No dinner Thurs.–Tues.*

$$ ✕ **White Dog Cafe.** The name of this eclectic town house restaurant near the Penn campus derives from the story of the 19th-century mystic Madame Blavatsky. She claimed that while she was living in the house, a white dog lay across her ailing leg and cured it. Innovative restaurateur Judy Wicks took her inspiration from the tale and sponsors all manner of events that would make Madame Blavatsky proud. The White Dog specializes in using locally grown products on an ever-changing creative menu; seasonings for the soups, fish, pasta, and other dishes can be overly ambitious, so choose carefully. The small, lively bar has eight American beers on tap and nine in bottles, mostly local brands. The wine list, too, is all-American. Tails, a Victorian piano parlor, provides a plush setting for a quiet drink in a smoke-free setting. ⊠ *3420 Sansom St., University City,* ☎ *215/386–9224. AE, D, DC, MC, V.*

$–$$ ✕ **Dock Street Brewery & Restaurant.** All the makings of a classic brasserie (which actually means "brewery" in French) were here from the day the restaurant opened: the machinery for producing the beer and the large, exuberant space in which to drink it. At first the food didn't live up to the promise, but that's not the case any longer. Olivier de St. Martin, a chef from the north of France whose family home nuzzles up to Alsace—where brasseries began—took over and metamorphosed the menu to include the dishes for which that region is famous. Hearty favorites like *choucroute* (sauerkraut cooked with white wine, juniper berries, assorted sausages, and duck confit) and cassoulet now dominate, although there are still plenty of standards such as steaks, fish, and burgers. Several flavors of the house-specialty boutique beer are available on a daily basis, along with a full bar. ⊠ *2 Logan Sq., Benjamin Franklin Pkwy.,* ☎ *215/496–0413. AE, MC, V.*

$–$$ ✕ **Restaurant School.** Here's the only place in Philadelphia where you have a chance to get haute cuisine and European service at a fraction of what you would normally pay at a fancy restaurant. A fixed price of $15–$17 buys an appetizer and an entrée; desserts and coffee are extra. It is managed and staffed entirely by students attending the Restaurant School, an institution that has produced many chefs for Philadelphia restaurants. A restored 1860 Victorian mansion near the University of Pennsylvania has a dining area that seats 120 in a glass-enclosed atrium. The menu sometimes lists Italian, Spanish, and German dishes but is mainly traditional French and American cuisine. Meals are occasionally extraordinary (especially for the price), but it depends on the level of training of the current kitchen staff. ⊠ *4207 Walnut*

St., University City, ☎ *215/222–4200. AE, D, DC, MC, V. Closed Sun. and Mon.*

$–$$ ✕ **Sonoma.** The first of Chef Derek Davis's ventures as an entrepreneur became the cornerstone of his mini-empire in trendy Manayunk (☞ River City Diner, *below*). The contemporary, airy design sets the stage for California-influenced food with Italian touches. The sandwiches on focaccia are standouts. Sonoma immediately earned a reputation as a hangout for people in the know; the bar, which regularly stock 135 varieties of vodka, cemented that reputation. ✉ *4411 Main St., Manayunk,* ☎ *215/483–9400. AE, D, DC, MC, V.*

$ ✕ **Tony Luke's.** The original location (at Front and Oregon, nearly under I–95) earned such a reputation from truckers who stopped for huge beef or pork sandwiches with Italian greens and cheese that the locals finally caught on and adopted the dinerlike restaurant for their own. The lines are long but move quickly, and seating (outside only, under cover) is relatively scarce, but people flock here from early morning to closing time for generous breakfasts and tasty sandwiches. For large orders, it's possible to call ahead and take food home. The new Northeast Philadelphia location doesn't open until 10. ✉ *39 E. Oregon Ave., South Philadelphia,* ☎ *215/551–5725;* ✉ *2998 Welsh Rd., Northeast Philadelphia,* ☎ *215/677–4820. Reservations not accepted. No credit cards. Closed Sun.*

Burmese

$–$$ ✕ **Rangoon.** The only Burmese restaurant in the city provides a surprising range of flavors and textures, some reminiscent of Thailand, some of India—and others that are unique to this cuisine. The curries, for example, incorporate familiar tastes from all the countries that surround Myanmar, as Burma is now known, into dishes that are quite special. The lentil fritters are well seasoned with ginger (some people find them hot) and make an unusual appetizer to drink with beer that is now stocked along with a moderate selection of other beverages. The inexpensive lunch special, on weekdays only, is an outstanding value. ✉ *112 N. 9th St., Chinatown,* ☎ *215/829–8939. MC, V. Closed Mon. No lunch weekends.*

Caribbean

$ ✕ **Jamaican Jerk Hut.** The scintillating flavors of the beautiful island of Jamaica are all here, tasting at least as good as on their original turf. The tiny storefront, overseen by the chef-owner who went to culinary school and decided to apply her training to the tastes of her homeland, is primarily takeout. There are a couple of doll-size tables (where people sit to wait for their orders), but you can eat in a charming back garden when the weather permits. Lovers of Jamaican patty—flaky pastries filled with meat or vegetables—will find them exceedingly well made. Pork or chicken jerk is lovingly tended over an authentic pit; the curries and *roti* (pancakes with fillings such as curried chickpeas or chicken) are exemplary. And it all costs, as they say, a "fish cake." ✉ *1436 South St., Center City,* ☎ *215/545–8644. No credit cards. Closed Sun.*

Chinese

$$–$$$$ ✕ **Susanna Foo.** The decor of Madame Foo's elegantly renovated restaurant now matches its national reputation for food. The chef has garnered all manner of top-notch awards for her cuisine, which incorporates a variety of Western ingredients into pure, essentially Chinese food. Such favorites as Hundred-Corner Crab Cakes and spicy

Mongolian lamb, along with a battery of exotic specials, bring repeat business from a loyal coterie of regulars, who compete for tables with out-of-towners. The Sunday brunch of ethereal dim sum is a recent addition. There is a full bar and a thoughtfully chosen, somewhat pricey wine list as well as imported beers. The restaurant has recently installed its own fine pastry chef, who prepares an array of French and Asian desserts. ⊠ *1512 Walnut St., Center City,* ☎ *215/545–2666. Reservations essential. AE, DC, MC, V.*

$–$$$ ✕ **Ocean Harbor.** At lunchtime, this is the closest place the city has to
★   a Hong Kong tea house, with multiple carts flying through the dining room with a dizzying selection of dim sum. There are the usual pork and shrimp dumplings, but this chef ranges far afield and incorporates vegetables, different kinds of seafood, and other specifically Chinese ingredients. You point at what you want and it is transferred to your plate and charged to your bill. The bill is in Chinese, and prices of portions vary, but it ends up a pretty reasonable meal. If you don't know what's in the dim sum, ask for a description—sometimes you get it. The clientele at lunch is mainly Chinese and the place is usually crowded. Evenings are quieter. ⊠ *1023 Race St., Chinatown,* ☎ *215/574–1398. MC, V.*

$–$$ ✕ **Joy Tsin Lau.** In recent years Chinatown has attracted a new assortment of restaurants, many run by people from Hong Kong and Vietnam. Joy Tsin Lau is a takeoff on Hong Kong Island (or perhaps Kowloon), with its gaudy exterior giving way to more of the same inside. Every Chinese symbol, including golden medallions, dragons, and the like, lines the walls and the ceiling. At lunchtime you'll find a direct re-creation of a Hong Kong tea house atmosphere, with carts of dim sum—little dishes that gladden the heart—being wheeled from table to table. You can also order from the rather predictable menu. ⊠ *1026–1028 Race St., Chinatown,* ☎ *215/592–7228. AE, D, DC, MC, V.*

$–$$ ✕ **Lee How Fook.** This restaurant has been serving Cantonese food to loyal fans of the genre for years, even when that style took a temporary backseat to the craze for Szechuan and Hunan dishes. Small and plain but clean, and just a block from the main Chinatown action, Lee How Fook manages to resurface every few years as it is "discovered" by yet another reviewer who extols its simple dishes, such as salt-baked shrimp or squid, beautifully cooked and seasoned asparagus (in season), and a variety of noodle dishes (except for the Singapore-style noodles, which, for whatever reason, emerge from the kitchen dry and lifeless in taste). ⊠ *219 N. 11th St., Chinatown,* ☎ *215/925–7266. No credit cards.*

$ ✕ **Sang Kee Peking Duck House.** Totally devoid of decor (unless you count the lacquered ducks and boneless pork loins hanging in the front window), this cramped, dingy hole-in-the-wall cooks the most delicious noodle soups in town. It's possible to order from a choice of egg or rice noodles in different widths and a selection of accompanying meats: duck, pork, beef brisket. And if you wish, you can have your soup with both noodles *and* overstuffed, tender wontons. Other traditional foods, besides the house specialty duck, are crisp fried shrimp balls and various seafood and fish dishes carried from the kitchen with more speed than style. This is not a place for leisurely dining, and the housekeeping could be more careful, but it's worth the adventure for the authentic food delivered by a generally pleasant staff. Beer is available. ⊠ *238 N. 9th St., Chinatown,* ☎ *215/925–7532. Reservations not accepted. No credit cards.*

Diners and Philly Food

Philadelphia's mayor, Ed Rendell, has gleefully enhanced the city's reputation as "the junk food capital of the country" by frequently appearing while stuffing his mouth with a hoagie or a cheese steak. Hoagies, a Philadelphia spin on the traditional Italian sandwich, hero, or sub of other cities, have been embraced by nearly everyone who tastes them. Soft pretzels (with mustard, to be authentic) are tolerated by many visitors, but the merits of Philadelphia cheese steaks often elude anyone not to the city born. Nevertheless, lovers of Philly food will be happy to know that gift packages of everything *but* cheese steaks can be shipped to any former residents or visitors by calling Philadelphia Favorites to Go (☎ 800/808–TOGO) or A Taste of Philadelphia (☎ 800/8–HOAGIE).

$–$$ ✕ **River City Diner.** With a startling amount of chrome-embellished decor that harks back to the '50s and forward to the 21st century, this huge new diner is another in the expanding Derek Davis empire of restaurants, all in Manayunk. Other eateries that clearly display the versatility and vitality of the chef are Arroyo Grill (✉ Main and Leverington St., Manayunk, ☎ 215/487–1400), strictly Southwestern in ambience and food preparation; the steak house Kansas City Prime (✉ 4417 Main St., Manayunk, ☎ 215/482–3700), which includes Kobe beef on its pricey menu; and Sonoma (☞ *above*). The River City Diner, however, offers diner standards like fried flounder with tartar sauce, augmented by some nostalgia dishes from the chef's mother and grandmother (chicken in a pot with matzo ball and noodles). In true diner style, the desserts are enormous. ✉ *3720 Main St., Manayunk,* ☎ *215/483–7500. AE, D, DC, MC, V.*

$ ✕ **Corned Beef Academy.** This simple, sparkling clean restaurant creates overstuffed sandwiches of juicy corned beef, pastrami, award-winning hand-sliced turkey, and more on a choice of rye, pumpernickel, marble bread, or kaiser rolls with all the various deli permutations. Everything is made on the premises, according to the owner, except the potato salad, which comes from a reliable purveyor who makes the best in town. Breakfast includes corned beef, too (with eggs). ✉ *1605 Walnut St., Center City,* ☎ *215/561–6222. No credit cards. Closed Sun.*

$ ✕ **Melrose Diner.** The food is nothing elaborate but this classic Philadelphia diner delivers fresh, top-quality ingredients at minimalist prices. Entrées cost $5–$9 ($11.50 for the sirloin). The Melrose is open around the clock, and you can get breakfast 24 hours a day, too. Popular dishes include deviled crab cutlet and fried shrimp with a rather heavy breading. The on-premises bake shop has eight bakers, who prepare favorite desserts such as hot apple pie with vanilla sauce and butter-cream layer cake. The busy waitresses, many of whom grew up in this South Philadelphia neighborhood, make you feel right at home. ✉ *1501 Snyder Ave., South Philadelphia,* ☎ *215/467–6644. No credit cards.*

$ ✕ **Pat's King of Steaks.** A cheese steak is a Philadelphia phenomenon—almost an addiction to some of the native-born. Shaved slices of beef, fried onions, and melted cheese (your choice of American, provolone, or Cheese Whiz) are loaded onto an untoasted roll, with oil and juices dripping onto everything: the wax paper, the outdoor metal tables, and even yourself. Add some greasy fries topped with more melted cheese and a Tastycake for dessert, and according to some locals, you've had the ultimate Philadelphia eating experience. It's an acquired taste. Pat's is open around the clock. ✉ *1237 E. Passyunk Ave., at intersection of 9th and Wharton Sts., South Philadelphia,* ☎ *215/468–1546. No credit cards.*

$ ✕ **Reading Terminal Market.** A Philadelphia treasure, the Reading
★ Terminal Market contains a profusion of more than 80 stalls, shops,
lunch counters, and food emporiums in a huge, exciting indoor market. You can choose from numerous raw ingredients and prepared
foods—Chinese, Greek, Mexican, Japanese, Thai, Middle Eastern,
Italian, soul food, vegetarian, and Pennsylvania Dutch. Food options
include an extensive salad bar, seafood, deli, baked goods, specialty
hoagie and cheese-steak shops, sushi bar, and the outstanding Bassett's
ice-cream counter. Get there early to beat the daily lunch rush. The Down
Home Diner has good farm-style breakfasts and lunches (and dinner
on some nights). Fisher's is the place to try a genuine Philadelphia soft
pretzel—with butter brushed on it as it emerges from the oven. The
market is open Monday–Saturday 8–6. ✉ *12th and Arch Sts., Center City,* ☎ *215/922–2317. Closed Sun.*

$ ✕ **Rocco's.** Fortunately for the hungry, one of Philadelphia's prime pur-
veyors of overstuffed hoagies has a convenient location at Reading Terminal Market. The sandwiches can be made with a variety of fillings,
but the classic Italian hoagies earn the most fans. Freshly sliced meats
including Genoa salami, *capicolla* (spiced ham), and others join aged
provolone and other cheeses in an overstuffed crisp roll specially baked
to hold the assortment without spilling over. The simple dressing is the
finishing touch. ✉ *Reading Terminal Market, 12th and Arch Sts.,
Center City,* ☎ *215/238–1223. No credit cards. Closed Sun.*

$ ✕ **Salumeria.** A local favorite, Salumeria specializes in hoagies that have
★ taken the basic sandwich one step up to a new level of consciousness.
This hoagie includes such ingredients as roasted pimientos and a house
dressing among its standard ingredients and offers house-marinated
artichoke hearts as an embellishment. Nobody can complain about gilding the lily, however, because all these additions somehow become incorporated into a delicious whole. ✉ *Reading Terminal Market, 12th
and Arch Sts., Center City,* ☎ *215/592–8150. No credit cards. Closed
Sun.*

French

$$$$ ✕ **Deux Cheminées.** This unique restaurant occupies a 19th-century
mansion filled with Oriental rugs, paintings, and fine objects that create a romantic setting for dining. The French food on the $68 prix-
fixe menu is rather classic in style, with touches that owner/chef Fritz
Blank feels are appropriate. Some signature dishes are rack of lamb
with truffle sauce, a rich crab bisque with Scotch, and a risotto with
black truffles, fontina cheese, and fresh shrimp. ✉ *1221 Locust St.,
Center City,* ☎ *215/790–0200. AE, DC, MC, V. Closed Sun., Mon.
No lunch.*

$$$$ ✕ **Le Bec-Fin.** For many years this outpost of Parisian and Lyonnais
★ food (with inspired touches from stellar owner-chef Georges Perrier)
was judged the finest in the city and, oftentimes, the country. Although
there has recently been some competition for that accolade, there are
still sufficient plaudits to require an advance reservation of several *months*
to garner a Saturday-night seat for the more than $100 per person fixed-
price dinner. Expect also to find this haute cuisine served in a luxurious setting of Louis XV furniture, apricot silk walls, and crystal
chandeliers. Le Bec-Fin translates as "Tip of the Beak" but is actually
a rather romantic term for the most sensitive part of the palate, a fitting name for a restaurant catering to people who appreciate exquisite
food in exquisite surroundings. Perrier is a perfectionist who spares
nothing to inject excellence into every detail of his prix-fixe dinner, which
includes a choice of appetizer, fish course, entrée, cheese or salad, and
an extravaganza of a dessert cart. The famous pressed lobster comes

with a $27 surcharge; *galette de crabe* (a sublime crab cake) is another popular signature dish. It's possible to indulge in a more limited selection of these dishes by reserving ahead for a three-course lunch for a relatively modest $36. Le Bar Lyonnais, just downstairs from the main dining room, has smallish portions of some specialty dishes such as lobster bisque for affordable prices. ⊠ *1523 Walnut St., Center City,* ☎ *215/567–1000. Reservations essential. Jacket and tie. AE, D, DC, MC, V. Closed Sun.*

$$–$$$$ ✕ **Chanterelles.** A ravishing menu of à la carte and set meals—including a three-course dinner, a five-course vegetarian feast, and a six-course tasting menu—makes up the fare at this small but stellar restaurant. Although owner-chef Philippe Chin claims that dress is casual, most people prefer to get a bit gussied up to eat his Asian-influenced French food. The venison dishes are Chin's particular pride, not to mention desserts and foie gras. The charming chef makes everything except the bread. ⊠ *1312 Spruce St., Center City,* ☎ *215/735–7551. Reservations essential. AE, DC, MC, V. Closed Sun.*

$$–$$$ ✕ **Ciboulette.** Bruce Lim, the owner-chef, has made his way through several incarnations of this French restaurant on the second floor of the stunning Bellevue Building. His current style is to serve all his entrées in appetizer-size portions while maintaining the complexity of preparation. Black bass in *barigoule* consists of the fish accompanied by artichoke bottoms, fennel, and arugula; salmon is presented over couscous with a basil vinaigrette. Some choices are intended to be kind to waistlines—or you can indulge in such pleasures as foie gras with mango or sinful desserts. ⊠ *200 S. Broad St., Center City,* ☎ *215/790– 1270. AE, DC, MC, V.*

$$–$$$ ✕ **Overtures.** A bit of Paris exists just off funky South Street. Not the food, exactly, since Overtures does not cook pure French but rather the inspired interpretations of the owner-chef, a genial man with definite ideas about how to operate his fine, moderately priced BYOB restaurant. Among the stylish decorative touches are extravagant flower arrangements, trompe l'oeil paintings, and black-and-white floor tiles. Although the menu changes periodically, there's always a lavender-scented rack of lamb, a genuine winner; and people who adore sweetbreads swear by Overtures' preparation. The Caesar salad may be the best in town. ⊠ *609–611 E. Passyunk Ave., Historic Area,* ☎ *215/ 627–3455. AE, DC, MC, V.*

Italian

$$–$$$$ ✕ **Il Portico.** Elegance begins at the gleaming brass-and-beveled-glass front doors of this relative newcomer to others of its pricey ilk on Rittenhouse Row. Inside, the theme continues with large old-world oil paintings and huge, contemporary crystal chandeliers. Classic Tuscan food is elegantly served by formally attired waiters who rush it steaming hot to the table. The chef does miraculous things with Portobello mushrooms and all forms of pasta; *papardelle alla lepre* (thick-cut pasta with hare), *caciucco* (seafood with vegetables) and the risotto with quail are good bets. The extensive wine list, heavy on Italian reds, includes some important bottles and is fairly priced. ⊠ *1519 Walnut St., Center City,* ☎ *215/587–7000. Reservations essential. AE, DC, MC, V.*

$$–$$$$ ✕ **Monte Carlo Living Room.** Two mirrored, candlelighted dining rooms
★   with crystal chandeliers create a refined atmosphere for sublime Italian cuisine. Chef Nunzio Patruno applies his deft, innovative touch to foods of the entire country. He is equally at home with all forms of protein, but fish and shellfish dishes, such as risotto with shrimp and peas, seem to bring out his very best instincts. Homemade pastas are ethereal, including ravioli flavored with squid ink surrounding lobster

mousse. The fresh gnocchi with duck ragout is admirable. If the chef is available to create a special menu, by all means consider the possibility. The multicourse tasting dinner costs $65. Dancing in a plush private club upstairs is free to diners. ✉ *150 South St., Historic Area,* ☎ *215/925–2220. Reservations essential. Jacket required. AE, MC, V.*

$$–$$$ ✕ **Assagi.** A casual, reasonably priced new restaurant has replaced the former (expensive) Osteria Romana at this location, with the same decor but with a change of style that includes assorted small-plate "samplings" of delicious pastas with a variety of sauces tasting of the Old World. Stucco walls are trimmed in dark wood, and the white tile floors are fashioned after a Roman *ristorante*. Octopus *alla Livornese* (sautéed with olive oil, olives, capers, and garlic) is a good choice; a new full-size menu item, available by advance reservation for six or more people, is a traditional roast suckling pig dinner for $40. The wine list is excellent. ✉ *935 Ellsworth St., South Philadelphia,* ☎ *215/339–0700. AE, DC, MC, V. Closed Mon.*

$$–$$$ ✕ **La Veranda.** Gaze out the window of either dining room at this riverside restaurant, and you'll see a charming marina of pleasure boats. Gaze at your plate, and you'll find the food of Italy, cooked the way the Centofanti family did at its original restaurant, near the Trevi Fountain in Rome. The antipasti of vegetables or seafood are outstanding; so are the pastas. Owner/chef Roberto and his nephews Domenico and Claudio rely on the best local and imported ingredients to replicate the flavors of the old country but with a decidedly modern spin, as in the risotto with shrimp and zucchini in cream sauce and fusilli with Portobello mushrooms. Check out the newest area upstairs (Caviar Ristorante) for the best views and snappy table-side preparations. ✉ *Pier 3, Penn's Landing (between Market and Arch Sts.), Historic Area,* ☎ *215/351–1898. Reservations essential. AE, DC, MC, V.*

$$–$$$ ✕ **Ristorante Primavera.** Get here early: This popular Italian bistro, owned by the same people as the Monte Carlo Living Room (☞ *above*), seats only 36 and takes no reservations. Cozy touches include soft track lighting, exposed brick walls, pink table linens, and wall-to-wall carpeting. *Insalata di frutti di mare* (seafood antipasto) with lemon juice, olive oil, and parsley is an excellent light seafood appetizer. Pastas and appetizers are the high points of the menu, but the veal chop is always delicious. For dessert try the tiramisu, from the recipe book of the owners' grandmother. The wine list is small but thoughtfully chosen. ✉ *146 South St., Historic Area,* ☎ *215/925–7832. Reservations not accepted. No credit cards.*

$$–$$$ ✕ **Tiramisu.** Oil paintings from Italy line the exposed-brick walls of a formerly intimate and now expanded restaurant serving what owner-chef Alberto Delbello describes as nouvelle Jewish-Roman cuisine. One outstanding appetizer is the baby artichokes prepared Jewish style, constantly pressed down as they are fried in olive oil until they emerge looking like flattened bronzed flowers. The eponymous dessert from which the restaurant takes its name is presented in large portions. ✉ *528 S. 5th St., Historic Area,* ☎ *215/925–3335. AE, DC, MC, V.*

$$–$$$ ✕ **Tre Scalini.** "Three little steps" are exactly what it takes to enter this restaurant deep in the heart of not Texas, but rather, South Philadelphia: locus of down-home Italian food. Somehow being in this smallish two-story eatery conveys the feeling of having entered someone's aunt's or grandmother's dining room, complete with paneling, mirrors, and a plethora of plastic hanging plants. The food, too, is more home style than professional kitchen, yet it is unmistakably carefully prepared, including such unusual (for South Philadelphia) appetizers as a tangle of wild mushrooms, beautifully sautéed with garlic and served on their own, without pasta as a base. If available, the teeny-tiny garlic-and-parsley-scented clams, about the size of a thumbnail, are a must. Sim-

ple pasta preparations are best; main courses suffer by comparison. ⊠ *1533 S. 11th St., South Philadelphia,* ☎ *215/551–3870. MC, V.*

$$ ✕ **Panorama.** The name refers to the inside mural rather than the window view of this lively Old City restaurant with the largest wine cruvinet in the world. The specially designed wine storage system allows Panorama to offer 120 wines by the glass; there is a huge selection of well-chosen bottles, too. The food is authentic northern Italian, simple and hearty, with special attention to such antipasto choices as calamari *alla Livornese* (squid sautéed in olive oil, garlic, capers, and olives) on grilled polenta or spinach, ricotta, and goat cheese in a potato crust served with tomato sauce. A large selection of outstanding pastas is also available along with salads and protein-rich main courses. The ambience is either ultranoisy or animated, depending on your tolerance level. ⊠ *14 N. Front St., Historic Area,* ☎ *215/922– 7800. Reservations essential. AE, DC, MC, V.*

$$ ✕ **Victor Cafe.** Looking for your waiter? He or she may be on the stairway singing a Verdi aria. At the Victor Cafe the waiters are opera singers, and the kitchen plays a very poor second fiddle to the music. Dishes are from southern and northern regions, but it's best to stick to simple pastas and chicken. Busts of composers adorn the shelves, and framed photos of opera singers line the walls. The family's record collection consists of 25,000 78 RPMs. ⊠ *1303 Dickinson St., South Philadelphia,* ☎ *215/468–3040. Reservations essential. AE, DC, MC, V.*

$$ ✕ **Villa di Roma.** This South Philadelphia classic in a central Italian Market location has endured many ups and downs but is still beloved for its basic southern Italian food. Daily specials such as delicious breaded asparagus spark the extensive regular menu. A must for dessert is the *tartufo* (a ball of chocolate ice cream rolled in cocoa), almost the equal of the one served to great acclaim at Tre Scalini in Rome. ⊠ *936 S. 9th St., South Philadelphia,* ☎ *215/592–1295. No credit cards.*

$–$$ ✕ **DiLullo Centro.** Occupying the premises of the former Locust Theater, this stunning restaurant across from the Academy of Music has two main-floor dining areas, a café-bar where light meals are served, and a wine cellar *cum* private dining room on the lower level. The main dining space and the bar are decorated with master painter look-alike murals. After a rocky few years of major management and kitchen changes, DiLullo Centro is now turning out fine, authentic food, which is occasionally slow to be delivered. *Tortelli di zucca* (half moon–shaped pasta stuffed with squash) with arugula pesto and *fregole con vongole* (semolina with clams, potatoes, and celery) are two options. The wine list is 75% Italian, with the addition of some good California and French choices. ⊠ *1407 Locust St., Center City,* ☎ *215/546–2000. AE, DC, MC, V. Closed Sun.*

$ ✕ **Triangle Tavern.** One of South Philadelphia's many neighborhood Italian bar-restaurants, only cheaper, the Triangle has lots of local color and "red gravy" (the South Philadelphia name for long-cooked tomato sauce). Mussels are the specialty of the house; calamari (squid) with tomato sauce is also popular. Dusty's Trio has been providing live entertainment on Friday and Saturday nights here for more than 40 years. ⊠ *10th and Reed Sts., South Philadelphia,* ☎ *215/467–8683. No credit cards.*

Japanese

$–$$ ✕ **Genji.** This place has been around University City for many years; at one time the majority of its following came from the nearby college crowd, both students and faculty. Now nearly everybody who is addicted to the cult of raw fish in its many guises trots both to Genji's older location, out of loyalty and because of regard for its familiar decor, and to its newer, even more simple Center City space. Attractive plates of all the standard raw and cooked Japanese dishes make their way to the tables. A talented Vietnamese sushi chef in University City draws raves from the regulars, and the beauty of his presentations makes it even more difficult for devotees to keep from running up the tab. ⊠ *4002 Spruce St., University City,* ☎ *215/387–1583;* ⊠ *1720 Sansom St., Center City,* ☎ *215/564–1720. AE, DC, MC, V.*

$–$$ ✕ **Hikaru.** If one location is good for people who find watching the preparation of Japanese food intriguing, then three must be even better, giving you a chance to drop in for a fix of your favorites without going too far afield. Each of the locations (Center City, Manayunk, South Street) has its special aficionados; sushi is a good bet at any of them. Reviews by some persnickety folks occasionally give these places mundane marks and call the food commercial: It's difficult to predict. ⊠ *108 S. 18th St., Center City,* ☎ *215/496/9950;* ⊠ *438 Main St., Manayunk,* ☎ *215/487–3500;* ⊠ *607 S. 2nd St., Historic Area,* ☎ *215/627–7110. AE, D, DC, MC, V.*

Mexican

$$ ✕ **Zocalo.** The freshly fine-tuned menu at this innovative contemporary Mexican outpost in University City continues to reflect experimentation with some favorite preparations such as guacamole and empanadas. A tasty Mayan appetizer, *xik-l-pak,* is a pumpkinseed salsa with habanero chile, cilantro, and tomato. Main courses range from venison and swordfish tacos to vegetable tostadas. At the bar, the lively crowd munches on appetizers and sips drinks from an ever-expanding stock of tequila. The light, airy decor is punctuated by shows of Mexican artifacts and contemporary art. ⊠ *3600 Lancaster Ave., University City,* ☎ *215/895–0139. AE, D, DC, MC, V.*

$–$$ ✕ **Tequila's.** Chef Carlos Molina makes Tequila's a prime Center City
★   choice for Mexican food—not the usual enchiladas but authentic south-of-the border dishes like chilies *rellenos,* moderately spicy *poblano* peppers stuffed either with cheese or ground meat mixed with raisins and nuts and baked in a tomato sauce or fried in a light batter. The chef also prepares fowl in complicated, multi-ingredient mole sauces or occasionally a delicious *pozole,* a Mexican pork and hominy dish. The decor is clearly Mexican, with photos of heroes such as Pancho Villa and Emiliano Zapata and alcoves containing Mexican glassware and ceramics. You can choose from a dozen different Mexican beers and 15 brands of tequila. ⊠ *1511 Locust St., Center City,* ☎ *215/546–0181. AE, DC, MC, V.*

Moroccan

$$ ✕ **Fez Moroccan Cuisine.** If you want your dining experience to be a bit exotic, Fez—with its Moroccan decor and its menu of Moroccan food cooked by a Middle Eastern chef—may fill the bill. The Queen Village location is cramped, but don't take it all too seriously and just enter into the spirit of eating with your hands (after having them washed by a waiter with water from an ornate kettle). People sit on low padded benches or hassocks as they crowd around tooled-brass tables. The best main-course choices are the lamb with honey and almonds or chicken with olives, both available on the $20 fixed-price seven-course banquet. The banquet also includes salads, *bastilla* (flaky dough stuffed with chicken, almonds, and scrambled eggs), couscous with vegetables, fresh fruit, baklava, and sweet mint tea. To top it off, the meal includes a performance by a belly dancer. ⊠ *620 S. 2nd St., Historic Area,* ☎ *215/925–5367. AE, D, DC, MC, V. No lunch.*

Russian

$$–$$$$ ✕ **Café Republic.** A tongue-in-cheek play on the theme of the failed Soviet Union (the name is spelled with a backward "R" on the menu), this establishment sprang up suddenly in a shabby bronze building in a nondescript restaurant no-man's land. The joke becomes apparent inside, with an ornately framed portrait of Lenin hanging over shabby leather chairs in the bar and an iconlike picture of Karl Marx in the highly stylized dining room. The restaurant serves caviar (five types) and vodka (50 types—some are international name brands and some house-infused flavors), and all the traditional accoutrements, such as featherlight *blini* and borscht. If you stick to the food without gobbling too much caviar and are moderate in your vodka consumption, this makes for an affordable, enjoyable experience. ✉ *2201 South St., Center City,* ☎ *215/545–8474. AE, DC, MC, V. No lunch.*

Seafood

$$$–$$$$
★ ✕ **Striped Bass Restaurant and Bar.** The opening of this all-seafood restaurant a couple of years ago caused the biggest splash on Philadelphia's dining scene in more than a decade. Capitalizing on the existing grandeur of a former brokerage house with soaring marble pillars, restaurateur-trendsetter (and now sole owner) Neil Stein created a visually stunning room with striking appointments that accent the 28-ft ceilings and muslin-draped windows. A spectacular 16-ft sculpture of a leaping striped bass overhangs the exhibition kitchen. A stellar new chef from Los Angeles should boost the restaurant to—or beyond—its former glory. Pan-roasted wild striped bass with ruby chard, porcini, and sage, and kasu-marinated Chilean sea bass with jasmine rice, garlic spinach, and ginger teriyaki are typical new dishes with Pacific Rim overtones. There is an extensive raw bar and a chef's table—strategically placed adjacent to the open-to-the-dining-room kitchen—which offers a grand feast at commensurately grand prices. ✉ *1500 Walnut St., Center City,* ☎ *215/732–4444. Reservations essential. AE, MC, V.*

$$–$$$$ ✕ **Old Original Bookbinder's.** Today the city's most famous restaurant has become more of a landmark (the original opened in 1865) than an essential stop for the devoted diner. There's a photo of Elizabeth Taylor and other celebrities and politicians with former owner John Taxin, whose daughter and grandson are the current owners. Booky's has two bars and seven dining rooms as well as a touristy gift shop, complete with cans of the restaurant's most popular soups, including snapper with sherry. It's often criticized for being overpriced (entrées range from $22 to $30), and you'll spring for the top end if you order one of the celebrated lobsters, which are selected from a tank and cooked to order. Still, the place remains a haunt of celebrities, politicians, and athletes who want to see and be seen. ✉ *125 Walnut St., Historic Area,* ☎ *215/925–7027. AE, D, DC, MC, V.*

$$–$$$ ✕ **Bookbinder's Seafood House.** This is the one that causes all the confusion: Bookbinder's is actually owned by a member of the original founding family, who sold the larger establishment (Old Original Bookbinder's) to new owners in the 1940s. It has typical seafood restaurant decor, such as stuffed swordfish mounted on the walls and fishermen's nets dangling from the ceiling. The fare is equally predictable, with a few daily specials that deviate from the normal dishes. The famous snapper soup is always good, as is the fresh crab salad; broiled local fish are a good choice. ✉ *215 S. 15th St., Center City,* ☎ *215/545–1137. AE, D, DC, MC, V.*

$–$$ ✕ Philadelphia Fish & Company. Owner-chef Kevin Meeker brings some
innovative approaches to a wide variety of seafood at this busy, lively
Old City–Society Hill oasis for lovers of protein that swims. Meeker
frequently hobnobs with his buddy, celebrity Hawaiian chef Sam Choy,
at either of their restaurants, and the menu includes many of the
bravura dishes cooked up by the two of them. There are many Asian
fish specialties, as well as stuffed shrimp with bouillabaise sauce. Outdoor dining and drinking takes place in season on a deck that overlooks busy Chestnut Street and is good for people-watching—and
traffic noise. ⊠ *207 South St., Historic Area,* ☎ *215/625–8605. AE,
D, DC, MC, V.*

Spanish

$–$$ ✕ Pamplona. Decorated with a huge faux-Picasso mural that overlooks
the lively, always crowded dining room, this Center City outpost
promises tapas, the Spanish snacks eaten with drinks at lunch and dinner. The renditions, however, are often like the muralcharming but not
exactly like the originals. Nevertheless, you can tailor your intake
(and expenditure) by the number and relative costliness of your selections. Try the grilled mushrooms filled with parsley and ham, potato
omelets cooked in olive oil, or the popular shrimp in garlic sauce. ⊠
225 S. 12th St., Center City, ☎ *215/627–9059. No credit cards.*

Steak

$$–$$$$ ✕ Palm. The Philadelphia branch of the celebrated Palm group holds
forth off the lobby of the Park Hyatt at the Bellevue. The pure steak-
house ambience comes complete with bare floors, harried waiters, and
huge steaks and chops and salads whizzing by. Nearly in the shadow
of City Hall and the surrounding courts, this is deal-making territory,
and local movers and shakers are frequently seen chatting it up at lunch
and dinner. Caricatures of nearly everyone who is anyone in the city
are on the walls, and it's fun to match up the people with their like-
nesses. The flavorful New York strip steak is fine at dinner, and the
stupendous steak sandwich (*no* relation to a Philly cheese steak) is a
lunchtime value: a large serving of hand-sliced sirloin, cooked to order
and served with crackling-crisp fried potato slices or hash browns—
or both. ⊠ *200 S. Broad St., Center City,* ☎ *215/546–7256. AE, D,
DC, MC, V.* .

$$$ ✕ Morton's of Chicago. The classy atmosphere of this steak house draws
mainly visitors familiar with the countrywide outpost of top-quality
red meat and humongous lobsters. A devoted coterie of local businesspeople favor Morton's as well. The house specialty, a juicy, tasty
24-ounce porterhouse, puts the most determined carnivore to the test.
Other fine cuts of meat are available, too, presented for selection from
a cart that is wheeled to the table. There are pristine whole fish and
unbelievable lobsters priced by the pound. Vegetable portions are
large—really enough for two—and are ordered à la carte. ⊠ *1 Logan
Sq. (on 19th St.), Benjamin Franklin Pkwy.,* ☎ *215/557–0724. AE,
DC, MC, V.*

$–$$ ✕ Outback Steakhouse. Everyone knows how much the folks from down
under hanker after beef. To get a sense of the passion they feel for huge,
juicy steaks, you just have to be prepared to drive to the 'burbs and
wait a long, long time to get a table. Then you will probably wait a
while longer before you can dive into a slab of decent beef (particularly good for the price). Another Aussie favorite, known as a "bloomin'
onion," is an onion cut and fried in such a way that you have a choice
of tucking it behind your ear—or eating it! (Eating is a better choice.)

This is a value-oriented steak house, but if you are longing for a beef fix without breaking the bank and you're patient, it's a decent choice. ⊠ *1162 Baltimore Pike, Springfield,* ☎ *610/544–9889;* ⊠ *610 Old York Rd., Jenkintown,* ☎ *215/886–5120. Reservations not accepted. AE, D, DC, MC, V.*

Thai

$–$$ ✕ **Thai Singa House.** Simple and unprepossessing, this pleasant family-run Thai outpost in University City cooks all the usual dishes plus an array of more unusual (for this country, at least) ones, such as venison and wild boar. Pad Thai, a noodle-dish staple that's a good choice if you're not certain you love Thai food, is particularly well prepared here, with an authenticity of texture and a fine meld of flavors. The family is fun to talk to, and the proprietor and his wife are helpful both to novices and to experts trying to fathom unfamiliar dishes on the menu. ⊠ *3939 Chestnut St., University City,* ☎ *215/382–8001. AE, D, DC, MC, V.*

Turkish

$$ ✕ **Dardanelles.** This unusual little restaurant, owned by a Turkish musician-artist-chef and his Philadelphia actress-waitress wife, specializes in authentic grilled fish dishes reminiscent of the scintillating tastes that emerge from kitchens on the Aegean or Bosporus or Black Sea around Turkey. Garlicky hummus, *baba ghanoush* (eggplant purée with tahini and seasonings), salads, and rice fill out an all-fish menu that sometimes includes appetizers of octopus and squid. Some people without a sense of humor have criticized the staff for having an attitude. Those who recognize that it's (mostly) all in fun flock to this place that has no sign on the door and other quirks as well. Bring your own wine or beer. ⊠ *213 Chestnut St., Historic Area,* ☎ *215/925–8333. No credit cards. Closed Mon. and Tues. No lunch.*

Vietnamese

$ ✕ **Vietnam.** This crowded family-run restaurant just next to a busy police station serves up an extensive selection of Vietnamese food. Restaurant owners from many of the city's other, much fancier restaurants often find each other here, comparing notes on which dishes are particularly good on that day. Occasionally, however, it seems as if the chef himself is "out to lunch," because the food lacks the customary sparkle. It's cheap enough, however, to forgive an occasional lapse without damaging the budget. So if the first couple of courses, like the soup and the generally ethereal, shatteringly crisp spring rolls, don't measure up to expectations, it's possible to leave and head to any of the similar places nearby to finish your meal. ⊠ *221 N. 11th St., Chinatown,* ☎ *215/592–1163. No credit cards.*

4 Lodging

From four-poster beds in primly historic digs to such grand-hotel gestures as plush towels and room-service foie gras, Philadelphia has lodgings for every style of travel. Thanks to the new Pennsylvania Convention Center, some midprice chains have spruced up their accommodations, making it easier to find a decent, moderately priced room—once a rarity. If you have greater expectations, you need look no further than the city's handful of swank hotels, each with its own gracious character.

PHILADELPHIA HOTELS RUN THE GAMUT from world class to commonplace, from a five-star 1,200-room hotel with every luxury to an endearingly personal nine-room Colonial inn. Although many are utilitarian hotels or national chains, others are experiences in themselves. Aside from bed-and-breakfasts and hostels, the city has a relatively small pool of moderately priced hotels; many are expensive.

By Rathe Miller

Updated by
Janet
Bukovinsky
Teacher

Because the number of rooms in the metropolitan area—17,000—is small for a city with a population of nearly a million and a half, it occasionally can be difficult to find a place to stay. The Philadelphia Marriott, adjacent to the Pennsylvania Convention Center, opened in 1995, giving the downtown area another 1,200 rooms. At the same time, however, demand for rooms has increased because of the rise in conventions and tourism. You're likely to encounter problems on the weekend of the Army-Navy football game (usually the weekend after Thanksgiving weekend) and when large conventions move into town. Advance reservations are usually advised. The city has no central reservation office.

The city will have 2,500 new rooms by the first quarter of the year 2000, according to the Philadelphia Convention and Visitors Bureau. New developments include a 610-room Loews hotel, to be built in the Pennsylvania Savings Fund Society (PSFS) Building, a 1932 modernist skyscraper at 12th and Market streets. The Philadelphia Marriott will add 220 concierge-level rooms in the old train shed area in front of historic Reading Terminal Market. Another significant new hotel in the works is the Courtyard by Marriott, with 500 rooms, just a block from the Pennsylvania Convention Center; it's expected to open by late 1999. Several other 300- to 400-room hotels are also planned.

Hotels are listed geographically, according to six neighborhoods. The Historic Area, on the east side of downtown, centers on Independence Hall and extends to the Delaware River. Old City and Society Hill lodgings are included here. Center City encompasses the heart of the downtown business district, centered around Broad Street and Market Street; Rittenhouse Square hotels are in this section. The Benjamin Franklin Parkway/Museum Area runs along the Benjamin Franklin Parkway from 16th Street to the Philadelphia Museum of Art. Several hotels are in University City, near the campus of the University of Pennsylvania in West Philadelphia. A half dozen hotels are clustered near Philadelphia International Airport, about 8 mi south (a 20-min drive) of Center City. Two are in the City Line Avenue area, northwest of downtown. Other options can be found in outlying areas, including Valley Forge and Bucks County (☞ Chapters 8 *and* 9).

Philadelphia has no off-season rates, but most hotels offer discount packages for weekends, when demand from businesspeople and groups subsides. Besides substantially reduced rates, these packages often include an assortment of free features, such as breakfast, parking, cocktails or champagne, and the use of exercise facilities. Tickets to popular museum shows have become a part of many special packages, too. Most downtown hotels charge an average of $15 a day for parking when it is not included as a package feature.

Although hotel facilities are listed here, it isn't specified whether they cost extra: When pricing accommodations, always ask what's included. In addition, assume that all rooms have private baths unless otherwise noted. Accommodations are ranked according to the following price categories. As noted, many hotels offer special weekend packages and rates, so be sure to ask.

CATEGORY	COST*
$$$$	over $200
$$$	$145–$200
$$	$85–$145
$	under $85

All prices are for a standard double room, excluding 13% tax.

Historic Area

Besides the hotels listed below, other accommodations in or around the Historic Area include the Shippen Way Inn, the Thomas Bond House, and the Bank Street Hostel (☞ Bed-and-Breakfasts *and* Hostels, *below*).

$$$$ ⌧ **Sheraton Society Hill.** Conveniently located for visits to the Historic District, this redbrick neo-Colonial building is two blocks from Penn's Landing, three blocks from Head House Square, and three blocks from Independence Hall. The hotel has a pleasant four-story atrium lobby framed by archways and balconies, filled with trees and plants, and lighted by wrought-iron lanterns. Rooms are furnished traditionally but have modern conveniences such as a bar, voice mail, modem ports in telephones, and coffeemakers. The fourth-floor rooms facing east toward the Delaware River have the best view. A pianist plays regularly in the atrium lobby. ✉ *1 Dock St., 19106,* ☎ *215/238–6000 or 800/325–3535,* 🖷 *215/922–2709. 365 rooms, 17 suites. Restaurant, bar, room service, indoor pool, health club, parking (fee). AE, D, DC, MC, V.*

$$$–$$$$ ⌧ **Omni Hotel at Independence Park.** The poshest accommodations
★   in the historic district, the elegant Omni has the feel of a much smaller hotel. An ornate fireplace dominates the lobby; you can have cocktails here in front of floor-to-ceiling windows overlooking the meticulously groomed park. The thoughtfully detailed rooms are notably spacious, and many have park views. The Azalea restaurant (☞ Chapter 3), once a pioneering venue for regional dishes, now serves more basic American fare, but still in a luxe atmosphere with cushioned armchairs and attentive service. The health club includes a lap pool, exercise pool, sauna, and whirlpool. This is an ideal location for visiting the art galleries and cafés of Old City as well as the Liberty Bell, Independence Hall, and other historic attractions. ✉ *4th and Chestnut Sts., 19106,* ☎ *215/925–0000,* 🖷 *215/925–1263. 147 rooms, 3 suites. Restaurant, no-smoking rooms, 2 indoor pools, health club, concierge, business services, parking (fee).*

$$–$$$ ⌧ **Best Western Independence Park Hotel.** From the rooms facing busy Chestnut Street you'll hear the clop-clop of carriage horses as well as the roar of city buses. The five-story building is a former dry goods warehouse, built in 1856; it opened in 1988 as a hotel. The high-ceiling guest rooms are modern but with Colonial touches and come standard and deluxe (deluxe includes king-size bed and parlor). VCRs and videos are available for a small charge. Complimentary Continental breakfast is served in a courtyard dining room with a glass ceiling. ✉ *235 Chestnut St., 19106,* ☎ *215/922–4443 or 800/624–2988,* 🖷 *215/ 922–4487. 36 rooms. In-room modem lines, parking (fee). AE, D, DC, MC, V.*

$$–$$$ ⌧ **Holiday Inn Independence Mall.** "Independence Mall" in the name is no exaggeration: This is one of the most convenient hotels to the downtown historic area. To complement its location, all rooms are done in Colonial decor with Ethan Allen furniture, including poster beds and wing chairs. ✉ *4th and Arch Sts., 19106,* ☎ *215/923–8660 or 800/*

THE–BELL, ℻ *215/923–4633. 364 rooms, 7 suites. 2 restaurants, bar, pool, parking (fee). AE, D, DC, MC, V.*

$$–$$$
★
🏨 **Penn's View Inn.** This cosmopolitan little hotel on the fringe of the city's oldest warehouse district, now an enclave of artists' galleries and studios known as Old City, has its own brand of urban charm. Housed in a refurbished 19th-century commercial building, it's owned by Italian-born restaurateurs, well regarded for their good taste and high quality, who run Panorama (☞ Chapter 3), the downstairs eatery (superb pasta!) and extensive wine bar, as well as another restaurant nearby. Deluxe rooms, done in somber tapestry, have whirlpool baths and windows overlooking the Delaware River. Accommodations are comfortable and rather European, if not strictly stylish, though street noise can be a concern. Complimentary Continental breakfast is served. ⊠ *14 N. Front St., 19106,* ☎ *215/922–7600 or 800/331–7634,* ℻ *215/922–7642. 28 rooms. Restaurant, bar, parking (fee). AE, DC, MC, V.*

$$
🏨 **Comfort Inn at Penn's Landing.** The low price is the most noteworthy attraction here, with complimentary Continental breakfast as an additional lure at this 10-story hotel, opened in 1987. Decor is contemporary, with oak furniture and a mauve color scheme. A bar enlivens the small, nondescript lobby. Tucked between the Benjamin Franklin Bridge, Delaware Avenue, and I–95, the location has more noise than charm—but if you have a room on an upper floor facing the river, you'll enjoy a good view of the Benjamin Franklin Bridge lighted up at night. A nice plus is the courtesy van service to points all over Center City; in a minute's time foot power will bring you to the nearby Betsy Ross House or to the RiverLink ferry to the New Jersey State Aquarium, in Camden. ⊠ *100 N. Columbus Blvd., 19106,* ☎ *215/627–7900 or 800/228–5150,* ℻ *215/238–0809. 182 rooms, 3 suites. Lobby lounge, no-smoking rooms, free parking. AE, D, DC, MC, V.*

Center City

$$$$
🏨 **Doubletree Hotel Philadelphia.** You can sit in the four-story atrium lobby lounge and observe one of the busiest corners of Philly's shopping and theater district, across the street from the Academy of Music. Guest rooms, renovated in 1994, are decorated in earth tones and have modern furnishings. The hotel's sawtooth design gives each room a peaked bay window with a whopping 180-degree view. East-side rooms get a panoramic view of the city, the Delaware River, and New Jersey. ⊠ *Broad St. at Locust St., 19107,* ☎ *215/893–1600 or 800/822–TREE,* ℻ *215/893–1663. 419 rooms, 8 suites. 2 restaurants, lobby lounge, indoor pool, sauna, health club, racquetball, parking (fee). AE, D, DC, MC, V.*

$$$$
🏨 **Philadelphia Marriott.** If you like big, bustling hotels, this is your place. Opened in 1995, this convention hotel—the biggest in Pennsylvania—takes up an entire city block and has corridors even the staff gets lost in. For an intrinsically impersonal place, the Marriott tries to meet special needs (iron and ironing board in each room, 24-hour workout room, kids' menu from room service) and offers some of the lowest rates in its price category. The five-story lobby atrium has a water sculpture, piano music (live and taped), and greenery (real and fake). The 1,200 guest rooms are big, beige, and bland; half come with two queen beds, the rest with kings; all have extra counter space in the bathrooms. You can request, at no additional cost, one of the 250 "rooms that work," with an adjustable work table and extra lighting and outlets. ⊠ *1201 Market St., 19107,* ☎ *215/625–2900 or 800/320–5744,* ℻ *215/625–6000. 1143 rooms, 57 suites. 2 restaurants, 2 lobby lounges, sports bar, room service, indoor pool, health club, concierge, business services, parking (fee). AE, D, DC, MC, V.*

Lodging

Adam's Mark, **4**

Airport Hilton, **30**

Bank Street Hostel, **23**

Best Western Center City, **1**

Best Western Independence Park Hotel, **25**

Chamounix Mansion, **3**

Clarion Suites Convention Center, **19**

Comfort Inn at Penn's Landing, **21**

Days Inn, **32**

Doubletree Hotel Philadelphia, **16**

Four Seasons, **8**

Holiday Inn City Line, **5**

Holiday Inn Express Midtown, **17**

Holiday Inn Independence Mall, **20**

Holiday Inn Philadelphia International Airport, **33**

Holiday Inn Select Center City, **9**

International House, **6**

KormanSuites Hotel, **2**

Latham, **12**

Omni Hotel at Independence Park, **24**

Park Hyatt Philadelphia at the Bellevue, **15**

Penn Tower, **7**

Penn's View Inn, **22**

Philadelphia Airport Marriott, **28**

Philadelphia Marriott, **18**

The Rittenhouse, **10**

Ritz-Carlton, **13**

Sheraton Society Hill, **27**

Shippen Way Inn, **34**

Thomas Bond House, **26**

Travelodge Hotel Stadium, **31**

The Warwick, **11**

Westin Suites, Philadelphia Airport, **29**

Wyndham Franklin Plaza, **14**

0   440 yards

0   400 meters

Willow St.

Callowhill St.

6th St.

Wood St.

Vine St.

30

Benjamin Franklin Bridge

Front St.

Franklin
Square

30   676

19

Race St.

Race St.

Quarry St.

U.S. Mint

Elfreth's
Alley

21

Cherry St.

2nd St.

Arch St.

Arch St.

20

Christopher Columbus Blvd (formerly Delaware Ave.)

Filbert St.

Commerce St.

22

Market St.

Letitia St.

Front St.

Delaware River

Ranstead St.

Bank St.

23

Penn's
Landing

**Independence
Hall**

24

Chestnut St.

25

10th St.

Sansom St.

**Independence
Square**

Ionic St.

26 Sansom
St.

Walnut St.

27

Washington
Square

5th St.

4th St.

3rd St.

Locust St.

9th St.

8th St.

7th St.

6th St.

Spruce St.

Delancey St.

2nd St.

95

Pine St.

N

KEY

Lombard St.

•••• Market-Frankford Subway
——— Broad St. Subway
– – – Subway-Surface Subway
——— Airport Train

28 – **33**

South St.

34
↓

↓

$$$$ ▦ **The Rittenhouse.** This small luxury hotel, which contains condo-
★ minium residences on other floors of the building, takes full advantage of its Rittenhouse Square location: Many of the rooms and both
restaurants overlook the city's classiest park. The expansive white-mar-
ble lobby leads to the Mary Cassatt Tearoom and Lounge and a cloistered garden. The 33-story building's sawtooth design gives the guest
rooms their unusual shape, with nooks and alcoves. Each room is out-
fitted with an array of amenities: two TVs, three telephones, an entertainment center in an armoire, a fully-stocked minibar, and a king-size
bed. Ninth-floor rooms facing the square have the best views. ⊠ *210
W. Rittenhouse Sq., 19103,* ☎ *215/546–9000 or 800/635–1042,* ℻
*215/732–3364. 87 rooms, 11 suites. 2 restaurants, bar, minibars, 3
no-smoking floors, room service, health club, concierge, business services, parking (fee). AE, D, DC, MC, V.*

$$$–$$$$ ▦ **Park Hyatt Philadelphia at the Bellevue.** A Philadelphia institution
for 94 years, the elegant Bellevue hotel reopened in 1989 with its
lower floors transformed into offices, upscale retail space, and a first-
rate food court. The Barrymore Room, topped by a 30-ft stained-glass
dome, and the seven-story Conservatory atrium are just two of the hotel's
lavish public areas. Founders, with views of the city from its 19th-floor
location, ranks among the most visually impressive dining rooms in
town. From the champagne toast available at registration to the tele-
phones in the bathrooms, a stay at the Bellevue promises luxury,
though service can be lax. Rooms are large, and each has an enter-
tainment center with color TV, stereo, and VCR. Guests have free use
of the Sporting Club, the best health club in town. ⊠ *Broad and Wal-
nut Sts., 19102,* ☎ *215/893–1776 or 800/221–0833,* ℻ *215/732–
8518. 170 rooms. Restaurant, bar, lobby lounge, room service, in-room
modem lines, minibars, shops, concierge, parking (fee). AE, D, DC,
MC, V.*

$$$–$$$$ ▦ **Ritz-Carlton.** Ritzy it is: a million dollars' worth of art on display,
★ mantelpieces from Italy, and silk walls in the bar. Opened in 1990, the
15-story building is nestled between the twin blue towers of Liberty
Place (and adjacent to the Shops at Liberty Place—more than 70 stores,
boutiques, and restaurants). The Grill Room, a beautiful formal room
with paintings and tapestries, rates as a major power spot for lunch
and dinner; the Dining Room serves, breakfast, lunch, and a superb
Sunday brunch. All guest rooms have an elegant Colonial motif; most
have king-size beds, although rooms with oversize twins are available.
All the typical luxury amenities are here: entertainment center in an
armoire, honor bar, complimentary shoeshine, valet laundry service,
bathroom telephone, terry robes, hair dryers, and bathroom scale.
You'll also find a complimentary copy of *Philadelphia* magazine and
a souvenir Ritz-Carlton bookmark. ⊠ *17th and Chestnut Sts. at Lib-
erty Place, 19103,* ☎ *215/563–1600 or 800/241–3333,* ℻ *215/564–
9559. 275 rooms, 15 suites. 2 restaurants, bar, lobby lounge, room
service, health club, baby-sitting, concierge, parking (fee). AE, D, DC,
MC, V.*

$$–$$$$ ▦ **Holiday Inn Select Center City.** This is an above-average Holiday Inn,
centrally located between Benjamin Franklin Parkway, Rittenhouse
Square, and City Hall. The 25-floor hotel opened in 1971; a 1994 renovation gave the good-size rooms a green-and-beige color scheme and
contemporary decor. Rooms designated Select have extra amenities, including voice mail, irons and ironing boards, coffeemakers, cable TV,
in-room modem lines, hair dryers, and *USA Today.* ⊠ *1800 Market
St., 19103,* ☎ *215/561–7500 or 800/HOLIDAY,* ℻ *215/561–4484.
443 rooms, 2 suites. Restaurant, bar, no-smoking floors, pool, exercise room, parking (fee). AE, D, DC, MC, V.*

$$$ ⛤ **Latham.** Once known as the finest hostelry in America for business travelers, this is a small, elegant hotel with a European accent and an emphasis on personal service. Doormen clad in vests and riding boots welcome you to the lobby. A concierge is on duty daily from 10 to 8. All rooms have marble-top bureaus and Louis XV–style writing desks, full-wall mirrors, hair dryers, and makeup mirrors; most have mini-bars. Guests have free access to a nearby health club. A weekend package includes a deluxe room, valet parking, and gourmet breakfast. ⊠ *135 S. 17th St., 1 block from Rittenhouse Sq., 19103,* ☎ *215/563–7474 or 800/528–4261,* ⅻ *215/568–0110. 139 rooms. Restaurant, piano bar, concierge, business services, parking (fee). AE, D, DC, MC, V.*

$$$ ⛤ **The Warwick.** Half the rooms here are apartments, which makes for an interesting mix of guests in business suits and residents in shorts and sneakers all crossing the lobby (nicely brightened by mirrors and 18-ft Palladian windows) in a constant stream of activity. The spacious guest rooms are decorated in English country style; bathrooms are marble, with an ivy green motif. A nice touch is the current issue of *Philadelphia* magazine in your room. You can use a nearby health club at no additional charge. ⊠ *1701 Locust St., 19103,* ☎ *215/735–6000 or 800/523–4210,* ⅻ *215/790–7766. 153 rooms, 47 suites. Restaurant, bar, coffee shop, parking (fee). AE, DC, MC, V.*

$$–$$$ ⛤ **Clarion Suites Convention Center.** Smack in the middle of Philadelphia's small but bustling Chinatown, this eight-story 1892 building, a former chair factory, is within walking distance of the Pennsylvania Convention Center, Reading Terminal Market, and Independence Mall. It's also near many Vietnamese, Thai, and Chinese eateries, some of which stay open late for dinner. The freshly renovated suites have a full-size kitchen, dining area, and two televisions. Exposed brick walls and wooden beams are reminders of the building's history. A complimentary Continental breakfast is served. ⊠ *1010 Race St., 19107,* ☎ *215/922–1730,* ⅻ *215/922–6258. 96 suites. Bar, café, fitness room, parking (fee).*

$$ ⛤ **Holiday Inn Express Midtown.** Rooms are more spacious than average here—perhaps because they're older (this Holiday Inn opened in 1964 and was renovated in 1992). All have contemporary furnishings and a light, floral motif. Rooms facing south to Walnut Street have the best views. The location is excellent: one block from the Broad Street subway, near the theater and shopping district, and three blocks from the Pennsylvania Convention Center. Continental breakfast is complimentary, and you have free access to a nearby health club. ⊠ *1305 Walnut St., 19107,* ☎ *215/735–9300 or 800/5–MIDTOWN. 166 rooms. No-smoking rooms, pool, parking (fee). AE, D, DC, MC, V.*

Benjamin Franklin Parkway/Museum Area

$$$$ ⛤ **Four Seasons.** If you were a film director who wanted a location
★ for a romantic hotel-room view of Philadelphia, you might well choose a room here overlooking the fountains in Logan Circle and the Benjamin Franklin Parkway. The eight-story U-shape hotel has the most attractive public areas, best service, and finest hotel dining in the city— and block-long hallways that some guests don't like. Guest-room furniture is Federal style, dark and stately. All rooms look out on either Logan Circle or the interior courtyard, thanks to picture windows (and in some rooms, private verandas). Then there are those Four Seasons touches: libraries in each room, a health-food menu available from room service and in the restaurant, and one-inch-thick bathroom rugs. Philadelphia's most expensive hotel provides terry robes and a complimentary shoeshine. The Fountain Restaurant (☞ Chapter 3) is one

of the best in town. Weather permitting, the Swann Courtyard Cafe is an excellent spot for a drink and a kiss. ⊠ *1 Logan Sq., 19103,* ☎ *215/963–1500 or 800/332–3442,* FAX *215/963–9506. 371 rooms. 2 restaurants, outdoor café, room service, 6 no-smoking floors, indoor pool, sauna, exercise room, concierge, parking (fee). AE, D, DC, MC, V.*

$$$$ ☷ **Wyndham Franklin Plaza.** This was Philadelphia's biggest and busiest hotel until the Philadelphia Marriott opened in 1995, but the public has benefited from the competition. All public areas and guest rooms have been updated and renovated, and although it is still primarily a convention hotel, it now caters to individual travelers with a variety of added amenities and services. Rooms have full-length mirrors, cable TV, voice mail, coffeemakers, and hair dryers. The 70-ft atrium lobby encompasses restaurants and numerous sitting areas. ⊠ *17th and Race Sts., 19103,* ☎ *215/448–2000 or 800/822–4200,* FAX *215/448–2864. 720 rooms, 38 suites. 2 restaurants, bar, no-smoking rooms, room service, indoor pool, barbershop, beauty salon, health club, concierge, parking (fee). AE, D, DC, MC, V.*

$$$ ☷ **KormanSuites Hotel.** The abstract neon blip that tops this luxury hotel and corporate apartment complex serves as a colorful landmark in the Philadelphia skyline. Just off the Benjamin Franklin Parkway, the business-oriented all-suite facility offers sumptuous city views from most of the spacious rooms, as well as fully equipped kitchens, dining/meeting areas, and washer/dryers in all accommodations. Its restaurant, the Grill at Catalina, specializes in traditional steaks, thick chops, and grilled fish; the bar stocks a full array of single-malt Scotches. Complimentary shuttle bus service is available throughout the city six days a week. ⊠ *2001 Hamilton St., 19130,* ☎ *215/569–7000,* FAX *215/469–0138. 100 suites. Restaurant, lounge, indoor pool, beauty salon, health club, concierge, business services, free parking.*

$$ ☷ **Best Western Center City.** If you're willing to stay a bit farther away from downtown and in accommodations that are only average, you'll find a bargain here—especially considering the free parking and easy proximity to the Philadelphia Museum of Art, a pleasant 15-minute walk. The three-story Y-shape building has guest rooms done in tranquil earth tones, with oak-finish furniture, individual climate controls, and cable TV. The best views face south toward the Benjamin Franklin Parkway, the Rodin Museum, and the downtown skyline. ⊠ *501 N. 22nd St., 19130,* ☎ *215/568–8300,* FAX *215/557–0259. 179 rooms, 4 suites. Restaurant, outdoor café, sports bar, room service, pool, free parking. AE, D, DC, MC, V.*

University City

This area just across the Schuylkill River in West Philadelphia is a 5- to 10-minute drive from Center City. Slightly less expensive than those downtown, the hotels here are on the campus of the University of Pennsylvania and are near Drexel University and the Civic Center, the city's secondary convention facility.

$$$ ☷ **Penn Tower.** The University of Pennsylvania purchased and improved this 21-floor former Hilton in 1987, converting half the space to medical offices. It is on the eastern edge of the campus, a good stone's throw from the Civic Center, University Museum, Franklin Field, the 30th Street Station, Drexel University, and University Hospital. All rooms were renovated in 1993 with traditional mahogany furnishings, cable TV, and data ports for personal-computer use. Rooms have excellent views east to Center City and west across campus. A big plus is free use of the university's own athletic facilities, including an Olympic-size pool. ⊠ *34th St. and Civic Center Blvd., 19104,* ☎ *215/387–8333 or*

800/356–PENN, ℻ 215/386–8306. 175 rooms, 7 suites. Restaurant, bar, room service, parking (fee). AE, D, DC, MC, V.

$ ⚄ **International House.** This residence for students and professors from around the world is on the University of Pennsylvania campus. Rooms are available year-round, but you must have an affiliation with an educational institution in order to register. The high-rise building has an unusual, poured-concrete, tiered design and an oddly barren atrium. Both the public areas and the rooms themselves have a rough-hewn, spartan feel. Single rooms share bath and living room; double rooms (fewer in number) have two single beds and a private bath. Lower rates are available for monthly stays. No children are permitted. ⊠ 3701 Chestnut St., 19104, ☎ 215/387–5125, ℻ 215/895–6535. 379 rooms, most with shared bath. Café, lobby lounge, parking (fee). MC, V.

Airport District

A 20-minute drive or taxi ride from most sightseeing and entertainment, these hotels about 8 mi south of Center City are less expensive than those found downtown. Although some are within sight of industrial parks, they all have a convenient location near the airport—a real plus for business travelers.

$$$ ⚄ **Airport Hilton.** You can take a swim in the unique lobby pool of this Hilton before jumping on a free shuttle bus for the ride to your airport terminal across the street. During the week this is mostly a business travelers' hotel. Rooms have wood-and-wicker dressing tables and bureaus, as well as cable TV. ⊠ 4509 Island Ave., 19153, ☎ 215/365–4150 or 800/445–8667, ℻ 215/365–3002. 328 rooms, 2 suites. Restaurant, sports bar, room service, pool, sauna, exercise room, free parking. AE, D, DC, MC, V.

$$$ ⚄ **Westin Suites, Philadelphia Airport.** A glass-walled elevator whisks
★   you to your floor at this freshly decorated all-suite hotel where front balconies overlook the light-flooded atrium lobby and restaurant. Suites are standard or deluxe; deluxe have a larger living room and a better view. Each accommodation has a king-size bed in the bedroom and a queen-size foldout in the living room, three telephones, two remote-control TV/clock-radios, and coffeemakers, plus complimentary in-suite coffee packages and daily newspapers. Some rooms have extra aids for business travelers, including speakerphones with data ports. At press time plans were under way to convert the restaurant to a steak house. ⊠ 4101 Island Ave., 19153, ☎ 215/365–6600 or 800/937–8461, ℻ 215/492–8471. 251 suites. Restaurant, lobby lounge, minibars, 1 indoor and 1 outdoor pool, exercise room, airport shuttle, free parking. AE, D, DC, MC, V.

$$–$$$ ⚄ **Philadelphia Airport Marriott.** Opened in 1995, this sprawling hotel in the Marriott style has a skybridge connecting directly to Philadelphia International Airport. Business travelers are accommodated with voice mail, data ports, and a speakerphone. Weekend packages are a good value here. ⊠ Arrivals Rd., ☎ 215/492–9000 or 800/228–9290, ℻ 215/492–6799. 419 rooms, 5 suites. Restaurant, lounge, indoor pool, exercise room, business services, meeting rooms, free parking.

$$ ⚄ **Days Inn.** Even though the Days Inn is surrounded by highways and is across the street from the airport, special construction makes it a quiet place. The sunny pastel green corridors of the five-story L-shape building lead to pleasant and spacious rooms. ⊠ 4101 Island Ave., 19153, ☎ 215/492–0400 or 800/325–2525, ℻ 215/365–6035. 177 rooms. Café, no-smoking rooms, pool, airport shuttle, free parking. AE, D, DC, MC, V.

$$ ⚏ **Holiday Inn Philadelphia International Airport.** The lobby sets a traditional tone, with green marble, dark colors, and fireplaces. The slightly oversize guest rooms have pastel color schemes with light-color wood furniture. Good weekend rates are available at this hotel, which is 3 mi south of the airport. ⊠ *45 Industrial Hwy., Rte. 291, Essington 19029,* ☎ *610/521–2400 or 800/HOLIDAY,* ℻ *610/521–1605. 307 rooms. Restaurant, pool, exercise room, airport shuttle, free parking. AE, D, DC, MC, V.*

$-$$ ⚏ **Travelodge Hotel Stadium.** This circular high-rise building is just five blocks from the city's major sports arenas. Rooms have coffeemakers, refrigerators, and remote-control cable TV. Upper floors have a good view of the city. ⊠ *20th St. and Penrose Ave., 19145,* ☎ *215/755–6500 or 800/578–7878,* ℻ *215/465–7517. 208 rooms. Restaurant, bar, airport shuttle, free parking. AE, D, DC, MC, V.*

City Line Avenue

If you prefer to stay outside the bustle of downtown and enjoy free parking, you may want to consider the two hotels here. City Line Avenue is only a 10-minute ride on the Schuylkill Expressway to Center City under favorable conditions; however, you should take note that the expressway is frequently under construction and heavily congested.

$$-$$$ ⚏ **Adam's Mark.** At 23 stories, the Adam's Mark is one of the tallest hotels in Philadelphia: Request a room on the upper floors facing south toward Fairmount Park and the downtown skyline for the best views. There's nothing special about the rooms, which are on the small side. The big attraction here is the nighttime activity: Quincy's, a turn-of-the-century-style nightclub, plus two restaurants (one in a re-created paneled English library, the other in a French orangery) and a sports bar. Lines form early for the action at all these spots. ⊠ *City Ave. and Monument Rd., 19131,* ☎ *215/581–5000 or 800/444–2326,* ℻ *215/581–5089. 459 rooms, 56 suites. 2 restaurants, sports bar, 1 indoor and 1 outdoor pool, health club, nightclub, free parking. AE, D, DC, MC, V.*

$$ ⚏ **Holiday Inn City Line.** This eight-story Holiday Inn is perfectly ordinary, but it's a good value in a choice location. You could stay here to save money and just walk across the parking lot to all the cateries and nightspots of the Adam's Mark hotel. A five-minute walk takes you to five other restaurants. In the lobby you can sink into an overstuffed easy chair and watch swimmers in the glass-enclosed pool. ⊠ *4100 Presidential Blvd., 19131,* ☎ *215/477–0200 or 800/642–8982,* ℻ *215/473–5510. 343 rooms. Restaurant, 1 indoor pool and 1 outdoor pool, free parking. AE, D, DC, MC, V.*

Bed-and-Breakfasts

Bed-and-breakfasts can be appealing for any number of reasons: a particularly gracious welcome, the personal touch of the owner, or rooms filled with antiques. These often less expensive alternatives to hotels are modeled after the European tradition of a room and meal in a private house or small hotel. B&Bs can offer considerable diversity depending on whether they are in urban, suburban, or rural settings. Services and policies vary. Some B&Bs accept children and pets; others offer monthly rates and provide free transportation from airports and bus or train terminals. Breakfasts range from hearty to elegant. The ones listed are in the Historic Area, but you can find B&Bs in a variety of neighborhoods.

$$–$$$ ⊞ **Thomas Bond House.** It doesn't get any more Colonial than this: You can spend the night in the heart of Old City the way Philadelphians did 229 years ago. Built in 1769 by a prominent local physician, this four-story house has undergone a faithful, meticulous restoration of everything from its molding and wall sconces to the millwork and flooring. All rooms have 18th-century features; two have marble fireplaces. Furnishings include four-poster Thomasville beds. During the week, your complimentary breakfast is Continental; a full breakfast is included on weekends. ⊠ *129 S. 2nd St., 19106,* ☎ *215/923–8523 or 800/845–BOND,* FAX *215/923–8504. 10 rooms, 2 suites. Breakfast room. AE, D, DC, MC, V.*

$–$$ ⊞ **Shippen Way Inn.** Imagine the historic Betsy Ross House turned into a bed-and-breakfast, and you'll have an idea of what to expect at the Shippen Way Inn. In 1987 Raymond Ruhle and his family restored two adjacent 18th-century working-class houses to create this Colonial-style inn. Guest rooms vary in size and appeal, but most have the original exposed wooden beams and wide plank floors, wall stenciling, and original and reproduction antiques. The communal living room has a fireplace and a TV. You can have tea in the enclosed garden out back before you walk a block to shops and nightlife along South Street. ⊠ *416–18 Bainbridge St., 19147,* ☎ *215/627–7266 or 800/245–4873,* FAX *215/271–2660. 9 rooms. AE, MC, V.*

B&B Reservation Services

$–$$$$ ⊞ **Bed and Breakfast Connections–Philadelphia.** Its selection of more than 100 host homes and inns includes a Colonial town house, a converted 1880s bank-style barn, and an 18th-century farmhouse on the Main Line. ⊠ *Box 21, Devon 19333,* ☎ *610/687–3565 or 800/448–3619. AE, MC, V.*

$–$$$ ⊞ **Association of B&Bs in Philadelphia, Valley Forge, and Brandywine.** You can choose from 300 rooms in town and country settings in the areas listed in the association's name, as well as in Bucks and Lancaster counties. *Box 562, Valley Forge 19481,* ☎ *610/783–7838 or 800/344–0123,* FAX *610/783–7783. AE, D, DC, MC, V.*

$–$$ ⊞ **Bed and Breakfast—The Manor.** This service has various locations throughout Philadelphia and surrounding areas, including Amish Country. Many hosts supply transportation for a nominal fee. Some accommodate travelers with disabilities. ⊠ *Box 416, 830 Village Rd., Lampeter 17537,* ☎ *717/464–9564. MC, V.*

Hostels

Hostels provide dormitory-style accommodations for less than you'd pay to park your car at a downtown hotel. They also offer a sense of adventure and a chance to share living, eating, and sleeping quarters with travelers from all over the world. The American Youth Hostel Regional Office and Travel Center is at 624 South 3rd Street (☎ 215/925–6004).

$ ⊞ **Chamounix Mansion.** Here's the cheapest place to stay in Philadelphia—$11 a night for American Youth Hostel members, and $14 for nonmembers. Set on a wooded bluff overlooking the Schuylkill River (and, unfortunately, the Schuylkill Expressway), it feels like it's out in the country. This restored 1802 Quaker country estate is loaded with character. The entrance hall is lined with flags; period rooms have antiques; walls display old maps, sketches, and paintings. There's a self-service kitchen. It's hard to find; call for directions. ⊠ *Chamounix Dr., 19131,* ☎ *215/878–3676 or 800/379–0017,* FAX *215/871–4313. 6* *rooms for 48 people, with shared baths. MC, V. Closed Dec. 15–Jan. 15.*

$ 🏨 **Bank Street Hostel.** A member of Hostel International, Bank Street opened in 1992 and, at $16 (members) to $19 (nonmembers) a night, is a downtown-Philly lodging bargain. Independently owned by David Herskowitz, it is on the cusp of Old City and Society Hill in a 140-year-old manufacturing building that's been combined with two neighboring buildings. Guests gather around the pool table and the 48-inch TV. ✉ *32 S. Bank St., 19106,* ☎ *215/922–0222 or 800/392–4678. 3 rooms for 70 people, with shared baths. No credit cards.*

5 Nightlife and the Arts

Philadelphia seems to have a rhythm of its own. Whether you're listening to the sounds of the Philadelphia Orchestra while picnicking on the lawn at the Mann Center for the Performing Arts, or having a jazz brunch at Zanzibar Blue, music adds depth to the Philadelphia experience. This is a city of neighborhoods, and you can find entertainment in all of them. From Broadway shows at the Forrest Theater in Center City to performance art and poetry readings at the Painted Bride in Old City, there's always something new to explore.

THEATER, DANCE, AND MUSIC from rock and to opera: Philadelphia has plenty going on after dark. The city's Avenue of the Arts cultural district on North and South Broad Street is one significant sign of the new energy in town. Of the 16 arts facilities here, some are old, such as the Academy of Music and the Merriam Theater; others, including the Wilma Theater and the Philadelphia Arts Bank, are new. The Avenue of the Arts spaces are providing forums for an even wider range of talents, both traditional and innovative, from local artists to international stars. On a lighter note, you can relax by partying on the Delaware River, or checking out some of the city's fine jazz.

Updated by
Janis
Pomerantz

NIGHTLIFE

In today's Philadelphia you can listen to a chanteuse in a chic basement nightclub, dance till 3 AM in a smoky bistro, and watch street jugglers, mimes, and magicians on a Society Hill corner. South Street between Front and 9th streets is still the hippest street in town. One-of-a-kind shops, bookstores, galleries, restaurants, and bars attract the young and the restless by droves. In the past few years Main Street in Manayunk, in the northwest section of the city, has become a smaller, tamer version of South Street. Dozens of new clubs have also opened up along the Delaware River waterfront, most near the Benjamin Franklin Bridge; a water taxi shuttles revelers between them.

Bars and clubs can change hands or go out of business faster than a soft pretzel goes stale. Many places are open until 2 AM; cover charges vary from free to $12. A few places do not accept credit cards, so carry some cash. For current information check the entertainment pages of the *Philadelphia Inquirer,* the *Philadelphia Daily News,* and *Philadelphia* magazine. You can also call the Events Hot Line of Temple University's jazz radio station, WRTI (☎ 610/337–7777, code 3234), for an extensive up-to-the-minute listing of music in town. For information about Penn's Landing events, call 215/923–4992.

Bars, Breweries, Lounges

The Bards. An authentic Irish pub, The Bards has an Irish crowd, Irish food, and great Irish music sessions on Sunday from 5 to 9. ⊠ *2013 Walnut St.,* ☎ *215/569–9585.*

Brasserie Perrier. The bar and banquette at Georges Perrier's (of Le Bec-Fin fame) new eatery attract a sophisticated, after-work crowd. ⊠ *1619 Walnut St.,* ☎ *215/568–3000.*

Dirty Frank's. Frank is long gone, but this place is still dirty, cheap, and a Philadelphia classic. An incongruous mixture of students, artists, journalists, and resident characters such as Clark DeLeon and F. Baggs Piglatano crowd around the horseshoe-shape bar and engage in friendly mayhem. It's open Monday–Saturday. ⊠ *347 S. 13th St.,* ☎ *215/732–5010.*

Dock Street Brewery and Restaurant. This brewery occupies a large, lively space. You can choose hearty Alsatian dishes with your beer or standards such as steaks and burgers. Several flavors of the house-specialty boutique beer are available on a daily basis. ⊠ *2 Logan Sq.,* ☎ *215/496–0413.*

Happy Rooster. Owner "Doc" Ulitsky provides the best selection of after-dinner drinks and liqueurs in the city. French, Russian, and Gypsy music plays in the background. It's open Monday–Saturday. ⊠ *118 S. 16th St.,* ☎ *215/563–1481.*

Il Bar. The wine bar at Panorama in the Penn's View Inn stands out for its 120-bottle selection, curved bar, and romantic atmosphere. It's open seven nights a week, with a separate entrance from the restaurant. ⊠ *14 N. Front St.,* ☎ *215/922–7800.*

Mia's. This upscale "meet market" bar and restaurant off the lobby of the Warwick Hotel is a popular after-work place for the business crowd. ⊠ *17th and Locust Sts.,* ☎ *215/545–4655.*

Swann Lounge. You can listen to piano music weekday evenings and dance on Friday and Saturday nights in this very elegant hotel lounge. ⊠ *Four Seasons Hotel, 18th St. and Benjamin Franklin Pkwy.,* ☎ *215/963–1500.*

Tin Angel Acoustic Cafe. Local and national musicians hold forth at a 105-seat acoustic cabaret above the Serrano restaurant (patrons get preferred seating). You can sit at candlelit tables or at the bar and hear music from blues to folk. Tickets are required except for Wednesday's open-mike evenings. ⊠ *20 S. 2nd St.,* ☎ *215/928–0978.*

Woody's. This is Philadelphia's most popular gay bar. ⊠ *202 S. 13th St.,* ☎ *215/545–1893.*

Comedy Clubs

Comedy Cabaret. Philly's one enduring comedy club presents national names and local talent. There's a two-drink minimum. ⊠ *1010 Race St., at the Clarion Suites Hotel,* ☎ *215/625–JOKE.*

David Brenner's Laugh House. Formerly Catch a Rising Star, this new comedy club is co-owned by the comedian, who was born in the city. The 250-seat club showcases local and national acts Thursday through Saturday. ⊠ *221 South St.,* ☎ *215/440–4242.*

Dance Clubs

Dave & Buster's. Call this a big amusement park for the somewhat grown-up. A short list of what's going on includes two restaurants, five bars, pool tables, pinball and video games, just-for-fun blackjack and poker, a virtual reality shooting game, and an outdoor deck overlooking the Delaware River. There's music and dancing, too. ⊠ *Pier 19 North, 325 N. Columbus Blvd.,* ☎ *215/413–1951.*

Katmandu. Large and usually crowded, this Delaware waterfront spot is an indoor/outdoor Caribbean restaurant and bar that has live music nightly—world, reggae, rock—and a "Wild Island" dance party on Saturday night. It's open from May to mid-October. ⊠ *Pier 25, Columbus Blvd. south of Spring Garden St.,* ☎ *215/629–7400.*

Maui Entertainment Complex. If you're idea of heaven is ersatz tropical ambience, beach volleyball, and waitresses in cutoffs and bikini tops hawking drinks to a crowd in their twenties, this place is for you. On the city's biggest dance floor, you can dance both indoors and out to live bands (rock, alternative, progressive) and to radio DJ dance-party broadcasts. It's open Thursday–Sunday. ⊠ *Pier 53 North, 1143 N. Columbus Blvd.,* ☎ *215/423–8116.*

Monte Carlo Living Room. The DJ at this sophisticated watering hole plays Top 40 hits, European sounds, and South American music for a mostly thirties to fifties crowd. A jacket and tie is required. All the furnishings, from the tapestries to the paintings, are European. It's open Wednesday–Sunday. ✉ *2nd and South Sts.,* ☎ *215/925–2220.*

Moshulu. This restored restaurant ship has fine riverfront views and an area for dancing from Wednesday through Saturday. ✉ *735 S. Columbus Blvd.,* ☎ *215/923–2500.*

River Cafe. Finished that Manayunk shopping spree? Stick around for a meal and dance to today's tunes, spun by a DJ. The restaurant is open nightly; dancing is Wednesday through Saturday. ✉ *4100 Main St., Manayunk,* ☎ *215/483–4100.*

Rock Lobster. From May to September you can join the party at this riverfront tent that resembles a yacht club. The over-30 set comes for reasonably priced meals and plenty of live music and dancing. ✉ *Pier 13–14, 221 N. Columbus Blvd,* ☎ *215/627–7625.*

Jazz and Blues

You can call the **Philadelphia Clef Club of Jazz & Performing Arts** (☞ *below*) for information. The monthly *Jazz Philadelphia* (☎ 215/473–4273) is available at the Philadelphia Visitors Center (✉ 16th St. and John F. Kennedy Blvd.).

Liberties. This handsomely restored Victorian pub has jazz Friday and Saturday. ✉ *705 N. 2nd St.,* ☎ *215/238–0660.*

Ortlieb's Jazz Haus. You'll hear good jazz in this 100-year-old bar. Celebrated jazz organist Shirley Scott and her quartet occasionally perform. There's music nightly from Monday through Saturday; Tuesday night includes a jam session for local musicians. ✉ *847 N. 3rd St.,* ☎ *215/922–1035.*

Philadelphia Clef Club of Jazz & Performing Arts. Dedicated solely to jazz, including its history and instruction, this organization also has a 250-seat cabaret-style theater for concert performances. ✉ *736–738 S. Broad St.,* ☎ *215/893–9912.*

Warmdaddy's. This rustic, down-home blues club and restaurant, owned by the people who run Zanzibar Blue (☞ *below*), serves up live blues and southern cuisine every night except Monday. ✉ *4–6 S. Front St., at Front and Market Sts.,* ☎ *215/627–8400 for reservations,* ☎ *215/627–2500 for hours and upcoming performances.*

Zanzibar Blue. A hip restaurant and bar adjoins the hottest jazz room in town. The best local talent plays on weeknights; nationally known names play on weekends. There's a jazz brunch on Sunday from 11 to 2 for $19.95 per person. ✉ *Downstairs at the Bellevue, Broad and Walnut Sts.,* ☎ *215/732–5200.*

Performance Arts Center

Painted Bride Art Center. By day it's a contemporary art gallery showing bold, challenging works. By night it's a "multidisciplinary, multicultural performance center," with performance art, prose and poetry readings, folk and new music, jazz, dance, and avant-garde theater. In 1998 this nonprofit educational institution celebrates its 29th season. The gallery is open Monday–Saturday 10–6; call for the performance schedule. ✉ *230 Vine St.,* ☎ *215/925–9914.*

Rock

Electric Factory. Electric Factory Concerts, which presents major rock concerts at various venues in the city, now has its own smaller rock club. ✉ *421 N. 7th St.,* ☎ *215/568–3222.*

The Khyber. This Old City spot is small and loud, with lots of action. The music is all live, including alternative and rock, performed by national and local talent. With more than 100 brands of beer, it has probably the best selection in town. The Khyber is open Monday–Saturday. ✉ *56 S. 2nd St.,* ☎ *215/238–5888.*

Polly Esther's. The music and decor of the '70s take center stage at a new hot spot, part of a national chain. The bar is painted to look like the Partridge family's bus, *Charlie's Angels* photographs adorn one wall, and there's a *Saturday Night Fever*–style disco floor. It's open Thursday through Saturday. ✉ *1201 Race St., next to the Pennsylvania Convention Center,* ☎ *215/851–0776.*

Trocadero. This spacious rock-and-roll club occupies a former burlesque house where W. C. Fields and Mae West performed. A lot of the old decor remains: mirrors, pillars, and balconies surround the dance floor. Most every up-and-coming band that's passing through Philly plays here to an under-30 crowd. On other nights local DJs host dance parties. ✉ *1003 Arch St., Chinatown,* ☎ *215/922–LIVE.*

THE ARTS

Of all the performing arts, it is music for which Philadelphia is most renowned and the Philadelphia Orchestra of which its residents are most proud. Considered one of the world's best symphony orchestras, it rose to fame under the batons of former conductors Leopold Stokowski, Eugene Ormandy, and Riccardo Muti. The orchestra performs at the Academy of Music, an acoustically superb concert hall built in 1857 and modeled after La Scala. Orchestra concerts during the September–May season are still among the city's premier social events. If you can get tickets, go. You'll see one of the city's finest groups in an opulent setting, with many Philadelphians dressed to match the occasion.

The Opera Company of Philadelphia also performs at the Academy. They gained national prominence a number of years ago with their performance of *La Bohème* on PBS's *Great Performances*—the most widely watched opera telecast in the history of public television.

There is no shortage of live entertainment, ranging from the Philly Pops to the Mellon PSFS Jazz Festival. There are also summer concerts of popular and classical music at the Robin Hood Dell East and at Fairmount Park's Mann Center for the Performing Arts. Many rock groups stop in Philadelphia on their national tours, playing at the new CoreStates Center and CoreStates Spectrum; the Keswick Theatre, in suburban Glenside; or the E-Centre in Camden.

Of course, Philly holds a special place in pop music history. *American Bandstand,* hosted by Dick Clark, began here as a local dance show. When it went national in 1957, it gave a boost to many hometown boys, including Fabian, Bobby Rydell, Frankie Avalon, and Chubby Checker. The city's rock-and-roll tradition began in 1955 with Bill Haley and the Comets. In the 1970s the Philadelphia Sound—a polished blend of disco, pop, and rhythm and blues—came alive through Kenny Gamble and Leon Huff; its lush sound has been kept alive by chart toppers such as Hall and Oates and Patti LaBelle.

For current performances and listings, the best guides to Philly's performing arts are the "Guide to the Lively Arts" in the daily *Philadelphia Inquirer*, the "Weekend" section of the Friday *Inquirer*, the "Friday" section of the *Philadelphia Daily News*, and the Donnelley Directory Events Hotline (☏ 215/337–7777, ext. 2540). Two free weekly papers, the *City Paper* and the *Philadelphia Weekly*, have extensive listings of concerts and clubs; they are available free in news boxes all over downtown. Check also at the Philadelphia Visitors Center (✉ 16th St. and John F. Kennedy Blvd., (☏ 215/636–1666). The Performing Arts Hot Line (☏ 215/573–ARTS) is another source for information about happenings. UpStages (☏ 215/569–9700) has tickets for many cultural events; there are walk-up locations at 1412 Chestnut Street and at Plays and Players Theatre (✉ 1714 Delancey Pl.); the Philadelphia Arts Bank (✉ 601 S. Broad St., at South St.) has regular-price tickets for performances on a given day. Discount tickets, often reduced up to 50%, are offered by UpStages on the day of the performance at 1412 Chestnut Street. TicketMaster (☏ 215/336–2000) sells tickets to rock concerts and other performing arts events.

Concerts

All-Star Forum. Impresario Moe Septee and his 57-year-old organization bring visiting orchestras, recitals by stars such as Itzhak Perlman and Isaac Stern, ballets, and special musical events to the Academy of Music. ☏ *215/735–7506.*

Blockbuster-Sony Music Entertainment Centre. Across the Delaware River in Camden, the E-Centre programs has everything from symphonies to rock and roll in a space that can seat 1,600 or up to 25,000 people. ✉ *1 Harbor Blvd., on the waterfront, Camden,* ☏ *609/635–1445 for ticket information and directions.*

Concerto Soloists of Philadelphia. Directed by Marc Mostovoy, this prestigious group performs chamber music from October to May at the Pennsylvania Convention Center (✉ 13th and Cherry Sts., ☏ 215/569–4690). There are also Sunday afternoon concerts from October to May at the Church of the Holy Trinity (✉ 19th and Walnut Sts.). ☏ *215/545–5451.*

CoreStates Spectrum and Core States Center. Rock concerts are often staged in these new facilities on the south side of the city. ✉ *Broad St. and Pattison Ave., off I–95,* ☏ *215/336–3600.*

Keswick Theatre. A 1,900-seat former vaudeville house with fine acoustics hosts rock, jazz, and country music concerts as well as musicals; call for directions. ✉ *Easton Rd. and Keswick Ave., Glenside,* ☏ *215/ 572–7650.*

Mellon PSFS Jazz Festival. A series of 40 concerts and events (most free or with low ticket prices) are presented in June at locations around town. Look for top names in jazz, including Pat Martino, Wynton Marsalis, and Chick Corea. ☏ *610/667–3559.*

Philadelphia Chamber Music Society. A classical music series of 40 concerts, including Music from Marlboro, is given at the Pennsylvania Convention Center (✉ 13th and Cherry Sts., ☏ 215/569–4690) from October to May. ☏ *215/569–8587.*

Philadelphia Folk Festival. First held in 1962, the oldest continuously running folk festival in the country takes place each year during the last week in August. Doc Watson, Taj Mahal, Joan Baez, and Judy Collins are just a few of the artists who have performed here. ✉ *Old Pool Farm, near Schwenksville,* ☏ *215/242–0150.*

Philadelphia Orchestra. The world-renowned ensemble performs at the Academy of Music from September to May. Musical director Wolfgang Sawallisch, who emphasizes the German repertoire, is finishing his fifth season with the orchestra. In June and July a series of noted soloists and guest conductors perform with the orchestra in an outdoor amphitheater, the **Mann Center for the Performing Arts** (⊠ West Fairmount Park, George's Hill near 52nd St. and Parkside Ave., ☎ 215/878–7707 for box office). In addition to regular seats, there is free seating on the lawn (bring a blanket), but you must reserve this by sending in a form well in advance. ⊠ *Broad and Locust Sts.,* ☎ *215/893–1999.*

Philly Pops. Conducted by Peter Nero, this group performs at the Academy of Music from October to May and occasionally at other local events. ☎ *215/735–7506.*

Robin Hood Dell East. This is the site for rhythm-and-blues and soul music concerts on Monday and Wednesday evenings in July and August. ⊠ *Strawberry Mansion Dr., East Fairmount Park,* ☎ *215/477–8810.*

Dance

The **Philadelphia Dance Alliance** (☎ 215/564–5270) is a good source of information on dance concerts and local companies.

Pennsylvania Ballet. This company, under artistic director Roy Kaiser, dances on the stages of the Academy of Music (⊠ Broad and Locust Sts.) and the Merriam Theater (⊠ 250 S. Broad St.) from October to June. The *Nutcracker* production at Christmastime is a city favorite. ☎ *215/551–7014.*

Philadelphia Dance Company. Modern dance performances are presented in September at the Philadelphia Arts Bank (⊠ 601 S. Broad St., ☎ 215/545–0590) and in May at the Annenberg Center (⊠ 3680 Walnut St., ☎ 215/898–6791). ☎ *Philadanco;* ☎ *215/387–8200.*

Film

For first-run commercial releases, the new **United Artist Riverview Plaza** (⊠ 1400 S. Delaware Ave., ☎ 215/755–2219) is a modern multiplex. Avoid what's left of the first-run theaters on Chestnut Street west of Broad Street—they're often frequented by rowdy urban youths.

International House. I-House on the University of Pennsylvania campus presents international film series throughout the year and also sponsors the popular Philadelphia Festival of World Cinema (☞ *below*).

Philadelphia Festival of World Cinema. Sponsored by International House (☞ *above*), this 12-day event in May is filled with screenings, seminars, and events attended by critics, scholars, filmmakers, and cinema buffs. ⊠ *3701 Chestnut St.,* ☎ *215/895–6593.*

Ritz Five and **Ritz at the Bourse.** These are the finest movie theaters in town for avant-garde and foreign films. Both have comfortable seats, clean surroundings, first-rate sound systems, and courteous audiences and staff. ⊠ *Ritz Five, 214 Walnut St.;* ⊠ *Ritz at the Bourse, 4th St. north of Chestnut St.;* ☎ *215/923–7900 for both.*

The Roxy. Philly's classic film repertory house has recently reopened, after two years of renovations, and has been restored to its original luster. ⊠ *2023 Sansom St.,* ☎ *215/923–6699.*

United Artists Main Street 6 Theatre. Manayunk now has a multiplex to complement its shopping and dining options. ⊠ *3720 Main St., Manayunk,* ☎ *215/482–6230.*

Opera

Opera Company of Philadelphia. The company stages four productions a year, between October and April, at the Academy of Music with such stars as Denyce Graves. All performances are in the original language, with computerized English "supertitles" above the stage. ⊠ *510 Walnut St.,* ☎ *215/928–2110.*

Savoy Company. The oldest Gilbert and Sullivan company in the country stages one G&S operetta each May or June at the Academy of Music and at Longwood Gardens in Kennett Square. ☎ *215/735–7161.*

Theater

Annenberg Center. The performing arts complex on the University of Pennsylvania campus has four stages, from the 120-seat Studio to the 970-seat Zellerbach Theater. Something is going on almost all the time—including productions of musical comedy, drama, dance, and children's theater. ⊠ *3680 Walnut St.,* ☎ *215/898–6791.*

Arden Theatre Company. The Arden, formed in 1988, has gained a reputation for innovative theatrical productions. It has a new home in Old City. ⊠ *400 N. 2nd St.,* ☎ *215/922–8900.*

Brick Playhouse. This fairly new theater group, with a space above the Montserrat Restaurant that seats 70, develops and produces new works by local playwrights and performance artists. ⊠ *623 South St.,* ☎ *215/592–1183.*

Forrest Theater. Here you can see productions of major Broadway shows, such as *Cats, La Cage aux Folles, Les Misérables,* and *Phantom of the Opera.* ⊠ *1114 Walnut St.,* ☎ *215/923–1515.*

Freedom Theater. The oldest and most active African-American theater in Pennsylvania has performances from September through June. ⊠ *1346 N. Broad St.,* ☎ *215/978–8497.*

Merriam Theater. Formerly the Schubert and part of the University of the Arts, the Merriam presents Broadway tours and student productions of musicals and dramas. ⊠ *250 S. Broad St.,* ☎ *215/732–5446.*

Philadelphia Arts Bank. A number of nonprofit arts groups use the 230-seat theater owned by the University of the Arts. The Arts Bank is part of the new Avenue of the Arts development. ⊠ *601 S. Broad St., at South St.,* ☎ *215/545–0590.*

Philadelphia Festival Theater for New Plays. This group focuses on works by new playwrights. Its season runs from October through May, and award–winning playwright Bruce Graham is the interim artistic director. ⊠ *3680 Walnut St.,* ☎ *215/898–3900.*

Philadelphia Theater Company. Philadelphia and world premieres of works by contemporary American playwrights are performed here. The company also produces Stages, a program showcasing new plays by American playwrights. ⊠ *1714 Delancey St., at Plays and Players,* ☎ *215/735–0630.*

Society Hill Playhouse. The main stage is for contemporary works; the Second Space Cabaret Theater has musical comedies. ⊠ *507 S. 8th St.,* ☎ *215/923–0210.*

Walnut Street Theatre. Founded in 1809, this is the oldest English-speaking theater in continuous use in the United States. The schedule includes musicals, comedies, and dramas in a lovely 1,052-seat auditorium where almost every seat is a good one. Smaller stages showcase workshop productions of new plays and are rented by other theater companies. ⊠ *9th and Walnut Sts.,* ☎ *215/574–3550.*

Wilma Theater. Under artistic director Blanka Zizka, the Wilma has gained favorable critical notices for innovative presentations of American and European drama. Its season runs from September to June. ⊠ *Broad and Spruce Sts.,* ☎ *215/546–7824.*

6 Outdoor Activities and Sports

Philadelphians are well-known sports fanatics. You can barely concentrate on a Phillies game when the fans are shouting at or cheering on the players, which is part of the fun, of course. Recreational athletes take full advantage of the city's natural resources, including its parks and rivers. Kelly and West River drives in Fairmount Park are quite a sight on spring weekends, when there is no car traffic and all the bikers, in-line skaters, and walkers are out enjoying the cherry blossoms.

Updated by
Janis
Pomerantz

PHILADELPHIA SPORTS FANS have lots to cheer about. Their professional teams—the Eagles (football), the Phillies (baseball), the Flyers (ice hockey), and the 76ers (basketball)—are all popular and occasionally make it to the play-offs. Crowds are the norm at the new 700,000-square-ft CoreStates Center sports complex and at Veterans Stadium: Philadelphians buy more tickets to pro sporting events than do residents of any other U.S. city.

There are many other sports attractions in the city, but two activities—and images—come immediately to mind. The first is one immortalized in a canvas by Thomas Eakins, Philadelphia's greatest painter, of an oarsman rowing on the Schuylkill River in an elegant single scull. Today, the scene that Eakins depicted in the 19th century is still enacted every week when scores of sculls are launched from Boathouse Row, a string of Victorian boathouses along Kelly Drive that are home to the city's many rowing clubs.

The second image, of course, is that of boxer Rocky Balboa, pungently captured by Sylvester Stallone in *Rocky* and its sequels. Had Rocky been a real Philadelphia boxer, he would have fought at the Blue Horizon, the legendary fight club at 1314 North Broad Street (☎ 215/763–0500): The club has more than a thousand seats—but every one is close to the action.

Participant Sports and Fitness

Philadelphia offers a wide variety of places for players to test their skills, whether the sport is canoeing, jogging, or tennis.

Biking

A treat for cyclists is to ride the paved path along the east side of the **Schuylkill River**, cross East Falls Bridge, and return on the west side of the river. It begins behind the Philadelphia Museum of Art and is parallel to Kelly Drive. This 8¼-mi loop is about an hour of casually paced biking. Another great ride is **Forbidden Drive** in the Wissahickon (☞ Fairmount Park *in* Chapter 2), a 5½-mi dirt-and-gravel bridle path along a stream.

The **Bicycle Club of Philadelphia** (☎ 215/735–2453) organizes bike tours, from afternoon outings to weeklong events. **Bike rentals** were available at 1 Boathouse Row, presently undergoing renovation for spring 1998 reopening. Call Fairmount Park (☎ 215/685–0000) for an update. You can also rent bikes ($15 a day) from **Bike Line** (✉ 13th and Locust Sts., ☎ 215/735–1503).

Boating and Canoeing

You can paddle or row through scenic Fairmount Park along the **Schuylkill River**, but yield the right of way to Olympic-caliber scullers speeding by. Call Fairmount Park (☎ 215/685–0000) for the latest rental information.

Fishing

On the banks of **Wissahickon Creek** and **Pennypack Creek**, you'll find good trout fishing in attractive natural settings; call Fairmount Park (☎ 215/685–0000) for information. Both creeks are stocked for the mid-April–December season. You'll need a license ($12.50–$25.50), available at some local sporting goods stores and at Kmart (✉ 424 Oregon Ave., ☎ 215/336–1778).

Golf

Philadelphia has six 18-hole courses that are open to the public. Cobbs Creek is the most challenging; Roosevelt is the easiest.

For golfers who love lots of action, **Cobbs Creek** and **Karakung** (⊠ 7200 Lansdowne Ave., ☎ 215/877–8707) are two adjacent courses. Cobbs Creek plays in and around the creek itself, making for lovely vistas and challenging shots. Karakung has hilly fairways and smaller greens. Both are par 71. Greens fees are $16–$22 weekdays, $19–$26 weekends and holidays.

Franklin D. Roosevelt (⊠ 20th St. and Pattison Ave., ☎ 215/462–8997) is a flat, relatively easy par 69; it's particularly recommended for beginners. Greens fees are $18 weekdays, $21 weekends.

J. F. Byrne (⊠ 9500 Leon St., ☎ 215/632–8666), a short but semichallenging course with small greens and water on six holes, is rated par 67. Greens fees are $16 weekdays, $20 weekends.

With lots of hills, trees, and the Frankford Creek running through it, **Juniata** (⊠ L and Cayuga Sts., ☎ 215/743–4060) is an impressive par 66. Greens fees are $16 weekdays, $19 weekends.

Narrow tree-lined fairways make **Walnut Lane** (⊠ 800 Walnut La., ☎ 215/482–3370), a short (4,500 yards) course, into a semichallenging par 62. Greens fees are $15 weekdays, $16 weekends.

Outside Philadelphia, the privately owned **Valley Forge Golf Club** (⊠ 401 N. Gulph Rd., King of Prussia, ☎ 610/337–1776), near Valley Forge National Historic Park, is open to the public. Trees, doglegs, and small greens make this course (6,000 yards, par 71) a challenging one. Greens fees are $19 weekdays, $23 weekends.

Health Clubs

Some downtown clubs allow nonmembers (with photo IDs) to have day guest privileges for around $10. Three good facilities are **Gold's Gym** (⊠ 834 Chestnut St., ☎ 215/592–9644); **12th Street Gym** (⊠ 204 S. 12th St., ☎ 215/985–4092); and **Rittenhouse Square Fitness Club** (⊠ 2002 Rittenhouse Sq., ☎ 215/985–4095).

Hiking

There are 25 mi of fine solo walks or hikes in Fairmount Park and 54 mi in the unspoiled Wissahickon, a northern section of Fairmount Park; call Fairmount Park (☎ 215/685–0000) for information. Hiking takes on an added dimension if you opt for some of the organized hikes in the area.

You can meet hikers at the **Batona Hiking Club** (☎ 215/659–3921) on Sunday mornings at a central Philadelphia location (such as Broad and Arch streets) and carpool to hiking areas within a two-hour drive of the city, including the Appalachian Trail, the Delaware Water Gap, and the New Jersey Pine Barrens. Hikes range from 7 to 12 mi and tend to be more strenuous than those of the other clubs.

The Department of Recreation sponsors the **Wanderlust Hiking Club** (☎ 215/580–4847). Relatively easy hikes of 5 to 8 mi, many through Fairmount Park and Pennypack Park, begin every Saturday afternoon at 1:30.

Horseback Riding

Of the numerous bridle paths coursing through Philadelphia, the most popular are the trails of the Wissahickon in the northwest, Pennypack Park in the northeast, and Cobbs Creek Park in the southwest. One riding academy that has instruction, trail rides, and rentals is **Circle K**

Stables (✉ 4220 Holmesburg Ave., ☎ 215/335–9975), which charges $30 per hour for lessons, $20 per hour to rent. **Ashford Farms** (✉ River Rd., Miquon, ☎ 610/825–9838), just over the northwestern border, has trail ride fees of $25 per hour and lessons for $30–$40 per hour.

Ice-Skating

You can skate outdoors—with the Delaware River and Benjamin Franklin Bridge as a backdrop—daily from November to March at the **Blue Cross RiverRink** (✉ Penn's Landing, Columbus Blvd. at Chestnut St., ☎ 215/925–RINK). The **University of Pennsylvania Class of 1923 Ice Rink** (✉ 3130 Walnut St., ☎ 215/898–1923) is open to the public from September to April.

Jogging

Joggers can be seen on streets all over the city, but probably no area is favored more than **Kelly and West River drives,** a scenic 8-mi route stretching from the Philadelphia Museum of Art along one bank of the Schuylkill River, across Falls Bridge, and back down the other bank to the museum. Then, of course, there are the steps of the art museum itself, host to Rocky-like runners who raise their arms in salute during early morning jaunts. For information about jogging and running in the city, contact the **Northeast Roadrunners of Philadelphia** (c/o Gerard Nolan, ✉ 3904 I St., 19124, ☎ 215/535–7335).

Fairmount Park (☎ 215/685–0000)—especially along the river drives and Wissahickon Creek—is a natural for joggers and runners. Forbidden Drive along the Wissahickon offers more than 5 mi of soft-surface trail along a picturesque creek in a secluded valley. Only runners, walkers, bikers, and horses can use the trail—no motor vehicles allowed.

Pennypack Park (☎ 215/685–0000), in the northeast section of the city, has an 8-mi macadam trail along Pennypack Creek. Those interested in the ultimate in running—through wide-open spaces on bike trails, horse trails, and grassy hills and dales—have to head outside Philadelphia to **Valley Forge National Park.**

From dawn to dusk the south walkway of the **Benjamin Franklin Bridge** provides a tough but rewarding 3½-mi round-trip run with a terrific view of the Delaware River waterfront.

Tennis

Fairmount Park has more than 100 free public courts, but many players must bring their own nets. Courts are first-come, first-served. The main courts are Chamounix Tennis Courts (✉ Chamounix Dr., off Belmont Mansion Dr., West Fairmount Park) and West Park Tennis Courts (✉ George's Hill, near 52nd and Parkside, adjacent to the Mann Center, West Fairmount Park). Call the **Department of Recreation** (☎ 215/686–3600) for information.

Spectator Sports

During the 1980s Philadelphia became known as the City of Champions, thanks to teams more accustomed to postseason play than not. Today Philadelphians remain avid sports fans who support both professional and collegiate teams.

The major-league sports teams play their home games in Veterans Stadium, the impressive CoreStates Center, or the CoreStates Spectrum. (At press time First Union was set to purchase CoreStates, so the stadiums' names may change.) These venues are located around Broad Street and Pattison Avenue, near I–95, at the southern edge of the city. The Broad Street subway stops nearby at Pattison Avenue; Bus C also runs down Broad Street. The Phillies and the Eagles play at Veterans Stadium; the 76ers and the Flyers call the CoreStates Center home. Some collegiate games are played in these stadiums, too; others are played on the campuses of the various colleges and universities.

Tickets to professional baseball, basketball, football, and hockey games are available at Veterans Stadium or the CoreStates Spectrum through TicketMaster (☎ 215/336–2000), at ticket agencies, and by mail and phone from the respective teams. You should plan to buy tickets as early as possible to avoid disappointment.

Baseball
The **Philadelphia Phillies** play from April to October at Veterans Stadium, (✉ 3501 S. Broad St., ☎ 215/463–1000).

Basketball
The **Philadelphia 76ers** play at the CoreStates Center (✉ Broad St. at I–95, ☎ 215/339–7676) from November to April.

Collegiate Big Five basketball (✉ Big Five Office, Hutchinson Gym, 220 S. 32nd St., ☎ 215/898–4747) features teams from LaSalle, St. Joseph's, Temple, the University of Pennsylvania, and Villanova. The season runs from December to March.

Bicycling
One of the world's top four bicycling events, the **CoreStates Pro Cycling Championship** (☎ 215/973–3546) is held each June. The 156-mi race starts and finishes at Benjamin Franklin Parkway, with 10 loops including the infamous Manayunk Wall.

Football
The **Philadelphia Eagles** can be seen in action at Veterans Stadium (✉ 3501 S. Broad St., ☎ 215/463–5500) from September to January. Many seats go to season ticket holders.

Hockey
The **Philadelphia Flyers** hit the ice at CoreStates Center (✉ Broad St. at I–95., ☎ 215/755–9700) from October to April.

The **Philadelphia Phantoms,** the city's new hockey team, are the Flyers' AHL affiliate. The team had its inaugural season in 1996–97. You can see them at the CoreStates Spectrum (✉ Broad St. and Pattison Ave., ☎ 215/465–4522) from October to May.

Horse Racing
Thoroughbred racing takes place at **Philadelphia Park** (✉ Street Rd., Bensalem, ☎ 215/639–9000). Post time is usually at 12:35 PM in the winter, 1:05 PM in the summer, Saturday–Tuesday year-round. At **Garden State Park** (✉ Rte. 70, Cherry Hill, NJ, ☎ 609/488–8400) the post time is 7:30 PM Friday and Saturday. Thoroughbred racing runs from January through June, harness racing from September through December. For offtrack betting, the **Turf Club Center City** (✉ 1635 Market St., ☎ 215/246–1556) is open daily 11–11.

Lacrosse
The **Philadelphia Wings,** an indoor lacrosse team, have won two major indoor Lacrosse League championships in three years. The team plays at the CoreStates Center (✉ Broad St. at I–95, ☎ 215/389–WINGS); the season runs from January through March.

Rowing
The elegant boathouses, the regattas, the placid Schuylkill River, and a climate that allows an average of 360 rowing days a year all make Philadelphia the rowing capital of the world. From February to Oc-

tober you can watch single and team races out on the river, usually from 5 AM to dusk. Dozens of major meets are held here, including the largest rowing event in the country, the **Dad Vail Regatta** (☎ 215/675–9227). This May event includes up to 500 sculls from more than 100 colleges. Free shuttle buses for spectators provide transportation from remote parking areas. The May **Stotesbury Cup Regatta** (☎ 215/332–8531) includes more than 2,500 students from 110 schools. More than a thousand individual and club member rowers compete in the 96-year-old **Independence Day Regatta** (☎ 215/332–8531), held around July 4.

Soccer

Philadelphia Kixx, the city's first national professional soccer team, just celebrated its inaugural season to crowds of exuberant fans at the CoreStates Spectrum (✉ Broad St. and Pattison Ave., ☎ 888/888–KIXX). You can catch the team in action from October through April.

Tennis

The **Advanta Tennis Championships** take place at the CoreStates Center (✉ Broad St. at I–95, ☎ 215/336–3600), usually in February. More than 60 of the world's top pros compete.

Track and Field

The **Penn Relays** (☎ 215/685–0052), the world's largest and oldest amateur track meet, held the last week of April at the University of Pennsylvania's Franklin Field, stars world-class performers in track and field. The **Philadelphia Distance Run** (☎ 215/685–0052), the nation's top half-marathon, takes place in September. The **Philadelphia Marathon** (☎ 215/685–0054) runs through Center City and along the Schuylkill River and is held the Sunday before Thanksgiving. The **Broad Street Run** (☎ 215/686–0841), a 10-miler down Broad Street, is a May event.

7 Shopping

Philadelphia's shopping scene is much like the city itself: a harmonious combination of the old and the new. Whether you're picking up a souvenir at the Bourse after seeing the historic sights surrounding Independence Mall or browsing in the very modern Shops at Liberty Place, there's something to suit all tastes. The choice is yours: check out the latest art trends at a chic Old City gallery, or hunt for fine cheese and olive oil in the Italian Market.

FOR CONSUMERS WITH CONSUMING PASSIONS, Philadelphia holds a vast array of goodies. Diamond baubles, bangles, and beads from Bailey, Banks, and Biddle? A photojournalist vest from Banana Republic? High-style Italian shoes from Bottino? A $500 reproduction of the inkwell used in the signing of the Declaration of Independence? Or for that matter, a $1 mini–Liberty Bell? From the homey to the haute, Philadelphia can be a great shopping town.

Updated by
Janis
Pomerantz

The city has an upscale shopping district centered on 17th and Walnut streets; Jewelers' Row and Antiques Row; the first downtown indoor shopping mall in the United States; and an outdoor food market that covers five city blocks. Bargains are available, too—from discount stores, street vendors, and factory outlets (for the lowdown on Philly thrift stores, check out the book *The Thrift Shop Maniac's Guided Tours,* by Nancy Berman).

Local stores have sales throughout the year. If you're looking for a particular item, check the daily newspapers. Most stores accept traveler's checks and Visa, MasterCard, and American Express; Diners Club and Discover are less widely accepted. Policies on personal checks vary. Pennsylvania has a 6% sales tax, and the city adds another 1%. These do not apply to clothing, medicine, and food bought in stores. Downtown shopping hours are generally 9:30 or 10 to 5 or 6. Many stores are open until 9 PM on Wednesday. Most downtown stores are closed on Sunday, but the Bourse and the Gallery are open 12–5.

Shopping Districts and Malls

Pine Street from 9th Street to 12th Street has long been Philadelphia's **Antiques Row.** The three-block area has dozens of antiques stores and curio shops, many specializing in expensive period furniture and Colonial heirlooms.

Across the street from the Liberty Bell is the **Bourse** (⊠ 21 S. 5th St., between Market and Chestnut Sts., ☎ 215/625–0300), an elegantly restored 1895 commodities exchange building. The six-story skylighted atrium contains a few fun shops catering to tourists, such as **Destination Philadelphia** (Philly-related T-shirts) and **Best of Philadelphia,** as well as a festive international food court.

The **Chestnut Street Transitway,** which extends from 8th to 18th streets, is somewhat seedy after dark but buzzes with urban vitality during the day. It has rare-book sellers, custom tailors, sporting goods stores, pinball arcades, and discount drugstores.

What attraction could there be in the cultural wasteland of northeast Philadelphia that rivals the Liberty Bell and the zoo in popularity? **Franklin Mills Mall** (⊠ Off I–95 at Exit 24, Rte. 63, Woodhaven Rd., ☎ 215/632–1500), with 1.7 million square ft, 220 stores, and two food courts, could be nicknamed the Disneyland of bargain shopping. Discount outlet stores include Ann Taylor, Saks Fifth Avenue Clearinghouse, and Last Call from Neiman Marcus. The mall, about 20 mi from downtown, is nearly a mile in length, and the parking lot holds almost 9,000 cars. You will get lost. For a break, you can visit one of the 14 theaters in the GCC Franklin Mills multiplex here (☎ 215/281–2750).

A block north of Chestnut Street is Philadelphia's landmark effort at urban-renewal-cum-shopping, the **Gallery at Market East** (⊠ Market St. between 8th and 11th Sts., ☎ 215/925–7162), America's first enclosed downtown shopping mall. The four-level glass-roofed structure near the Pennsylvania Convention Center contains 170 mid-price retailers. It includes 40 food outlets and two department stores—JCPenney (☎ 215/238–9100) and Strawbridge's (☎ 215/629–6000), which has somewhat higher-quality merchandise.

If you want local color, nothing compares with South Philadelphia's **Italian Market.** On both sides of 9th Street from Christian Street to Washington Street and spilling out onto the surrounding blocks, hundreds of outdoor stalls and indoor stores sell such food items as spices, cheeses, pastas, fruits, vegetables, and freshly slaughtered poultry and beef, not to mention household items, clothing, shoes, and other goods. It's crowded and smelly, and the vendors can be less than hospitable—but the food is fresh, and the prices are reasonable. Food shops include the **Spice Corner, DiBruno Brothers House of Cheese, Claudio's,** and **Talluto's Authentic Italian Foods. Fante's** is well-known for cookware. The market's hours are Tuesday–Saturday 9–5:30; some vendors open earlier, and others close around 3:30. Some shops are open Sunday from 9:30 to 12:30.

Jewelers' Row, centered on Sansom Street between 7th and 8th streets, is one of the world's oldest and largest markets of precious stones: More than 350 retailers, wholesalers, and craftspeople operate here. The 700 block of Sansom Street is a brick-paved enclave occupied almost exclusively by jewelers.

Lord & Taylor (✉ Between 13th, Juniper Sts., Market, and Chestnut Sts., ☎ 215/241–9000) now occupies the former John Wanamaker department store, a Philadelphia landmark. Its focal point is the nine-story grand court with its 30,000-pipe organ—the largest ever built—and a 2,500-pound statue of an eagle, both remnants of the 1904 Louisiana Purchase Exposition in St. Louis. The new owners promise to continue the famous Christmas sound-and-light show and the organ performances.

For browsing, a trip to the historic and newly hip **Manayunk** neighborhood (☎ 215/482–9565) is worth the 7-mi trip from Center City. Clothes and crafts are the highlights; for antiques, art galleries, clothing, and gifts and souvenirs, *see* the listings in Specialty Stores, *below.* Many stores are on Main Street from number 4400 to 3900. For background on this area, *see* Manayunk *in* Chapter 2; for some of the area's good dining options, *see* Chapter 3.

Market Place East (✉ Market St. between 7th and 8th Sts., ☎ 215/592–8905), across from the Gallery, is in a historic building saved from the wrecker's ball at the 11th hour. The century-old former Lit Brothers department store went through a $75 million renovation to emerge as an office building with a five-level atrium with stores and restaurants.

Serious shoppers will want to make a trip to **The Plaza & The Court at King of Prussia** (✉ Rte. 202 at the Schuylkill Expressway, ☎ 610/265–5727 for the Plaza, ☎ 610/337–1210 for the Court), the largest retail shopping complex on the East Coast. A recent $6.4 million renovation project turned the two malls into an elegant place to stroll and shop, with 450 specialty shops and nine department stores, including **Nordstrom, Neiman Marcus, Lord & Taylor,** and **Bloomingdale's.** The mall is about 20 mi from downtown; SEPTA Bus 124 or 125 runs here from 17th Street and John F. Kennedy Boulevard.

At 17th and Chestnut you'll find the **Shops at Liberty Place** (✉ 1625 Chestnut St., ☎ 215/851–9055), the city's newest shopping complex, with popular stores including **Benetton, Barami, The Coach Store, Speedo Authentic Fitness, The Body Shop,** and **Country Road Australia.**

More than 70 stores and restaurants are arranged in two circular levels within a strikingly handsome 90-ft glass-roof atrium.

If you've finally decided on that new tattoo or need supplies for your next witches' sabbath, head to **South Street,** just south of Society Hill. One of the city's main entertainment strips is also one of its major shopping areas, with most shops open in the evenings. From Front Street near the Delaware River to 9th Street you'll find more than 300 unusual stores—high-fashion clothing, New Age books and health food, avant-garde art galleries—and 100 restaurants. You'll find a few of the national chains, but 95% of the stores are individually owned, selling things you won't find in the mall back home.

Most shop-till-you-droppers first head for the main shopping area of **Walnut Street,** between Broad Street and Rittenhouse Square, and the intersecting streets just north and south. These blocks are filled with boutiques, art galleries, jewelers, fine clothing stores, and many other unusual shops. At Broad and Walnut, the **Shops at the Bellevue** include **Polo/Ralph Lauren, Nicole Miller,** and **Tiffany & Co.** On 18th Street in the block north of Rittenhouse Square, you'll find entrepreneurs both indoors and out: the youthful and trendy department store **Urban Outfitters,** a sidewalk vendor selling handmade Peruvian shawls, street artist Joe Barker painting watercolors of Philadelphia cityscapes, and a shop—**Scoop De Ville**—that sells more than 40 flavors of frozen yogurt.

Specialty Stores

Antiques
Many dealers in higher-priced wares cluster on Antiques Row—Pine Street between 9th and 12th streets. There are also some less expensive shops off South Street, on Bainbridge Street between 4th and 8th Streets.

Antique Marketplace. The 100 antiques and collectibles dealers with stalls in this brick building display vintage clothes, toys, glassware, furniture, and more. ⊠ *3797 Main St., Manayunk,* ☎ *215/482–4499.*

Architectural Antiques Exchange. Victorian embellishments from saloons and apothecary shops, stained and beveled glass, gargoyles, and advertising memorabilia entice many shoppers. ⊠ *715 N. 2nd St.,* ☎ *215/922–3669.*

Calderwood Gallery. Art nouveau and art deco furniture, glass, bronzes, and rugs tempt discerning collectors at this fine establishment. ⊠ *1427 Walnut St.,* ☎ *215/568–7475.*

Freeman Fine Arts. This is not only the city's most prominent auction house but also America's oldest (founded in 1805). Examine furniture, china, prints, and paintings on Monday and Tuesday; bid for them on Wednesday. Freeman's auctioned one of the original flyers on which the Declaration of Independence was printed and posted throughout the city. It sold for $404,000 in 1968. ⊠ *1808 Chestnut St.,* ☎ *215/ 563–9275.*

Gargoyles. You can wander through 11,000 square ft of displays of antiques and reproduction decorative and architectural pieces—archways, mantels, entranceways, carousel horses, stained-glass windows, and ornate mirrors. ⊠ *512 S. 3rd St.,* ☎ *215/629–1700.*

G. B. Schaffer Antiques. Eighteenth, 19th-, and early 20th-century American furnishings, stained glass, silver, porcelain, paintings, and prints are the specialties here. ⊠ *1014 Pine St.,* ☎ *215/923–2263.*

M. Finkel and Daughter. Late 18th- and early 19th-century American furniture, quilts, needlework, samplers, and folk art make this an important outpost for Americana buffs. ⊠ *936 Pine St.,* ☎ *215/627–7797.*

Vintage Instruments. Antique strings and woodwinds are displayed; the store specializes in violins and also carries American fretted instruments—banjos, guitars, and mandolins. ⊠ *1529 Pine St.,* ☎ *215/545–1100.*

W. Graham Arader. This is the flagship store of a highly respected chain that stocks the world's largest selection of 16th- to 19th-century prints and maps, specializing in botanicals, birds, and the American West. ⊠ *1308 Walnut St.,* ☎ *215/735–8811.*

Art Galleries

For current shows in Philadelphia's numerous galleries, see the listings in *Philadelphia* magazine or the Weekend section of the Friday *Philadelphia Inquirer.* Many galleries are near Rittenhouse Square; others are on South Street or scattered about downtown. In recent years Old City has become the hottest gallery area. One evening a month from October to June, on what is called First Friday, you can wander 2nd and 3rd streets above Market Street going from gallery to gallery. It's like a refined block party, with refreshments and performance artists.

American Pie Contemporary Crafts and Judaica. Artists from around the country produce the handcrafted jewelry, blown glass, and Judaica items such as menorahs and seder plates shown here. ⊠ *127 S. 18th St.,* ☎ *215/751–2752;* ⊠ *327 South St.,* ☎ *215/922–2226;* ⊠ *4303 Main St., Manayunk,* ☎ *215/487–0226.*

Clay Studio. A nonprofit organization runs the gallery and conducts classes as well as an outreach program to inner city schools. There are clay works and pottery by well-known artists; the gallery has juried shows and group exhibits. ⊠ *139 N. 2nd St.,* ☎ *215/925–3453.*

David David Gallery. American and European paintings, drawings, and watercolors from the 16th to the 20th centuries are on display. ⊠ *260 S. 18th St.,* ☎ *215/735–2922.*

Fleisher Ollman Gallery. You'll find fine works by 20th-century self-taught American artists here. ⊠ *211 S. 17th St.,* ☎ *215/545–7562.*

Helen Drutt. This gallery presents contemporary American and European artists, with a focus on ceramics and jewelry. ⊠ *1721 Walnut St.,* ☎ *215/735–1625.*

I. Brewster. The specialty here is contemporary paintings and prints by such artists as Louis Icart, Erté, Andy Warhol, and Red Grooms. ⊠ *1628 Walnut St.,* ☎ *215/731–9200.*

Gilbert Luber Gallery. Japanese antique and contemporary prints and Thai and Balinese artifacts are offered. ⊠ *1220 Walnut St.,* ☎ *215/732–2996.*

Gross McCleaf Gallery. This is a good place to see works by both prominent and emerging artists, with an emphasis on Philadelphia painters. ⊠ *127 S. 16th St.,* ☎ *215/665–8138.*

Locks Gallery. Shows present works by an impressive assortment of contemporary regional, national, and international painters, sculptors, and mixed-media artists. ⊠ *600 Washington Sq. S,* ☎ *215/629–1000.*

Muse Gallery. Established in 1978 by the Muse Foundation for the Visual Arts, Muse Gallery is a women's cooperative in Old City committed to increasing the visibility of women's artwork and presenting experimental work in a variety of media. ⊠ *60 N. 2nd St.,* ☎ *215/ 627–5310.*

Newman Galleries. This gallery carries a range of works from 19th-century paintings to contemporary lithographs and sculpture. It's strong on 20th-century painters from the Bucks County area. ⊠ *1625 Walnut St.,* ☎ *215/563–1779.*

Nexus Foundation for Today's Art. A group of artists started this non-profit organization in 1975. The emphasis is on experimental art as well as new directions in traditional media. ⊠ *137 N. 2nd St.,* ☎ *215/ 629–1103.*

Paul Cava Fine Art. Vintage and contemporary photography and contemporary art distinguish this Old City gallery. ⊠ *54 N. 3rd St.,* ☎ *215/922–2126.*

Schmidt/Dean Gallery. Contemporary paintings, sculpture, prints, and photographs are shown; the specialty is work by Philadelphia artists. ⊠ *1636 Walnut St.,* ☎ *215/546–7212;* ⊠ *1721 Spruce St.,* ☎ *215/ 546–9577.*

School Gallery of the Pennsylvania Academy of Fine Arts. Stop here to see rotating exhibits of works by faculty, alumni, and students in the school's attractively renovated building near the Pennsylvania Convention Center. ⊠ *1301 Cherry St.,* ☎ *215/972–7600.*

Schwarz Gallery. Eighteenth- to 20th-century American and European paintings are the focus, with an emphasis on Philadelphia artists of the past. ⊠ *1806 Chestnut St.,* ☎ *215/563–4887.*

Snyderman Gallery. One-of-a-kind handmade furniture pieces and glass objects are displayed at this Old City gallery. ⊠ *303 Cherry St.,* ☎ *215/238–9576.*

University of the Arts' Rosenwald-Wolf Gallery. The school's gallery presents works by faculty and students, and local, national, and international artists. ⊠ *333 S. Broad St.,* ☎ *215/875–1116.*

The Works. This Old City gallery showcases contemporary American crafts in wood, fiber, ceramics, and metals. ⊠ *303 Cherry St.,* ☎ *215/ 922–7775.*

Works on Paper. The contemporary prints here have won the gallery a reputation as one of the city's best. ⊠ *1611 Walnut St.,* ☎ *215/988– 9999.*

Bookstores

AIA Bookstore. Run by the Philadelphia chapter of the American Institute of Architects (AIA), this shop specializes in books on architectural theory, building construction, interior design, and furnishings. It also carries blueprint posters, international magazines, and unusual gifts. ⊠ *117 S. 17th St.,* ☎ *215/569–3188.*

Borders. Some locals find this the friendliest bookstore in Philadelphia. You can sit on a couch, listen to live guitar music, and read for hours. The 110,000 titles and more than half-million books are spread over a three-level 20,000-square-ft selling floor. There's a second-floor espresso bar, and Saturday-morning children's programs are held at 11:30. ⊠ *1727 Walnut St.,* ☎ *215/568–7400.*

Encore. A discount chain with several locations in the area, Encore offers 30% off *New York Times* best-sellers and up to 80% off close-outs and remainders. ⊠ *609 Chestnut St.,* ☎ *215/627–4557.*

Giovanni's Room. Focusing on books dealing with feminist, gay, and lesbian topics, this store stocks an extensive inventory and sponsors many author appearances. ⊠ *345 S. 12th St.,* ☎ *215/923–2960.*

How-to-Do-It Bookshop. Want to build a computer, grow rutabagas, groom your poodle? If there's a book telling you how to do something, chances are this unique place (with more than 40,000 titles) will have it. ⊠ *1608 Sansom St.,* ☎ *215/563–1516.*

Joseph Fox. This small bookstore specializes in art, architecture, and design. ⊠ *1724 Sansom St.,* ☎ *215/563–4184.*

Rittenhouse Bookstore. Known as the best medical bookstore in Philadelphia, this establishment may be able to get the book you want overnight if you can't find it in stock. ⊠ *1706 Rittenhouse Sq.,* ☎ *215/ 545–6072.*

Rizzoli Bookstore. Art lovers will rejoice in this elegant store filled with every kind of coffee table book imaginable. Art, architecture, and design are strengths here. ⊠ *Shops at the Bellevue, Broad and Walnut Sts.,* ☎ *215/546–9200.*

Robin's Bookstore. Not the biggest bookstore in town and maybe not the best, but it's definitely the sentimental favorite of devotees of literature, poetry, and minority studies. Owner Larry Robin has been promoting literature and fighting literary censorship for more than 30 years. Robin's has an exceptional variety of hard-to-find intellectual titles. Book fans are drawn to its frequent poetry readings and book signings by local authors. ⊠ *108 S. 13th St.,* ☎ *215/735–9600.*

Tower Books. Famous for its magazine selection, the biggest in the city, this is a great place to browse on a Saturday night; so is its companion music store, Tower Records (☞ *below*), farther up South Street. You'll be mesmerized by the huge travel section. ⊠ *425 South St.,* ☎ *215/925–9909.*

University of Pennsylvania Barnes and Noble Bookstore. With more than 60,000 popular and scholarly titles, this bookstore is especially strong in business, computers, psychology, and sociology. The Middle East section may be the only place in town to buy a book on Kurdish grammar. ⊠ *3729 Locust Walk,* ☎ *215/898–7595.*

Whodunit. The city's only store specializing in mysteries, spy stories, and adventure books also stocks out-of-print mysteries. Owner Art Bourgeau has published six mysteries and a nonfiction book on mystery writing. ⊠ *1931 Chestnut St.,* ☎ *215/567–1478.*

RARE AND USED BOOKS

Bauman Rare Books. An antiquarian bookstore with volumes dating as far back as the 15th century, this is a treasure trove for collectors in the fields of law, science, literature, travel, and exploration. There is also a print and map collection. ⊠ *1215 Locust St.,* ☎ *215/546– 6466.*

Book Trader. You'll find great browsing on the two floors of this eclectic used-book store, though prices are on the high side. It's open daily 10 AM–midnight. ⊠ *501 South St.,* ☎ *215/925–0219.*

Hibberd's. Rare and used books, remainders, and a large selection of unusual art books are the sizable draws for book aficionados. ⊠ *1306 Walnut St.,* ☎ *215/546–8811.*

William H. Allen Bookseller. This store carries one of the city's best collections of used and scholarly books; specialties are history, literature, and philosophy. Note the extensive collection of books on ancient Greece and Rome, in English and the original Greek or Latin. ⊠ *2031 Walnut St.,* ☎ *215/563–3398.*

Cameras and Photographic Equipment

Kosmin's Camera Exchange. Come here for film, motion picture equipment, slide projectors, screens, darkroom supplies, and a half-dozen brands of cameras. ⊠ *927 Arch St.,* ☎ *215/627–8231.*

Mid-City Camera. This major stock house carries a large line of darkroom equipment and all major camera brands in all formats. It also buys and sells used cameras and has a service department and rentals. ⊠ *1316 Walnut St.,* ☎ *215/735–2522.*

Roth Camera Repairs. If you have camera trouble, here's the place to go. The store prides itself on extra-quick service. ⊠ *1015 Chestnut St., Jefferson Bldg. lobby, Room 102,* ☎ *215/922–2498.*

Clothing

CHILDREN'S CLOTHING

Born Yesterday. The selection of clothing and toys for tots includes handmade goods, imported fashions, and styles you won't find elsewhere. ⊠ *1901 Walnut St.,* ☎ *215/568–6556.*

Children's Boutique. This store carries a look between conservative and classic in infant to preteen clothes; you can buy complete wardrobes, specialty gifts, and handmade items. ⊠ *1717 Walnut St.,* ☎ *215/563–3881.*

Kamikaze Kids. Unique designer fashions for infants to preteens are showcased in a kid-friendly atmosphere, with cloud-painted walls and play areas. ⊠ *527 S. 4th St.,* ☎ *215/574–9800.*

MEN'S AND WOMEN'S

Banana Republic. This store is part of the chain that helped make famous—and still sells—the photojournalist vest (with a plethora of pockets) and the Kenya convertible pants (with hidden zippers that convert them into shorts). ⊠ *1716 Walnut St.,* ☎ *215/735–2247.*

Burberrys Ltd. Named after Thomas Burberry, who designed the trench coat in the mid-1850s, this British-owned establishment stocks British raincoats, overcoats, sport coats, and cashmere sweaters. Quality is high, and so are prices. ⊠ *1705 Walnut St.,* ☎ *215/557–7400.*

Destination Philadelphia. Every item bears some form of Philadelphia logo or design—from a soft pretzel to a line drawing of Billy Penn. You'll find hats, jackets, sweatshirts, and more than 40 styles of T-shirts. ⊠ *Bourse Bldg., 21 S. 5th St.,* ☎ *215/440–0233.*

Hats in the Belfry. Designer hats, practical hats, formal hats, silly hats, Panama hats, baseball caps and more add the finishing touch to your outfit. ⊠ *245 South St.,* ☎ *215/922–6770.*

Neo Deco. Shop here for European-style contemporary clothing and accessories: sportswear, shoes, and jewelry. ⊠ *414 South St.,* ☎ *215/928–0627;* ⊠ *4409 Main St., Manayunk,* ☎ *215/487–7757.*

Nicole Miller. This successful designer for men and women even produced a T-shirt for a city tourist campaign. The men's line includes golf apparel and a notable selection of ties. The women's section has sportswear and evening wear, in addition to loads of the designer's signature scarves and handbags. ⊠ *Shops at the Bellevue, Broad and Walnut Sts.,* ☎ *215/546–5007;* ⊠ *4249 Main St., Manayunk,* ☎ *215/930–0307.*

Polo/Ralph Lauren. The city's entry in the Lauren retail empire carries the designer's women's, men's, boys' and home collections. ⊠ *Shops at the Bellevue, 200 S. Broad St.,* ☎ *215/985–2800.*

Ultimate Sock. You'll find designer socks and hosiery by Hue, DKNY, Calvin Klein, and Hot Sox, plus hundreds of novelty socks—some even play music. Prices range from $4 to $20. ⊠ *Shops at Liberty Place, 1625 Chestnut St.,* ☎ *215/567–0801.*

Urban Outfitters. What started out as a storefront selling used jeans to students in West Philadelphia is now a trend-setting chain on campuses across the country. A Beaux Arts mansion now houses the flagship store, selling hip clothing, books, unusual toys, and apartment accessories. ⊠ *1801 Walnut St.,* ☎ *215/569–3131.*

Zipperhead. As you enter this place, chances are you'll have to step around a teenager and his parents arguing about whether to go in. For 17 years this has been the alternative clothing landmark for the spiked-hair-and-nose-ring set. Offerings here include motorcycle jackets, rock band T-shirts, and hard-to-find body jewelry for those hard-to-pierce places. ⊠ *407 South St.,* ☎ *215/928–1123.*

MEN'S CLOTHING

Allure. Classic and stylish Italian clothing and furnishings draw a cosmopolitan crowd. Brioni, Pal Zileri, Verri, Donna Karan, and Canali are some of the designers here. ⊠ *1509 Walnut St.,* ☎ *215/561–4242;* ⊠ *4358-B Main St., Manayunk,* ☎ *215/482–5299.*

Boyd's. The largest single-store men's clothier in the country has nine shops that present the traditional English look, avant-garde Italian imports, and dozens of other styles and designers. There are shops for extra tall, large, and short men; an excellent café for lunch; valet parking; and 60 tailors on the premises. Women will find a small selection of high-quality designer clothes, too. ⊠ *1818 Chestnut St.,* ☎ *215/564–9000.*

Brooks Brothers. The oldest men's clothing store in America (founded in New York in 1818), Brooks is synonymous with Ivy League business clothing: conservative suits, button-down shirts, and striped ties. ⊠ *1513 Walnut St.,* ☎ *215/564–4100.*

Structure. This hip, stylish store has relatively decent prices for casual clothes, such as silk shirts and baggy pleated pants in bold colors. Sales can yield real bargains. ⊠ *Shops at Liberty Place, 1625 Chestnut St.,* ☎ *215/851–0835.*

Wayne Edwards. You'll find exclusive lines of classic contemporary clothing from Italy, Japan, France, and the United States. Barbera, Quinto, and Armani are representative designers. ⊠ *1521 Walnut St.,* ☎ *215/563–6801.*

WOMEN'S CLOTHING

Asta De Blue. A boutique in a brownstone off Rittenhouse Square is a hot place for upbeat urban-contemporary clothing, jewelry, accessories, and gifts. Key collections include Zelda, Ghost, and Annie Kwan. The owners say they have the largest collection of Arche footwear outside Manhattan. ⊠ *265 S. 20th St.,* ☎ *215/732–0550.*

Knit Wit. High-fashion clothes and accessories from sportswear to cocktail dresses are the focus here. ⊠ *1721 Walnut St.,* ☎ *215/564–4760.*

Ma Jolie. Spacious and lovely, this boutique is run by three sisters, native Philadelphians. It specializes in clothing that is comfortable and

Pick up the phone.
Pick up the miles.

1-800-FLY-FREE

Is this a great time, or what? :-)

Now when you sign up with MCI you can receive up to 8,000 bonus frequent flyer miles on one of seven major airlines.

Then earn another 5 miles for every dollar you spend on a variety of MCI services, including MCI Card® calls from virtually anywhere in the world.*

You're going to use these services anyway. Why not rack up the miles while you're doing it?

Speakeasy.

Fodor's and Living Language® bring you the most useful, up-to-date language course for travelers. Phrasebook/dictionary, two cassettes, booklet.

www.fodors.com/

flattering to all sizes, including suits, evening dresses, and sweaters. Children's clothes and toys are a new addition; the mezzanine has a café and gift shop. ☒ *4340 Main St., Manayunk,* ☎ *215/483–8850.*

Mendelsohn. Classic European and specialty clothing attract a devoted clientele. ☒ *229 S. 18th St.,* ☎ *215/546–6333.*

Plage Tahiti. A leading showcase for promising young high-fashion designers carries a wide selection of chic and charming swimwear. ☒ *128 S. 17th St.,* ☎ *215/569–9139.*

Toby Lerner. Expensive high-fashion apparel with strong classic lines, plus a full line of shoes, is the store's strength. ☒ *117 S. 17th St.,* ☎ *215/568–5760.*

Discount Shopping

Franklin Mills Mall (☞ Shopping Districts and Malls, *above*) is the big draw, but there are a number of other spots closer to downtown.

Cambridge Clothing Factory Outlet. This is a manufacturers' outlet for men, with 10 national brands starting at 40% off retail. Out-of-towners can get immediate alterations. ☒ *1520 Sansom St., 2nd floor,* ☎ *215/568–8248.*

Daffy's. Housed in an attractive Egyptian deco–style building, Daffy's carries higher-end American and European designs for men, women, and children at 40–75% off list (sometimes even more with special markdowns). ☒ *1700 Chestnut St.,* ☎ *215/963–9996.*

Thos. David Factory Store. Upstairs they make it; downstairs they sell it. High-quality men's and women's business clothing and sportswear are sold at almost wholesale prices. ☒ *401 Race St.,* ☎ *215/922–4659.*

Food

The Italian Market (☞ Shopping Districts and Malls, *above*) is a classic Philly experience and the Reading Terminal Market (☞ Diners and Philly Food *in* Chapter 3) is a city gem, but you'll find other good food options, too.

Chef's Market. Philly's ultimate gourmet supermarket prepares 60 to 70 entrées every day, stocks several hundred kinds of cheeses, sells goods from its own bakery, and is a fish market and meat market. Packaged items include 150 varieties of imported jams, 40 olive oils, and 60 flavored vinegars. ☒ *231 South St.,* ☎ *215/925–8360.*

Fante's. One of the oldest gourmet supply stores in the country has the largest selection of coffeemakers and cooking equipment in the United States. Family owned since 1906, Fante's is famous for oddball kitchen gadgets such as truffle shavers and pineapple peelers; restaurants and bakeries all over the country and overseas order from the store. It's in the Italian Market, so you can combine a visit here with other food shopping. ☒ *1006 S. 9th St.,* ☎ *215/922–5557.*

Food Hall at Strawbridge's. You can eat in or take out breads, cheeses, salads, and ice cream. There are frequent cooking demonstrations with free samples—and check out the large candy department and charcuterie. ☒ *8th and Market Sts.,* ☎ *215/629–6000.*

Godiva Chocolatier. At $3 for a single piece of hand-dipped fruit to $29 for a one-pound box in the classic gold packaging, it doesn't get any sweeter than this. ☒ *Shops at Liberty Place, 1625 Chestnut St.,* ☎ *215/963–0810.*

Kitchen Kapers. This is a good source for fine cookware, French copper, cutlery, coffees, and teas. ☒ *213 S. 17th St.,* ☎ *215/516–8059.*

Gifts and Souvenirs

Best of Philadelphia. Here's a fun place for cheap Philly souvenirs: There are more than 100 different items, including earrings, flags, jigsaw puzzles, coloring books, Ben Franklin key chains, T-shirts, and, of course, Liberty Bells. ✉ *Bourse Bldg., 21 S. 5th St.,* ☎ *215/440–7016.*

Country Floors. Decorators love the ceramic and terra-cotta hand-painted tiles from the United States and all over Europe (mostly for floors and walls, but individual tiles can make great decorative art). ✉ *1706 Locust St.,* ☎ *215/545–1040.*

Hand of Aries. You'll find everything for the discriminating witch—books, candles, incense, tarot cards, ritual robes, capes, and long dresses (black only). ✉ *620 S. 4th St.,* ☎ *215/923–5264.*

Holt's Tobacconist. The city's oldest (1898) and largest purveyor of tobacco, cigars, and lighters, Holt's also has the city's largest selection of writing instruments. ✉ *1522 Walnut St.,* ☎ *215/732–8500.*

Home Grown. Unique tableware, including ceramic serving pieces from around the United States and Europe, is the focus of an upscale home accessories shop that carries everything from Calvin Klein dinnerware to Mackenzie Childs pottery. ✉ *4321 Main St., Manayunk,* ☎ *215/482–1910.*

Touches. Upscale shoppers come to this attractive shop for its handmade shawls, handbags, belts, unusual jewelry, and children's gifts. ✉ *225 S. 15th St.,* ☎ *215/546–1221.*

Urban Objects. This store carries an eclectic collection of contemporary gifts, home accessories, antiques (both authentic and reproductions), lamps, and pictures. Many objects are imported from Europe and Asia but are reasonably priced. (✉ *1724 Sansom St.,* ☎ *215/557–9474.*

Warner Bros. Store. For those who love Bugs, Sylvester, Daffy, and Tweety on their mugs, T-shirts, key chains, puzzles, and golf club covers, this is the place. The store's gallery of animation art has 'toon lithographs for $150 and original cels for up to $2,400. (✉ *Shops at Liberty Place, 1625 Chestnut St.,* ☎ *215/981–0680.*

Xenos Candy and Gifts. Asher chocolates and Philly souvenirs from key chains to T-shirts are stocked here. ✉ *231 Chestnut St.,* ☎ *215/ 922–1445.*

Jewelry

Philadelphia is a fine town for shopping for jewelry from antique to contemporary, with good choices on Jewelers' Row (☞ Shopping Districts and Malls, *above*) and beyond.

Bailey, Banks & Biddle. This old-line store, in business since 1832, is known for diamond and gold jewelry, objets d'art, silver, crystal, and a good gift-wrap department. ✉ *16th and Chestnut Sts.,* ☎ *215/564–6200.*

Harry Sable. Harry "king of the wedding bands" Sable has been selling engagement rings, diamond rings, gold jewelry, and watches for more than 50 years. ✉ *8th and Sansom Sts.,* ☎ *215/627–4014.*

J. E. Caldwell. A local landmark since 1839, the store is adorned with antique handblown crystal chandeliers by Baccarat, making it as elegant as the jewels it sells. Along with traditional and modern jewelry, Caldwell has one of the city's largest selections of giftware and stationery. ✉ *1339 Chestnut St.,* ☎ *215/864–7800.*

Jack Kellmer Co. Diamonds, gold jewelry, and gifts are offered at below retail price. ⊠ *717 Chestnut St.,* ☎ *215/627–8350.*

Lagos—The Store. Here you'll find the largest selection of Lagos jewelry, handcrafted and designed in Philadelphia by Ann and Steven Lagos. Lagos is famous for its "golden wheat" collection of 22-karat contemporary gold jewelry, sold in the boutiques of upscale department stores; this is its only retail store. ⊠ *200 S. 17th St.,* ☎ *215/735–4630.*

Richard Kenneth. On display is jewelry from the late-Georgian, Victorian, art nouveau, art deco, and '40s-retro periods. Kenneth also specializes in repairs and appraisals. ⊠ *202 S. 17th St.,* ☎ *215/545–3355.*

Tiffany & Co. This is the local branch of the store, famous for its exquisite gems, fine crystal and china, and, of course, its signature blue gift box. ⊠ *Shops at the Bellevue, 1414 Walnut St.,* ☎ *215/735–1919.*

Luggage and Leather Goods

Robinson Luggage. The shop carries popular, moderate to expensive brands of luggage, leather, and travel accessories. The selection of briefcases and attaché cases is the largest in the Delaware Valley. ⊠ *201 S. Broad St.,* ☎ *215/735–9859.*

Music

HMV. Known for the huge selection of music in its vast 25,000-square-ft store, HMV also has helpful staff and listening booths. ⊠ *1510 Walnut St.,* ☎ *215/875–5100.*

Theodor Presser. The best selection of sheet music in Center City draws musicians from far and wide. The store specializes in classical but also carries pop and will special order anything. ⊠ *1718 Chestnut St.,* ☎ *215/568–0964.*

Third Street Jazz and Rock. There's still some vinyl here (a few hard-to-find jazz and soul records), but now it's mostly CDs, with a focus on rock, New Wave, reggae, Caribbean, and African music. Salespeople are particularly knowledgeable. ⊠ *20 N. 3rd St.,* ☎ *215/627–3366.*

Tower Records. Open 9 AM to midnight 365 days a year, Tower stocks more than 250,000 CDs and tapes—the largest selection in the city. You can watch music videos on the 20 screens on three floors. Classical music lovers head to the annex across the street. ⊠ *610 South St.,* ☎ *215/574–9888.*

Perfumes

Body Shop de le Parfumier. This "scent boutique" for men and women imports new fragrances, some not yet available elsewhere in the United States. The shop also carries cosmetics, perfume bottles, discontinued scents, and accessories. ⊠ *Bourse Bldg., 21 S. 5th St.,* ☎ *215/922–7660.*

Crabtree and Evelyn. Toiletries and soaps, many imported from Britain and France, as well as specialty foods, fill the shelves. ⊠ *Bourse Bldg., 21 S. 5th St.,* ☎ *215/625–9256).*

Parfumerie Douglas Cosmetics. A wide selection of major brands of perfume, cosmetics, and beauty accessories are found here. ⊠ *Shops at Liberty Place., 1625 Chestnut St.,* ☎ *215/569–0770.*

Shoes

Beige. You'll find a good selection of women's Italian leather shoes in sizes 4–12, priced toward the high end. ⊠ *1715 Walnut St.,* ☎ *215/564–2395.*

Bottino. Men's shoes and accessories are the stars here, all handmade and imported from Italy. Some very big feet get shod here, including those of regular customers Michael Jordan and Sylvester Stallone. ⊠ *121 S. 18th St.,* ☎ *215/854–0907.*

Sherman Brothers Shoes. This off-price retailer of men's shoes has name-brand merchandise and excellent service. The store carries 28 lines of shoes and stocks extra-wide and extra-narrow widths, as well as sizes up to 16. ⊠ *1520 Sansom St.,* ☎ *215/561–4550.*

Strega. There's a wide range of looks for men here, including some exclusive footwear, the custom-made Edward Green line from England, and many top Italian designers. ⊠ *1521 Walnut St.,* ☎ *215/ 564–5932.*

Sporting Goods

City Sports. Beside sports equipment from in-line skates to bike helmets, the store carries plenty of brand-name active wear and its own line of clothing. ⊠ *1608 Walnut St.,* ☎ *215/985–5860.*

Everyone's Racquet. As you might guess, this store's specialty is goods related to racket sports: tennis, racquetball, badminton, squash. Next-day racket-stringing service is available. ⊠ *132 S. 17th St.,* ☎ *215/ 665–1221.*

I. Goldberg. This army-navy-and-everything store isn't stylish, but it is practical, with an emphasis on sporting apparel and camping gear. Goldberg's is crammed with government-surplus, military-style clothing, jeans and work clothes, unusual footwear, and exclusive foreign imports. Rummaging here is a sport in itself. ⊠ *902 Chestnut St.,* ☎ *215/925–9393.*

Rittenhouse Sports. The focus is on shoes and gear for triathlon sports—running, swimming, and cycling—but the store also stocks aerobic and workout shoes and gear. ⊠ *126 S. 18th St.,* ☎ *215/569–9957.*

Toys

Einstein Presents of Mind. The spacious Einstein's has everything from a large selection of nonfiction children's books to Madame Alexander dolls, chess sets, pull toys, and mechanical toys for executives. There are plenty of unique items and a museum, too. ⊠ *1627 Walnut St.,* ☎ *215/665–3622.*

Fat Jack's Comicrypt. For more than 20 years Fat Jack (his real name is Mike) has been buying and selling old and new comics at catalog prices. With more than 500,000 available, this is the largest selection in the Philadelphia area. ⊠ *2006 Sansom St.,* ☎ *215/963–0788.*

Wine and Liquor

Pennsylvania liquor stores are state operated. State stores (as they're known) are generally open Monday and Tuesday 11–7, Wednesday–Saturday 9–9. You may find chilled beer at delis and gourmet shops. For general information, call 215/560–5316.

Wine and Spirits Shoppe. This shop carries one of the best selections of fine wines and liquors in a city where liquor stores are state run. ⊠ *819 Chestnut St.,* ☎ *215/560–6190.*

8 Side Trips from Philadelphia

The Brandywine Valley

Valley Forge

Reading and Environs

Updated by
Janet
Bukovinsky
Teacher

EXPAND YOUR VIEW of the Philadelphia area by taking one or more easy day trips less than two hours from the city. Head southwest from Philadelphia, and in less than an hour you can be immersed in a whole new world. Make that worlds: First you can see the verdant hills and ancient barns of the Brandywine Valley, home to three generations of Wyeths and other artists inspired by the rural landscapes outside their windows. Then you can visit the extravagant realm of du Pont country, whose attractions include Longwood Gardens in nearby Kennett Square and Winterthur, an important repository of American decorative furnishings, over the border in Delaware. Or you can visit the Revolutionary War battlefield of Brandywine, at Chadds Ford. These attractions are favorites of Philadelphians, and area B&Bs and inns make the Brandywine appealing as an overnight or weekend trip as well as a day excursion.

The historical park at Valley Forge adds another dimension to the revolutionary story that began in Independence Hall. Not far away, the town called King of Prussia dates to that period, but today it's primarily synonymous with shopping, thanks to two huge upscale malls just a half hour from Philadelphia and easily accessible by public transportation. For retail consumption on an even grander scale, visit Reading, 65 mi northwest of Philadelphia, a small 19th-century city with major-league outlet centers.

Pleasures and Pastimes

Dining

It seems that most restaurants in the Brandywine Valley serve what is called Continental-American cuisine, yet most also have local specialties—fresh seafood from the Chesapeake Bay and dishes made with Kennett Square mushrooms. For price-category information *see* Chapter 3, which has the dining price chart for Philadelphia.

Gardens

Anyone who has ever paused to admire the simple beauty of spring's first crocus will thrill to the horticultural splendors of the greater Philadelphia area. The Brandywine area alone, at the state's southeast point, is home to some of America's most spectacular botanic sights, including the renowned Longwood Gardens. While touring the Hagley Museum and Library, as well as nearby Winterthur, take time to step outside and appreciate the gorgeous natural backgrounds designed to complement the architecture. The grounds of Rockwood, a rural Gothic manor in Wilmington, Delaware, have splendid landscaping.

Spring, of course, is the most obvious time to visit these glorious oases, but other seasons can be rewarding too: Longwood Gardens, a treat at any time of year, has one of the world's largest conservatories, and Rockwood has a similarly stunning, though smaller, Victorian cast-iron-and-glass garden room. At the Brandywine River Museum, the Brandywine Conservancy's Wildflower and Native Plant Gardens are a riot of fall colors, as are the grounds surrounding the French-inspired parterres of the Hagley Museum and Library.

Lodging

Many Brandywine Valley accommodations call themselves bed-and-breakfasts because they provide beds and serve breakfast, but they are far from the typical B&B—which is usually a room in a private home—and are more accurately characterized as inns or small hotels. Reading has many rooms for shoppers in motels and hotels. For price-category information *see* Chapter 4, which has the lodging price chart for Philadelphia.

THE BRANDYWINE VALLEY

Chances are that travelers journeying to the Brandywine Valley will feel a strong sense of déjà vu. Every hundred yards there seems to be a scene so hauntingly familiar that first-time visitors feel they've seen this area before, a vista so picturesque it virtually seems to spring from a canvas. When Andrew Wyeth immortalized the special landscape of the Brandywine Valley—creating some of the most beloved works in 20th-century American art—he caused many travelers to flock to this valley and fall in love with its peaceful byways. Using colors quintessentially Brandywine—the earthen brown of its hills, gray slate of its stone farmhouses, and dark green of its spruce trees—the famous American realist artist captured the unique personality of the valley: decidedly private, unostentatiously beautiful. Although parts of the valley have become more suburban and U.S. 1 is lined with the usual stores and gas stations, off the main paths there are still enough places to make you feel that you have discovered a tucked-away treasure.

KINGDOM OF THE DU PONTS

The Brandywine Valley actually incorporates parts of three counties in two states: Chester and Delaware counties in Pennsylvania and New Castle County in Delaware. Winding through this scenic region (about 25 mi south of Philadelphia), the Brandywine River flows lazily from West Chester, Pennsylvania, to Wilmington, Delaware. Although in spots it's more a creek than a river, it has nourished many of the valley's economic and artistic endeavors. Although paintings of the Wyeth family distilled the region's mystery, it was the regal du Pont family that provided more than a bit of its magnificence, recontouring the land with grand gardens, mansions, and mills. Their kingdom was founded by the family patriarch, Pierre-Samuel du Pont, who had escaped with his family from post-Revolutionary France and settled in northern Delaware. The Du Pont company was founded in 1802 by his son Éleuthère Irénée (E. I.), who made the family fortune, first in gunpowder and iron and later in chemicals and textiles.

E. I. and five generations of du Ponts lived in Eleutherian Mills, the stately family home on the grounds of a black-powder mill that has been transformed into the Hagley Museum. The home, from which Mrs. Henry du Pont was driven after accidental blasts at the powder works, was closed in 1921. Louise du Pont Crowninshield, a great-granddaughter of E. I., restored the house fully before opening it to the public. Louise's relatives were busy, too. Henry Francis was filling his country estate, Winterthur, with furniture by Duncan Phyfe, silver by Paul Revere, decorative objects, and entire interior woodwork fittings salvaged from homes built between 1640 and 1840.

Pierre devoted his life to horticulture. He bought a 1,000-acre 19th-century arboretum and created Longwood Gardens, where he entertained his many friends and relatives. Today 350 acres of the meticulously landscaped gardens are open to the public. Displays range from a tropical rain forest to a desert; acres of heated conservatories, where flowers are in bloom year-round, create eternal summer. Pierre also built the grand Hotel du Pont in downtown Wilmington adjacent to company headquarters. No expense was spared; more than 18 French and Italian craftspeople labored for two years, carving, gilding, and painting. Alfred I. du Pont's country estate, Nemours, was named after the family's ancestral home in north-central France. It encompasses 300 acres of French gardens and a mansion in Louis XVI style.

WYETH COUNTRY

For many travelers the Brandywine Valley will always be Wyeth country first and foremost, for here is where three generations of artists found landscapes worthy of their talents. Although Andrew Wyeth is the most famous local artist, the area's artistic tradition began long before, when artist-illustrator Howard Pyle started a school in the valley. He had more than 100 students, including Andrew's father, N. C. Wyeth; Frank Schoonover; Jessie Willcox Smith; and Harvey Dunn. It was that tradition which inspired Andrew and his son Jamie.

In 1967 local residents formed the Brandywine Conservancy to prevent industrialization of the area and pollution of the river. In 1971 they opened the Brandywine River Museum in a preserved 19th-century gristmill. It celebrates the Brandywine School of artists in a setting much in tune with their world.

OTHER PLEASURES

The valley is also the site of one of the more dramatic turns in the American Revolution, the Battle of Brandywine, and an offbeat museum that celebrates the mushroom. Antiques shops, fine restaurants, cozy country inns, and reliable bed-and-breakfasts dot the region. Your best bet is to rent a car and explore on your own with the help of a map (☞ Visitor Information *in* Brandywine Valley A to Z, *below*).

If you start early enough, you can tour the valley's top three attractions—the Brandywine River Museum, Longwood Gardens, and Winterthur—in one day. You'd have to limit your time at each stop, however. If you have more time to spend in the valley, you can stop in to see the additional sites in Pennsylvania and then move on to Delaware.

Numbers in the text correspond to numbers in the margin and on the Brandywine Valley map.

Wawa

20 mi southwest of Philadelphia.

For visitors, the highlight of this small town is the museum of a well-known private mint. The **Franklin Mint Museum,** operated by the company that creates well-known collectibles, displays uniquely designed coins, precision die-cast model cars, porcelain dolls, objets d'art from the House of Igor Carl Fabergé, and sculptures in crystal, pewter, and bronze. You can also see original works by Andrew Wyeth and Norman Rockwell here. ⊠ *U.S. 1,* ☎ *610/459–6168.* ☑ *Free.* ☺ *Mon.– Sat. 9:30–4:30, Sun. 1–4:30.*

Lodging

$$$–$$$$ ⊞ **Sweetwater Farm.** A handsome 18th-century fieldstone farmhouse
    ★   has been lovingly restored into a homey inn serving hearty breakfasts. A shaded porch lined with rockers overlooks the 50-acre horse farm; no other houses are in sight. Rooms have fresh flowers, fragrant potpourri, and reproductions of period furnishings, including some canopy beds. Rooms in the newer section (circa 1815) of the house are larger. The farm is off U.S. 1. ⊠ *50 Sweetwater Rd., Glen Mills 19342,* ☎ *610/459–4711 or 800/SWEETWATER. 6 rooms, 5 cottages. Pool, horseback riding. AE, MC, V.*

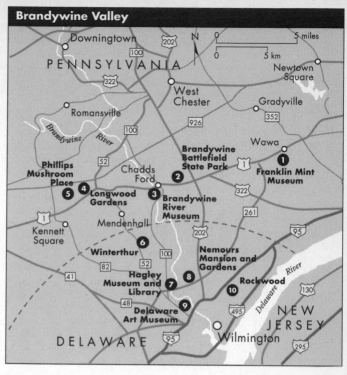

Brandywine Valley

Chadds Ford

10 mi southwest of Wawa.

A Revolutionary War battlefield park and a museum celebrating area artists make this historic town appealing. There are some pretty side roads to explore as well as the Chaddsford Winery (⊠ U.S. 1, ☎ 610/388–6221).

② **Brandywine Battlefield State Park** is near the site of the Battle of Brandywine, where British general William Howe and his troops defeated George Washington on September 11, 1777. The Continental Army then fled to Lancaster, leaving Philadelphia vulnerable to British troops. The visitor center has audiovisual materials and displays about the battle that are a good introduction to the area's history. On the site are two restored Quaker farmhouses that once sheltered Washington and Lafayette. The 50-acre park is a fine place for a picnic. ⊠ *U.S. 1,* ☎ *610/459–3342.* ⊠ *Park free; house tours $3.50.* ☉ *Tues.–Sat. 9–5, Sun. noon–6.*

★ **③** In a converted Civil War–era gristmill, the **Brandywine River Museum** showcases the art of Chadds Ford native Andrew Wyeth, a major American realist painter, and his family: his father, N. C. Wyeth, illustrator of many children's classics; his sisters Henriette and Carolyn; and his son Jamie. The collection also emphasizes still life, landscape paintings, and American illustration, with works by such artists as Howard Pyle and Maxfield Parrish. The glass-walled lobby overlooks the river and countryside that inspired the Brandywine School earlier in the century. The museum uses a system of filters, baffles, and blinds to direct natural light. Outside the museum, you can visit a garden with regional wildflowers and follow a 1-mi nature trail along the river.

The N. C. Wyeth Studio, where N. C. painted, is open part of the year; this highlight gives an intimate feeling for his artistic process and is worth the extra fee. The 1911 studio, set on a hill, holds many of the props N. C. used in creating his illustrations. A shuttle (departures every 50 minutes) takes you from the museum to the studio for a 30-minute guided tour. ⊠ *U.S. 1 and Rte. 100,* ☎ *610/388–2700.* 💶 *$5; $2.50 additional for studio.* ☉ *Museum: daily 9:30–4:30; studio: Apr.–Oct., Wed.–Sun. 10–3:15.*

OFF THE BEATEN PATH	**ROUTE 100 –** For a scenic, curving route to Wilmington, or just a pretty drive, follow Route 100 south from Chadds Ford. This is the countryside captured in the works of the Wyeths and other artists, and if you take time to study their paintings at the Brandywine River Museum before you begin, you'll see the land in a new light. You can also drive Route 100 north toward West Chester. If you do, stop at Baldwin's Book Barn (⊠ 865 Lenape Rd., Rte. 100, ☎ 610/696–0816), a barn packed with used books, prints, maps, and more.

Dining and Lodging

$$–$$$ ✕ **Chadds Ford Inn.** Within walking distance of the Brandywine River Museum, the inn was once a lively rest stop on the Wilmington-Philadelphia-Lancaster commerce route. The inn now welcomes you to a Colonial-period dining room, complete with candlelight, stone hearts, and Wyeth prints. Continental-American dishes, such as roasted salmon with fresh ginger and sun-dried tomato purée and pecan-wood-smoked free-range chicken with roasted corn and andouille, are served up in generous portions. ⊠ *Rte. 100 and U.S. 1,* ☎ *610/388–7361. AE, DC, MC, V.*

$$ 🏨 **Brandywine River Hotel.** This small, modern two-story hotel across the highway from the Brandywine River Museum has tasteful Queen Anne furnishings, classic English chintz, and florals that create a homey feeling. Suites have fireplaces and whirlpool baths. Complimentary Continental breakfast and afternoon tea are served in a pretty room with a fireplace. The hotel's restaurant, the Chadds Ford Inn (☞ *above*) is adjacent. Ask about special packages. ⊠ *Rte. 100 and U.S. 1, 19317,* ☎ *610/388–1200. 30 rooms, 10 suites. Restaurant, business services, meeting rooms. AE, D, DC, MC, V.*

Kennett Square

7 mi west of Chadds Ford.

This town has a long history that has left its downtown full of interesting buildings in different styles, but most people come here to visit Longwood Gardens and perhaps to stop at the mushroom museum that has information about one of the area's most important businesses.

★ ❹ **Longwood Gardens,** 3 mi northeast of Kennett Square, has established an international reputation for its immaculate, colorful gardens full of flowers and blossoming shrubs. In 1906 Pierre Samuel du Pont bought a simple Quaker farm, famous for its trees, and turned it into the ultimate early 20th-century estate garden. Fabulous seasonal attractions include magnolias and azaleas in spring, roses and water lilies in summer, fall foliage and chrysanthemums, and winter camellias, orchids, and palms. You can stroll in the Italian water garden or explore a meadow full of wildflowers on the garden's 350 acres. Bad weather is no problem here, as 3½ acres of exotic foliage, cacti, ferns, and bonsai are housed in heated conservatories; it's easy to spend an hour or more touring these. The Heritage exhibit in the 1730 Peirce–du Pont House traces the last 300 years of evolution, historical and horticultural, of the Longwood area. The spectacular illuminated fountain displays on Tuesday, Thursday, and Saturday evenings in summer are very popular; the gardens stay open until almost 10. The cafeteria (open year-round) and dining room (closed January–March) serve pleasant, reasonably priced meals. ⊠ *U.S. 1,* ☎ *610/388–1000.* ⌑ *$10 ($6 Tues.).* ☉ *Apr.–Oct., daily 9–6; Nov.–Mar., daily 9–5; plus some evenings in summer and Thanksgiving–Christmas.*

❺ Phillips Mushroom Place is a small museum devoted exclusively to a fungus—the mushroom. Mushrooms are Pennsylvania's number-one cash crop, and most are grown in Kennett Square, which labels itself the "mushroom capital of the world." The history, lore, and growing process of mushrooms is explained with dioramas, exhibits, and an 18-minute film. The gift shop sells a mushroom gift pack suitable for mailing. ⊠ *909 E. Baltimore Pike, U.S. 1,* ☎ *610/388–6082.* ⌑ *$1.25.* ☉ *Daily 10–6.*

Dining and Lodging

$$–$$$$ ✕ **Mendenhall Inn.** Continental and American cuisine is served in this 1790s Quaker mill building, which still has its old beams intact. Seafood, prime rib, and game are specialties. For lunch request a table with a courtyard view; at Saturday dinner ask for the Mill Room upstairs. ⊠ *Rte. 52, Mendenhall, 1 mi south of U.S. 1, 3 mi east of Kennett Square,* ☎ *610/388–1181. Reservations essential. Jacket and tie. AE, D, DC, MC, V.*

$$–$$$ ▦ **Fairville Inn.** Ole and Patti Retlev's inn, halfway between Longwood Gardens and Winterthur, has bright, airy rooms furnished with Queen Anne and Hepplewhite reproductions. There's a main house, built in 1826; a remodeled barn; and a carriage house. Request a room in the back of the property, away from traffic. The main house has a striking living room with a large fireplace. The Fairville serves a complimentary light breakfast and afternoon tea. Note that this inn is not suitable for children under 10 and is totally no-smoking. ⊠ *506 Rte. 52, Kennett Pike, Mendenhall 19357,* ☎ *610/388–5900,* 𝔽𝔸𝕏 *610/388–5902. 13 rooms, 2 suites. Business services. AE, D, MC, .*

$$ ▦ **Meadow Spring Farm.** Anne Hicks's farmhouse is a gallery for her family's antiques, dolls, teddy bears, and Santas. Rooms have Amish quilts and televisions. A full country breakfast is served daily on the glassed-in porch. Children are welcome here, and they will particularly enjoy the farm animals. ⊠ *201 E. Street Rd., 19348,* ☎ *610/444–3903. 6 rooms, 4 with bath. Pool, hot tub, fishing. No credit cards.*

Wilmington

15 mi southeast of Kennett Square.

Surrounded by bigger cities, Wilmington is one of the quieter stops on the eastern corridor. It began in 1638 as a Swedish settlement and later was populated by employees of various du Pont family businesses and nearby poultry ranches. Today the state's pro-business policies have enticed many multinational corporations. Outside the compact city center are some good museums, including some that are legacies of the du Ponts.

 ★ ❻ Henry Francis du Pont housed his 89,000 objects of American decorative art in a nine-story mansion called **Winterthur**; today the collection is recognized as one of the nation's finest. The 1640–1860 furniture, silver, paintings, and textiles are displayed in 175 period room settings in the original house; a selection of those can be seen on guided tours. The galleries have permanent displays and changing exhibits of decorative arts and crafts; you can tour these on your own. Surrounding the museum are 200 acres of landscaped lawns and gardens, worth a visit in themselves, especially in spring when the azaleas and other plants are flowering. Winterthur's Yuletide Tour (November 15–December 31) showcases the holiday traditions of early America. Gift shops sell high-quality licensed merchandise, books, and more, and there is a cafeteria and a restaurant. ⊠ *Rte. 52, 5 mi south of U.S. 1,* ☎ *302/888–4600.* ☞ *$8–$21 (depending on tour selected, but all include garden tram);* ☉ *Mon.–Sat. 9–5, Sun. 12–5.*

❼ Hagley Museum and Library offers a glimpse of the du Ponts at work and an illuminating look at the development of early industrial America. A restored mid-19th-century mill community on 240 landscaped acres, Hagley is the site of the first Du Pont black-powder mills, built by E. I. du Pont. Exhibits, including a restored workers' community complete with schoolhouse and worker's house, depict the dangerous work of the early explosives industry. One building holds dioramas and working models. Admission includes a bus ride with stops at Eleutherian Mills, an 1803 Georgian-style home furnished by five generations of du Ponts, and a French Renaissance–style garden. Allow about two hours for your visit. The coffee shop is open for lunch except in winter. ⊠ *Rte. 141 between Rte. 100 and U.S. 202,* ☎ *302/658–2400.* ☞ *$9.75.* ☉ *Mar. 15–Dec., daily 9:30–4:30; Jan.–Mar. 14, weekends 9:30–4:30; winter tours, weekdays at 1:30.*

❽ For a look at how the wealthy and tasteful lived, visit **Nemours Mansion and Gardens,** a 300-acre country estate built for Alfred I. du Pont in 1910. This modified Louis XVI château showcases 102 rooms of European and American furnishings, rare rugs, tapestries, and art dating to the 15th century. The gardens, reminiscent of those at Versailles, are landscaped with fountains, pools, and statuary. The estate can only be seen on the guided two-hour tours. ⊠ *Rockland Rd., between Rte. 141 and U.S. 202,* ☎ *302/651–6912.* ☞ *$10;* ☉ *May–Nov.; tours Tues.–Sat. at 9, 11, 1, and 3; Sun. at 11, 1, and 3 (reservations required).*

❾ The **Delaware Art Museum** has a several notable strengths, including a good collection of the paintings of Howard Pyle (1853–1911), a Wilmington native known as the "father of American illustration," and his students—N. C. Wyeth, Frank Schoonover, and Maxfield Parrish. Pyle's work has an appealingly direct realism. Other American artists represented include Benjamin West, Winslow Homer, Edward Glackens, and Edward Hopper. The museum also houses the largest American collection of 19th-century English pre-Raphaelite paintings and decorative arts and a children's participatory gallery. ⊠ *2301 Kentmere Pkwy.,* ☎ *302/571–9590.* ☞ *$5.* ☉ *Tues.–Sat. 10–5, Sun. noon–5.*

❿ Rockwood, a quietly elegant English-style country house and a fine example of rural Gothic architecture, stands in contrast to the opulent French-inspired du Pont homes in the area. Built in 1851 by Joseph Shipley, a Quaker merchant, the house is now a museum filled with 17th- to 20th-century American, European, and Asian decorative arts and furnishings. There is a guided tour of the mansion. ⊠ *610 Shipley Rd.,* ☎ *302/761–4340.* ☞ *$5.* ☉ *Jan.–Feb., Tues.–Sat. 11–3; Mar.–Dec., Tues.–Sun. 11–3.*

Dining and Lodging

$$$–$$$$ ✕ **Green Room.** For years Philadelphians have trekked to Wilmington
★ to celebrate special occasions in the famous Hotel du Pont restaurant.
Classic French cuisine is served in Edwardian splendor under a gold-
encrusted ceiling with massive Spanish chandeliers and high French win-
dows. Harp music accompanies formal dinners. ⊠ *Hotel du Pont, 11th
and Market Sts.,* ☎ *302/594–3100. Reservations essential. Jacket re-
quired. AE, D, DC, MC, V.*

$$–$$$$ ▦ **Hotel du Pont.** Built in 1913 by Pierre-Samuel du Pont, the hotel is
an elegant 12-story building with an old-world feel. The lobby has a
spectacular decorative ceiling, polished marble walls, and carved paneling. Spacious guest rooms have high ceilings, 18th-century reproduction
furnishings, and original art. ⊠ *11th and Market Sts., Wilmington, DE
19801,* ☎ *302/594–3100 or 800/441–9019,* ℻ *302/594–3108. 216
rooms. 3 restaurants, lobby lounge, theater. AE, D, DC, MC, V.*

Brandywine Valley A to Z

Arriving and Departing

BY BUS

From Philadelphia, **Greyhound Lines** (☎ 215/931–4075 or 800/231–
2222) operates out of the terminal at 10th and Filbert streets, just north
of the Market East commuter rail station. There are about 10 daily
departures to the Wilmington terminal at 101 North French Street. The
trip takes one hour.

BY CAR

Take U.S. 1 south from Philadelphia; the Brandywine Valley is about
25 mi from Philadelphia, and many attractions are on U.S. 1. To reach
Wilmington, pick up U.S. 202 south just past Concordville or take I–
95 south from Philadelphia.

BY TRAIN

Amtrak (☎ 215/824–1600 or 800/872–7245) has frequent service from
Philadelphia's 30th Street Station to Wilmington, at Martin Luther King
Jr. Boulevard and French Street on the edge of downtown. It's a 25-
minute ride.

Getting Around

Driving is the easiest way to see the area's spread-out attractions.

Contacts and Resources

B&B RESERVATION AGENCIES

This is a popular area for B&Bs; for information ☞ Chapter 4.

GUIDED TOURS

Colonial Pathways (⊠ Box 879, Chadds Ford 19317, ☎ 610/388–
2654) guides escort you—in your car—for full-day excursions. You can
plan the itinerary or have them do it for you. Call for reservations.

Brandywine Tours (⊠ 20 Woodland Dr., Glen Mills 19342, ☎ 610/
358–5445) will pick you up at your Philadelphia hotel on Tuesday,
Friday or Saturday morning for full-day excursions in a 15-person van.
Call for reservations.

VISITOR INFORMATION

The **Brandywine Valley Tourist Information Center** (⊠ U.S. 1 north of
Kennett Sq., ☎ 610/388–2900 or 800/228–9933), in the Longwood
Progressive Meeting House at the entrance to Longwood Gardens, has
information on attractions, lodging, and restaurants. It's open daily
10–6 from May to September and 10–5 from October to April. The

Brandywine information center is run by the **Chester County Tourist Bureau,** which has its main office at the Government Services Center (⊠ 601 Westtown Rd., Suite 170, West Chester 19382, ☎ 610/344–6365).

For good road maps and guides, contact the **Delaware County Convention and Visitors Bureau** (⊠ 200 E. State St., Suite 100, Media 19063, ☎ 610/565–3679 or 610/565–3666 for tape of events). The **Greater Wilmington Convention and Visitors Bureau** (⊠ 100 W. 10 St., Wilmington, DE 19801, ☎ 302/652–4088) has maps and information.

VALLEY FORGE

A visit to the monuments, markers, huts, and headquarters in Valley Forge National Historical Park, 20 mi from Center City, Philadelphia can illuminate early American history. The park preserves the area where George Washington's Continental Army endured the bitter winter of 1777–78. This is an area rich in history, offering an awesome beauty that seems to whisper of the past. If the weather is fine, consider renting a bicycle or packing a lunch and picnicking in the park.

Other nearby attractions are Mill Grove, the home of naturalist John James Audubon; the studio and residence of craftsman Wharton Esherick; and The Plaza & The Court, one of the nation's largest shopping complexes.

Numbers in the text correspond to numbers in the margin and on the Valley Forge map.

Valley Forge

20 mi from Philadelphia.

Near the village of Valley Forge is a major site of the Revolutionary War. The town was named because of an iron forge built in the 1740s.

★ ❶ **Valley Forge National Historical Park,** administered by the National Park Service, is the location of the 1777–78 winter encampment of General George Washington and the Continental Army. Stop first at the visitor center for an 18-minute orientation film, exhibits, and a map for a 10-mi self-guided auto tour of the attractions in the 3,600-acre park. Stops include reconstructed huts of the Muhlenberg Brigade and the National Memorial Arch, which pays tribute to the soldiers who suffered through the infamous winter. Other sites are the bronze equestrian statue on the encampment of General Anthony Wayne and his Pennsylvania troops; Artillery Park, where the soldiers stored their cannons; and the Isaac Potts House, which served as Washington's headquarters. From June through September you can purchase an auto-tour cassette tape for $8 or rent a tape and player for $10.

Here's the background: The army had just lost the battles of Brandywine, White Horse, and Germantown. While the British occupied Philadelphia, Washington's soldiers were forced to endure horrid conditions—blizzards, inadequate food and clothing, damp quarters, and disease. Many men deserted, and although no battle was fought at Valley Forge, 2,000 American soldiers died.

The troops did win one victory that winter—a war of will. The forces slowly regained strength and confidence under the leadership of Prussian drillmaster Friedrich von Steuben. In June 1778 Washington led his troops away from Valley Forge in search of the British. Fortified, the Continental Army was able to carry on the fight for five years more.

The park contains 7 mi of jogging and bicycling paths and hiking trails,

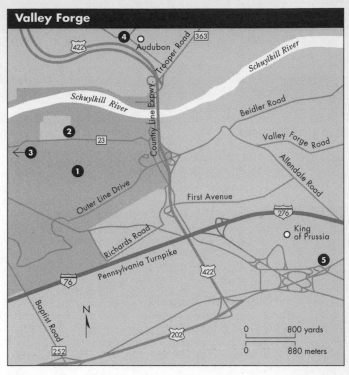

and you can picnic at any of three designated areas. A leisurely visit to the park will take no more than half a day. ✉ *Rtes. 23 and 363, Box 953, Valley Forge 19481,* ☎ *610/783–1077.* ✎ *Washington's head-quarters: $2.* ☉ *Daily 9–5.*

❷ The **Valley Forge Historical Society Museum** tells the Valley Forge story with military equipment and Colonial artifacts plus a large collection of items that belonged to Martha and George Washington. The nearby Chapel Cabin Shop sells homemade goodies such as Martha's 16-Bean Soup and blue-barb jam. ✉ *Alongside the Washington Memorial Chapel on Rte. 23,* ☎ *610/783–0535.* ✎ *$1.50.* ☉ *Mon.–Sat. 9:30–4:30, Sun. 1–4:30.*

On the Horseshoe Trail, 2 mi west of Valley Forge National Histori-
❸ cal Park, is the **Wharton Esherick Museum,** the former home and stu-dio of the "Dean of American Crafts." Best known for his sculptural furniture, Esherick shaped a new aesthetic in decorative arts by bridg-ing art with furniture. The museum houses 200 samples of his work—paintings, woodcuts, furniture, and wood sculptures. The studio, in which everything from the light switches to the spiral staircase is hand-carved, is one of his monumental achievements. ✉ *1520 Horseshoe Trail,* ☎ *610/644–5822.* ✎ *$6.* ☉ *Mar.–Dec., Sat. 10–5, Sun. 1–5 for hourly guided tours (reservations required). Group tours (at least 5 people) weekdays.*

Audubon

2 mi north of Valley Forge.

The main reason to visit Audubon is its connection with the early Amer-
❹ ican naturalist of the same name. **Mill Grove** was the first American home of Haitian-born artist and naturalist John James Audubon. Built

in 1762, the house is now a museum displaying Audubon's major works, including reproductions, original prints, his paintings of birds and wildlife, and the double-elephant folio of his *Birds of America*. The attic has been restored to a studio and taxidermy room. The Audubon Wildlife Sanctuary has 170 acres with a marked hiking trail along Perkiomen Creek. ⊠ *Audubon and Pawlings Rds.,* ☎ *610/666–5593.* ▣ *Free.* ☉ *Museum: Tues.–Sat. 10–4, Sun. 1–4. Grounds: Tues.–Sun. dawn–dusk.*

King of Prussia

5 mi southeast of Audubon.

⑤ Shopping is a main draw in this busy suburban town. For lunch or an afternoon of browsing, head for **The Plaza & The Court,** one of the nation's largest shopping complexes (☞ Shopping Districts and Malls *in* Chapter 7). These two adjacent malls contain more than 35 restaurants, 450 shops and boutiques, and nine major department stores, including Bloomingdale's, Nordstrom, and Neiman Marcus. ⊠ *Rte. 202 at the Schuykill Expressway, 160 N. Gulph Rd.,* ☎ *610/265–5727 for the Plaza,* ☎ *610/337–1210 for the Court.* ☉ *Mon.–Sat. 10–9:30, Sun. 11–5.*

Dining and Lodging

$$$ ✕ **Kennedy Supplee Restaurant.** French and northern Italian cuisine is served in the seven dining rooms of a circa 1852 Italian Renaissance mansion overlooking Valley Forge National Historical Park. ⊠ *1100 W. Valley Forge Rd.,* ☎ *610/337–3777. Jacket required. AE, MC, V. No lunch weekends.*

$$ ✕ **Lily Langtry's Dinner Theater.** This lavishly appointed Victorian-era restaurant/cabaret serves American and Continental dishes, but the campy Las Vegas–style entertainment—corny comedians, showgirls, and some fine singers and dancers—is the real draw here. ⊠ *Valley Forge Sheraton Hotel, 1160 1st Ave.,* ☎ *610/337–5459. Reservations required. AE, D, DC, MC, V.*

$–$$ ✕ **Jefferson House.** When a venerable classic undergoes change, people are sometimes slow to catch on. Tom Groff, general manager and executive chef, has wrought just such changes by installing his own elegant dishes in addition to the standards that diners at this large beautiful restaurant are used to ordering, both for every day and special occasions. White truffle gnocchi, Black Angus beef crusted with aged provolone, and game dishes (in season) are among his signature dishes. The lush grounds of this Prohibition-era mansion, complete with currently inactive subterranean speakeasy, are worth a stroll. ⊠ *2519 DeKalb Pike, Norristown, 4 mi northeast of King of Prussia,* ☎ *610/ 275–3407. AE, DC, MC, V.*

$$ ▥ **Valley Forge Sheraton Hotel and Convention Center.** Two bustling high-rises cater to groups and couples escaping to Jacuzzi-equipped fantasy theme suites—a prehistoric cave, a wild-and-woolly jungle, the outer-space-like "Outer Limits." Regular rooms and executive suites are contemporary in style. There are excellent champagne-and-dinner-theater packages at **Lily Langtry's Dinner Theater** (☞ *above*). ⊠ *1160 1st Ave., 19406,* ☎ *610/337–2000 or 800/325–3535,* ℻ *610/768–3222. 398 rooms, 50 suites, 40 fantasy suites. 4 restaurants, piano bar, pool, health club, comedy club, theater, convention center. AE, D, DC, MC, V.*

Valley Forge A to Z

Arriving and Departing

BY BUS

On weekdays **SEPTA** (☎ 215/580−7800) Bus 125 leaves from 16th Street and John F. Kennedy Boulevard (departing hourly starting at 5:30 AM) for King of Prussia (including The Plaza & the Court) and continues on to Valley Forge National Historical Park. On Saturday transfer at the plaza to the Royersford, Bus 99, which goes through the park. Bus 99 departs hourly. On Sunday Bus 99 does not run; Bus 125 goes as far as the Valley Forge Sheraton Hotel, less than a mile from the park but along busy roads.

BY CAR

Take the Schuylkill Expressway (I−76) west from Philadelphia to Exit 25 (Goddard Boulevard). Take Route 363 to North Gulph Road and follow signs to Valley Forge National Historical Park. Exit 25 also provides easy access to the Plaza & the Court shopping complex.

Getting Around

You can get to several sites, such as Valley Forge National Historical Park and The Plaza & The Court by bus, but a car is helpful for touring the large park and for traveling between sights.

Contacts and Resources

B&B RESERVATION AGENCIES

This is a popular area for B&Bs; for information ☞ Chapter 4.

GUIDED TOURS

The **Valley Forge National Historical Park Bus Tour** (☎ 610/783−1077) is a narrated minibus tour that originates from the park's visitor center (✉ Rte. 23 and N. Gulph Rd.). Passengers can alight, visit sites, and reboard. Tours are scheduled from June through September; times vary. Tours cost $5.50.

VISITOR INFORMATION

Valley Forge Convention and Visitors Bureau (✉ 600 W. Germantown Pike, Suite 130, Plymouth Meeting 19462, ☎ 610/834−1550 or 800/441−3549). Call or write for information packet. **Valley Forge Country Funline** (☎ 610/834−8844) offers information about special events and exhibits 24 hours a day.

READING AND ENVIRONS

Northwest of Philadelphia lies Reading (*Red*-ing), a city of 78,000 residents, but one whose population often swells considerably thanks to hordes of shop-till-you-droppers. They arrive by car, bus, and train, attracted to the city's claim to fame as the "outlet capital of the world."

Reading is an easy 90-minute drive from Philadelphia, and the major outlets can be scanned in a day. Most outlet complexes have cafeterias or food courts. If you want another day to shop or sightsee, you have numerous overnight options; the success of the outlet stores has led to a hotel and restaurant renaissance.

Sitting prettily atop Mt. Penn on Skyline Drive is the Pagoda, a seven-story building of Japanese design, which provides an expansive view of the city. Skyline Drive is a meandering road with miles of unspoiled vistas. The Daniel Boone Homestead, the frontiersman's renovated home, and the Mary Merritt Doll Museum make good diversions after a shopping spree.

Numbers in the text correspond to numbers in the margins and on the Reading Environs and Reading maps.

Morgantown

55 mi from Philadelphia.

❶ Stop in this town off the Pennsylvania Turnpike if you can't wait until Reading to load up your shopping bag. The **Home Furnishing and Fashion Outlet Mall,** formerly Manufacturers Outlet Mall, is a typical suburban enclosed shopping mall, with 23 stores on one level, including Van Heusen, Pennsylvania House Furniture, Drexel Heritage and Oak Gallery, Arrow, and London Fog. Attached to the mall is a 200-room Holiday Inn (☎ 610/286–3000) and indoor recreation center with pool. The food court serves lunch and dinner. ✉ *Exit 22, Pennsylvania Turnpike, Rtes. 23 and 10,* ☎ *610/286–2000.* ◷ *Mon.–Wed. 10–6, Thurs.–Sat. 10–9, Sun noon–6.*

Reading

65 mi from Philadelphia.

Once the city had a claim to fame other than shopping: Founded by William Penn's sons Thomas and Richard, it was celebrated in the 19th-century as the terminus of the Reading Railroad. Today most visitors hop off the bus and head straight for the outlets. Not for nothing does the city continue to draw thousands of bargain hunters enticed by those alluring promises of savings up to 75% off retail: There are outlets for clothing, pretzels, candy, luggage, jewelry, shoes, pet food—even tropical fish!

This method of merchandising began when local factories and mills started selling overruns and seconds to employees. Eventually, small stores sprang up inside the factories. About 10 million visitors a year, many on bus excursions from all over the East Coast, now visit some 300 outlets within a 4-mi radius of Reading. A large number of outlets are grouped together in former factory complexes.

In recent years outlets with narrow wooden stairs and sawdust on the floors have given way to upscale shopping. Most outlets are indistinguishable from normal retail stores, complete with carpeting, fitting rooms, sales clerks, and classical music playing in the background. Designer labels, including Ralph Lauren, Calvin Klein, Karl Lagerfeld, Mark Cross, Coach, and Yves Saint Laurent, are discounted.

It's easy to get caught up in the buying frenzy as you browse through racks marked $10 and under, but not all the buys are bargains. If an item is marked IRREGULAR, look it over carefully. It may be fine, or it may have noticeable imperfections. An added shopping bonus is that Pennsylvania has no sales tax on clothing.

❷ The **VF Outlet Village** offers some of the best buys and the largest variety of goods in the city. In what was once the world's largest hosiery mill, the complex originally sold surplus hosiery, sleepwear, and lingerie. Today it consists of nine major buildings on more than 900,000 square ft, with over 90 outlets. The VF factory outlet store carries a vast selection of Lee jeans, women's sleepwear, and lingerie from Vanity Fair and Lollipop, Healthtex, and Jantzen and Jansport active wear, all at half price. Designers Place has a three-story glass atrium, with a food court and about 15 upscale outlets, including Anne Klein, Perry Ellis, Carole Little, and Tommy Hilfiger. Shuttle buses take shoppers

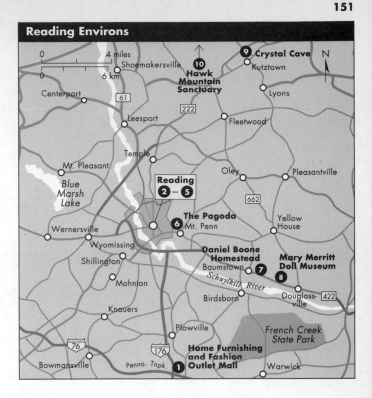

Reading Environs

0   4 miles
0   6 km

Centerport
Shoemakersville
9 Crystal Cave
Kutztown
10 Hawk Mountain Sanctuary
Lyons
Leesport
Fleetwood
Temple
Mt. Pleasant
Blue Marsh Lake
Oley
Pleasantville
Reading 2 – 5
Wernersville
The Pagoda 6 Mt. Penn
Yellow House
Wyomissing
Daniel Boone Homestead
Baumstown **7**
Mary Merritt Doll Museum 8
Shillington
Schuylkill River
Mohnton
Birdsboro
Douglass-ville
Knauers
Plowville
French Creek State Park
Bowmansville
Penna. Tnpk.
Home Furnishing and Fashion 1 Outlet Mall
Warwick

to and from the parking lot. ✉ *Park Rd. and Hill Ave.,* ☎ *610/378–0408 or 800/772–8336.* ☉ *Weekdays 9–9, Sat. 9–7 (July–Dec., 8–9), Sun. 10–5.*

❸ The **Reading Outlet Center** occupies a former silk-stocking mill in the heart of the city and houses more than 70 shops on four floors plus stores in nearby buildings. Items for sale range from coffee and cosmetics to sporting goods and wine. There's a Polo/Ralph Lauren outlet, Fashion Flair's Izod Lacoste clothes, Timberland, Burberry's, and Corning. The Russ-Villager-Crazyhorse occupies a site nearby, at 832 Oley Street. The center has a restaurant, too. ✉ *801 N. 9th St.,* ☎ *610/ 373–5495.* ☉ *Mon.–Sat. 9:30–8, Sun. 11–5.*

❹ **Outlets on Hiesters Lane** is a grouping of three outlet buildings along one city block at the north end of downtown Reading. Some of the stores here are the Mikasa Factory Store, Burlington Coat Factory Warehouse, Luxury Linen, Baby Depot, and Kids Depot. ✉ *Corner of Hiesters La. and Kutztown Rd.,* ☎ *610/921–8130.* ☉ *Most stores Mon.–Sat. 9:30–9, Sun.10–5.*

❺ **Reading Station** bills itself as the "upscale outlet experience." This $23 million outlet complex is modeled after a turn-of-the-century Pennsylvania railroad village on the site of the former Reading Company railroad. The five buildings surrounding the courtyard display railroad memorabilia and house restaurants and about 30 factory outlet stores, including WestPoint Steven's Bed, Bath & Linens, Calvin Klein, and He-Ro Group, featuring Oleg Cassini. ✉ *951 N. 6th St.,* ☎ *610/478–7000.* ☉ *Mon.–Thurs. 9:30–7, Fri.–Sat. 9:30–8, Sun. 11–5.*

❻ The **Pagoda,** a seven-story Japanese castle attached to the top of Mt. Penn by 10 tons of bolts, provides a panoramic view of the Reading

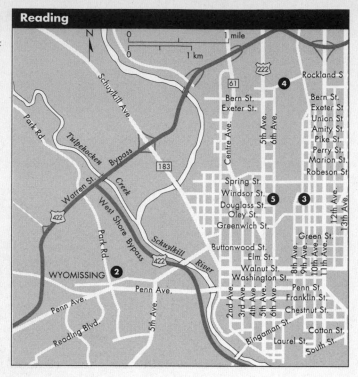

Reading

area. Built in 1908 as a mountaintop resort, it is now the home of the Berks Arts Council. An art gallery on the second floor has changing exhibits. ⊠ *Skyline Dr.,* ☎ *610/655–6374.* 🎫 *Free.* ⊙ *Daily 11–5.*

OFF THE
BEATEN PATH

BLUE MARSH LAKE – This 6,300-acre park with an 1,150-acre lake is run by the U.S. Army Corps of Engineers as a recreational park, with hiking, picnicking, and swimming. ⊠ *Leesport, 5 mi northwest of Reading on Rte. 183,* ☎ *610/376–6337.* ⊙ *Daily 8–dusk.*

Dining and Lodging

$$–$$$ ✕ **Dans.** Named for two guys called Dan who run the place, this restaurant across from City Park is one of the region's best bets for contemporary American cuisine. Each menu selection seems more tantalizing than the last: orange-glazed achiote pork loin, pasta with sausage and sage. Save room for the strawberries Chantilly—berries served with whipped cream on flaky pastry floating in caramel sauce. At lunchtime moderately priced salads and sandwiches entice. Thanks to the tranquil decor, a great glass of wine, and attentive service, dining at Dans is always a relaxed affair—and a welcome relief for shoppers after a hectic day. ⊠ *1049 Penn St., at 11th St.,* ☎ *610/373–2075. Reservations essential. AE, D, MC, V. Closed Sun.– Mon.*

$–$$$ ✕ **Joe's Bistro 614.** The success of local chef Jack Czarnecki's *Joe's Book of Mushroom Cookery* and *A Cook's Book of Mushrooms* (the definitive mushroom cookbooks) has created new legions of mushroom fans. Joe's, the Reading restaurant established by Czarnecki's father, was a mecca for those aficionados. After his father's death, Czarnecki closed the family restaurant and opened this engaging bistro across town. Then he headed west to Oregon, leaving chef Harry Holden to run the eatery. Look for salmon poached in lobster sauce with exotic mushrooms, New York strip steak with Portobellos, onions, and blue cheese, and roast chicken. The legendary wild mushroom soup, prepared according to the venerable Czarnecki recipe, remains a don't-miss dish. ⊠ *614 Penn Ave., West Reading,* ☎ *610/371–9966. AE, D, DC, MC, V. Closed Sun.–Mon.*

$–$$ ✕ **Arner's.** This chain of family restaurants has four locations, all with the look and feel of spruced-up diners. The menu highlights American favorites with a Pennsylvania Dutch influence, such as pork chops, chicken potpie, meat loaf, apple dumplings, and homemade pastries and pies. The bountiful salad bar and daily specials make this a hard-to-beat bargain. ⊠ *9th and Exeter Sts.,* ☎ *610/929–9795;* ⊠ *Howard Blvd., Mt. Penn,* ☎ *610/779–6555;* ⊠ *1714 Bern Rd., Berkshire Mall,* ☎ *610/372–6101;* ⊠ *4643 Pottsville Pike, Tuckerton,* ☎ *610/926–9002. AE, D, MC, V.*

$–$$ ✕ **Peanut Bar.** Free peanuts (throw the shells on the floor), video games, and good burgers and fries make this 1930s-style tavern and restaurant a fun outing. Besides such casual foods as Buffalo chicken wings and cheese balls, the chef serves up some gourmet meals, including Maryland crab cakes and tandoori chicken. Beers from local breweries are served. ⊠ *332 Penn St.,* ☎ *610/376–8500 or 800/515–8500. AE, D, MC, V. Closed Sun.*

$$ ⊞ **Inn at Reading.** This hotel, housed in a well-kept, elegant complex a few miles west of Reading, has large rooms with remote-control cable TV and traditional cherry-wood furnishings, including some four-poster beds. Request a room close to the lobby. The Publick House restaurant serves excellent meals. ⊠ *1040 Park Rd., at Warren St., Wyomissing 19610,* ☎ *610/372–7811 or 800/383–9713,* ℻ *610/372–4545. 250 rooms. Restaurant, pool, nightclub, playground, meeting rooms. AE, DC, MC, V.*

$$ ⊞ **Sheraton Berkshire Inn.** Renovations, including the addition of a striking art deco lobby and marble-tile floors, have made this an exceptionally attractive property. It's worth the extra $20 a night to upgrade from a standard room to an extra large executive room in the tower. Wyomissing is just west of Reading, over the Schuylkill River. ⊠ *U.S. 422 W, on Papermill Rd., Wyomissing 19610,* ☎ *610/376–3811 or 800/325–3535,* ℻ *610/375–7562. 256 rooms, 4 bilevel suites. 2 restaurants, indoor pool, putting green, exercise room, nightclub. AE, D, DC, MC, V.*

$–$$ ⊞ **Hampton Inn.** This small hotel a few miles west of the city has stylish contemporary rooms. The spacious King Special, just $5 more than a double, has a separate sitting area, a king-size bed, and a remote-control cable TV. A complimentary deluxe Continental breakfast is served. ⊠ *1800 Papermill Rd., Wyomissing 19610,* ☎ *610/374–8100 or 800/426–7866,* ℻ *610/374–2076. 125 rooms. Exercise room, business services. AE, D, DC, MC, V.*

Baumstown

10 mi east of Reading.

➐ This tiny town contains a slice of history. The **Daniel Boone Homestead** is where the great frontiersman lived until the age of 16. The rebuilt homestead has been furnished to typify rural life in this part of the state. You can take a half-hour house tour and a self-guided tour of the blacksmith shop, sawmill, and a log cabin built in 1737. ⊠ *Daniel Boone Rd. off U.S. 422,* ☎ *610/582–4900.* ⊡ *$4.* ⊙ *Tues.–Sat. 9–5, Sun. noon–5. Closed Mon. except Memorial Day, Labor Day, and July 4.*

Douglassville

> *3 mi east of Baumstown, 13 mi east of Reading.*

8 A small town holds a small world—of dolls. At the **Mary Merritt Doll Museum** you'll find rare dolls—rag dolls, French bisque dolls, mechanical dolls, and more—crafted between 1725 and 1900. Also on display are toys, exquisitely fashioned miniature period rooms, and elaborate dollhouses. **Merritt's Museum of Childhood,** in a separate building, has an eclectic collection of 18th-century Pennsylvania Dutch Fraktur (hand-painted birth and marriage certificates), tin and iron toys, Colonial lighting devices, and early baby carriages. If all this tempts you, you can purchase dolls and more at two shops here. ⊠ *Rte. 422, 1 mi east of Boone Homestead,* ☎ *610/385–3809.* ⌑ *$3 (both museums).* ⊘ *Mon.–Sat. 10–5, Sun. 1–5.*

Kutztown

> *15 mi north of Reading.*

Many descendants of Pennsylvania Germans live in this town, which is noted for its annual Pennsylvania Dutch Folk Festival (☎ 610/375–4085 or 800/963–8824), held in late June or early July.

9 **Crystal Cave,** just west of town, has 45-minute guided walking tours that wind through illuminated stalactites and stalagmites in distinctive formations like the "ice-cream cone," "totem pole," and many others. ⊠ *U.S. 222 north from Reading, Kutztown exit and follow signs,* ☎ *610/683–6765.* ⌑ *$8.* ⊘ *Mar.–Nov., daily 9–5 (longer in summer).*

Hawk Mountain Sanctuary

10 *28 mi north of Reading.*

This 2,330-acre refuge is visited by more than 20,000 migrating raptors—hawks, bald eagles, ospreys, and falcons—each fall. In other seasons you can spot songbirds, grouse, and white-tailed deer and other mammals; you can also hike along the sometimes rocky trails and picnic at a lookout offering a bird's-eye view of the spectacular scenery. Bring binoculars and proper footgear. No pets are allowed. From Reading take Route 61 north to Route 895E and follow the signs; it's about 8 mi west of Kempton. ⊠ *Hawk Mountain Rd.,* ☎ *610/756–6961.* ⌑ *$4; Sept.-Nov., weekends $6.* ⊘ *Trails: sunrise–sunset. Visitor center: Dec.–Aug., daily 9–5; Sept.–Nov., daily 8–5.*

Reading A to Z

Arriving and Departing

BY BUS

Greyhound Lines (☎ 215/931–4075 or 800/231–2222) operates out of the terminal at 10th and Filbert streets, just north of the Market East commuter rail station. It has frequent runs to the Intercity Bus Terminal, Third and Court streets, in Reading. Most buses make the trip in 90 minutes, although some locals take more than three hours. Check the schedule carefully.

BY CAR

Take the Schuylkill Expressway (I–76) west from Philadelphia to the Pennsylvania Turnpike. Go west to Exit 22, take I–176 north to U.S. 422 and then west into downtown Reading.

Getting Around

If you arrive by bus, you can walk or take a cab between the outlets. To see other area attractions, you'll need a car.

Contacts and Resources

CANOEING

From April through October, **Northbrook Canoe Co.** (⊠ 1810 Beagle Rd., West Chester 19382, ☎ 610/793–2279) helps you explore the Brandywine River by canoe, tube, or splash boat on trips of different length.

VISITOR INFORMATION

Reading & Berks County Visitors Bureau (⊠ Factory Village Complex, Park Rd. and Hill Ave., Box 6677, Wyomissing 19610, ☎ 610/375–4085 or 800/963–8824) provides outlet maps and guides. It's open January–June, weekdays 9–5, Saturday 10–2; July–December, weekdays 9–7, Saturday 10–3, Sunday 10–2.

9 Bucks County

It's no wonder so many artists have found glorious inspiration in this Delaware River valley countryside. Despite inevitable pockets of development, the area remains a feast of lyrical landscapes—canal and river vistas, rolling hills, ancient stone barns—with plenty of low-key diversions. Quiet little towns, important historic sites, charming overnight inns, dozens of antiques shops, and one of the most dramatic drives in the state continue to make Bucks County the classic weekend getaway from Philadelphia.

BUCKS COUNTY, about an hour's drive northeast of Philadelphia, could have remained 625 square mi of sleepy countryside full of old stone farmhouses, lush rolling hills, and covered bridges if it hadn't been discovered in the '30s by New York's Beautiful Brainy People. Such luminaries as writers Dorothy Parker and S. J. Perelman and composer Oscar Hammerstein bought country homes here, a short drive from Manhattan. Pulitzer Prize– and Nobel Prize–winning author Pearl S. Buck chose to live in the area because it was "a region where the landscapes were varied, where farm and industry lived side by side, where the sea was near at hand, mountains not far away, and city and countryside were not enemies." Author James A. Michener, who won the 1947 Pulitzer Prize for his *Tales of the South Pacific,* was raised and worked in Doylestown. The region quickly gained a nickname: the Genius Belt.

Updated by
Janet
Bukovinsky
Teacher

Over the years Bucks County has become known for art colonies and antiques, summer theater, and country inns. And although parts of the county have fallen prey to urban sprawl and hyperdevelopment, many areas of central and upper Bucks County remain as bucolic as ever. One of Bucks County's agrarian pursuits is a cottage vineyard industry. Five local wineries have opened their doors for tours and tastings.

A BIT OF HISTORY

Named after England's Buckinghamshire, Bucks County was opened by William Penn in 1681 under a land grant from Charles II. The county's most celebrated town, New Hope, was settled in the early 1700s as the industrial village of Coryell's Ferry. (One of the original gristmills is the home of the Bucks County Playhouse.) The town was the Pennsylvania terminal for stagecoach traffic and Delaware River ferry traffic. Barges hauled coal along the 60-mi Delaware Canal until 1931.

Commerce built up New Hope, but art helped sustain it. The art colony took root in the late 19th century and was revitalized first in the 1930s by New York theater folk and more recently with the formation of the New Hope–Lambertville Gallery Association, a cooperative network of gallery owners, artists, and the community. Today New York artists are again relocating to the region. In 1988 the James A. Michener Art Museum, showcasing 19th- and 20th-century American art, opened in the renovated former Bucks County jail.

INNS AND ADVENTURES

Although you can see all the major attractions in a day-long whirlwind tour of Bucks County, many people plan overnight stays at some of the prettiest inns in the Mid-Atlantic region. A number of houses and mills, some dating back to a half century before the Revolution, are now bed-and-breakfasts and excellent restaurants. A hearty meal, blissful sleep, and a day spent driving leisurely along River Road (Route 32) are what make visits to Bucks County most enjoyable.

Among the leading destinations is New Hope, a hodgepodge of old stone houses, narrow streets and alleys, pretty courtyards, and charming restaurants. Summer weekends can be frantic here, with traffic jams along Main Street and shoppers thronging the tiny boutiques and galleries. The Delaware Canal threads through town, and you can glide lazily along it in a mule-pulled barge.

Doylestown, the county seat, was an important coach stop in the 18th century. Today the town is best known as the home of Henry Chapman Mercer, curator of American and Prehistoric Archaeology at the University of Pennsylvania Museum, master potter, self-taught architect, and writer of Gothic tales. When Mercer died in 1930, he left a legacy of artistic creativity, along with a magnificently bizarre castle named Fonthill, a museum displaying 50,000 implements and tools, and a pottery and tile works that still makes Mercer tiles.

The county is also a treasure trove for Colonial history buffs. Among the most interesting sites is Pennsbury Manor, a careful reconstruction of the brick Georgian-style mansion and estate William Penn built for himself in the late 1600s. On the banks of the Delaware, the 500-acre Washington Crossing Historic Park is situated where George Washington and his troops crossed the icy river on Christmas night 1776 to surprise the Hessian mercenaries at Trenton, New Jersey.

The Delaware River and the canal that follows its path offer opportunities for canoeing, kayaking, and fishing. Thousands float down the river each year in inner tubes or on rubber rafts. Joggers, hikers, bicyclists, cross-country skiers, and horseback riders take full advantage of the 60-mi canal towpath.

The town of Lahaska is the center of shopping in Bucks County. The bargain-price American treasures that made the area an antiques hunter's paradise are now few and far between, but there is good prowling between New Hope and Doylestown all along U.S. 202. In the 70 shops in Peddler's Village in Lahaska, you can find fine furniture, handcrafted chandeliers, hand-woven wicker, and homespun fabrics.

For families a premier attraction in Langhorne is Sesame Place, a theme park based on the public television series. There are shows starring Bert and Ernie, water play such as Big Bird's Rambling River raft ride, a computer gallery, and lots of colorful structures on which to climb and jump.

Pleasures and Pastimes

Antiques
Bucks County has long been known for antiques shops full of everything from fine examples of early American craftsmanship to fun kitsch. There are formal and country furnishings plus American, European, and Asian antiques. Many shops are along a 4-mi stretch of U.S. 202 between Lahaska and New Hope and on intersecting country roads. You can walk across the bridge from New Hope to Lambertville, New Jersey, for dozens more shops full of treasures that include armoires from Provence and vintage 20th-century toy rocket ships. Shops are generally open on weekends, with weekday hours by appointment only: It's best to call first.

Covered Bridges
Eleven covered bridges are all that remain of the 36 originally built in Bucks County. Although the romantically inclined call them "kissing bridges" or "wishing bridges," the roofs were actually intended to protect the supporting beams from the ravages of the weather. The bridges are examples of the lattice-type construction of overlapping triangles, without arches or upright beams. They are delightful to stumble upon, but if you're serious about seeing them, contact the Bucks County Tourist Commission (☞ Visitor Information *in* Bucks Country A to Z, *below*). Directions, driving distances, and a brief history of each bridge are printed on the back of the map that comes with the county's Visitors Guide.

Dining
Bucks County has no regional specialties to call its own, but you will discover some *very* sophisticated restaurants as well as casual country spots. What makes dining here unique are the enchanting settings, rang-

ing from a French-style auberge to Colonial-era manor. Fine meals of French or contemporary American fare are served in restored mills, pre-Revolutionary taverns, stagecoach stops, small cafés, and elegant Victorian mansions. For price-category information *see* Chapter 3, which has the dining price chart for Philadelphia.

Lodging

Bucks County has relatively limited lodging options for families; larger inns, hotels and motels, and campgrounds are the best bets. It does offer numerous choices to couples. Accommodations ranging from modest to elegant can be found in historic inns, small hotels, and bed-and-breakfasts. Most hostelries include breakfast with their room rates. Plan and reserve early—as much as three months ahead for summer and fall weekends. You should also ask about minimum stays; many accommodations require a two-night minimum stay on weekends and a three-night minimum on holiday weekends. Many inns prohibit or restrict smoking. Since some inns are historic homes furnished with fine antiques, the owners may not accept children or may have age restrictions. For price-category information *see* Chapter 4, which has the lodging price chart for Philadelphia.

Outdoor Activities and Sports

Many travelers compare the heart of Bucks County to the Cotswolds region of England, and one of the best ways to experience the beauty of Bucks is to stroll along the grassy towpath of the Delaware Canal, one of Pennsylvania's most picturesque byways. Dotted with fieldstone bridge-tender houses and clapboard toll-collector offices—now private studios and homes—and shaded by magnificent trees, the path runs parallel to the Delaware River and River Road (Route 32). Constructed in 1832 to allow access for coal barges, the canal and towpath are known today as the Delaware Canal State Park. You can enjoy the 60-mi towpath for biking, hiking, jogging, and in the winter, cross-country skiing. In winter the canal freezes over to form a great ice-skating rink. Tubing or canoeing the Delaware River rates as another popular activity. County parks have plenty of places for hiking, fishing, and boating.

Exploring Bucks County

Many Bucks County sights are contained within the triangle formed by the towns of New Hope, Doylestown, and Newtown. Other interesting places are along River Road (Route 32) from Pennsbury Manor north to pretty river villages such as Erwinna. Lambertville, New Jersey, a five-minute walk across the Delaware River bridge from New Hope, functions as an appealing adjunct to Bucks County, replete with inns, restaurants, and engrossing antiques shops.

Numbers in the text correspond to numbers in the margin and on the Bucks County map.

Great Itineraries

It's entirely possible to "do" Bucks County as a day trip from Philadelphia, but a few days more will allow you to sample many of the area's pleasures. If you have young children along, you may want to spend half a day at Sesame Place in the southern part of the county rather than some of the nearby historic attractions.

IF YOU HAVE 1 DAY

Start in **Doylestown** ⑤ at Fonthill, the fantastic mansion built by local Renaissance man Henry Chapman Mercer. As lunchtime approaches, wend your way along U.S. 202, stopping at any antiques shops displaying wares along the roadside, usually indicating they're open for business. Have lunch in **New Hope** ⑩, take a quick stroll through town to check out the eclectic boutiques and gracious historic buildings, and then head north on River Road (Route 32) for a stirring drive along the Delaware River up to **Lumberville** ⑧ or **Erwinna** ⑨. Have dinner at one of the inns in these towns.

IF YOU HAVE 2 DAYS

Begin at **Washington Crossing Historic Park** ③, where you can see where George Washington set off across the river with his troops on that fateful Christmas night in 1776. Then drive up River Road (Route 32) to ⛴ **New Hope** ⑩ and have lunch, perhaps outside. In the afternoon head west to explore Mercer Mile in **Doylestown** ⑤ and return to New Hope to spend the night at an inn. On Day 2 check out **Lambertville**'s antiques shops across the river and then drive upriver in Pennsylvania on River Road for about 17 mi. Stop to stretch your legs along the way with a stroll on the scenic Delaware Canal towpath. Have dinner and spend the night at an inn in ⛴ **Erwinna** ⑨ or ⛴ **Upper Black Eddy.**

IF YOU HAVE 3 DAYS

Drive up River Road to ⛴ **Erwinna** ⑨. In season—roughly from May to October—even the mildly athletic will enjoy an 11-mi canoe trip south on the Delaware River, beginning at the rental facility Bucks County River Country Canoe and Tube, in **Point Pleasant.** It's a terrific way to appreciate the area's natural splendors and get some fresh-air exercise. Afterward you're justified in lounging for a few hours on the veranda of your inn with a good book. As an alternative, rent bikes in **Lumberville** ⑧ and take a ride on the river's bucolic towpath.

On Day 2 drive downriver to **New Hope** ⑩ for breakfast at Mother's. Shop and see the town, then head west on U.S. 202. Visit the museums on Mercer Mile in **Doylestown** ⑤. If you enjoy art, linger in Doylestown and spend the afternoon at the James A. Michener Art Museum, where many paintings by the Pennsylvania Impressionists are on permanent display. Another choice is to spend the afternoon at Peddler's Village in **Lahaska,** an expansive parklike shopping complex with exemplary landscaping; check out its boutiques full of delicious nonessentials. Back in New Hope for the evening, consider dinner and window-shopping just across the river in **Lambertville.**

History buffs can fill their plate on Day 3 by starting out with a tour of the pre-Revolutionary village of **Fallsington** ① and **Pennsbury Manor** ②, William Penn's country retreat, both near Morrisville in the southern part of the county. Have lunch in **Newtown** ④, ideal for strolling and browsing. Drive toward the river in the afternoon, and you'll end up at **Washington Crossing Historic Park** ③, where a visitor center, two historic buildings, and a walk through the glorious parkland can easily occupy the rest of the day.

When to Tour Bucks County

Spring, summer, or fall—each time of year has its own pleasures and seasonal festivals. Summer and fall weekends are very busy, so you need to make reservations well ahead and be ready for some crowds; a weekday trip could be more relaxing. Winter has its appeal here, too, especially around the holidays; the snow-covered buildings and fields are lovely.

Langhorne

25 mi west of Philadelphia.

For years families have visited this town because of a popular TV-themed attraction. The good times roll, crawl, climb, and jump at **Sesame Place,**

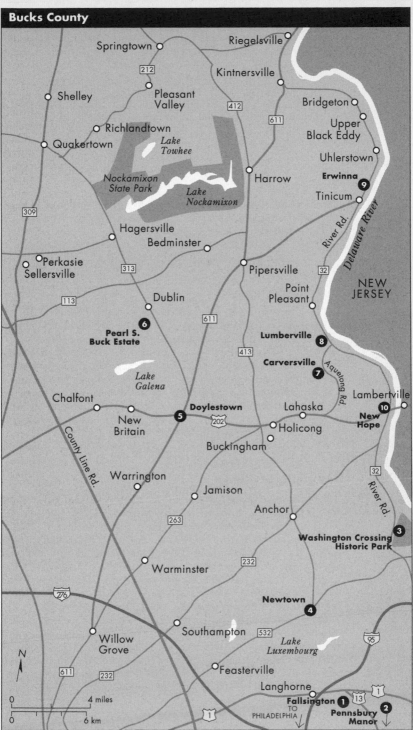

a recreation park designed for children—ages 3 to 13—who love the show. Kids go wild playing on Cookie Mountain, and their imaginations can run free in Twiddlebug Land, the larger-than-life attraction themed around the tiny critters in the flower box outside Ernie and Bert's window. What kid could resist climbing a giant bag of marbles or discovering Ernie's Bed Bounce? There's even Sesame Island, a tropical-style water park. Tots splish-splash at the Rubber Duckie Pond, while adults love the Big Slipper or the Sesame Streak. Don't forget your bathing suit! The highlight for most is Sesame Neighborhood, a replica of the street on the popular public-TV show. ⊠ *100 Sesame Rd., off Oxford Valley Rd. near junction of U.S. 1 and I–95,* ☎ *215/ 757–1100.* ☞ *$24.95; parking $5.* ☉ *Mid-May–mid-Sept., daily; early May and mid-Sept.–mid-Oct., weekends. Peak season hrs (July– Aug.) 9–8; call for spring and fall hrs.*

☺ **Sportland America,** just up the road from Sesame Place, is a huge indoor arcade that offers batting cages, miniature golf, roller skating, a gladiator wall climb, and a Velcro jumping wall. ⊠ *9 Cabot Blvd. E,* ☎ *215/547–7766.* ☉ *Sun.–Thurs. 10–10, Fri.–Sat. 10* AM*–12:30* AM.

Fallsington

❶ *2 mi east of Langhorne.*

Fallsington, the pre-Revolutionary village where William Penn attended Quaker meetings, displays 300 years of American architecture, from a simple 17th-century log cabin to the Victorian excesses of the late 1800s. Ninety period homes surround the village, which is listed on the National Register of Historic Places. Many private homes are open to the public on the second Saturday in October. Three historic buildings, including a log cabin, have been restored and opened for guided tours by **Historic Fallsington Inc.** ⊠ *4 Yardley Ave., Tyburn Rd. W off U.S. 13,* ☎ *215/295–6567.* ☞ *$3.50.* ☉ *May–Oct., Mon.–Sat. 10– 4, Sun. 1–4.*

Morrisville

3 mi east of Fallsington.

The reason to visit this town across the river from Trenton lies a few miles south of the town itself. On a gentle rise 150 yards from the ❷ Delaware River, **Pennsbury Manor** is a reconstruction of the Georgian-style mansion and plantation William Penn built as his country estate. Living-history demonstrations at the manor house and work buildings on 43 of the estate's original 8,400 acres provide a glimpse of everyday life in 17th-century America. Among the antique furnishings in the house are some fine William and Mary and Jacobean pieces, including William Penn's own furniture. Formal gardens, orchards, an icehouse, a smokehouse, a bake-and-brew house, and collections of tools attest to the self-sufficient nature of Penn's early community. They also hint that although history portrays Penn as a dour Quaker, as governor of the colony he enjoyed the good life by importing the finest provisions and keeping a vast retinue of servants and slaves. These extravagances led to financial difficulties that resulted in Penn spending nine months in a debtor's prison. The house can only be seen on the tour. ⊠ *400 Pennsbury Memorial Rd., Tyburn Rd. E off U.S. 13, between Morrisville and Bristol,* ☎ *215/946–0400.* ☞ *$5.* ☉ *Tues.– Sat. 9–5, Sun. noon–5; tours are at 10, 11:30, 1:30, 3:30.*

Washington Crossing Historic Park

❸ *7 mi north of Fallsington.*

You can revisit a slice of American history at this lovely Delaware River park. It was here on Christmas night in 1776 that General Washington and 2,400 of his men crossed the Delaware River, surprised the mercenary Hessian solders, and captured Trenton. A tall granite shaft surrounded by 13 cedar trees marks the point from which the soldiers embarked that snowy night. Attractions are divided between the Lower and the Upper Park, which are about 5 mi apart.

In the Lower Park, the fieldstone **Memorial Building and Visitors Center,** on Route 32, 7 mi south of New Hope, displays a reproduction of Emanuel Leutze's famous painting of the crossing (the original hangs in the Metropolitan Museum of Art in New York). Descendants of men who made that crossing sometimes come to gaze upon the painting and point out the resemblance between themselves and the soldiers in the boat. It's a vain and useless exercise: Leutze was in Düsseldorf, Germany, when he painted the figures, and for his models he used either young men from villages along the Rhine River or American artists living abroad. But past and present do merge—magically—during the annual Christmas Day reenactment of the crossing, when local businessmen don Colonial uniforms and brave the elements in small boats (and it's a delightful experience to walk into nearby restaurants later in the day to discover troops, still in uniform, enjoying their holiday bird). The **McConkey Ferry Inn** is where Washington and his staff had Christmas dinner while waiting to cross the river. It's near the Memorial Building. You can tour the **Taylor Mansion,** a completely restored 19th-century residence in the Lower Park.

In the Upper Park, about 5 mi north of the Memorial Building on Route 32, stop at the landmark **Bowman's Hill Tower,** named after a surgeon who sailed with Captain Kidd. Washington used the hill as a lookout point. You can get a much better view of the countryside than he did by riding the elevator up the 110-ft-tall memorial tower. It's open April–November, Tuesday–Sunday 10–4:30.

A half mile north of Bowman's Hill Tower, the 80-acre **Wildflower Preserve** (☎ 215/862–2924) has been planted with hundreds of species of wildflowers, trees, shrubs, and ferns native to Pennsylvania. Take the guided tour (offered March–October for $2 per person) or follow the short trails, which are clearly marked to bring you back to your starting point. At the same location, the **Platt Bird Collection** displays more than 100 stuffed birds and 600 eggs. The **Thompson-Neely House,** an 18th-century farmhouse, is furnished just as it was when the Colonial leaders planned the attack on Trenton its kitchen.

✉ *Washington Crossing Historic Park, Rtes. 532 and 32,* ☎ *215/493–4076.* 🎟 *Grounds free. 45-min walking tour of 5 historic park buildings plus tower: $4, available at visitor center, Thompson–Neely House, and Bowman's Hill Tower.* ☉ *Tours: Tues.–Sat. 9:30, 11, 12:30, 2, 3:30; Sun. 12:30, 2, 3:30. Park: Tues.–Sat. 9–5, Sun. noon–5.*

Newtown

❹ *6 mi west of Washington Crossing Historic Park.*

Until the real estate boom of the 1980s, Newtown was a busy village serving the commercial needs of the surrounding rural community. Today it's the bustling center of sprawling suburban development. Still, the town takes pride in its many 18th- and 19th-century homes and inns; the downtown historic district is on the National Register of Historic Places. The **Newtown Historic Association** (⊠ Court St. and Center Ave., ☎ 215/968–4004) has regional antiques and paintings by renowned local artist Edward Hicks. An association brochure provides a walking tour of the town.

Dining and Lodging

$$$–$$$$ ✕ **Jean Pierre's.** Owner-chef Jean Pierre Tardy, formerly executive
★   chef at Philadelphia's distinguished Le Bec-Fin, prepares classic French cuisine in a country French setting. Salmon stuffed with lobster and herb-encrusted rack of lamb with a rosemary lamb jus are two of the chef's favorites. ⊠ *101 S. State St.,* ☎ *215/968–6201. Reservations essential. AE, D, DC, MC, V. Closed Mon. No lunch weekends.*

$$ ✕🖿 **Temperance House.** This meticulously restored 1772 inn and hostelry also contains a restaurant ($$–$$$$) that serves fine Continental cuisine. Homemade soup stocks and an in-house charcuterie ensure an appealing range of dishes, including rack of lamb, roast Long Island smoked duck, and pork; beef, fresh-catch, and chicken preparations change each day. Listen to live jazz Friday and Saturday nights and enjoy a Cajun brunch accompanied by Dixieland jazz on Sunday. Each room in the 1772 inn is decorated with a different style of furniture: the Benetz Suite has bent willow and twig furniture; the Edward Hicks Suite has rich period mahogany and walls stenciled in a pattern derived from a "Peaceable Kingdom" mosaic tile. Continental breakfast is served in the dining room. ⊠ *5–11 S. State St., 18940,* ☎ *215/860–0474. 13 rooms. Restaurant. AE, DC, MC, V.*

Buckingham

8 mi north of Newtown.

You can visit one of the area's wineries outside this town. The **Buckingham Valley Vineyard & Winery** is a small family-owned operation that produces distinguished estate-bottled varietal wines. It was one of the state's first farm wineries. The vineyards and wine cellars are open to tours and tastings. ⊠ *1521 Rte. 413, 2 mi south of U.S. 202,* ☎ *215/794–7188.* 🖿 *Free self-guided tour.* ☉ *Tues.–Fri. noon–6, Sat. 10–6, Sun. noon–4. Winter hours may vary.*

Outdoor Activities and Sports

Kiddle Cyclery (⊠ Rtes. 413 and 202, ☎ 215/794–8958) rents 3- to 10-speed road bicycles. It's closed some Sundays.

Shopping

At **Brown Brothers** (⊠ Rte. 413 south of Rte. 263, ☎ 215/794–7630) three or four auctioneers simultaneously offer auctions in various categories—jewelry, silver, linens, tools, books, frames, furniture, and box lots. ☉ *Sept.–May, Sat. 8–3; June–Aug., Thurs. 3–9:30.*

Doylestown

⑤ *5 mi west of Buckingham, 12 mi north of Newtown.*

Doylestown, the county seat, is a showcase of American architecture, with the stately Federal brick buildings of Lawyers' Row, and gracious Queen Anne, Second Empire, and Italianate homes. The historic district, with its nearly 1,200 buildings, is listed on the National Register of Historic Places. Three walking tours highlighting the architecture and history of Doylestown are mapped out in a brochure available at the **Central Bucks Chamber of Commerce** (☞ Visitor Information *in*

Bucks County A to Z, *below*) and at area B&Bs, inns, and bookstores. The town has interesting shops and restaurants and is also home to the James A. Michener Art Museum and the National Shrine of Our Lady of Czestochowa, a Polish pilgrimage and spiritual center that includes a monastery and church.

The most unusual buildings in Doylestown are those created by Henry Chapman Mercer. Bucks County has seen its share of eccentrics, but even in such august company Henry Mercer stands out. Expert in prehistoric archaeology, a homespun architect and writer of Gothic tales, Mercer is best remembered for the three brilliantly theatrical structures, including his home and the Mercer Museum, found on what is known as **Mercer Mile.** All are constructed with reinforced concrete, a method perfected by Mercer in the early part of this century.

★ You almost expect to see a dragon puffing smoke outside **Fonthill,** Henry Chapman Mercer's storybook home and surely one of the most unique abodes in the country. Mercer, a Harvard-educated millionaire, designed the house in 1910, modeling it after a 13th-century Rhenish castle. Outside, the stone mansion bristles with turrets and balconies. Inside, the multilevel structure is truly mazelike: Mercer built his castle from the inside out—without using blueprints!—and Gothic doorways, sudden stairways, dead-ends, and inglenooks follow one after the other, all creating a fairy tale effect. Fonthill's wealth of books, prints, and Victorian engravings is enhanced by the setting: The ceilings and walls are embedded with tiles from Mercer's own kilns and with ancient tiles from around the world. As a final touch, every chamber has a different shape. ✉ *E. Court St. and Swamp Rd. (Rte. 313),* ☏ *215/348– 9461.* ⛶ *$5.* ◷ *Mon.–Sat. 10–5, Sun. noon–5. Hr-long guided tours.*

The **Moravian Pottery and Tile Works,** on the grounds of the Fonthill estate (☞ *above*), still produces unique Arts and Crafts–style picture tiles. These "Mercer" tiles adorn such structures as Graumann's Chinese Theater in Hollywood, the Pocantico Hills residence of John D. Rockefeller, and the Harvard Lampoon Building. As author and Bucks County resident James Michener described them, "Using scenes from the Bible, mythology, and history, Henry Chapman Mercer produced wonderfully archaic tiles about 12 or 14 inches square in powerful earth colors that glowed with intensity and unforgettable imagery." Reproductions of Mercer's tiles can be purchased in the Tile Works Shop. The factory, built in 1912, resembles a Spanish mission, with an open-ended courtyard. ✉ *130 Swamp Rd., Rte. 313,* ☏ *215/345–6722.* ⛶ *$3.* ◷ *Daily 10–4:45. 45-min self-guided tours every ½ hr; last tour at 4.*

The **Mercer Museum,** opened in 1916, displays Mercer's collection of tools, representing every craft and including more than 50,000 objects from before the age of steam. An archaeologist, Mercer worried that the rapid advance of progress would wipe out evidence of America's productivity before the industrial revolution. Consequently, from 1895 to 1915 he scoured the back roads of eastern Pennsylvania buying folk art, tools, and articles of everyday life. This must be one of the most incredible attics in the world: The four-story central court is crammed with log sleds, cheese presses, fire engines, boats, and bean hullers, most suspended by wires from the walls and ceiling. The **Spruance Library,** on the third floor, holds 20,000 volumes on Bucks County history. ✉ *84 S. Pine St.,* ☏ *215/345–0210.* ⛶ *$5.* ◷ *Mon. and Wed.–Sat. 10– 5, Tues. 10–9, Sun. noon–5; self-guided tours.*

The **James A. Michener Art Museum,** across the street from the Mercer Museum, has a permanent collection and changing exhibits (photography, crafts, textiles, sculpture, and painting) that focus on 19th- and 20th-century American art and Bucks County art. It was endowed by the late best-selling novelist, a native of Doylestown. The Pennsylvania Impressionists, who worked in the area in the early part of the century, are represented by such artists as Edward Redfield and Daniel Garber.

The museum occupies the buildings and grounds of the former Bucks County Jail, which dates from 1884. A 23-ft-high fieldstone wall surrounds seven exhibition galleries, an outdoor sculpture garden, and a Gothic-style warden's house. There is also a re-creation of Michener's Doylestown study. The Mari Sabusawa–designed Michener Wing, which debuted in 1996, added a library, archives, and a room with 12 interactive exhibits, each honoring a prominent Bucks County arts figure such as Pearl S. Buck and Oscar Hammerstein. ⊠ *138 S. Pine St.,* ☎ *215/340–9800.* ☞ *$5.* ☉ *Tues.–Fri. 10–4:30, weekends 10–5.*

The **National Shrine of Our Lady of Czestochowa,** a Polish spiritual center, has drawn millions of pilgrims, including Pope John Paul II, many U.S. presidents, and Lech Wałesa, since its opening in 1966. The complex includes a modern church with huge panels of stained glass depicting the history of Christianity in Poland and the United States. The gift shop and bookstore sell religious gifts, many imported from Poland, and the cafeteria serves hot Polish and American food on Sunday. ⊠ *Ferry Rd. off Rte. 313,* ☎ *215/345–0600.* ☉ *Daily 9–4:30.*

Dining and Lodging

$$–$$$$ ✕ **Cafe Arielle.** This French bistro serves delicious grilled seafood
★ dishes (including tuna steak), prime meats, and pistachio-encrusted rack of lamb in a setting of country French furnishings and striking artwork. ⊠ *100 S. Main St., in the Doylestown Agricultural Works,* ☎ *215/ 345–5930. AE, DC, MC, V. Closed Mon.–Tues.*

$$–$$$ ✕ **Russell's 96 West.** Chef-proprietor Russell Palmer artistically presents classical French cuisine—with an accent on southern France—in a restored 1846 town house. The seasonally changing menu may include rack of lamb, sautéed duck with soy and ginger, and Norwegian salmon with a reduction sauce of tomato, scallion, and bacon. Vegetables are bought from local organic farmers. Dinner and the lighter lunch are also served on the patio in warm weather. ⊠ *96 W. State St.,* ☎ *215/345–8746. AE, D, DC, MC, V. Closed Sun.*

$$ ✕▥ **Sign of the Sorrel Horse.** Catering to weary (and hungry) travelers, this inn has one of the finest restaurants in the area. The 1714 gristmill houses the formal Escoffier Room ($$–$$$$; jacket required). Chef Jon Atkin grows his own herbs and does wonders with fresh game dishes. His wife, Monique, oversees the dining rooms and his son, Christian, combs area stores for the best varietal wines. For espresso and desserts, repair to the Waterwheel Lounge. If you plan to stay the night, you'll be put up in a 1714 gristmill that once supplied flour for Washington's army and lodged Lafayette and is now decorated in the style of a French auberge. Guest rooms are filled with period antiques; one has a fireplace, and one has a whirlpool bath. ⊠ *4424 Old Easton Rd., 18901,* ☎ *215/230–9999,* ℻ *215/230–8053. 6 rooms. Restaurant. AE, DC, MC, V. Inn and restaurant closed Mon.–Tues.*

$$$ ▥ **Pine Tree Farm.** This Colonial farmhouse dating back to 1730 has been redecorated with cheerful country antiques set in light and airy rooms. The glass-enclosed garden room in the rear of the house overlooks 16 acres of pine trees, a pond, and the pool. Breakfast, served poolside in summer, may include poached eggs Florentine and apple

muffins. Room 1 is a favorite. This B&B is no-smoking. ✉ *2155 Lower State Rd., 18901,* ☎ *215/348–0632. 4 rooms, 2 with bath. Pool. AE, MC, V.*

$$–$$$ 🏠 **Inn at Fordhook Farm.** The Burpee family (of seed catalog fame) country estate is now a B&B set on 60 lovely acres and loaded with family memorabilia and antiques. Built in 1760 and purchased in 1888 by W. Atlee Burpee, the house has high-ceiling spacious bedrooms (two with Mercer tile fireplaces) brightened with floral prints, a large Federal-style living room, and a dining room with another tile fireplace. The full country breakfast, with oatmeal-buttermilk pancakes and cream-cheese-filled French toast, is served in the Burpee family dining room. The carriage house, with its dark wood paneling and vaulted cathedral ceiling, is a more modern alternative to the main house. ✉ *105 New Britain Rd., 18901,* ☎ *215/345–1766,* ℻ *215/345–1791. 7 rooms, 5 with bath. Badminton, croquet. AE, MC, V.*

$$ 🏠 **Highland Farms.** If only this house could talk . . .or rather, sing. This
★ Bucks County estate was the home of lyricist Oscar Hammerstein from 1941 to 1960. Not far from the field where the *Oklahoma* cocreator could enjoy what he originally called "corn as high as an elephant's eye," this pretty 1840s Federal-style country home often hosted the greats of Broadway and even Hollywood. Today the house is elegantly furnished with antiques and Hammerstein family memorabilia. A four-course country breakfast is served in the formal dining room or on the brick patio overlooking the 60-ft pool; at night you can settle in with a film from the video library stocked with Rodgers and Hammerstein favorites. ✉ *70 East Rd., 18901,* ☎ *215/340–1354. 4 rooms, 2 with bath. Pool, tennis court, library. AE, MC, V.*

$–$$ 🏠 **Doylestown Inn.** In the middle of town at the crossroads of Route 611 and U.S. 202, this Victorian hotel dates to 1902. Some guest rooms have richly stained furnishings and moldings, while others are furnished with painted country-pine armoires and hand-stenciled walls. Mercer tiles are found in the lobby, and there's a Mercer tile in each bathroom floor. A nice plus is live musical entertainment most nights in the restaurant and lounge. ✉ *18 W. State St.,* ☎ *215/345–6610,* ℻ *215/345–4017. 21 rooms, 1 suite. AE, D, DC, MC, V.*

Perkasie

6 mi north of Doylestown.

Outside this small town (but closer to Dublin) is the country home of writer Pearl S. Buck. Two of the area's covered bridges are nearby, too.

❻ The **Pearl S. Buck Estate** is filled with the writer's collection of Asian and American antiques and personal belongings. Green Hills Farm, Buck's country home (built in 1835), is where she wrote nearly 100 novels, children's books, and works of nonfiction while raising seven adopted children and caring for many others. The house still bears the imprint of the girl who grew up in China and became the first American woman to win both the Nobel and Pulitzer prizes. She is best known for *The Good Earth.* The Pearl S. Buck Foundation, which supports displaced children in Asia, has offices on the property. ✉ *520 Dublin Rd., off Rte. 313,* ☎ *215/249–0100 or 800/220–2825.* ⬛ *$5.* ⊙ *Mar.– Dec., farmhouse tours Tues.–Sat. 10:30, 1:30, and 2:30; Sun. 1:30 and 2:30.*

Outdoor Activities and Sports

Haycock Riding Stables (✉ 1035 Old Bethlehem Rd., off Rte. 313, ☎ 215/257–6271) escorts riders on one- and two-hour trips through lovely Nockamixon State Park, 4 mi to the north. You need to make a reservation.

Carversville

❼ *8 mi east of Doylestown.*

One pleasure of traveling in Bucks County is driving on lovely back roads and discovering tiny old mill villages such as Carversville. If you're traveling east from Doylestown, take a scenic detour by making a left turn onto Aquetong Road and straight into one of the most beautiful byways of the state, the drive along the Delaware Canal towpath. You'll wind through fields and woods dotted with old houses and barns before you arrive at the village. Stop at the **Carversville General Store** (⊠ Carversville and Aquetong Rds., ☎ 215/297–5353), where locals gather for gossip and take-out coffee and pick up picnic supplies.

Dining

$$–$$$ ✕ **Carversville Inn.** Its out-of-the-way location has made this circa-1813
★   inn one of the area's best-kept secrets. Chef Will Mathias's regional American cuisine with a Southern flair is now a local favorite. The menu changes seasonally, but you can always count on innovative sauces such as roast red-pepper horseradish on grilled filet mignon or rosemary demiglacé sauce on roast duck. On Friday evening look for complimentary hors d'oeuvres at the bar. ⊠ *Carversville and Aquetong Rds.,* ☎ *215/297–0900. AE, MC, V. Closed Mon.*

Lumberville

❽ *3 mi northeast of Carversville.*

In tiny Lumberville you can picnic along the Delaware Canal or on Bull's Island, accessible by the footbridge across the Delaware River. Open since 1770, the **Lumberville Store** is the focus of village life, the place to mail letters, buy groceries (and picnic supplies), and rent a bicycle (☞ Outdoor Activities and Sports, *below*). Across the street stands the Black Bass Hotel, a famous Colonial-period inn (☞ Dining and Lodging, *below*) that was once the country retreat of President Grover Cleveland. To get here from Carversville, continue to Fleecydale or Old Carversville roads (ignore the ROAD CLOSED sign—it's been there for years.) Both of these backcountry roads lead to River Road (Route 32) and Lumberville.

Dining and Lodging

✕🏠 **Black Bass Hotel.** This inn has been a favorite stopover along the Delaware River for more than 240 years. Although it sits snug within a region that witnessed many events of the American Revolution, don't look for any GEORGE WASHINGTON SLEPT HERE plaques: the hotel and its clientele were loyalists to the British Crown, and, coincidentally, its current owner, Herb Ward, is as Anglophile as they come. He's even adorned the inn with a fabulous collection of British royal memorabilia. A wayside inn (and we do mean wayside, since the hotel's facade sits directly on Route 32), the Black Bass also has an excellent restaurant ($$–$$$) and an outdoor deck overlooking the river—just the place for a picture-perfect summer dinner. ⊠ *Rte. 32,* ☎ *215/297–5770,* 🆔 *215/297–0262. 9 rooms, 2 with bath. AE, DC, MC, V.*

Outdoor Activities and Sports

A recommended 6-mi route for hikers and bikers starts here. Cross the pedestrian bridge to Bull Island State Park; go south on the New Jersey side along the Delaware and Raritan Canal to Stockton. Cross the river again to Center Bridge, Pennsylvania, and head back up the Delaware Canal towpath to Lumberville.

Lumberville Store Bicycle Rental Co. (✉ River Rd., ☎ 215/297–5388) rents mountain bikes with wide tires from April through October; daily rental is $24. They can direct you to scenic bike routes.

Point Pleasant

2 mi north of Lumberville.

This town's location on the Delaware River makes it a focus for recreational activities. It's a lovely area to explore, and two of the county's covered bridges are a few miles northwest of town. Two fine parks, **Tohickon Valley County Park** (Point Pleasant) and **Ralph Stover State Park** (Pipersville), are joined along Tohickon Creek near town.

More than 100,000 people a year—from toddlers to grandparents eighties—negotiate the Delaware on inner tubes or in canoes from **Bucks County River Country Canoe and Tube** (✉ Byron Rd. at River Rd., ☎ 215/297–5000). The cost is around $15 per person, and the company also rents rafts and kayaks during its April through October season. A bus transports people upriver to begin three- or four-hour tube or raft rides down to the base. No food, cans, or bottles are permitted on the tube rides. Wear sneakers you don't mind getting wet and lots of sunscreen. Life jackets are available at no charge. Reservations are required.

En Route   Between the villages of Point Pleasant and Erwinna run some of the most Edenic stretches of the **Delaware Canal towpath,** parallel to River Road. This is the section of Bucks County that is reminiscent of the Cotswolds of England, with bridge-keeper lodges, corkscrew bends in the road, and vistas so picturesque they seem to drip off the canvas (drivers, beware of the artists often painting at easels by the side of the road).

Erwinna

⑨ *7 mi north of Point Pleasant.*

The bucolic river town of Erwinna is a fine place to unwind. There are three covered bridges nearby, and you can visit a park and a local winery. Nearby Tinicum was once home to Dorothy Parker and S. J. Perelman.

One of the most active in the county parks system, 126-acre **Tinicum Park** (✉ River Rd., ☎ 215/757–0571) has hiking, boating, fishing and more. You can also tour the **Erwin-Stover House,** an 1800 Federal house with 1840 and 1860 additions.

Sand Castle Winery opens it doors for tastings and tours of its vineyard and underground wine cellar. Ask about longer 2½-hour VIP tours, too. ✉ *755 River Rd., Rte. 32,* ☎ *610/294–9181.* 🖾 *$3–$7.50 for tours.* ☉ *Weekdays 9–6, Sat. 10–6, Sun. 11–6.*

Dining and Lodging

$$–$$$ ✕🏨 **Evermay on-the-Delaware.** The Barrymores used to play croquet
★   on the lawn in front of this cream-color clapboard house, a fine Victorian mansion along the Delaware. Today, Evermay is as popular for its restaurant ($$$$; open Friday–Sunday for one dinner seating) as for its stylish hostelry; reservations a month in advance are essential. Ron Strouse serves an impressive prix-fixe six-course dinner. His contemporary American menu offers a choice of two entrées, such as grilled tuna with fresh tomato salsa or chicken on linguine with basil and pine nuts, and includes champagne, hors d'oeuvres, and a cheese course. Upstairs (try to book a room with a river view) and in the nearby

carriage house, guest rooms are filled with antiques and fresh flowers. A breakfast of fresh fruit compote, croissants, juice, and coffee is served in the glassed-in conservatory. Could anything be nicer than taking predinner sherry or afternoon tea in the stately parlor warmed by its twin fireplaces? ✉ *River and Headquarters Rds., 18920,* ☎ *610/ 294–9100. 16 rooms. Restaurant. MC, V.*

$–$$ ✕🖼 **Golden Pheasant Inn.** One of the prettiest places along the Delaware
★   Canal, this 1857 Bucks County landmark has been restored into a rustic yet elegant French auberge by Michel and Barbara Faure, a husband-and-wife team of chef and hostess. In the solarium of the restaurant ($$–$$$), diners eat beneath potted plants—and the stars—in a renovated greenhouse. Other diners prefer the fieldstone room—all gleaming copper cooking vessels and pierced tin chandeliers. An ex-chef at Paris's Ritz Hotel, Michel Faure deliciously melds the culinary traditions of the New and Old Worlds: Medallions of boned duck with a marinade of apricot brandy and salmon in a lobster-and-champagne sauce adorned with Kennett Square mushrooms are favored choices. Upstairs there are six guest rooms, all with four-poster beds and river or canal views and often booked months in advance (note that some rooms front River Road, at times a heavily trafficked thoroughfare). ✉ *River Rd., 18920,* ☎ *610/294–9595. 6 rooms. Restaurant. AE, MC, V.*

$$–$$$ 🖼 **Isaac Stover House.** This 1837 brick mansion is a delightful B&B
★   full of personality. The inn was completely redecorated in 1996 in formal Federal style, with Persian carpets, French antiques, Pierre Deux wallpapers, and Chippendale pieces. The Victorian sitting room is now a tranquil study in white on white, making it easy for guests to sink into romantic dreams at night. Full breakfast is served on a sunny porch, weather permitting, or in the taproom. The inn is set on 13 acres of woods and meadows across River Road from the Delaware River. At press time (fall 1997), Isaac Stover House was up for sale by its owner, talk-show host Sally Jesse Raphael. ✉ *845 River Rd., 18920,* ☎ *610/ 294–8044. 7 rooms, 4 with bath. MC, V.*

Outdoor Activities and Sports

Keystone State Balloon Tours organizes hot-air balloon flights over Bucks County followed by a champagne reception back on land. Flights are scheduled at dawn or in late afternoon, when the winds are best. Reservations are required. ✉ *Van Sant Airport, just off Rte. 611, Headquarters and Cafferty Rds.,* ☎ *610/294–8034.* 🎫 *$150 per person.* ⊙ *Weekends only, weather permitting.*

Upper Black Eddy

6 mi north of Erwinna.

This is another Bucks County river town that's a fine place in which to relax or explore the countryside. You can drive across the river here to Milford and explore the Jersey side of the Delaware. A few miles south of Milford are the antiques shops and restaurants of pretty Frenchtown; then you can recross to Uhlerstown and drive back north to Upper Black Eddy. Another scenic route takes you north of town on River Road; a 6-mi drive will bring you to Riegelsville.

If you're here in fall, you can try a **Haunted Hayride,** a spook-filled evening ride through 256 acres of sinister woods, complete with a visit to a haunted house. ✉ *Bucks County River Country,* ☎ *215/297–8406.* 🎫 *$12–$15.* ⊙ *Oct., Thurs.–Sun. at 6 PM.*

Lodging

$–$$$ ⊡ **Bridgeton House on the Delaware.** Wide, screened porches and a terrace provide close-up views of the Delaware River and the bridge to Milford, New Jersey. Guest rooms are decorated with wall and ceiling folk murals by the self-described artist-in-residence. The informal sitting room has white wood walls and a glass wall overlooking the river. A two-course gourmet country breakfast is served, as is afternoon tea and sherry. Request a river view: Although other rooms face the road directly outside the front entrance, riverfront rooms have French doors to private screened porches. In the penthouse the marble fireplace and huge windows are delightful. ⊠ *River Rd., 18972,* ☎ *610/ 982–5856. 8 rooms, 3 suites. AE, MC, V.*

New Hope

⑩ *18 mi south of Upper Black Eddy.*

The cosmopolitan village of New Hope is a mecca for artists, shoppers, and lovers of old homes—and hordes of day-trippers and backpackers on summer weekends. The town, listed on the National Register of Historic Places, is easy to explore on foot; the most interesting sights and stores are clustered along four blocks of Main Street and on the cross streets—Mechanic, Ferry, and Bridge streets—which lead to the river. Unfortunately, lower Main Street has succumbed to tourist blight, but if you take a walk on Ferry Street or along the towpath, there's still plenty of charm. For a good orientation to New Hope, take the Bucks County Carriages horse-drawn tour (☞ Guided Tours *in* Bucks County A to Z, *below*), which starts by the cannon alongside the Logan Inn. And if you're eager for more country charm (and more antiques), you can take Bridge Street over the Delaware River to Lambertville (☞ *below*) in New Jersey.

The **Parry Mansion,** a stone house built in 1784, is notable because the furnishings reflect decorative changes from 1775 to the Victorian era—including candles, whitewashed walls, oil lamps, and wallpaper. Wealthy lumber-mill owner Benjamin Parry built the house, which was occupied by five generations of his family. ⊠ *S. Main and Ferry Sts.,* ☎ *215/862–5460.* ⊡ *$3.* ☉ *Apr.–Dec., Fri.–Sat. 1–5.*

NEED A
BREAK?
Family-owned **Gerenser's Exotic Ice Cream** (⊠ 22 S. Main St., ☎ 215/ 862–2050) has been making ice cream—with 14% butterfat—since 1943. "Exotic" is no exaggeration: Polish plum brandy, African violet, and Indian loganberry are 3 of the more than 40 flavors.

Beginning in 1832, coal barges plied the Delaware Canal. Today the canal is a state park, and you can ride a mule-pulled barge from the **New Hope Mule Barge Co.** The one-hour narrated excursion travels past Revolutionary-era cottages, gardens, and artists' workshops. A barge historian/folk singer is aboard. ⊠ *New and S. Main Sts.,* ☎ *215/ 862–2842.* ⊡ *$7.50.* ☉ *Apr. and Nov. 1–Nov. 15, Wed. and weekends at 11:30, 1, 2, 3, and 4:30; May 1–Oct. 31, daily 11:30, 1, 2, 3, 4:30, and 6.*

The **New Hope & Ivyland Rail Road** makes a 9-mi, 50-minute scenic run from New Hope west to Lahaska. The train crosses a trestle used in the rescue scenes in the old "Perils of Pauline" movies. The New Hope depot is an 1891 Victorian gem. Theme rides, which require reservations, include wine-and-cheese trains, Halloween haunted trains, Santa trains at Christmas, and Sunday brunch trains. ⊠ *W. Bridge and Stockton Sts.,* ☎ *215/862–2332.* ⊡ *$7.95.* ☉ *May–Oct., daily; Nov.*

Wed.–Mon.; Dec., Fri.–Sun.; Jan.–Apr., weekends and holidays; trains run hourly 11–4.

Dining and Lodging

$$$$ ✕ **La Bonne Auberge.** Some critics consider this to be Bucks County's
★   most elite and expensive restaurant, thanks to the owners—chef Gerard Caronello, a native of Lyon, France, and his wife, Rozanne, of Great Britain. Consistently classic French cuisine is served in a pre-Revolutionary farmhouse. The Terrace Room, used for dining, has a modern country French ambience. Some specialties are grilled salmon with a light lobster sauce and rack of lamb. The five-course table d'hôte menu, available Wednesday and Thursday evenings in addition to the regular menu, is a bargain. The restaurant is within a residential development called Village 2; when you call for reservations, travel directions will be provided. ⊠ *Village 2 off Mechanic St.,* ☎ *215/862–2462. Reservations essential. Jacket required. AE. Closed Mon.–Tues.*

$$–$$$ ✕ **Martine's.** Reminiscent of an English pub with its beamed ceiling, plaster-over-stone walls, and fireplace, Martine's has an eclectic menu that includes filet mignon au poivre, pasta, duckling, and seafood paella. Try the French onion soup. Outdoor dining is on a small patio. ⊠ *7 E. Ferry St.,* ☎ *215/862–2966. AE, MC, V.*

$$–$$$ ✕ **Odette's.** In 1961 Parisian actress Odette Myrtil Logan converted a former canal lock house into a restaurant. The atmosphere is French country bistro; the cuisine, Continental, with a menu that changes seasonally. Sunday brunch is buffet style. You may want to request a table at one of the dining rooms with a river view. Entertainment consists of a nightly session around the piano bar, legendary among local showtune buffs, plus occasional cabarets and art shows. ⊠ *S. River Rd., ½ mi south of Bridge St.,* ☎ *215/862–2432. AE, DC, MC, V.*

$$ ✕ **Hotel du Village.** You can feast on country French fare in a converted private school. Chef-owner Omar Arbani prepares tournedos Henri IV, a beef fillet with béarnaise sauce; sweetbreads with mushrooms in Madeira sauce; and fillet of sole in curried butter, all topped off by extravagant desserts. Dinner is served in a Tudor-style room or on the sunporch. ⊠ *2535 N. River Rd.,* ☎ *215/862–5164 or 215/862–9911. AE, DC. Closed Mon.–Tues. No lunch.*

$$ ✕ **Mother's.** Once one of New Hope's most popular dining spots, Mother's main claim is still its truly sinful desserts, such as chocolate mousse bombe and mocha Amazon. Homemade soups, pastas, and unusual pizzas are offered on the extensive menu, but your best bet is to visit for breakfast. In summer meals are also served in the garden. Expect to wait; it's often crowded here. ⊠ *34 N. Main St.,* ☎ *215/862–9354. AE, D, MC, V.*

$–$$ ✕ **Havana Bar and Restaurant.** Hickory-grilled specialties enhance the American regional and contemporary fare at the Havana. Menu items include sesame onion rings, a Chinese vegetable sandwich, and spice-fried redfish. The bar is enlivened by jazz bands from Thursday through Sunday nights and by karaoke on Monday night. The view of Main Street is ideal for people-watching, especially from the outdoor patio. ⊠ *105 S. Main St.,* ☎ *215/862–9897. AE, D, DC, MC, V.*

$$ ✕▣ **Logan Inn.** Established in 1727 as an extension of the Ferry Tavern, this inn accommodated passengers who used the Delaware River ferry to Lambertville. George Washington is said to have stayed here at least five times—and one can only imagine what he would think of the crowds of shoppers who stroll right outside the inn, smack dab in the busiest part of town. Rooms have original and reproduction Colonial and Victorian furnishings and canopy beds; some have river views.

Full or Continental breakfast on the tented patio is included. As for the friendly restaurant ($$–$$$), the Logan serves three menus: lunch (11:30–4), dinner (4:30–closing), and a popular all-day café menu, with such favorites as nachos, buffalo wings, salads, burgers, and pizzas. ✉ *10 W. Ferry St., 18938,* ☎ *215/862–2300. 16 rooms. Restaurant. AE, D, DC, MC, V.*

$$$–$$$$ ★   🖫 **Mansion Inn.** Romantic luxury and calm surround you inside this elegant 1865 Second Empire–style Victorian inn, although busy Main Street is just steps away from the massive front door. Even the pool and English garden feel pleasantly private. Depression glass, local art, antiques, and comfortable furniture fill the inviting, high-ceilinged yellow and beige sitting rooms. Guest rooms (two in a separate building) have antique pieces, plush linens, and modern baths, some with whirlpool tubs. Breakfast includes everything from fresh muffins and fruit to an egg dish or French toast. There's a two-night minimum on weekends, three on holidays; no smoking is allowed. ✉ *9 S. Main St., 18938,* ☎ *215/862–1231,* FAX *215/862–0277. 5 rooms, 4 suites. Breakfast room, air-conditioning, pool. AE, MC, V.*

$$–$$$ 🖫 **Whitehall Inn.** Guest rooms at the 18th-century manor house of what was once a gentleman's horse farm are furnished with period antiques, canopy beds, and patterned wallpaper. You get a bowl of fresh fruit and bottle of mineral water upon arrival and will find chocolate truffles and velour robes in your room. A spacious parlor has sofas and rocking chairs facing a fireplace. The four-course candlelit gourmet breakfast is served at tables set with white linen, English china, and heirloom silver; in the afternoon, high tea is served. Smoking is not allowed here. ✉ *1370 Pineville Rd., 18938,* ☎ *215/598–7945. 6 rooms, 4 with bath. Pool. AE, D, DC, MC, V.*

$–$$$ ★   🖫 **Wedgwood Inn.** Three buildings comprise the Wedgwood Inn B&B lodgings: a blue "painted lady" 1870 Victorian house with a gabled roof, porch, and a porte cochere; a Federal-style 1840 stone manor house; and the Aaron Burr House, another 1870 Victorian building. Minutes from downtown, the collection of inns has landscaped grounds with gazebos and gardens. Wedgwood pottery, antiques, fireplaces, and wood-burning stoves add to its charm. A Continental-plus breakfast and afternoon tea are served on the sunporch, gazebo, or your room. For a fee you can have tennis and pool privileges at a nearby club. The inn is no-smoking. ✉ *111 W. Bridge St., 18938,* ☎ *215/862–2570. 15 rooms, 4 suites. Concierge. AE, MC, V.*

$$ 🖫 **Best Western New Hope Inn.** This serviceable motel is a few minutes from New Hope and 30 minutes from Sesame Place. It's handy for single-night accommodations on busy fall weekends, when the country inns are often all booked up. ✉ *6426 Lower York Rd. (Rte. 202), 18938,* ☎ *215/862–5221 or 800/467–3202,* FAX *215/862–5847. 159 rooms. Restaurant, lobby lounge, pool, tennis court. AE, D, DC, MC, V.*

$$ 🖫 **Hotel du Village.** Flower-filled grounds surrounding the large, old stone boarding school create the feeling of an English manor house. The guest rooms have country furniture, and a Continental breakfast is served in the parlor. ✉ *2535 N. River Rd. (Rte. 32), 18938,* ☎ *215/ 862–5164 or 215/862–9911. 20 rooms. Pool, 2 tennis courts. AE, DC.*

Nightlife and the Arts

The **Bucks County Playhouse** (✉ 70 S. Main St., ☎ 215/862–2041), housed in a historic mill, stages Broadway musical revivals—most recently *Oklahoma!* The season runs from April through December.

The **New Hope Performing Arts Festival,** held just outside New Hope at the Solebury School (✉ Phillips Mill Rd., ☎ 215/862–9894 in

July–Aug. or ☎ 215/862–9307 for off-season information) is dedicated to innovative works in theater, music, and performing arts. The summer festival, in July and August, includes classical music and children's programming.

Outdoor Activities and Sports

West End Farm (✉ River Rd. in Phillips Mill, north of New Hope, ☎ 215/862–5883) offers one-hour escorted trail rides along the Delaware Canal; call to make a reservation.

Shopping

New Hope's streets are lined with shops selling crafts and handmade accessories, art, antiques, campy vintage items, and contemporary wares.

ANTIQUES

Hobensack & Keller (✉ Bridge St., New Hope, ☎ 215/862–2406) stocks antique and authentic reproduction garden ornaments, cast-iron furniture, fencing, and Oriental rugs. **Olde Hope Antiques** (✉ U.S. 202 and Reeder Rd., ☎ 215/862–5055) carries hooked rugs, Pennsylvania German textiles, hand-painted furniture, and folk art. **Katy Kane** (✉ 34 W. Ferry St., New Hope, ☎ 215/862–5873) is the place for antique, vintage, and designer clothing, accessories, and fine linens; it's by appointment only. The **Pink House** (✉ W. Bridge St., ☎ 215/862–5947) has magnificent European 18th- and 19th-century furnishings and textiles.

ART GALLERIES

Many artists have relocated to Bucks County, and more than 30 galleries in New Hope and neighboring Lambertville (across the river in New Jersey) showcase paintings, prints, and sculpture. The New Hope Information Center (☞ Bucks County A to Z, *below*) can tell you about other galleries. The **Golden Door Gallery** (✉ 52 S. Main St., New Hope, ☎ 215/862–5529) displays works by Bucks County painters, sculptors, and print makers.

BOOKSTORE

The crowded shelves at **Farley's Bookshop** (✉ 44 S. Main St., ☎ 215/862–2452) hold plenty of choices for readers, including books about the area.

Lambertville

Across the Delaware River from New Hope.

If you're interested in all that New Hope has to offer but prefer it in a lower key, this New Jersey village is just a walk or short drive away, over the Delaware River; use the bridge on New Hope's Bridge Street. You'll find more charm and even better antiques, as well as a delightfully chic assemblage of shops, galleries, Federal and Victorian houses, and fine restaurants. The Hamilton Grill Room (✉ 8½ Coryell St., ☎ 609/397–4343) a Mediterranean eatery, is one good dining choice. For an overnight stay try the newly reopened Lambertville House (✉ 32 Bridge St., ☎ 609/397–0200), a historic lodging with 25 rooms.

Lahaska

3 mi west of New Hope.

Shopping packs in the crowds here, primarily because of the boutiques at Peddler's Village (☞ Shopping, *below*). If bargains are your goal, you can also find outlets here. Along U.S. 202 between New Hope and Lahaska you will see many antiques stores.

Dining and Lodging

$$–$$$ ✗ **Jenny's.** American regional cuisine is served in a Victorian or a country French room. Lobster and crab sauté and filet Chesterfield (filet mignon with cheddar cheese, bacon, and horseradish sauce) are favorites. You can hear live jazz and blues Friday and Saturday nights, and there's Dixieland during Sunday brunch. ⊠ *U.S. 202, Peddler's Village,* ☎ *215/794–4020. AE, D, DC, MC, V. No dinner Mon.*

$–$$ ✗ **Spotted Hog.** This casual country bistro in the Golden Plough Inn (☞ *below*) serves American cuisine such as New York strip steak, grilled chicken with macadamia-lime butter, Philadelphia cheese steaks, interesting pizzas, and sundaes. The bar stocks 35 American microbrewery beers. Live bands play folk, country, and pop on Thursday, Friday, and Saturday evenings and Sunday afternoons. ⊠ *Peddler's Village, Rte. 202 and Street Rd.,* ☎ *215/794–4030. AE, D, DC, MC, V.*

$$–$$$ 🏨 **Barley Sheaf Farm.** If Bucks County was once known as the Ge-
★ nius Belt, this famous estate was probably its buckle. Home to play-
wright George S. Kaufman—author of and collaborator on such jewels as *Dinner at Eight* and *You Can't Take It with You*—the house was then called Cherchez la Farm. The inn's 30-acre parklike setting includes the 1740 fieldstone mansion, a duck pond, a pool, and a meadow full of sheep. You retire to bedrooms that are a medley of floral prints, brass, and four-poster beds. A hearty breakfast is served on the glass-enclosed sunporch. Rooms in the adjacent cottage are smaller but share the same country antique decor. Barley Sheaf Farm is in Holicong, a mile west of Lahaska. ⊠ *5281 York Rd. (U.S. 202), Holicong 18928,* ☎ *215/794–5104,* FAX *215/794–5332. 10 rooms. Pool, badminton, croquet, meeting rooms. AE, MC, V.*

$$–$$$ 🏨 **Golden Plough Inn.** Nestled within Peddler's Village, this inn has
★ 22 spacious guest rooms, many with four-poster beds, rich fabrics, and cozy window seats that beautifully evoke 19th-century Bucks County. All rooms are equipped with air-conditioning, remote control TV, a small refrigerator, and a complimentary bottle of champagne, and some have a fireplace or a Jacuzzi. Thirty-eight other guest rooms are scattered about the village—in an 18th-century farmhouse, a historic carriage house, and in Merchant's Row. There is a complimentary Continental breakfast or a credit toward breakfast on the à la carte menu. ⊠ *Peddler's Village, Rte. 202 and Street Rd., 18931,* ☎ *215/794–4004,* FAX *215/794–4008. 60 rooms. Restaurant. AE, D, DC, MC, V.*

$$ 🏨 **Ash Mill Farm.** This country B&B is a handsome 18th-century field-
stone manor house set on 10 acres. High ceilings, ornate moldings, and deep-sill windows add character to the parlor; rooms have Irish and American antiques and thoughtful extras such as thick terry-cloth robes, hair dryers, and down comforters on canopy or four-poster beds. A full country breakfast is served to the strains of Mozart or Vivaldi. Afternoon tea and home-baked treats are offered by a cozy fire, in the garden, or on the porch, which has a view of resident sheep. This B&B is just west of Lahaska. ⊠ *5358 Old York Rd., Rte. 202, Holicong 18928,* ☎ *215/794–5373. 3 rooms, 2 suites. No credit cards.*

Shopping

Peddler's Village (⊠ U.S. 202 and Rte. 263, ☎ 215/794–4000) began in the early 1960s, when Earl Jamison bought a 6-acre chicken farm, moved local 18th-century houses to the site, and opened a Carmel, California–inspired collection of 70 specialty shops and restaurants. Today the 42-acre village peddles books, cookware, toys, leather goods, clothes, jewelry, dried wreaths, posters, candles, and a host of other decorative items. Carousel World has a carousel museum, circus art, and an operating 1926 Dentzel Grand merry-go-round. Crowd-drawing seasonal events include the Strawberry Festival, in May; the Teddy Bear's Picnic, in July; and the Scarecrow Festival, in September. On the grounds is the Golden Plough Inn (☞ Dining and Lodging, *above*).

Penn's Purchase Factory Outlet Stores (✉ 5881 York Rd., at U.S. 202, ☎ 215/794–0300), on the site of the former Lahaska Antique Court, is now home to more than 50 stores selling name-brand merchandise at 20% to 60% off regular retail prices. You'll find Anne Klein, Coach, Easy Spirit, Geoffrey Beene, Izod, Orvis, Nautica, Nordic Track, and more, as well as restaurants. All 11 buildings in this new complex have been designed in an Early American country style that harmonizes with the look of Peddler's Village, right across the road.

ANTIQUES

The **Heritage Collectors' Gallery** (✉ 161 Peddler's Village, ☎ 215/794–0901) exhibits and sells historical artifacts and original documents owned or signed by everyone from Washington and Napoléon to Elvis and Freud. You might see a baseball inscribed by Babe Ruth, letters signed by Lincoln, or an autographed copy of Amelia Earhart's book. Prices for original items range from $200 to $30,000.

FLEA MARKETS

Rice's Sale and Country Market (✉ Green Hill Rd., Solebury, near Peddler's Village, ☎ 215/297–5993) is a mostly open-air market with bargains on canned goods, clothing, linens, shoes, back-issue magazines, and plants; there are a few antiques, too. It opens Tuesday around 6:30 AM and closes at 1:30 PM. There are Call for additional Saturday and holiday openings.

BUCKS COUNTY A TO Z

Arriving and Departing

By Bus
Greyhound Lines (☎ 800/231–2222) has three buses a day to Doylestown from Philadelphia. The trip takes 75–90 minutes and costs $7 one-way, $14 round-trip.

By Car
From Philadelphia the most direct route to Bucks County is I–95 north, which takes you near sights in the southern part of the county. I–95 crosses Route 32, which runs along the Delaware River past Washington Crossing Historic Park and on to New Hope. New Hope is about 40 mi from Philadelphia.

By Train
SEPTA (☎ 215/580–7800) provides frequent service from Philadelphia's Market Street East, Suburban, and 30th Street stations to Doylestown on the R5 line. The trip takes up to 85 minutes, depending on the number of local stops.

Getting Around

Bucks County is a large area—40 mi long and up to 20 mi wide—and is almost impossible to tour without a car.

Contacts and Resources

Emergencies

Dial **911** in an emergency. There is an emergency room at **Doylestown Hospital** (⊠ 595 W. State St., Doylestown, ☎ 215/345–2200).

Fishing

Fishermen are drawn to the Delaware River and Lake Nockamixon for smallmouth bass, trout, catfish, and carp. The most popular event is the annual shad run (from early April to early June), which has spawned a festival in Lambertville, New Jersey, the last weekend in April. The required fishing license can be purchased at any area sporting goods shop. A three-day tourist license costs $15, and a seven-day license is $30; a trout stamp costs an extra $5.50. For a license and tips on where to fish, try the **Nockamixon Sports Shop** (⊠ 808 Doylestown Pike, Quakertown, ☎ 215/538–9553) or **Dave's Sporting Goods** (⊠ 1127 N. Easton Rd., Rte. 611, north of Doylestown, ☎ 215/766–8000).

Guided Tours

Bucks County Carriages (☎ 215/862–3582) offers 20-minute horse-drawn carriage tours. Horses are "parked" at Logan Inn in New Hope, near the bakery in Peddler's Village, and at the Lambertville station in Lambertville, New Jersey. There are daytime and evening rides depending on the season and departure location. A ride to a catered picnic and customized tours are available by reservation.

Coryell's Ferry Ride and Historic Narrative (☎ 215/862–2050) is a half-hour sightseeing ride on the Delaware River in a 65-ft, 49-passenger stern-wheeler.

Ghost Tours of New Hope (☎ 215/957–9988) leads a one-hour lantern-led walk that explores the haunting tales of the area.

Marlene Miller of Executive Events Inc. (☎ 215/766–2211) has customized group tours and tour groups for individual travelers in 28-passenger minivans. Some tour themes include covered bridges, historic mansions, arts, wineries, antiques, and shopping.

PERSONAL GUIDE

Nancy Neely (☎ 215/283–8778) will drive you around the county in your car. A Bucks County tour guide for more than 20 years, she will take you off the main roads, show you the covered bridges, and amuse you with colorful local stories. Reservations are required.

Parks

Many parks throughout the county have canoes for rent, trails for biking and hiking, and camping facilities. The largest and best equipped is **Nockamixon State Park** (⊠ Rte. 563, Quakertown, ☎ 215/529–7305), which has a 1,450-acre lake, boating and boat rentals, swimming pool, bike path and bike rentals, hiking trails, ice-skating and sledding in winter, and picnic areas. Call the county park (☎ 215/757–0571) or state park (☎ 215/453–5000) office for further information.

The **Delaware Canal State Park** (⊠ 11 Lodi Hill Rd., Upper Black Eddy, ☎ 610/982–5560) follows the path of the Delaware Canal for 60 mi and is a National Historic Landmark. If you're interested in nature walks and guided tours, call the **Friends of the Delaware Canal** (☎ 215/862–2021) for their seasonal calendar of events.

Visitor Information

Bucks County Tourist Commission (⊠ 152 Swamp Rd., Doylestown 18901, ☎ 215/345–4552 or 800/836–2825) is on the Fonthill property. It's open weekdays 9–5:30.

Central Bucks Chamber of Commerce (⊠ Fidelity Bank Building, 115 W. Court St., Doylestown 18901, ☎ 215/348–3913) has brochures with walking tours and other information. It's open weekdays 8:30–4:30.

New Hope Information Center (⊠ 1 W. Mechanic St., at Main St., New Hope 18938, ☎ 215/862–5880 for an automated menu of information, or ☎ 215/862–5030 for a travel counselor) is a convenient place to stop or to contact in advance for information about New Hope and its surroundings. The center also has a free lodging referral service. It's open daily, usually 10–5, but hours vary seasonally.

10 Lancaster County, Hershey, and Gettysburg

In Lancaster County, especially among the Amish, an entirely different past and culture come alive for you. Farmers drive horses in the fields, and drivers slow down for buggies on country roads. You can eat hearty Pennsylvania Dutch cooking and shop at farmers and antiques markets, quilt shops, and outlet stores. Beyond Lancaster County are the battlefield and museums at Gettysburg and the amusement parks and chocolate-themed pleasures of Hershey.

Updated by
Bob Brooke

NEATLY PAINTED FARMSTEADS dot the countryside of Lancaster County, nearly 65 mi west of Philadelphia. Wooden fences outline pastures, and the land looks like a huge quilt of neat rectangles. On country roads horse-drawn buggies jockey with horn-tooting cars for position. Though it's the 20th century, it looks more like the 19th, for this is Pennsylvania's Amish Country, a place where time seems to stand still.

Here, the plain and fancy live side by side. You can glimpse what rural life was like 100 years ago because whole communities of the "Plain" people—as the Old Order Amish are called—shun telephones, electricity, and the entire world of American gadgetry. Clinging to a centuries-old way of life, the Amish, one of the most conservative of the Pennsylvania Dutch sects, shun the amenities of modern civilization, using kerosene or gas lamps instead of electric lighting, horse-drawn buggies instead of automobiles. Ironically, in turning their backs on the modern world, they have attracted its attention.

Today the area's main roads are lined with souvenir shops and attractions of varying quality and can be crowded with busloads of tourists. The area's proximity to Philadelphia and Harrisburg has brought development as non-Amish farmers sell land. In fact, in 1997 the World Monuments Watch put Lancaster County on its annual list of the world's 100 most endangered cultural sites because of rapid suburbanization. But if you look beyond the commercialism and development, there's still much charm in the general stores, one-room schoolhouses, country lanes, and picturesque farms. There are instructive places to learn about the Amish way of life, pretzel factories to tour, quilts to buy, and a host of museums for railroad buffs.

THE CULTURE OF THE PENNSYLVANIA DUTCH

The country's largest and oldest settlement of Plain people—70,000 people in more than 41 Amish, Mennonite and Brethren sects—make Lancaster County their home. Collectively, they're known as the Pennsylvania Dutch. Despite their name, they aren't Dutch at all, but descendants of German and Swiss immigrants who came to the Lancaster area to escape religious persecution. Because of a corruption of the word *Deutsch,* meaning German, they became known as the "Dutch."

The Mennonite movement, named after its leader, Dutch Catholic priest Menno Simons, began in Switzerland in the early 16th century, the time of the Reformation. This radical religious group advocated nonviolence, separation of church and state, adult baptism, and individual freedom in choosing a religion. In 1710 eight families led by Mennonite bishop Hans Herr accepted William Penn's invitation to settle in Lancaster County.

In 1693 Swiss Mennonite bishop Jacob Amman, whose stricter interpretation of church tenets had attracted a following, broke off from the movement and formed his own group to adhere more to the founding beliefs and practices. This group became known as the Amish. Like the Mennonites, the Amish came to live in Lancaster County.

Today there are 137,000 Amish people living in North America, in 20 states and one Canadian province. Lancaster County has the second-largest community in the country, with 17,000 Old Order Amish (Holmes County, Ohio, is first). That the number of Amish has doubled in the last two decades suggests that theirs is still a viable lifestyle.

The eight Amish, 24 Mennonite, and nine Brethren groups differ in their interpretations of the Bible, their use of technology, the value they place on education, their use of English, and their degrees of interaction with outsiders. Brethren and Mennonite groups make use of modern conveniences more than Old Order Mennonites and Amish sects, particularly the Old Order Amish, who shun modern technology.

The Amish religion and way of life stress separation from the world, caring for others of the faith, and self-sufficiency. What may appear as unusual behavior results from religious convictions based on biblical interpretation. The Amish, who reject compulsory school attendance and military registration, do not accept social security benefits or purchase life or property insurance.

Old Order Amish send their children to one-room schoolhouses with eight grades to a room. They avoid larger public schools to prevent the exposure of their children to the influence of "outsiders." Though Amish students study many of the traditional subjects, they learn less about science and technology than their worldly counterparts. The Supreme Court has ruled that Amish children need not attend school beyond the eighth grade, after which students learn agriculture, building trades, and homemaking skills at home.

Farmers work with teams of mules to plow, plant, and harvest their crops. The average farm is small, about 55 acres, but good farming practices make them extremely productive; tobacco is one of the most conspicuous crops. When the tobacco leaves mature in September, whole families take to the fields to cut stalks, after which they hang them in rows from floor to ceiling in tobacco sheds.

As Lancaster County's most visible sect, the Amish can be recognized by their clothing, which is similar to that worn by their ancestors. Their dress and grooming symbolize their role in Amish society. Men must begin to grow a beard upon marriage, and wear several different styles of hats to distinguish their age, status, and their religious district. Amish women wear full-length dresses, capes, and aprons. Those who are baptized wear white organdy caps and don't cut their hair. For a further look into the world of the Amish, *see* "Portrait of the Amish" *in* Chapter 11.

Although some changes have been thrust upon them by the government, the Amish do change and update some rules themselves. Some have telephones in their barns or on the edge of their property, for emergency use only; many will accept a ride in an automobile or take public transportation. They live a lively, rich life of discipline and caring. They seek to be at peace with themselves, their neighbors, their surroundings, and their God.

HISTORIC LANCASTER, HERSHEY, AND GETTYSBURG

The Amish are not the only lure to Lancaster County. Lancaster, which the English named after Lancashire, is an intriguing city to explore. This charmingly residential city of row houses served as the nation's capital for one day during the American Revolution, when Congress fled Philadelphia after the Battle of Brandywine. It is also one of the nation's oldest inland cities, dating from 1710. Historic sites in the area include Wheatland, the home of James Buchanan, Pennsylvania's only contribution to the White House. Around Lancaster you can visit the Landis Valley Museum, an exhibit devoted to rural life before 1900. Ephrata Cloister provides a look at a religious communal society of the 1700s. And Main Street in Lititz, founded in 1756, offers an architectural treat for strollers.

Western Lancaster County, which includes the towns of Marietta, Mount Joy, and Columbia, is a quieter part of the county, where you can bicycle down winding lanes, sample local wines and authentic Mennonite cooking, and explore uncrowded villages. Its history is rooted in the Colonial period. The residents are of Scottish and German descent, and architecture varies from log cabins to Victorian homes. There are a number of good restaurants, inns, and farms that accept guests.

If you've brought your children as far as Lancaster, you may want to continue northwest to Hershey, the "Chocolate Town" founded in 1903 by Milton S. Hershey. Here the number-one attraction is Hersheypark, an 87-acre theme park with kiddie rides and thrill rides, theaters, and live shows. Finally, you may wish to journey southwest to the battlefields and museums of Gettysburg, also within driving distance. Here—as in many other area destinations—you can journey back in time.

Pleasures and Pastimes

History and Culture
A visit to Lancaster County and the surrounding area captures a lot of history in a relatively small space. In towns such as Bird-in-Hand and Intercourse, you can see the Amish living their traditional lifestyle. Museums and activities help interpret complex social and religious history; a drive along country roads off the beaten path will also give you a deeper feeling for this way of life. The city of Lancaster has Revolutionary War sites and President James Buchanan's home, Wheatland. Even if you're not a history buff, a trip to Gettysburg, site of the pivotal 1863 Civil War battle, can be a moving experience.

Dining
Like the German cuisine that influenced it, Pennsylvania Dutch cooking is hearty and uses ingredients from local farms. To sample regional fare, eat at one of the bustling restaurants in the area where diners sit with perhaps a dozen other people and the food is passed around in bowls family style. Meals are plentiful and basic—fried chicken, ham, roast beef, dried corn, buttered noodles, mashed potatoes, chowchow (pickle relish), bread, pepper cabbage—and that's only a partial listing. Entrées are accompanied by traditional "sweets and sours," vegetable dishes made with a vinegar-and-sugar dressing. This is the way the Amish, who hate to throw things out, preserve leftover vegetables.

Don't forget to indulge your sweet tooth with shoofly pie (made with molasses and brown sugar), *snitz* (dried apple) pie, and all kinds of other pies, even for breakfast. Bake shops proudly point out that this is the region that invented the hole in the doughnut (by cutting out the center of *fastnacht* cakes)—so it's not surprising that even the English word *dunk* comes from the Pennsylvania Dutch *dunke*.

Lancaster County offers numerous smorgasbords and reasonably priced family restaurants, along with a number of Continental and French restaurants in contemporary settings and quaint historic inns. Unless otherwise noted, liquor is served. For price-category information, *see* Chapter 3, which has the dining price chart for Philadelphia.

Lodging
Lancaster County lodgings are much like the people themselves—plain or fancy. You can rough it in one of the many campgrounds in the area, stay at an historic inn, or indulge yourself at a full-frills resort. A good selection of moderately priced motels caters to families. Though hotels welcome guests year-round, rates are highest in summer and lower at other times. Some inns and bed-and-breakfasts may have minimum stays in high season.

Twenty-two working Amish and non-Amish farms throughout Lancaster County welcome visitors to stay for a few days and allow them to observe and even participate in farm life. Operated as bed-and-breakfast establishments with a twist, they invite you to help milk the cows and feed the chickens and afterward share a hearty breakfast with the farmer and his family or participate in a number of other farm chores. Reservations must be made weeks in advance as most farms are heavily booked during the summer season. Some are listed with the towns in this chapter; the Pennsylvania Dutch Convention & Visitors Bureau (☞ Lancaster Country A to Z, *below*) has a listing of all area B&Bs and farms that welcome guests. For price-category information, *see* Chapter 4, which has the dining price chart for Philadelphia.

Shopping

There's something for every shopper in Lancaster County, from farmers markets to outlet malls. With several hundred outlet stores, it seems as if Lancaster is trying to compete with Reading as a factory outlet capital. Some are factory stores, with top-quality goods at big discounts. Others call themselves outlets but don't have good bargains. It's best to know the actual retail prices of items before leaving home; don't be misled by so-called sales.

On Sundays antiques hunters frequent the huge antiques malls along Route 272 between Adamstown and Denver. As many as 5,000 dealers may turn up on Extravaganza Days, held in late spring, summer, and early fall. You can spend hours browsing among old books and prints and looking at Victorian clothing, pewter, silver, pottery, and lots of furniture. Or you can stop in a store along a country road to shop for the crafts and handmade quilts for which the area is famous. Galleries, boutiques, roadside stands, and farmers markets abound, offering a wide variety of merchandise.

Exploring Lancaster County

The city of Lancaster, near the center of the county, is close to the heart of Pennsylvania Dutch Country. East of it lie towns such as Intercourse and Bird-in-Hand, with markets, outlet shops, and sights that interpret Amish life. Also nearby is Strasburg, with its railroad museums. Less than half an hour north of Lancaster, the historic towns of Ephrata and Lititz are near farmers markets and antiques malls. The quiet western part of Lancaster County has the Susquehanna River towns of Columbia and Marietta, as well as country towns to the north. For those on an extended tour of south-central Pennsylvania, Gettysburg and Hershey, which are both west of the county, are also included.

Great Itineraries

Most visitors come to Lancaster County to get a glimpse of the Amish and their lifestyle. The territory covered is not that large, and you can see many area sights in a week, though you could spend twice that time. If you have only a couple of days, you'll probably want to concentrate on key Amish towns and Lancaster. With a few more days you can explore the area north of Lancaster or visit Strasburg. If you have up to a week, you can see the quieter towns in the western part of the county and continue on to Hershey or Gettysburg.

Numbers in the text correspond to numbers in the margin and on the Lancaster County map.

IF YOU HAVE 2 DAYS

Begin your tour of Amish Country in **Intercourse** ⑤ and visit People's Place, a cultural interpretation center with good introductory films and an exhibit for children. If you'd rather see the area by Amish buggy, follow Route 340 west to **Bird-in-Hand** ⑥ and take a tour with Aaron & Jessica's Buggy Rides, the only Amish-owned and -operated tour of its kind in the area. Also in this area are such sights as the Amish Farm and House. Farmers markets and shops will easily fill the day before you head to **Lancaster** ① for the night. On Day 2 explore this historic city. The Heritage Center Museum shows the work of Lancaster County artists and craftspeople, past and present. The Historic Lancaster Walking Tour, given at midday, is a 90-minute stroll through the heart of town. On Tuesday or Friday be sure to visit the Central Market, with its open-air stalls brimming with produce and baked goods. Antique lovers will want to see Historic Rock Ford Plantation, with its exhibits of antiques and folk art.

IF YOU HAVE 4 DAYS

Follow the two-day itinerary above for the beginning of your trip. On Day 3 continue on in the **Lancaster** ① area. While in the city visit **Wheatland** ②, the home of former president James Buchanan, and the **Hans Herr House** ③, on the south side of the city. Take an hour or two to explore the country roads east of the city. Drive the side roads between Routes 23 and 340 to see Amish farms (the ones with windmills and green blinds) along the way. You can stop at roadside stands and farms with signs advertising quilts and fresh produce. Then head up the Oregon Pike (Route 272) to visit the **Landis Valley Museum** ④, an outdoor museum of Pennsylvania German rural life and folk culture before 1900, and drive on to ⊡ **Ephrata** ⑧ and ⊡ **Lititz** ⑨, either of which is good for an overnight. On Day 4 you can visit the Ephrata Cloister, tour a pretzel or chocolate museum in Lititz, or, depending on the day of the week, spend the day shopping for antiques. Another choice for Day 4 is to spend your time in ⊡ **Strasburg** ⑦, which has the Railroad Museum of Pennsylvania and the don't-miss Strasburg Rail Road ride. Also here is the Amish Village, including a blacksmith shop, one-room schoolhouse, and smokehouse.

IF YOU HAVE 7 DAYS

Follow the four-day itinerary for the beginning of your trip. On Day 5 head west to the sleepy towns of Marietta, Columbia, and Mount Joy; any of these is fine for your overnight. The river town of ⊡ **Columbia** ⑩ has the excellent Watch and Clock Museum of the National Association of Watch and Clock Collectors, as well as Wright's Ferry Mansion, the former residence of English Quaker Susanna Wright, whose family helped found the town. The restored town of ⊡ **Marietta** ⑪ is perfect for strolling and browsing. You can tour a historic brewery in ⊡ **Mount Joy** ⑬ or take the wine-tasting tour at the **Nissley Vineyards and Winery Estate** ⑫, near Bainbridge. On Day 6 you have a choice, depending on your interests. You can visit ⊡ **Hershey** ⑮, with its amusement park, zoo, and Chocolate World, or tour the Civil War battlefields and museums of ⊡ **Gettysburg** ⑯.

When to Tour Lancaster County, Hershey, and Gettysburg

Lancaster County can be hectic, especially on summer weekends and in October, when the fall foliage attracts crowds. Its main arteries, U.S. 30 (also known as the Lincoln Highway and Lancaster Pike) and Route 340 (sometimes called the Old Philadelphia Pike), are lined with gift shops and outlets. Farmers markets and family-style restaurants overflow with people. The trick is to visit the top sights and then get off the beaten path. If possible, plan your trip for early spring, September, or Christmas season, when it is less crowded. You should note that although many restaurants, shops, and farmers markets close Sunday for the Sabbath, commercial attractions remain open.

Lancaster County

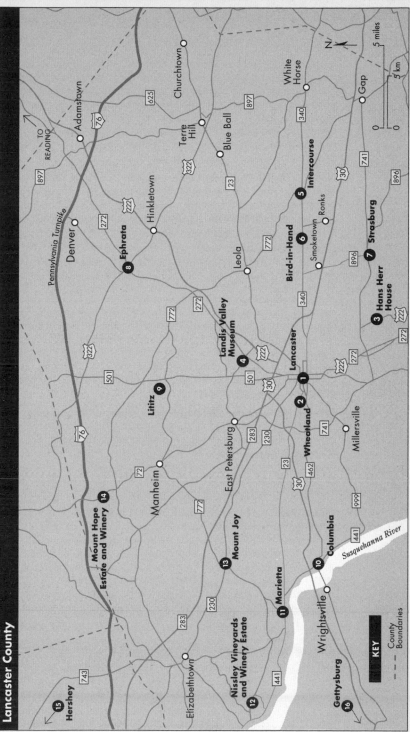

AROUND LANCASTER
Heart of Pennsylvania Dutch Country

In roughly the center of Lancaster County, Lancaster has plenty to see and also makes a good base for exploring the surrounding countryside. The area east of Lancaster, centered around Intercourse, makes up the heart of Amish Country. Here, between Routes 340 and 23 in towns with names like Blue Ball, Paradise, and Bird-in-Hand, live most of Lancaster County's Amish community. Strasburg, to the southeast, has sights for train buffs. No more than 12 mi north of Lancaster, Ephrata and Lititz are lovely, historic towns.

One note: When you are visiting among the Amish, remember to respect their values. They believe that photographs and videos with recognizable reproductions of them violate the biblical commandment against making graven images. You will be asked to refrain from photographing or making videos of the Amish, and you should comply.

Lancaster

❶ *75 mi west of Philadelphia.*

The heart of Pennsylvania Dutch Country, Lancaster is a colorful small city that combines the Colonial past with the Pennsylvania Dutch present. During the French and Indian War and the American Revolution, its craftsmen turned out fine guns, building the city's reputation as the arsenal of the colonies. And on September 27, 1777, Lancaster became the national capital for a day, as Congress fled the British in Philadelphia. Today you will find markets and museums that preserve the area's history.

The **Historic Lancaster Walking Tour,** a 90-minute stroll through the heart of this charming old city, is conducted by costumed guides who impart anecdotes about 50 points of architectural and historical interest covering six square blocks. Tours depart from the visitor center downtown. ⊠ *S. Queen and Vine Sts. near Penn Sq.,* ☎ *717/392–1776.* ⊡ *$5.* ⊙ *Tours April.–Oct., Tues. and Fri.–Sat. at 10 and 1, Sun., Mon., Wed.–Thurs. at 1; Nov.–Mar., by reservation only.*

★ **Central Market,** which began with open-air stalls in 1742, is where locals shop for fresh fruit and vegetables, meats (try the Lebanon bologna), flowers, and baked goods such as sticky buns and shoofly pie. The current Romanesque building, in the heart of town, was constructed in 1889 and is one of the oldest covered markets in the country. It's a good place to pick up food for a picnic. ⊠ *Penn Sq.,* ☎ *717/291–4723.* ⊙ *Tues. and Fri. 6–4, Sat. 6–2.*

The **Demuth Foundation** includes the restored 18th-century home, studio, and garden of Charles Demuth (1883–1935), one of America's first modernist artists. A watercolorist, Demuth found inspiration in the geometric shapes of machines and modern technology. A few of his works are usually on display. The complex includes a museum shop and the oldest operating tobacco shop (1770) in the country. ⊠ *114 E. King St.,* ☎ *717/299–9940.* ⊡ *Free.* ⊙ *Feb.–Dec., Tues.–Sat. 10–4, Sun. 1–4.*

The Old City Hall, reborn as the **Heritage Center Museum,** shows the work of Lancaster County artisans and craftsmen—clocks, furniture, homemade toys, Fraktur (documents in a style of calligraphy with folk art decorations), and Pennsylvania long rifles. Some exhibits are on display permanently, while others rotate. ✉ *King and Queen Sts. on Penn Sq.,* ☎ *717/299–6440.* ✉ *Donation requested.* ⊘ *Tues.–Sat. 10–4.*

Historic Rock Ford Plantation is the restored home of General Edward Hand, Revolutionary War commander, George Washington's adjutant, and member of the Continental Congress. Eighteenth-century antiques and folk art are displayed in a 1794 Georgian-style house. The **Kauffman Museum,** in the restored 18th-century barn, holds the Zoe and Henry Kauffman collection of pewter, brass, copper, tin, firearms, and furniture. ✉ *Lancaster County Park, at 881 Rock Ford Rd.,* ☎ *717/392–7223.* ✉ *$4.50.* ⊘ *Apr.–Oct., Tues.–Sat. 10–4, Sun. noon–4.*

★ ❷ **Wheatland** was the home of the only president from Pennsylvania, James Buchanan, who served from 1857–1861. The restored 1828 Federal mansion displays the 15th president's furniture just as it was during his lifetime. A one-hour tour includes a profile of the only bachelor to occupy the White House. ✉ *1120 Marietta Ave., Rte. 23, 1½ mi west of Lancaster,* ☎ *717/392–8721.* ✉ *$5.50.* ⊘ *Apr.–mid-Dec., daily 10–4.*

★ ❸ The **Hans Herr House,** the oldest in Lancaster County, is considered the best example of medieval-style German architecture in North America. The subject of several paintings by Andrew Wyeth, the house was the Colonial home of the Herr family, to whom the Wyeths are related. Today the house is owned by the Lancaster Mennonite Historical Society, which educates the public about the Mennonite religion by using exhibits about their way of life in its visitor center. The 45-minute tours cover the grounds and the 1719 sandstone house, a former Mennonite meeting place. ✉ *1849 Hans Herr Dr., 5 mi south of Lancaster off U.S. 222,* ☎ *717/464–4438.* ✉ *$3.50.* ⊘ *Apr.–Nov., Mon.–Sat. 9–4.*

❹ The **Landis Valley Museum** is an outdoor museum of Pennsylvania German rural life and folk culture before 1900. Owned by brothers Henry and George Landis, the farm and village are now operated by the Pennsylvania Historical and Museum Commission. You can visit more than 15 historical buildings, from a farmstead to a country store. From May through October there are demonstrations of such skills as spinning and weaving, pottery making, and tinsmithing, the products of which are for sale in the Weathervane Shop. ✉ *2451 Kissel Hill Rd., off Oregon Pike, Rte. 272,* ☎ *717/569–0401.* ✉ *$7.* ⊘ *Mar.–Oct., Tues.–Sat. 9–5, Sun. noon–5.*

☾ With 44 acres of games and rides, **Dutch Wonderland** amusement park is ideally suited for families with younger children. Most rides are tame. The rides are supplemented by diving shows, an animated bear show, and concerts. ✉ *2249 U.S. 30, east of Lancaster,* ☎ *717/291–1888.* ✉ *$19 for unlimited rides.* ⊘ *Memorial Day–Labor Day, daily 10–7 or later; Labor Day–Oct. 31 and Easter–Memorial Day, Sat. 10–6, Sun. 11–6.*

Dining and Lodging

$$ ✕ **The Log Cabin.** Steak, lamb chops, and seafood are prepared on a
★ charcoal grill in this 1928 expanded log cabin, which was a speakeasy during Prohibition. The atmosphere is elegant, and the setting is embellished with an impressive art collection. ✉ *11 Lehoy Forest Dr., off Rte. 272, 6 mi northeast of Lancaster, Leola,* ☎ *717/626–1181. AE, D, MC, V. No lunch.*

$$ ✕ **Market Fare.** The cuisine is American, and steaks, seafood, and veal are served in a cozy dining room with upholstered armchairs and 19th-century paintings, drawings, and photographs. Homemade soups and breads highlight the diverse menu. A children's menu and a light menu are also available. The café upstairs offers a light breakfast, quick lunch, and takeout. ⊠ *Market and Grant Sts. across from Central Market,* ☎ *717/299–7090. AE, D, DC, MC, V.*

$$ ✕ **Olde Greenfield Inn.** Continental cuisine and a fine wine cellar form part of the appeal in this gracious circa-1780 restored farmhouse. House specialties include roast duckling with raspberry sauce, Cajun beef with shrimp, and jumbo lump crab cakes. Lighter entrées, such as seafood crepes, are also available. A piano player provides entertainment in the lounge on weekends. In good weather you can dine on the patio. ⊠ *595 Greenfield Rd.,* ☎ *717/393–0668. AE, D, DC, MC, V. No dinner Sun.*

$–$$ ✕ **Center City Grill.** This casual but elegant bar and restaurant has a convenient downtown location for those exploring the city center. The varied international menu gives you a choice of anything from Thai chicken in peanut-and-ginger sauce to gourmet pizzas to quiche Lorraine. Most nights there is dancing to DJ-spun tunes, and you can listen to live jazz on Sunday evening. A children's menu is available. ⊠ *10 S. Prince St.,* ☎ *717/299–3456. AE, D, DC, MC, V.*

$ ✕ **Lancaster Dispensing Co.** Fajitas, salads, sandwiches, and nachos are served until midnight in this stylish Victorian pub. The selection of imported beers is extensive. On the weekend you can hear live music. ⊠ *33–35 N. Market St.,* ☎ *717/299–4602. AE, MC, V.*

$ ✕ **The Pressroom.** The menus look like newspapers, and headline banners hang over the bar in this upscale bistro in an old warehouse. The open kitchen has an exposed baking hearth. The menu runs toward sandwiches (named after newspaper cartoon characters), salads, pizza, and pasta dishes. In summer you can sit in the park outside. ⊠ *16–18 W. King St.,* ☎ *717/295–1316. AE, MC, V.*

$$–$$$ 🏨 **Holiday Inn Lancaster Host Resort and Conference Center.** This sprawling family resort has a striking marble lobby and comfortable, contemporary rooms with cherry-wood furnishings. The golf course and grounds are beautifully landscaped. A camp program for children ages 1–12 is offered daily during the summer and on weekends throughout the year. ⊠ *2300 Lincoln Hwy. E, Rte. 30, 17602,* ☎ *717/299–5500 or 800/233–0121. 330 rooms. 2 restaurants, piano bar, indoor-outdoor pool, 27-hole golf course, miniature golf, 12 tennis courts. AE, DC, MC, V.*

$$–$$$ 🏨 **Willow Valley Family Resort and Conference Center.** This mom-and-pop operation has blossomed into a large, stylish family resort. The striking skylighted atrium lobby is surrounded by attractive rooms; the ones overlooking the atrium are the most attractive and the most expensive. Since the resort is Mennonite owned, there is no liquor permitted on the premises. ⊠ *2416 Willow St. Pike, 17602,* ☎ *717/ 464–2711 or 800/444–1714,* FAX *717/464–4784. 353 rooms. 2 restaurants, outdoor pool, 2 indoor pools, hot tub, sauna, steam room, 9-hole golf course, 2 tennis courts, exercise room, recreation room. AE, D, DC, MC, V.*

$$ 🏨 **Best Western Eden Resort Inn.** Spacious contemporary rooms (request a room poolside) and attractive grounds contribute to a pleas-
★ ant stay here. The inn has a stunning tropical indoor pool and whirlpool under a retractable roof. The award-winning chef in Arthur's is noted for seafood and pasta dishes; casual fun food is presented in Garfield's. ⊠ *222 Eden Rd., U.S. 30 and Rte. 272, 17601,* ☎ *717/569–6444 or*

800/528–1234, FAX 717/569–4208. 275 rooms, 40 suites. 2 restaurants, indoor pool, outdoor pool, sauna, tennis court, exercise room. AE, D, DC, MC, V.

$$ ☎ **King's Cottage.** This elegant Spanish mansion on the National Register of Historic Places has been transformed into a B&B furnished with antiques and 18th-century English reproductions. A library and an outdoor goldfish pond are additional pleasures. The price includes breakfast and afternoon tea. ✉ *1049 E. King St., 17602,* ☎ *717/397–1017 or 800/747–8717, FAX 717/397–3447. 9 rooms. Library. D, MC, V.*

$$ ☎ **Lancaster Hilton Garden Inn.** An elegant, contemporary hotel popular with corporate travelers offers oversize rooms, many with cathedral ceilings and large desks. There's a complimentary Continental breakfast, as well as free coffee in rooms. ✉ *101 Granite Run Dr., intersection of Rtes. 72 and 283, 17601,* ☎ *717/560–0880. 155 rooms. Restaurant, indoor pool, exercise room. AE, D, DC, MC, V.*

Nightlife and the Arts

The **American Music Theatre** (✉ 2425 Lincoln Highway E, ☎ 717/397–7700 or 800/648–4102) is a new 1,500-seat facility that presents full-scale productions, such as "From Branson to Broadway," especially designed to celebrate American music. There are afternoon and evening shows daily.

The draws at the 400-seat **Dutch Apple Dinner Theater** (✉ 510 Centerville Rd., at U.S. 30, ☎ 717/898–1900) are a candlelight buffet plus Broadway musicals and comedies, such as *Camelot* and *Fiddler on the Roof.* Call for reservations for matinees and dinner shows.

A National Landmark, the 19-century **Fulton Opera House** (✉ 12 N. Prince St., ☎ 717/397–7425) is home to the Fulton Theater Company, the Actors Company of Pennsylvania, the Lancaster Symphony Orchestra, and the Lancaster Opera.

Outdoor Activities and Sports

The **Holiday Inn Lancaster Host Resort and Conference Center** (✉ 2300 Lincoln Hwy. E, ☎ 717/299–5500) has 27 holes of regulation golf; carts aren't required. Greens fees are $28 for 18 holes, $11.50 per person for a cart. Rental clubs are available.

Shopping

CRAFTS

Although craftspeople in the Lancaster County area produce fine handiwork, folk art, quilts, and needlework, much of the best work is sold to galleries nationwide and never shows up in local shops.

The **Olde Mill House Shoppes** (✉ 105 Strasburg Pike, ☎ 717/299–0678), one of Lancaster's oldest country stores, carries a fine choice of pottery, folk art, country and Shaker furniture, and primitive ceiling and table lighting.

Pandora's Antiques (✉ 2014 Old Philadelphia Pike, just east of U.S. 30, ☎ 717/299–5305) sells antique quilts and textiles made in Lancaster County. Call ahead.

The **Tin Bin** (✉ 20 Valley Rd., off Rte. 501, north of Lancaster in Neffsville, ☎ 717/569–6210) stocks handmade tinware and pottery and reproductions of 18th-century lighting devices.

Among the few places that carry fine local crafts is the **Weathervane Shop** (✉ 2451 Kissel Hill Rd., ☎ 717/569–9312), at the Landis Valley Museum, where craftspeople sell the wares they make on-site—tin, pottery, leather, braided rugs, weaving, and caned chairs.

OUTLETS

U.S. 30 is lined with outlets of varying quality; be sure to check the retail prices of whatever you want before you leave home. With more than 120 stores, from Lenox to London Fog and the huge Reading China & Glass, the **Rockvale Square Factory Outlet Village** (⊠ U.S. 30 and Rte. 896, ☎ 717/293–9595) is the largest outlet center in Lancaster. The **Tanger Outlet at Millstream** (⊠ 311 Outlet Dr., Rte. 30 E, ☎ 717/392–7202) is a collection of 53 designer outlets, including Ann Taylor and Brooks Brothers. The **Dutch Gems and Jewelry Outlet** (⊠ 2208 Lincoln Hwy. E, ☎ 717/396–0810) sells unusual gems and jewelry, especially gemstone jewelry and handmade rings, pendants, earrings, and bracelets.

Intercourse

⑤ *10 mi east of Lancaster.*

Intercourse is a center for Amish life. Many places that will help you better understand this community can be found between here and Bird-in-Hand (☞ *below*). The town is at the intersection, or intercourse, of two roads (today's Routes 340 and 772), which is how it got its name in Colonial times.

★ ☺ The **People's Place,** a "people-to-people interpretation center," provides an excellent introduction to the Amish, Mennonite, and Hutterite communities. A 30-minute multiscreen slide show titled *Who Are the Amish?* has close-ups of Amish life and perceptive narration. Geared toward children, **Amish World** is a hands-on exhibit on transportation, dress, schools, and mutual aid in Amish society. Children can try on bonnets and play in the "feeling box." Don't miss the collection of wood carvings by Aaron Zook. *Hazel's People,* a feature film starring Geraldine Page and set in the Mennonite community, is shown Monday–Saturday from Memorial Day through Labor Day at 7:30 PM (with a separate admission fee). There's a bookstore, too. ⊠ *3513 Old Philadelphia Pike, Rte. 340,* ☎ *717/768–7171.* 🎫 *$3.50.* ☾ *Memorial Day–Labor Day, Mon.–Sat. 9:30–9:30; Labor Day–Memorial Day, Mon.–Sat. 9:30–5.*

NEED A BREAK?	For a rest from sightseeing, head to the ☺ **Lapp Valley Farm,** which sells 18 flavors of homemade ice cream and root beer and has animals to entertain the children. ⊠ *Mentzer Rd. between Intercourse and New Holland, from Intercourse follow Rte. 340 1 mi east, turn left on New Holland Rd., left on Peters Rd., and right on Mentzer Rd.,* ☎ *717/354–7988.* ☾ *Mon.–Thurs. noon–dark, Fri. 8–dark, Sat. 8–7 or later.*

Dining and Lodging

$ ✕ **Kling House.** The Kling family home has been converted into a charming, casual restaurant that serves American cuisine throughout the day. Cranberry chicken, London broil, and *knepp* (ham) entrées come with complimentary appetizer of red-pepper jam and cream cheese with crackers. The soups are homemade, and the desserts are luscious. A children's menu is available. ⊠ *Kitchen Kettle Village, Rtes. 340 and 772,* ☎ *717/768–8261. D, MC, V. Closed Sun. No dinner Mon.–Wed.*

$ ✕ **Stoltzfus Farm Restaurant.** Homemade Pennsylvania Dutch foods are served family style in a small country farmhouse, with most ingredients grown on the farm. Most dishes are so tasty (especially the ham loaf with vinegar and brown sugar) you'll want the recipes—and the owners will happily supply you with them. ⊠ *Rte. 772E, ½ mi east* *of Rte. 340,* ☎ *717/768–8156.* ⊙ *May–Oct., Mon.–Sat.; call for limited hours in Apr. and Nov.*

$ ⚏ **Spring Gulch Resort Campground.** Glorious farmland and forest are the setting for the campsites (pleasantly shaded) and a limited number of more expensive rental cottages (two-night minimum stay is $148). A full schedule of weekend activities includes country dances and chicken barbecues. ⊠ *Rte. 897 between Rtes. 340 and 322, New Holland 17557,* ☎ *717/354–3100 or 800/255–5744. 500 sites, 4 cottages. 2 pools, lake, spa, miniature golf, tennis courts, volleyball, fishing, recreation room.*

Shopping

The **Country Market at Intercourse** (⊠ 3504 Old Philadelphia Pike, ☎ 717/768–8058) has the handmade works of local Amish families, including toys, quilts, and furniture. Within the market Amishland Prints (☎ 717/768–7273) sells prints depicting the Amish in rural daily life as well as landscapes by artist and folklorist Xtian Newswanger.

Kitchen Kettle Village (⊠ Rte. 340, ☎ 717/768–8261 or 800/732–3538) consists of 32 shops showcasing local crafts, including decoy carving, furniture making, leather tooling, relish, jam, and jelly making, and tin punching. The shops are closed Sunday. The Kling House (☞ Dining and Lodging, *above*) is here, too.

The **Old Country Store** (⊠ 3510 Old Philadelphia Pike, ☎ 717/768–7101) carries items from more than 450 local craftspeople. It also has a large selection of quilts and discounted fabrics.

The **Old Road Furniture Company** (⊠ 3457 Old Philadelphia Pike, ☎ 717/768–7171) has lovely furniture handcrafted by Amish craftspeople, including harvest and farm tables, chairs, chests, and desks.

Bird-in-Hand

❻ *3 mi west of Intercourse.*

This village, like many others, took its name from the sign on an early inn and tavern. Today it is a center for the Pennsylvania Dutch farming community.

★ ☾ **Aaron & Jessica's Buggy Rides** is the only one owned and operated by Amish. Tour the countryside in an authentic Amish carriage in one of three different half-hour tours. ⊠ *Rte. 340 between Bird-in-Hand and Intercourse at Plain & Fancy Farm,* ☎ *717/768–8828.* 🎟 *$10.* ⊙ *Mon.–Sat., 8–dusk.*

On **Abe's Buggy Rides** Abe chats about the Amish during a 2-mi spin down country roads in an Amish family carriage. ⊠ *2596 Old Philadelphia Pike, no phone.* 🎟 *$10.* ⊙ *Mon.–Sat. 8–dusk.*

The **Amish Experience** is a multimedia theater presentation about the history of the Amish, using 3-D sets, multiple screens and special effects. In *Jacob's Choice,* the teenage main character struggles between traditional ways and the temptations of the present. ⊠ *Rte. 340 between Bird-in-Hand and Intercourse at Plain & Fancy Farm,* ☎ *717/768–8400.* 🎟 *$6.* ⊙ *Apr.–June, Mon.–Sat. 9–5, Sun. 10–5; July–Oct., Mon.–Sat. 8:30–8, Sun. 9:30–6; Nov.–Mar., daily 10–5; shows on the hour.*

At the **Amish Country Homestead,** a re-creation of a nine-room Old Order Amish house, you can learn about the clothing of the Amish and how they live without electricity. ⊠ *Rte. 340 between Bird-in-Hand*

and Intercourse at Plain & Fancy Farm, ☎ *717/768–8400.* 🍴 *$9.* ☉
*July–Oct., Mon.–Sat. 9:45–6:45; Apr.–June and Nov., Mon.–Sat. 9:45–
4:45; Dec.–Mar., weekends 10–4:45.*

The **Amish Farm and House** offers 40-minute tours through a 10-
room circa-1805 house furnished in the Old Order Amish style. A map
guides you to the farmstead's animals, waterwheel, and barns. ✉ *2395
Lincoln Hwy. E, 4½ mi east on U.S. 30, in Smoketown,* ☎ *717/394–
6185.* 🍴 *$5.* ☉ *Spring and fall, daily 8:30–5; winter, daily 8:30–4;
summer, daily 8:30–6.*

The **Folk Craft Center and Museum,** housed in early 18th-century
buildings, has displays of pottery, household implements, toys, glassware, quilts, and early Pennsylvania Dutch memorabilia. An antique
loom is on exhibit in a log cabin built in 1762. Woodworking and print
shop demonstrations show early techniques. In spring and summer the
ornamental and herb gardens come alive with color. ✉ *445 Mt. Sid-
ney Rd., ½ mi west of town, north of Rte. 340 in Witmer,* ☎ *717/397–
36091.* 🍴 *$3.50.* ☉ *Apr.–Nov., Mon.–Sat. 9–5, Sun. 10–4.*

Dining and Lodging

$ ✕ **Amish Barn Restaurant.** Pennsylvania Dutch cuisine is served fam-
ily style, which means generous helpings of meat and produce, breads,
and pies. Apple dumplings and shoofly pie are specialties. You can choose
from an à la carte menu or order a family-style meal. No liquor is served.
✉ *3029 Old Philadelphia Pike, Rte. 340, between Bird-in-Hand and
Intercourse,* ☎ *717/768–8886. AE, D, MC, V.*

$ ✕ **Bird-in-Hand Family Restaurant.** This family-owned diner-style
★ restaurant has a good reputation for hearty Pennsylvania Dutch home
cooking. The menu is à la carte, but there's a lunch buffet weekdays.
It's an excellent place to sample local specialties such as apple dumplings
and chicken potpie. No liquor is served. ✉ *2760 Old Philadelphia Pike,
Rte. 340,* ☎ *717/768–8266. MC, V. Closed Sun.*

$ ✕ **Good 'N Plenty.** Don't bother to ask for a menu here: They just bring
★ out heaps of Pennsylvania Dutch cuisine. Share a table with about a
dozen other customers and be treated to hearty regional fare, including traditional "sweets and sours." More than 650 can be served at
this bustling family-style restaurant, nicely set within a remodeled
Amish farmhouse. ✉ *Rte. 896, ½ mi north of U.S. 30,* ☎ *717/394–
7111. MC, V. Closed Sun. and Jan.*

$ ✕ **Miller's Smorgasbord.** Miller's presents a lavish spread with a good
★ selection of Pennsylvania Dutch foods. Breakfast (served end of May–
October) is sensational here, with omelets, pancakes, and eggs cooked
to order, fresh fruits, pastries, bacon, sausage, potatoes, and much more.
It's one of the few area restaurants open Sunday. ✉ *2811 Lincoln Hwy.
E, U.S. 30 in Ronks, south of Bird-in-Hand,* ☎ *717/687–6621 or 800/
669–3568. AE, D, MC, V.*

$ ✕ **Plain and Fancy Farm.** This family-style restaurant serves heaping
helpings of stick-to-your-ribs Pennsylvania Dutch food. There are specialty shops on the grounds, too. ✉ *Rte. 340 between Bird-in-Hand
and Intercourse,* ☎ *717/768–8281. AE, MC, V.*

$–$$ 🏨 **Bird-in-Hand Family Inn.** Plain, clean, comfortable rooms and a
friendly staff are the highlights of this family-run motel. There's complimentary coffee in rooms. ✉ *2740 Old Philadelphia Pike, 17505,*
☎ *717/768–8271 or 800/537–2535,* ℻ *717/768–1768. 100 rooms.
Restaurant, indoor pool, outdoor pool, tennis court, playground. AE,
D, DC, MC, V.*

$–$$ 🏨 **Hershey Farm Restaurant and Motor Inn.** This continually expanding motel south of Bird-in-Hand overlooks a picture-perfect pond and a farm. Ask for one of the large rooms in the newer building. The handy restaurant offers a buffet and reasonably priced à la carte meals. ✉ *240 Hartman Bridge Rd., Ronks 17572,* ☎ *717/687–8635 or 800/ 827–8635,* 🅵🅰🆇 *717/687–8638. 59 rooms. Restaurant, no-smoking rooms, pool. AE, D, MC, V.*

$–$$ 🏨 **Village Inn of Bird-in-Hand.** The Victorian flavor of this three-story country inn, built in 1734 to serve travelers along the Old Philadelphia Pike, is tempered by the modern comforts of down-filled bedding, cable TV, and phones. Continental breakfast, an evening snack, and a two-hour tour of the area are complimentary. Guests have pool and tennis privileges at the nearby Bird-in-Hand Family Inn (☞ *above*). ✉ *2695 Old Philadelphia Pike, Rte. 340, 17505,* ☎ *717/293–8369 or 800/914–2473. 5 rooms, 6 suites. AE, D, MC, V.*

$ 🏨 **Mill Stream Motor Lodge.** Long a popular choice, this motel overlooks a picturesque stream. Request a room in the rear to get the prettiest view. Breakfast is available in the restaurant, but no alcohol is served. Guests have exercise and pool privileges at Willow Valley, a sister property. ✉ *Rte. 896, 17576,* ☎ *717/299–0931,* 🅵🅰🆇 *717/295–9326. 52 rooms, 3 suites. Restaurant. AE, D, MC, V.*

$ ⛺ **Mill Bridge Village and Campresort.** This campground is attached to a restored 18th-century village. Guests have free admission to village and buggy rides. ✉ *S. Ronks Rd., ½ mi south of U.S. 30, Ronks 17579,* ☎ *717/687–8181 or 800/645–2744. 101 sites. Snack bar, fishing.*

Shopping

Bird-in-Hand Farmers Market (✉ Rte. 340, ☎ 717/393–9674) is an indoor market with produce stands, baked goods, gift shops, outlets, and a snack counter. It's open Wednesday–Saturday from April to November, Friday and Saturday the rest of the year.

Strasburg

❼ *5 mi south of Bird-in-Hand.*

Although settled by French Huguenots, the village of Strasburg, is today a community of Pennsylvania Dutch. It is best known as the railroad center of eastern Pennsylvania; railroad buffs can easily spend a day here. You can also visit the Amish Village, which has buildings typical of the community.

☾ The **Strasburg Rail Road** offers a scenic 9-mi round-trip excursion from Strasburg to Paradise on a rolling antique chartered in 1832 to carry milk, mail, and coal. Called America's oldest short line, the Strasburg run has wooden coaches pulled by an iron steam locomotive. You can lunch in the dining car or buy a box lunch in the restaurant at the station and have a picnic at Groff's Grove along the line. ✉ *Rte. 741,* ☎ *717/687–7522.* 🎫 *$7.50 round-trip.* ☉ *Apr.–June and Sept., daily 11– 4; July–Aug., daily 10–7; Oct.–Mar., weekends noon–3; closed 1st 2 wks in Jan. Trains depart every 30–60 mins depending on season; call for an exact schedule.*

★ ☾ The **Railroad Museum of Pennsylvania,** across the road from the Strasburg Rail Road, holds 75 pieces of train history, including 13 colossal engines built between 1888 and 1930; 12 railroad cars including a Pullman sleeper that operated from 1855 to 1913; sleighs; and railroad memorabilia documenting the history of Pennsylvania railroading. More than 50 of the pieces are kept indoors in the Hall of Rolling

Stock. ⊠ *Rte. 741,* ☎ *717/687–8628.* ⊞ *$6.* ☉ *May–Oct., Mon.–Sat. 9–5, Sun. noon–5; Nov.–Apr., Tues.–Sat. 9–5, Sun. noon–5.*

★ ℭ The **National Toy Train Museum,** the showplace of the Train Collectors Association, displays antique and 20th-century model trains. There are five huge operating layouts, with toy trains from the 1800s to the present, plus hundreds of locomotives and cars in display cases and nostalgia films. Take the kids to see the special hands-on layouts every Friday from June through August. ⊠ *Paradise La. just north of Rte. 741,* ☎ *717/687–8976.* ⊞ *$3.* ☉ *May–Oct. and Christmas wk, daily 10–5; Apr. and Nov.–mid-Dec., weekends only.*

The **Gast Classic Motorcars Exhibit** has an ever-changing collection of more than 50 mint-condition antique, classic, celebrity, and high-performance cars. A gift shop sells books and auto memorabilia. ⊠ *Rte. 896,* ☎ *717/687–9500.* ⊞ *$6.* ☉ *Memorial Day–Labor Day, daily 9–9; Labor Day–Memorial Day, Sun.–Thurs. 9–5, Fri.–Sat. 9–9.*

ℭ **Choo-Choo Barn, Traintown, USA,** is a family hobby that got out of hand: What started in 1945 as a single train chugging around the Groff family Christmas tree is now a 1,700-square-ft display of Lancaster County in miniature, with 16 trains and 140 figures and vehicles in O-gauge. Every five minutes a house catches on fire, and fire engines turn on their hoses to extinguish the blaze. Flag bearers march in a Memorial Day parade, and animals perform in a three-ring circus. Periodically the overhead lights dim, and it becomes night, when streetlights glow and locomotive headlights pierce the darkness. ⊠ *Rte. 741,* ☎ *717/687–7911.* ⊞ *$3.* ☉ *Apr.–Dec., daily 10–5 (later in summer).*

The **Amish Village** offers guided tours through an authentically furnished Amish house. Afterward you can wander about the grounds of the village, which includes a one-room schoolhouse, a blacksmith shop, and an operating smokehouse built for the Amish Village by Amish craftsmen. ⊠ *Rte. 896 between U.S. 30 and Rte. 741,* ☎ *717/687–8511.* ⊞ *$6.50.* ☉ *Spring and fall, daily 9–5; summer, daily 9–6; winter, house tours weekends 10–4.*

Dining and Lodging

$$ ✕ **Iron Horse Inn.** This rustic, candlelighted restaurant is housed in the original 1780s Hotel Strasburg. Best bets are the catch of the day, the homemade breads, and for dessert, the great warm apple pie. There's live entertainment on weekends and an extensive wine list. ⊠ *135 E. Main St., Rte. 741,* ☎ *717/687–6362. AE, D, DC, MC, V. Closed Mon. Dec.–May.*

$–$$ ✕ **Washington House Restaurant.** One of the restaurants at the Historic Strasburg Inn (☞ *below*) offers fine candlelight dining in two Colonial-style dining rooms. The American menu features steaks, jumbo lump crab cakes, and wild game. The lunch buffet is bountiful. ⊠ *Rte. 896, Historic Dr.,* ☎ *717/687–7691 or 800/872–0201. AE, D, DC, MC, V.*

$$ ▥ **Fulton Steamboat Inn.** At Lancaster County's busiest intersection,
★ across from rows of outlet stores, are a small lake, waterfalls, the piped-in sounds of a river, and a hotel that looks just like a steamboat. Named after Lancaster native Robert Fulton, who built the first successful passenger steamer in 1807, the hotel aims to please all landlocked boaters. Inside, the decor is coordinated, right down to the costumed staff in the Victorian-style lobby. The inn has three levels: The uppermost deck has whirlpool baths and private outdoor decks; the middle level has staterooms with two queen-size beds; and the bottom level has cabins with nautical nuances and bunk beds. Rooms have

turn-of-the-century-style furnishings, microwaves, and mini-refrigerators. Package plans include meals and admission to area attractions. ⊠ *Rtes. 30 and 896, Box 333, 17579,* ☎ *717/299–9999 or 800/922–2229 outside PA,* FAX *717/299–9992. 95 rooms. Restaurant, indoor pool, exercise room, recreation room. AE, MC, V.*

$$ ⊞ **Historic Strasburg Inn.** Just a whistle stop from all of Strasburg's railroad attractions, this Colonial-style inn with five buildings is set on 58 peaceful acres overlooking farmland. The rooms come with double beds; a Continental-plus breakfast is included. ⊠ *Rte. 896, Historic Dr., 17579,* ☎ *717/687–7691 or 800/872–0201. 101 rooms. 2 restaurants, pool, exercise room, volleyball. AE, D, DC, MC, V.*

$–$$ ⊞ **Strasburg Village Inn.** This historic circa-1788 house has rooms el-
★ egantly appointed in the Williamsburg style. Most have a canopy or a four-poster bed; two have whirlpool baths. A sitting/reading room is on the second floor; an old-fashioned porch overlooks Main Street. Full breakfast in the adjacent ice cream parlor is included, except on Sunday, when it's Continental only. ⊠ *1 W. Main St., 17579,* ☎ *717/687–0900 or 800/541–1055. 11 rooms. AE, D, MC, V.*

$–$$ ⊞ **Timberline Lodges.** Beautiful lodges nestled on a hillside put you close enough to Strasburg to hear the train whistles but far away enough to hear the birds. The lodges, which sleep between two and eight people, have stone fireplaces, balconies, and furnished kitchens. ⊠ *44 Summit Hill Dr., 17579,* ☎ *717/687–7472. 11 lodges, 5 motel units. Restaurant, bar, pool, playground. AE, D, MC, V.*

$ ⊞ **Red Caboose Motel.** With 37 railroad cabooses that have been converted into a string of rooms, this motel provides nostalgic accommodations for railroad buffs, who will appreciate the N5-style cabooses, some dating to 1910, perched on railroad tracks. Half a caboose sleeps two; a family gets a whole car (one double bed, four bunks). Even the furnishings are fun—TV sets are built into pot-bellied stoves. ⊠ *303 Paradise La., off Rte. 741, 17579,* ☎ *717/687–6646. 40 units, including 7 suites. Restaurant, playground. AE, D, MC, V.*

Ephrata

⑧ *22 mi north of Strasburg, 12 mi northeast of Lancaster.*

Ephrata has a well-known farmers market and Ephrata Cloister, which preserves the legacy of an early religious community. North of town, antiques markets draw huge crowds.

You can visit the remains of an 18th-century religious communal society at **Ephrata Cloister.** It was founded in 1728, when dissident brethren split from a group that had arrived four years earlier. A living example of William Penn's "Holy Experiment," the monastic Protestants of Ephrata lived an ascetic life of work, study, and prayer. They ate one meal a day of grains, fruits, and vegetables and encouraged celibacy (the last sister died in 1813). The society was best known for its a cappella singing, its Fraktur, its medieval German architecture, and its publishing center. Robed guides lead 45-minute tours of three restored buildings, after which visitors can browse through the stable, print shop, and craft shop by themselves. ⊠ *Rtes. 272 and 322,* ☎ *717/733–6600.* ▨ *$5.* ☉ *Mon.–Sat. 9–5, Sun. noon–5.*

★ The **Green Dragon Farmers Market and Auction** is a traditional agricultural market with a country carnival atmosphere. Each Friday livestock and agricultural commodities are auctioned in the morning. Local Amish and Mennonite farmers tend many of the 450 indoor and outdoor stalls selling meats, fruits, vegetables, fresh-baked pies, and dry goods. One of the state's largest farmers markets (occupying 30 acres), it also has a flea market and an evening auction of small animals. Try the sticky buns at Rissler's Bakery and the sausage sandwiches at Newswanger's. ⊠ *955 N. State St., off Rte. 272,* ☎ *717/738–1117.* ⊙ *Fri. 9 AM–10 PM.*

Dining and Lodging

$$ ✕ **The Restaurant at Doneckers.** Classic and country French cuisine is served downstairs amid Colonial antiques and upstairs overlooking a country garden. The kitchen is known for its chateaubriand for two, sautéed Dover sole with strawberry sauce, steak au poivre, the daily chef's veal special, and salmon. The service is fine, the wine cellar extensive. From 2:30 to 4 light fare is served. ⊠ *333 N. State St.,* ☎ *717/738–9501. AE, D, DC, MC, V. Closed Wed.*

$$ ✕ **Stoudt's Black Angus.** Prime rib cut from certified Angus beef is the
★ specialty of this Victorian-style restaurant, adjacent to the Black Angus Antiques Mall. Also notable are its raw oyster bar and German dishes such as Wiener (veal) and *Schwabian* (pork) schnitzel. Stoudt's beer, brewed right next door, is on tap. On weekends from July through October, a Bavarian Beer Fest with German bands, a pig roast, and ethnic food takes over Brewery Hall. There are brewery tours Saturday at 3 and Sunday at 1. ⊠ *Rte. 272, Adamstown, 6 mi northeast of Ephrata,* ☎ *717/484–4385. AE, DC, MC, V. No lunch Mon.–Thurs.*

$–$$$ ⊞ **Smithton Inn.** This B&B, a historic former stagecoach inn built in
★ 1763, has lovingly furnished guest rooms and one four-room suite. The rooms have antiques and reproductions, fireplaces, and canopy beds; the third-floor suite has a skylight, cathedral ceiling, and Franklin stove fireplace. Nice touches abound: oversize goose-down pillows, nightshirts, magazines, and flowers. Outside are a lily pond, a fountain, English lawn furniture, and a lovely garden. Full breakfast is included, as is complimentary coffee and tea. ⊠ *900 W. Main St., at Academy Dr., 17522,* ☎ *717/733–6094. 7 rooms, 1 suite. AE, MC, V.*

$–$$ ⊞ **The Inns at Doneckers.** Four properties dating from the 1770s to 1920s have been tastefully furnished with French country antiques and decorated by hand-stenciling. Rooms are light and airy, and the price includes Continental breakfast. Suites have fireplaces and whirlpool baths. You can shop for crafts (☞ Shopping, *below*) and clothing here, too. ⊠ *318–324 N. State St., 17522,* ☎ *717/738–9502. 27 rooms, 13 suites. Shops. AE, D, DC, MC, V.*

Shopping

ANTIQUES

Large antiques malls line Route 272 north of Ephrata between Adamstown and Denver and offer plenty of temptations.

Heritage I and II Antique Centers (⊠ Heritage I, Rte. 272, 1 mi north of Pennsylvania Turnpike Exit 21, ☎ 717/484–4646; ⊠ Heritage II, Rte. 272, 2 mi south of Pennsylvania Turnpike Exit 21, ☎ 717/336–0888), two of the area's many antique cooperatives, have more than 200 dealers set up in over 25,000 square ft of indoor space. Both are open daily from 9 to 5.

The huge **Renninger's Antique and Collector's Market** (⊠ Rte. 272, ½ mi north of Pennsylvania Turnpike Exit 21, Adamstown, ☎ 717/336–2177) draws thousands of collectors and dealers on Sunday from 7:30 to 5. Nearly 400 indoor stalls, open year-round, overflow with every conceivable type of antique, while the outdoor flea market adds to the selection on good-weather days.

Shupp's Grove (⊠ Just off Rte. 897, south of Adamstown, ☎ 717/484–4115), the oldest of the Adamstown antique markets, has acres of dealers in an outdoor tree-shaded grove. Tables are piled with antiques, art, and collectibles. The market is open weekends from April through October, 7–5.

At **Stoudt's Black Angus Antiques Mall** (⊠ Rte. 272, Adamstown, ☎ 717/484–4385), more than 200 indoor dealers and 100 outdoor ones display old books and prints, estate jewelry, linens, china and glassware, coins, and lots of furniture. There's also a restaurant (☞ Dining and Lodging, *above*) on the grounds. The mall is open Sunday from 7:30 to 5.

CRAFTS

The **Artworks at Doneckers** (⊠ 100 N. State St., ☎ 717/738–9503) houses studios where you can watch painters, sculptors, and potters at work. There are also art, fine crafts, and antiques galleries. It's closed Wednesday.

The Mennonite Central Committee operates **Selfhelp Crafts of the World Gifts and Tea Room** (⊠ Rte. 272 just north of the Cloister, ☎ 717/721–8400). A job-creation program designed to aid developing countries, the store has more than 3,000 items—including jewelry, Indian brass, onyx, needlework, baskets, toys, and handwoven rugs—from Bangladesh, Botswana, Brazil, and about 30 other countries. Sales in January and July offer some terrific bargains. Each week for lunch the Nav Jiwan (Hindi for "new life") Tea Room features the cuisine of a different country. The store is open daily except Sunday.

Lititz

9 *10 mi southwest of Ephrata.*

Lititz was founded in 1756 by Moravians who settled in Pennsylvania to do missionary work among the Native Americans. Its tree-shaded main street, lined with 18th-century cottages and shops selling antiques, crafts, clothing, and gifts, is a fine place for a walk. Around the main square are the Moravian communal residences, a church dating from 1787, and a hospital that treated the wounded during the Revolutionary War. You can pick up a Historical Foundation walking tour brochure at the General Sutter Inn (☞ Lodging, *below*) or at the Johannes Mueller House (⊠ 137–139 Main St., ☎ 717/626–7958).

At the **Julius Sturgis Pretzel House,** the nation's oldest pretzel bakery, pretzels are twisted by hand and baked in brick ovens the same way Julius Sturgis did it in 1861. At the end of the 20-minute guided tour, you can try your hand at the almost extinct art of pretzel twisting. ⊠ *219 E. Main St.,* ☎ *717/626–4354.* ☞ *$2.* ☉ *Mon.–Sat. 9–4:30.*

★ ☺ The first thing visitors notice in Lititz is the smell of chocolate emanating from the **Wilbur Chocolate Company's Candy Americana Museum and Factory Candy Outlet,** which has a candy-making demonstration (with free samples), a small museum of candy-related memorabilia, and a retail store. ⊠ *48 N. Broad St.,* ☎ *717/626–1131.* ☞ *Free.* ☉ *Mon.–Sat. 10–5.*

Lodging

$$ 🏨 **Swiss Woods.** Innkeepers Werner and Debrah Mosimann designed this Swiss style chalet while they were still living in Werner's native Switzerland. They planted it on 30 acres, creating a comfortable, friendly European-style bed-and-breakfast with light pine furnishings, a contemporary country decor, and goose-down comforters. The chalet is surrounded by extensive flower gardens and is nestled on the edge of the woods overlooking Speedwell Forge Lake. ⊠ *500 Blantz Rd.,*

17543, ☎ 717/627–3358 or 800/594–8018, FAX 717/627–3483. 6 rooms, 1 suite. Hiking, boating, fishing. D, MC, V.

$–$$ 🏨 **General Sutter Inn.** Built in 1764, the oldest continuously run inn
★ in Pennsylvania was named after the man who founded Sacramento
in 1839, 10 years before the discovery of gold on his California property started the gold rush. This Victoriana lover's delight has furnishings that range from Pennsylvania folk art to Louis XIV sofas and
marble-top tables. The inn stands at the crossroads of town, within
easy walking distance of the buildings of the historic district. The tavern is a good place to mingle with locals, and its brick patio is an inviting spot to linger in summer. ✉ *14 E. Main St., corner of Rtes. 501
and 772, 17543, ☎ 717/626–2115, FAX 717/626–0992. 10 rooms, 2
suites. Restaurant, bar, coffee shop. AE, D, MC, V.*

WESTERN LANCASTER COUNTY
Peaceful Backwaters

You can avoid the crowds and commercialism of parts of eastern Lancaster County by staying in the sleepy towns along or near the Susquehanna River, including Columbia, Marietta, and Mount Joy. There's
plenty of scenery and Colonial history to explore, and you can sample good Mennonite food here.

Columbia

⑩ *10 mi west of Lancaster.*

It's a quiet town now, but Columbia and other river communities
were very important in the days when rivers were one of the easiest
methods of transportation. Eighteenth-century Quaker missionary
John Wright worked in this area, and two of this sons set up a ferry
here that became an important transportation point for settlers moving west. Today museums and the tranquil countryside provide diversions.

★ The **Watch and Clock Museum of the National Association of Watch
and Clock Collectors** displays a large and varied collection of timepieces,
specialized tools, and related items from the primitive to the modern.
There's a 19th-century Tiffany globe clock, a German Black Forest organ
clock with 94 pipes, and the showstopper, the Engle Clock—an 1877
timepiece intended to resemble the famous astronomical cathedral
clock of Strasbourg, France. It took clock maker Stephen D. Engle 20
years to complete and has 48 moving figures. ✉ *514 Poplar St., ☎
717/684–8261.* 🎟 *$3.50.* ☉ *Oct.–Apr., Tues.–Sat. 9–4; May–Sept.,
Tues.–Sat. 9–4, Sun. noon–4.*

The **Market House and Dungeon,** built in 1869, is one of the oldest
continuously operating farmers markets in the state. You can buy
handcrafted jewelry, baked goods, meat, fruits, and vegetables from
local farms. The basement of the market used to be a dungeon; you
can still see the ground-level windows through which prisoners were
shoved down a chute into the darkness. ✉ *308 Locust St., off Rte. 441,
☎ 717/684–2468.* ☉ *Farmers market: Fri. 7–4, Sat. 7–noon. Dungeon by appointment only; contact* ✉ *Susquehanna Heritage Visitors
Center, 3rd and Linden Sts., ☎ 717/684–5249.*

You can capture a bit of the state's history at **Wright's Ferry Mansion,**
the former residence of English Quaker Susanna Wright, a silkworm
breeder whose family helped open Colonial Pennsylvania west of the

Susquehanna. The 1738 stone house showcases period furniture in the Philadelphia William & Mary and Queen Anne styles and a great collection of English needlework, ceramics, and glass, all predating 1750. ⊠ *38 S. 2nd St.,* ☎ *717/684–4325.* ⊠ *$5.* ☉ *May–Oct., Tues.–Wed. and Fri.–Sat. 10–3.*

En Route For a commanding view of the Susquehanna River as it snakes through the valley, follow the trail from the parking area at **Chickies Rock County Park** (⊠ Rte. 441 between Columbia and Marietta) to Chickies Rock, an outcropping high above the water. Bring a picnic lunch.

Lodging

$–$$ ⊞ **The Columbian.** You can relax in this Victorian mansion with a fancy stained-glass window and tiered staircase. Antiques and queen beds fill the rooms. The rate includes an ample country breakfast. ⊠ *360 Chestnut St., 17512,* ☎ *717/684–5869. 5 rooms. MC, V.*

Marietta

⓫ *8 mi northwest of Columbia.*

Almost 50% of the buildings in the town of Marietta are listed on the National Historic Register; the architecture ranges from log cabins to more recent Federal and Victorian homes. The restored river town, now seeing new life as an artists' community, is perfect for a stroll that takes you past the well-preserved facades and art galleries and antiques shops.

⓬ At the 52-acre **Nissley Vineyards and Winery Estate,** you can review the grape-growing process on a self-guided tour of this scenic operating winery, which produces award-winning vintage wines. You can purchase bottles on the grounds, too. ⊠ *140 Vintage Dr., northwest of Marietta near Bainbridge, 1½ mi off Rte. 441,* ☎ *717/426–3514.* ⊠ *Free.* ☉ *Mon.–Sat. 10–5, Sun. 1–4.*

Dining and Lodging

$–$$ ✕⊞ **Railroad House.** The restaurant in a historic hotel on the east bank of the Susquehanna River has a split personality. Upstairs, classic American cuisine reigns, with steaks, seafood, veal, poultry, and pastas flavored with herbs from the on-premises garden; downstairs, a light tavern menu offers gourmet pizza, wings, sandwiches, soups, and salads. In warm weather you can dine out on the patio in the garden. On Saturday night the Victorian era is re-created with strolling minstrels. The adjoining bed-and-breakfast was originally built in 1820 to service canal and river traffic. Refurbished Victorian-style rooms have antiques and Oriental rugs. A full breakfast is served. ⊠ *280 W. Front St., 17547,* ☎ *717/426–4141. 12 rooms, 8 with bath. Restaurant. MC, V.*

$ ⊞ **Olde Fogie Farm.** Milk the goats and bottle-feed the calves on this organic farm. The old frame home has an Amish cookstove, a petting farm, a creek, a pond, and a new stable for pony rides. ⊠ *106 Stackstown Rd., 17547,* ☎ *717/426–3992. 2 rooms, 1 with bath; 2 efficiency apartments. No credit cards.*

Shopping

George's Woodcrafts (⊠ 9 Reichs Church Rd., ☎ 717/426–1004 or 800/799–1685) sells handcrafted furniture in walnut, oak and cherry for every room in the house. You can watch items being made and then put in an order. The store is closed Sunday.

Mount Joy

⑬ *5 mi northeast of Marietta.*

This small town holds a historic brewery and some good restaurants. Dating from before the Civil War, **Bube's Brewery** (☞ Dining and Lodging, *below*) is the only brewery in the United States that has remained intact since the mid-19th century. A guided tour takes you 43 ft below the street into the brewery's vaults and passages, which were built in a cave; these passages also served as part of the Underground Railroad. It's a pleasant way to learn about beer making in Victorian times. ⊠ *102 N. Market St.,* ☎ *717/653–2056.* 🎫 *$3.50.* ☉ *Tours Memorial Day–Labor Day, daily 10–5.*

Dining and Lodging

$–$$ ✕ **Bube's Brewery.** The only intact pre-Prohibition brewery in the country contains three unique restaurants. The Bottling Works, in the original bottling plant of the brewery, serves steaks, light dinners, salads, burgers, and subs. Alois's offers prix fixe six-course international dinners (reservations required; closed Monday) in a Victorian hotel attached to the brewery. The Catacombs serves traditional steak and seafood dishes in the brewery's aging cellars below street level. A feast master presides over a medieval-style dinner (reservations required) every Sunday night. Wine and ale flow, musicians entertain, and diners participate in the festivities. In addition, Bube's Brewery has an outdoor beer garden in summer. ⊠ *102 N. Market St.,* ☎ *717/653–2056. AE, D, MC, V. No lunch Sun.*

$–$$ ✕ **Groff's Farm.** Abe and Betty Groff's 1756 farmhouse restaurant has
★ received national attention for its hearty Mennonite fare. Candlelight, fresh flowers, and original Groff Farm country fabrics and wall coverings contribute to the homey ambience. House specialties include chicken Stoltzfus, farm relishes, and cracker pudding. Dinner begins with chocolate cake. Lunch is à la carte, dinner à la carte or family style but served at your own table. ⊠ *650 Pinkerton Rd.,* ☎ *717/653–2048. Reservations essential. AE, D, DC, MC, V. Closed Sun.–Mon.*

$–$$ ✕🏠 **Cameron Estate Inn.** A sprawling Federal redbrick mansion, once
★ the summer home of Simon Cameron, Abraham Lincoln's first secretary of war, the Cameron Estate Inn welcomes guests to both its hostelry and fine restaurant. The candlelighted Federal-style dining room (reservations essential) specializes in American cuisine presented with French flair; on the menu are such dishes as veal Cameron (medallions sautéed with wine and capers served over pasta) and broiled Norwegian salmon with pineapple and sweet pepper relish. Rooms beckon with Oriental rugs, antique and reproduction furniture, and canopy beds; seven have working fireplaces. The lovely porch overlooks the inn's 15 wooded acres, and guests have access to tennis courts and a pool nearby. Continental breakfast is included. ⊠ *Donegal Springs Rd., 17552,* ☎ *717/653–1773,* 🖷 *717/653–9432. 18 rooms, 16 with bath. Restaurant. AE, D, DC, MC, V.*

$ 🏠 **Rocky Acre Farm.** Here you can sleep in a 200-year-old stone farmhouse that was once a stop on the Underground Railroad. This is a dairy farm with calves to feed, cows to milk, and dogs, kittens, roosters, and sheep—in the meadow, of course—to enjoy. There's fishing and boating in the creek, too. A full hot breakfast is served daily. ⊠ *1020 Pinkerton Rd., 17552,* ☎ *717/653–4449. 5 rooms, 2 efficiency units share bath. Boating, fishing. No credit cards.*

Manheim

7 mi northeast of Mount Joy.

Baron Henry William Stiegel founded the small town of Manheim and manufactured Stiegel flint glassware here in the 18th century. Today a major draw is a winery a few miles north of town.

⑭ The **Mount Hope Estate and Winery** is an elegant 19th-century mansion with a vineyard on the grounds. Originally built in 1800 in the Federal style, the house was Victorianized and enlarged to its current 32 rooms in 1895. Turrets, hand-painted 18-ft ceilings, Egyptian marble fireplaces, gold-leaf wallpaper, and crystal gas chandeliers are just some of the decorative elements. Tours, led by costumed guides, are followed by a formal wine tasting of Mount Hope Wines in the billiards room. Afterward you can take a stroll through the estate greenhouse and gardens. ⊠ *5 mi north of Manheim on Rte. 72, ½ mi from Exit 20 of Pennsylvania Turnpike,* ☎ *717/665–7021, ext. 125.* ⌦ *$5.* ☉ *Tours May–June, weekends; July–Sept., daily; by reservation only.*

Lodging

$ 🏠 **Jonde Lane Farm.** Breakfast with the family is served every day but Sunday at this working dairy and poultry farm where ponies, chickens, and cats are conspicuous. The four guest rooms include a family room that can sleep seven people. You can fish on the property. ⊠ *1103 Auction Rd., 17545,* ☎ *717/665–4231. 4 rooms, 2 with bath. Fishing. No credit cards. Closed Thanksgiving–Easter.*

Nightlife and the Arts

The seasonal **Pennsylvania Renaissance Faire,** on the grounds of the Mount Hope Estate and Winery (☞ *above*), transforms the winery into a 16th-century English village with human chess matches, jousting and fencing tournaments, knighthood ceremonies, street performances, craft demonstrations, jesters, and Shakespearean plays performed on 11 outdoor stages. ⊠ *5 mi north of Manheim on Rte. 72, ½ mi from Exit 20 of Pennsylvania Turnpike,* ☎ *717/665–7021.* ⌦ *$15.95.* ☉ *Aug.–Labor Day, Sat.–Mon. 11:30–7; Sept.–mid-Oct., weekends 10:30–6.*

HERSHEY AND GETTYSBURG

Beyond Lancaster County

If you have the time, it's easy to combine a trip to Lancaster County with two popular sights not more than an hour's drive from Lancaster. Hershey, to the northwest, has an amusement park and some chocolate-themed attractions. Gettysburg, to the southwest, is the county seat of Adams County and the site of Gettysburg National Military Park and museums that help convey the significance of the critical Civil War battle.

Hershey

⑮ *30 mi northwest of Lancaster.*

Hershey is Chocolate Town, a community built around a chocolate factory and now home to an amusement theme park, the Hershey Museum, and other diversions for children and adults. Founded in 1903 by confectioner Milton S. Hershey, a Mennonite descendant, it celebrates chocolate without guilt, from streetlights shaped like foil-wrapped kisses to avenues named Chocolate and Cocoa. Hershey is also known as a fine golf center. You can call 800/HER–SHEY for brochures and room reservations.

Ⓒ At **Hersheypark** they take seriously the saying "You are what you eat" seriously. Where else can you find walking Hershey Bars and dancing Reese's Peanut Butter Cups? On 100 landscaped acres are 50 rides, games of chance, five theaters, and ZooAmerica (☞ *below*), with animals from North America. Begun in 1907 as a playground for Hershey chocolate factory employees, it has been called America's cleanest and greenest theme park. Among its historic rides are the Comet, a 1946-vintage wooden roller coaster, and a carousel built in 1919 with 66 hand-carved wooden horses. ⊠ *Hersheypark Dr., Rte. 743 and U.S. 422,* ☎ *717/ 534–3090.* ⊡ *$24.95, includes ZooAmerica.* ⊙ *Memorial Day– Labor Day, daily 10:30–10 (some earlier closings); May and Sept., weekends only.*

Ⓒ **ZooAmerica,** on the grounds of Hersheypark (☞ *above*), is an 11-acre wildlife park, with more than 250 animals from throughout North America in re-creations of their natural habitats. ⊠ *Rte. 743 and U.S. 422,* ☎ *717/534–3860.* ⊡ *$4.75 (or included in Hersheypark admission price).* ⊙ *Mid-June–Aug., daily 10–8; Sept.–May, daily 10–5.*

★ Ⓒ At **Hershey's Chocolate World,** a 10-minute automated ride takes you through the steps of producing chocolate (the crowds are now too large for actual factory tours). It also serves as the town's official visitor center. Chocolate aficionados get to see the entire process from picking the cocoa beans to making candy bars in Hershey's candy kitchens. Afterward you may taste-test your favorite Hershey confection and buy gifts in a spacious conservatory filled with tropical plants. ⊠ *Park Blvd.,* ☎ *717/534–4900.* ⊡ *Free.* ⊙ *Fall–spring, Mon.–Sat. 9–5; summer, daily 9–8.*

★ The **Hershey Museum of American Life** preserves the story of Milton S. Hershey, who founded the town bearing his name and just about everything in it. The main exhibition, *Built on Chocolate,* displays Hershey artifacts and memorabilia. Displays of chocolate bar wrappers and cocoa tins show their evolution through the years, while black-and-white photos of the town from the '30s, '40s, and '50s are hung side by side with color photos of the same sites today. *Adam Danner's World* documents the daily lives of Pennsylvania Germans, and the American Indian Collection has exhibits about the life and culture of Native Americans. A children's area provides a hands-on experience. ⊠ *170 W. Hersheypark Dr.,* ☎ *717/534–3439.* ⊡ *$4.25.* ⊙ *Memorial Day– Labor Day, daily 10–6; Labor Day–Memorial Day, daily 10–5.*

Hershey Gardens began with a single 3½-acre plot of 8,000 rose bushes and has grown to include 10 themed gardens on 23 landscaped acres, with 1,200 varieties of roses and 22,000 tulips. The gardens come to life in spring as thousands of bulbs burst into bloom. Flowering displays last until fall, when late roses open. ⊠ *Hotel Rd. near Hotel Hershey,* ☎ *717/534–3439.* ⊡ *$4.25.* ⊙ *Apr.–Oct., daily 9–5.*

Chocolatetown Square is a 1-acre park downtown where free concerts are held. ⊠ *Intersection of Cocoa and E. Chocolate Aves., near wooden gazebo,* ☎ *717/534–3411 for information on upcoming events.*

OFF THE   **INDIAN ECHO CAVERNS** – One of the largest caves in the northeastern
BEATEN PATH   United States has a 45-minute guided walking tour of its underground
                  wonderland. Bring a sweater; no strollers are allowed. The kids will
                  enjoy panning for gold at Gem Hill Junction; there are horse carriage

rides and a petting zoo, a gift shop, and a picnic area. The caverns are about 3 mi west of Hershey. ⊠ *Off U.S. 322, Hummelstown,* ☎ *717/ 566–8131.* ⊡ *$8.* ☉ *Memorial Day–Labor Day, daily 9–6; Labor Day– Memorial Day, daily 10–4.*

Dining and Lodging

$ ✕ **Pippin's.** Pub-style food in an Early American setting is a good value at this family-oriented restaurant, in Tudor Square just outside Hersheypark. It's a short walk from Chocolate World and the Hershey Museum. ⊠ *100 W. Hersheypark Dr.,* ☎ *717/534–3821. AE, D, MC, V. Closed Jan.–Mar.*

$$$$ ✕⊡ **Hotel Hershey.** The grande dame of Hershey, this gracious Mediter-
★ ranean villa-style hotel is a quiet and sophisticated resort with lots of options for recreation, starting with the golf course that lushly surrounds the hotel. Opened in 1933 as part of Milton S. Hershey's building program to lift his town out of the Great Depression, the Hershey was nicely refurbished in time for the hotel's 60th anniversary. Rooms have an evocative old-world feel and are popular with families because of the hotel's proximity to Hersheypark. Dining options are the Fountain Cafe, the casual Clubhouse Café, and the formal Circular Dining Room, serving gourmet delights. Some packages include meals. ⊠ *Hotel Rd.,* ☎ *717/533–2171 or 800/533–3131. 241 rooms. 3 restaurants, indoor-outdoor pool, sauna, 9-hole golf course, 3 tennis courts, bowling, exercise room. AE, D, DC, MC, V.*

$$–$$$ ⊡ **Hershey Lodge & Convention Center.** This bustling, expansive modern resort caters to families and has two casual restaurants where kids can be kids, plus a somewhat more formal room for adult dining. The hotel caters to groups of up to 1,300 in its Chocolate Ballroom, and it can be hectic during conventions. By fall 1998 the lodge plans to add another 200 rooms and additional meeting space. ⊠ *W. Chocolate Ave. and University Dr., 17033,* ☎ *717/533–3311 or 800/533–3131. 457 rooms. 3 restaurants, indoor pool, outdoor pool, miniature golf, 2 tennis courts, exercise room, cinema, nightclub, playground, convention center. AE, D, DC, MC, V.*

Outdoor Activities and Sports

The **Country Club of Hershey** (⊠ 1000 E. Derry Rd., ☎ 717/533–2464) maintains two private 18-hole courses, which are available to guests of the Hotel Hershey. Greens fees are around $60. The **Hotel Hershey** (⊠ Hotel Rd., ☎ 717/533–2171) offers 9 holes on the hotel grounds. Greens fees are $14–$17. A public 18 holes known as the **South Course** (⊠ 600 W. Derry Rd., ☎ 717/534–3450) is short but demanding. Greens fees are $22–$43. **Spring Creek Golf** (⊠ 450 E. Chocolate Ave., ☎ 717/ 533–2847), a nine-hole course, was originally built by Milton Hershey for youngsters to hone their stroke. Greens fees are $9.

Shopping

Ziegler's Antiques Mall (⊠ Intersection Rtes. 322 and 743, ☎ 717/533– 7990) has 75 dealers and an assortment of antiques and collectibles. It is housed in Hershey's largest parabolic barn, which formerly belonged to the Milton Hershey School. The mall is open Thursday–Monday 10–5:30.

Ziegler's in the Country (⊠ Rte. 743, ☎ 717/533–1662) is on a restored 1850s homestead, with several buildings from that era. An air-conditioned barn has space for 92 dealers and an herb and spice shop (open on weekends). You can shop Thursday–Monday 9–5.

Gettysburg

⑯ *53 mi west of Lancaster on U.S. 30.*

The events that took place in Gettysburg during a few days in 1863 affected the course of American history. From July 1 to 3, 51,000 Americans were killed, wounded, or counted as missing in the bloodiest battle of the Civil War. The Union soldiers held their ground, and some would say that this battle was the turning point of the war. At the battlefield park and the 20 museums in Gettysburg, you can recapture the power of these momentous days.

The **Gettysburg Travel Council,** housed in the former Western Maryland Railroad Passenger Depot, has free brochures and maps of area attractions. Be sure to pick up a self-guided walking tour map of the town's Historic District, which has more than 90 restored buildings. ⊠ *35 Carlisle St.,* ☎ *717/334–6274.* ⊙ *Daily 9–5.*

The **Gettysburg Tour Center** is the departure point for two-hour narrated tours of the battlefield. Open-air double-decker buses depart every 15 to 45 minutes. ⊠ *778 Baltimore St.,* ☎ *717/334–6296.* ☷ *$10.95.* ⊙ *Daily 9–5, later in summer.*

★ **Gettysburg National Military Park** honors the casualties of the battle with more than 1,000 markers and monuments spread over 5,700 acres. The turning point of the Civil War came here when General Robert E. Lee and his Confederate troops encountered the Union forces of General George Meade for three days of fighting in July 1863. More than 30 mi of marked roads lead through the site, highlighting key battle sites. It's best to begin your exploration at the visitor center (☞ *below*). ⊠ *97 Taneytown Rd.,* ☎ *717/334–1124.* ☷ *Free.* ⊙ *Park roads 6 AM– 10 PM.*

The Gettysburg National Military Park **Visitor Center** offers a free map with an 18-mi driving tour through the battlefield, as well as an orientation program, Civil War exhibits, and current schedules of ranger-conducted programs and talks. The park service also provides free walking-tour maps, which have short 1-mi loops that include the sites of some of the battle's most pivotal engagements; 3½- and 9-mi trails also are marked.

To best understand the battle, begin by viewing the **Electric Map,** which uses colored lights to illustrate deployments and clashes during the three days of fighting. Sit on the south side for the best view. Private, licensed guides may also be hired at the center. ⊠ *97 Taneytown Rd.,* ☎ *717/334–1124.* ☷ *Free; Electric Map $2.50.* ⊙ *Daily 8–5, later in summer; map shows every 45 mins.*

The **Cyclorama Center** contains a 19th-century in-the-round painting that puts you in the center of Pickett's Charge, the South's ill-fated frontal assault during the last day of the battle. ⊠ *Taneytown Rd., adjacent to the visitor center,* ☎ *717/334–1124.* ☷ *$2.50* ⊙ *Showings daily, every 30 mins, 9–4:30.*

★ The **Gettysburg National Cemetery,** dedicated by President Abraham Lincoln in his famous Gettysburg Address, is now the final resting place of more than 7,000 honorably discharged servicemen and their dependents. ⊠ *Off Baltimore Pike, across the street from the visitor center.* ☷ *Free.* ⊙ *Daily dawn–dusk.*

The **National Civil War Wax Museum** presents the story of the Civil War era and the Battle of Gettysburg through 200 life-size figures in 30 scenes, including a reenactment of the Battle of Gettysburg and an animated Abraham Lincoln delivering his Gettysburg Address. ✉ *297 Steinwehr Ave.,* ☎ *717/334–6245.* 🎫 *$4.50.* ⊙ *Mar.–Dec., daily 9–7; Jan.–Feb., weekends 9–5.*

The **Hall of Presidents and First Ladies** re-creates in wax the nation's chief executives from Washington to Clinton, as well as their wives (with reproductions of their inaugural gowns). ✉ *789 Baltimore St.,* ☎ *717/334–5717.* 🎫 *$5.25.* ⊙ *Summer, daily 9–9; spring and fall, daily 9–5; closed Dec.–Feb.*

Soldier's National Museum depicts 10 major battles of the Civil War in miniature dioramas plus a life-size encampment scene from the night of July 2, 1863. ✉ *777 Baltimore St.,* ☎ *717/334–4890.* 🎫 *$5.25.* ⊙ *Summer, daily 9–9; spring and fall, daily 9–5; closed Dec.–Feb.*

The **Lincoln Train Museum** brings to life Lincoln's journey from Washington to Gettysburg in November 1863 to dedicate the national cemetery. A 12-minute ride simulates the sights, sounds, and most of all the feel of traveling on a period railcar. The museum also houses the Alexander Model Train and Military Rail Collection. ✉ *425 Steinwehr Ave.,* ☎ *717/334–5678.* 🎫 *$5.25.* ⊙ *Summer, daily 9 AM–10 PM; spring and fall, daily 9–5; closed Dec.–Feb.*

The **Lincoln Room Museum,** along U.S. 30, which runs through the center of town, houses the bedroom where President Lincoln finished writing his famous address. Feel the spirit of Lincoln and hear a re-creation of him speaking his thoughts, doubts, and dreams on November 18, 1863, as he wrote the final draft of his speech. ✉ *12 Lincoln Sq.,* ☎ *717/334–8188.* 🎫 *$3.50.* ⊙ *Summer, daily 9–7:30; reduced hrs off-season.*

General Lee's headquarters, one of the few original houses in Gettysburg open to the public, is west of town on U.S. 30. Here, on July 1, 1863, Lee planned his strategy for the now-famous battle. The old stone building houses a fine collection of Civil War relics. ✉ *Rte. 30W, 8 blocks west of Lincoln Sq.,* ☎ *717/334–3141.* 🎫 *$2.* ⊙ *Mar.–Nov., daily 9–9.*

★ The **Eisenhower National Historic Site** offers a glimpse into the life and times of General and later President Dwight D. Eisenhower. This bucolic farm was his peaceful retreat from 1951 until his death in 1969. In addition to the brick-and-stone farmhouse, preserved in 1950s style, there are various other outbuildings. The farm adjoins the battlefield and is administered by the park service, which offers daily ticketed tours only on a first-come, first-served basis from the visitor center. ☎ *717/334–1124.* 🎫 *$3.75; tickets at Gettysburg National Military Park Visitor Center (☞ above).* ⊙ *Apr.–Oct., daily 9–5; Nov.–Mar., Wed.–Sun. 9–5; closed mid-Jan.–mid.-Feb.*

Dining and Lodging

$–$$ ✕ **Farnsworth House Inn.** Housed in an 1810 building that still shows bullet holes from the battle, the restaurant at this B&B serves up Civil War–era dishes such as game pie, peanut soup, pumpkin fritters, and spoon bread. The outdoor garden, with sculptures and fountains, makes a tranquil setting in which to ponder the events of 1863. ✉ *401 Baltimore St.,* ☎ *717/334–8838. AE, D, MC, V. No lunch.*

$$ ✕🏠 **Historic Dobbin House Tavern.** This unique old tavern in the His-
★ toric District was built in 1776, making it the oldest building in town. Fine Continental cuisine and 18th-century specialties are served in restored rooms filled with hand-carved woodwork, fireplaces, and antiques. The Alexander Dobbin Restaurant has six rooms in which you

can dine by candlelight seated in wing chairs in the parlor or at a table in the dining room. Lighter fare is served in the Springhouse Tavern. The adjacent Gettystown Inn has rooms decorated with antiques and four-poster beds. Rates include full breakfast and tea and coffee in the parlor of the 1860s home. ⊠ *89 Steinwehr Ave., 17325,* ☎ *717/334–2100. 5 rooms, 1 suite. Restaurant. AE, MC, V.*

$$ 🏨 **Best Western Gettysburg Hotel 1797.** The hotel is a pre–Civil War
★ structure in the heart of the historic downtown district, but the interior was completely rebuilt in 1991. Rooms are furnished in traditional style, and suites have fireplaces and whirlpool baths. Ask about the cannonball from the Battle of Gettysburg that is still embedded in the brick wall across the street. Coffee and tea are complimentary. ⊠ *1 Lincoln Sq., 17325,* ☎ *717/337–2000,* 🖷 *717/337–2077. 60 rooms, 23 suites. Restaurant, pool. AE, D, DC, MC, V.*

$–$$ 🏨 **Baladerry Inn.** This restored home, built in 1812 and on the edge of the battlefield, once served as a field hospital during the Battle of Gettysburg. The inn is set on extensive landscaped grounds and has interiors filled with antiques. The full breakfast is complimentary, as are coffee and tea. ⊠ *40 Hospital Rd., 17325,* ☎ *717/337–1342. 8 rooms. Tennis court. AE, D, MC, V.*

$ 🏕 **Artillery Ridge Campground.** You can pitch a tent or park an RV a mile south of the military park visitor center. There's a pond for fishing. ⊠ *610 Taneytown Rd., 17325,* ☎ *717/334–1288. 45 tent sites, 105 camper or RV sites. Pool, horseback riding, fishing, bicycles. D, MC, V.*

Shopping

Old Gettysburg Village (⊠ 777 Baltimore St., ☎ 717/334–8666), a collection of shops in the center of the tourist district, has an art gallery showing paintings of the battle by Dale Gallon, the town's artist-in-residence.

The Horse Soldier (⊠ 777 Baltimore St., within Old Gettysburg Village shopping center, ☎ 717/334–0347) provides a shopping experience that's more like visiting a museum. Carrying one of the country's largest collections of military antiques—everything from bullets to discharge papers, the shop even offers its customers help in researching their ancestors' war records prior to 1910.

LANCASTER COUNTY A TO Z

Arriving and Departing

By Bus
Greyhound Lines (☎ 800/231–2222) has three runs daily between Philadelphia and the R&S Bus Terminal (⊠ 22 W. Clay St.), in Lancaster. The ride takes about 2 ½ hours.

By Car
From Philadelphia take the Schuylkill Expressway (I–76) west to the Pennsylvania Turnpike. Lancaster County sights are accessible from Exits 20, 21, and 22. For a slower, more scenic route, follow U.S. 30 (Lancaster Pike) west from Philadelphia. It's about 65 mi to the Pennsylvania Dutch Country.

By Train
Amtrak (☎ 215/824–1600 or 800/USA–RAIL) has regular service from Philadelphia's 30th Street Station to the Lancaster Amtrak station (⊠ 53 McGovern Ave.). Trips take 80 minutes.

Getting Around

By Car

A car is the easiest way to explore the spread-out sights in the area; it also lets you get off the main roads and into the countryside. Lancaster County's main arteries are U.S. 30 (also known as the Lincoln Highway and Lancaster Pike) and Route 340 (sometimes called the Old Philadelphia Pike). Some pleasant back roads can be found between Routes 23 and 340. Vintage Road is a country road running north over U.S. Route 30 and then along Route 772 west to Intercourse. You get a look at some of the best farms in the area and also see Amish schoolhouses, stores, and the Amish themselves. Remember that you must slow down for horse-drawn buggies when you're driving along country roads.

Contacts and Resources

B&B Reservation Agencies

Lancaster County Bed-and-Breakfast Inns Association (⌧ 2835 Willow Street Pike, Willow Street 17548, ☎ 717/464–5588 or 800/848–2994) is a group of 16 B&Bs in the area. For other agencies, *see* B&B Reservation Services *in* Chapter 3.

Emergencies

Dial 911 **for police, fire,** or **ambulance.**

Guided Tours

Amish Country Tours (⌧ Rte. 340 at Plain and Fancy Farm, between Bird-in-Hand and Intercourse, ☎ 717/768–3600 or 800/441–3505) has large bus or minivan tours. Most popular is the four-hour Amish farmlands trip, with stops at an Amish farmhouse, a wine tasting, and shopping for crafts. On Tuesday tours to Hershey are available.

Brunswick Tours (⌧ National Wax Museum, U.S. 30E, Lancaster, ☎ 717/397–7541) provides private guides who will tour with you in your car, as well as a self-guided auto audiotape tour with 28 stops which takes three to four hours, beginning at the Pennsylvania Dutch Convention & Visitors Bureau.

Glick Aviation (⌧ 311 Airport Dr., off Rte. 340, Smoketown, ☎ 717/394–6476), at Smoketown Airport, offers 18-minute flights in a four-seater plane (pilot plus three), with a splendid aerial view of rolling farmlands.

Lancaster Bicycle Touring (⌧ 3 Colt Ridge La., Strasburg 17579, ☎ 717/396–0456) can show you the area by bicycle.

The **Mennonite Information Center** (⌧ 2209 Millstream Rd., Lancaster, ☎ 717/299–0954) has local Mennonite guides who will join you in your car. These knowledgeable guides will lead you to country roads, produce stands, and Amish crafts shops and also acquaint you with their religion.

Hospitals

There are three **emergency rooms** in the city of Lancaster: Community Hospital of Lancaster (⌧ 1100 E. Orange St., ☎ 717/397–3711); Lancaster General Hospital (⌧ 555 N. Duke St., ☎ 717/299–5511); and St. Joseph's Hospital (⌧ 250 College Ave., ☎ 717/291–8211). For nonemergency referrals call the **Lancaster City & County Medical Society** (☎ 717/393–9588).

Pharmacies

Strasburg Pharmacy (⌧ 326 Hartman Bridge Rd., Rte. 896, 2 mi south of Rte. 30, Strasburg, ☎ 717/687–6058) is open weekdays 9–9, Saturday 9–5. **Weis Pharmacy** (⊠ 1603 Lincoln Hwy. E, Lancaster, ☎ 717/394–9826) is open weekdays 9–9, Saturday 9–6.

Visitor Information

The **Pennsylvania Dutch Convention & Visitors Bureau** (⊠ 501 Greenfield Rd., Lancaster 17601, ☎ 717/299–8901 or 800/735–2629) has many brochures and maps, direct phone connections to local hotels, and a 14-minute multi-image slide presentation ($2 charge) *There Is a Season,* which serves as a good introduction to the area. It's open daily 8:30–5, later in summer.

The **Mennonite Information Center** (⊠ 2209 Millstream Rd., Lancaster 17602-1494, ☎ 717/299–0954) serves mainly to "interpret the faith and practice of the Mennonite Church to all who inquire." It has information on local inns and Mennonite guest homes as well as a 20-minute video about the Amish and Mennonite people. Next door is the "only actual-size model" of the Hebrew Tabernacle ($4 charge). It's open Monday–Saturday 8–5.

Intercourse Tourist Information Center (⊠ 3614 Old Philadelphia Pike, Intercourse 17534, ☎ 717/768–3882) provides travel advice on one of the Dutch Country's most popular towns. It's open March–December, Monday–Saturday 10–5.

The **Susquehanna Heritage Tourist Information Center** (⊠ 445 Linden St., Box 510, Columbia 17512, ☎ 717/684–5249) has information about visiting the Susquehanna River town of Columbia.

11 Portraits of Philadelphia and the Pennsylvania Dutch Country

Portrait of an Amish Family

Books and Videos

PORTRAIT OF AN AMISH FAMILY

YOU'LL SPOT JOSEPH Stoltzfus working his fields with a team of horses as you drive the back roads of Lancaster County. You will certainly encounter his somber black buggy on one of the traffic-choked highways. You might exchange a few words with his wife, Becky, in her plain dark dress and white cap, if you happen to stop by their farmhouse to buy fresh eggs or inspect the homemade quilts she has for sale. If you're on the right road at the right time, you might see their younger children playing in the yard of a one-room schoolhouse. And on certain Sundays you may pass the farmhouse where the Stoltzfus family and other Amish people gather to worship.

Stoltzfus is the most common of a dozen Amish family names; Jacob and Becky and their seven children are fictitious but typical of the more than 17,000 Amish (pronounced *Ah*-mish) in this area. Their roots and religious traditions reach back to 16th-century Europe. Every detail of their lives, from their clothing to the way they operate their farms, is an expression of their faith in God and their separateness from "the world"; every detail is dictated by the *Ordnung,* the rules of their church.

Becky Stoltzfus, like Amish women of any age, wears a one-piece dress in a dark color (bright colors and printed patterns are forbidden). The sleeves are long and straight, and her full skirt is hemmed modestly halfway between knees and ankles. The high, collarless neck is fastened shut in front with straight pins; buttons and safety pins are forbidden, although the Ordnung of some church districts allows hooks and eyes. Over her shoulder she wears a shawl the same color as her dress, pinned in front and back to the waistband of an apron, also in the same color. Since apron strings tied in a bow are considered frivolous and are therefore forbidden, her apron is also pinned. She wears black stockings rolled below the knee and black low-heeled oxfords. At home in warm weather Becky and her family go barefoot.

Soon after her daughters were born, Becky made sure they wore the white organdy prayer cap. When Katie turned 12, she changed to a black cap for the Sunday preaching; after she marries she will wear the white cap all the time. The head coverings may look identical to outsiders, but subtle differences tell the Amish a great deal about one another. The width of the front part, the length of the ties, the style of the seams, and the way the pleats are ironed all indicate where the woman lives and how conservative or liberal her church district is.

Becky has never cut or curled her hair, nor has she let it hang loose. She pins it in a plain knot at the back of her neck. She parts little Hannah's hair in the middle, plaits it, and fastens the two little braids in the back. When Becky is away from home, she wears a black bonnet with a deep scoop brim over her prayer cap.

The clothes Jacob wears are also carefully dictated by the Ordnung of his church district. For Sunday preaching he wears a *Mutze,* a long black frock coat with split tails and hook-and-eye closings but no collar or lapels. His vest is also fastened with hooks and eyes. Jacob's broadfall or "barn-door" trousers have no zipper, just a wide front flap that buttons along the sides; they have no creases and no belt—homemade suspenders hold them up. There are buttons on his shirt, the number specified by the Ordnung. Colored shirts are permitted, but stripes and prints are out. Neckties are forbidden.

When he's not dressed up, Jacob hangs up his Mutze and puts on a *Wamus,* a black sack coat with either a high, round neck or V-neck but neither lapels nor outside pockets. Sometimes the Wamus has hooks and eyes, but more liberal church districts allow buttons. Buttoned sweaters are sometimes permitted, and there are also buttons on the long greatcoats some older men wear in cold weather.

In winter Jacob and his sons wear broad-brimmed black felt hats; in summer they switch to straw. Ben and Ezra, Jacob's younger boys, have been wearing hats with three-inch brims since they were little. Sam, the oldest son, wears a hat with a crease around the top of the crown, a sign (along with his sprouting beard) that he is newly married. The hat is a status symbol among the Amish. The grandfather's hat is higher in the crown than the father's, and its brim is four inches wide. At the top of the hierarchy, the bishop who preaches at the Sunday service is recognizable by his hat's high rounded crown and its brim, the broadest in the district.

The width of an Amish man's hat brim also signifies his degree of conservatism: the broader the brim, the more conservative the wearer. Young rebels like Jacob's middle son Joe sometimes trim their hat brims to slightly less than the prescribed width. Jacob's long beard is as much the mark of an Amish man as a broad-brimmed hat. He shaves only his upper lip, since mustaches are against the rules. He cuts his hair straight around, well below the ears. Ben and Ezra have theirs parted in the middle, with bangs across the forehead. Cutting it short—up to the earlobe, as Joe did—is another form of rebellion.

THE STYLE OF THE AMISH BUGGY is as carefully prescribed as the style of the hat. The Stoltzfus family owns a black carriage with a gray top and big wooden wheels. The battery-powered side lamps, reflectors, and bright orange triangles have been added as required by Pennsylvania state law. The iron-tire wheels are precisely set, toed in slightly, farther apart at the top than at the bottom. A gear assembly at the pivot of the front axle adds stability. The brakes are operated by hand, an iron block pressed hard against the rear tire. This kind of brake is prescribed by the Ordnung; different groups permit different kinds of brakes. The Ordnung tells the buggy owner whether or not he may have roll-up side curtains or sliding glass doors, and if he is allowed a dashboard, a whipsocket, and other variations. The Stoltzfus family also owns a farm wagon, and young Joseph was given his own horse and open one-seater when he turned 16.

The waiting list is long for handmade buggies. Carriage making used to be a non-Amish occupation, but the growing Amish population, the toll of wrecked carriages, and the need for approved work in addi-tion to farming have brought some Amish into the trade. The carriage maker is in a more liberal church district that allows power tools.

Incidentally, the Amish can—and do— ride in cars owned by non-Amish people and travel on trains, buses, and even airplanes and taxis. But they are not allowed to *own* a car. Teenage Amish boys sometimes manage to buy a car and hide it out of sight of their families. They are not subject to the rules of the Ordnung until they have been baptized, an event that takes place in their late teens or early twenties, after they've had time to sow some wild oats.

No electric wires lead from the power lines along the road into the neat, well-kept buildings of the Stoltzfus farm, a difference that distinguishes Amish farms from those of their non-Amish neighbors. The farms are small, no more than 50 or 60 acres, which is all that can be handled by a farmer limited to horse power. Tractors, like electricity, are taboo among most Amish.

The Stoltzfus house is spacious and uncluttered. There is no wall-to-wall carpeting to vacuum; instead, plain and unpatterned linoleum covers the floor. There are no curtains to wash or draperies to clean; although some church districts allow plain curtains on the lower half of the windows, this district permits only dark-green roller shades. There are no slipcovers to launder or upholstery to shampoo because upholstered furniture is not allowed.

Becky has a large kitchen where the family eats around a big wooden table. Afterward Becky and Katie and Hannah clean up the kitchen, wash the dishes, and put away leftover food in the gasoline-operated refrigerator. A one-cylinder engine in the cellar chugs noisily, powering the water pump, but many Amish families still rely on windmills or water power. A creek that runs through a farm also supplies water. Although labor-saving devices are generally forbidden, Becky does have a washing machine that runs by gasoline. Her stove burns kerosene; she would prefer bottled gas, but that is forbidden by the Ordnung of her district. She uses a treadle sewing machine and sews by the bright and steady light of a gasoline lamp.

About once a year it is the Stoltzfuses' turn to host the every-other-Sunday preaching service. As many as 175 people may attend: There are 90 members in the district, and double that number when unbaptized children are counted. The removable partitions built into the downstairs walls are folded back and furniture moved aside. The district's backless oak benches are brought in and set up in rows. For that one Sunday morning the entire district fills the big house for the long service, staying on for a hearty lunch that Becky has been preparing for days.

Jacob and Becky Stoltzfus are fluent in English, but the language they speak among themselves is Pennsylvania Dutch, a German dialect related to the dialects spoken in the part of Germany from which their Amish ancestors came. It is primarily a spoken language and spelling varies with the writer. "Dutch" actually means *Deutsch,* or German, and some scholars call the dialect Pennsylvania German. Many Pennsylvanians of German descent speak the dialect, but among the Amish it is the mother tongue, the first language an Amish child learns to speak and another mark of separation from the world.

When Hannah, Becky's youngest child, starts school, she will learn to speak and read and write in the language of "the world." Jacob and Becky want their children to know English because their survival depends on good business relationships with English-speaking people. Sometimes when the Amish converse in English, they use a literal translation of their dialect. The results are the expressions that amuse tourists and inspire souvenir manufacturers to decorate switchplates and cocktail napkins with "typical Amish" expressions like "Outen the light" and "Throw Papa down the stairs his hat."

About the same time Hannah Stoltzfus starts to learn English, she will also be taught High German, the language of religion. The family Bible is written in High German, and she and her brothers and sisters must learn to read it. By the time they are baptized, in their late teens, they will be able to understand most of the Sunday sermon and to join in the prayers and hymns. Most Amish can't carry on a conversation in High German and have no need to do so unless they are ordained church officials who must preach sermons and pray. But everyone needs to be able to read and to listen.

THE OUTSIDER MAY NOT NOTICE the inconspicuous building on a back road where Ben and Ezra and Annie Stoltzfus attend school, along with eight grades of children in one room. They are taught by a young Amish woman with only an eighth-grade education. Amish children are not sent to public school, and Amish schools continue only as far as the eighth grade. That's time enough to learn the basics of reading, writing, and arithmetic: The *real* education for their lives takes place at home, on the farm.

At age five Hannah Stoltzfus would be old enough for kindergarten—if the Amish had one. But they believe children should be at home with their parents until they are six. Annie loves school and wishes she could continue, while her brothers can hardly wait until their 14th birthdays, the end of school for them. Schools are built to serve children within a 2-mile radius so that no one has far to walk. Some children go to old one-room schoolhouses once owned by the public school district. When districts consolidated, the Amish bought the obsolete schools and remodeled them—not modernizing them but ripping out the electric wiring. Since none was available near the Stoltzfus farm, the Amish fathers in that area built a plain cinder-block structure with big windows to take advantage of natural light.

Stepping into an Amish schoolhouse is like entering a time machine and emerging 70 or more years in the past. At 8:30 the teacher pulls the rope to ring the old-fashioned bell on the roof. Ben and Ezra and Annie come early, after they've finished their farm chores, so they have a chance to play before school begins. When the bell rings, the children line up and file through the big front door into the cloakroom. They hang their hats and jackets on pegs, line up their lunch boxes, and go quietly to their carefully refinished old-fashioned desks.

The school day begins with the roll call. During peak periods of farm work, the Amish close down the schools for a few days; they stop earlier in the spring than the public schools. They make up for the time by taking only a short Christmas break and celebrating none of the national holidays. Except in the case of illness, everyone stays home to work or goes to school to learn.

Next, the teacher reads to the pupils from the German Bible, then everyone recites the Lord's Prayer in German. Except for the lessons in reading German Scriptures and prayers, the teacher speaks exclusively English in the classroom.

Beside the teacher's desk is a "recitation bench." There are more than 30 students in the eight grades, and each class of three or four or five comes forward by turns to recite its lessons. There is no competition to come up with the answer first, and they all respond in a singsong chorus.

Because it is essential to the work of a farmer, arithmetic is considered very important. Picking readers (books) for the pupils was not easy. The parents want the subject matter to be farm children, not city life; they want the stories to teach a moral lesson; fairy tales, myths, and fantasies are taboo. The Amish think most modern readers are too worldly, showing families with clothes, cars, and too many material possessions. Outsiders would consider the books they use hopelessly outdated.

During the 15-minute morning recess, Ezra and Ben and the other boys resume their baseball game. One of the rules of the Amish schoolyard is that children are never allowed to stand around by themselves; everyone must be included in the group. Annie and the older girls play blindman's bluff; the younger ones, joined by their teacher, race around in a game of tag.

During recess and lunchtime the yard rings with conversation in English, Pennsylvania Dutch, and mixtures of the two. Parents disagree about which language should be used in the schoolyard. More pragmatic parents want their children to become as fluent as possible in English. The more traditional argue that using English when it's not necessary helps to drive a wedge between the Amish child and the Amish community.

The Amish want their children to learn to work together as a group, not to compete as individuals. Preserving tradition is a goal; reasoning abstractly is not. Asking too many questions is not acceptable. Discipline is strict; the only voices heard in

the schoolroom are those of the teacher and the pupils who are reciting. The Amish expect pupils to master the material unquestioningly: Memorization replaces reasoning in a culture dominated by oral tradition. Rapid learning is not considered an advantage; thoroughness is valued more. Teachers believe that intellectual talents are a gift from God and that children should be encouraged to use the gift by helping others in the school.

BEFORE THE DAY IS OVER, there is time for singing. Singing is a vital part of the Amish tradition, important in their religious life and in their social life as well. There are no songs with harmonization for the Amish; unaccompanied unison singin is the universal rule. The Amish have their own style of singing, in which the leader (*Vorsanger*) sings the first word and everybody else joins in for the rest of the line.

When it's time to go home, students put away their books, sweep out the room, line up the desks neatly, wash the old-fashioned slate blackboards, and clap the erasers until they are clean. In cold weather they carry in the wood for the stove and take turns cleaning out the ashes and banking tomorrow's fire.

For years public school authorities were in conflict with the Amish. Truancy laws were enforced, and Amish fathers were often arrested and jailed for refusing to send older children to school. But in 1972 the United States Supreme Court ruled that the Amish are exempt from state compulsory education laws that require a child to attend beyond the eighth grade; they found that such laws violate Constitutional rights to freedom of religion.

Today the Amish accept the idea of sending their children to school for eight years to learn what they need to survive in the 20th-century rural economy. But what Amish children really need to know in order to survive in the Amish culture they learn from their parents and from other adults in the community. Most of the practical knowledge of farmers and housewives is acquired not in books but in a family apprenticeship.

The marriage of Jacob and Becky Stoltzfus is a very practical affair. The Amish are quite realistic about their expectations.

They do not marry for love or romance but out of mutual respect and the need for a partner in the kind of life they expect to live. The farmer needs a wife, and they both need children. Marriage is essential to the Amish community; divorce is unknown; separation is rare. Marriage is the climax of the rite of passage that begins with baptism, the signal of the arrival of adulthood and sober responsibility. It signifies that young people have really joined the community.

From the time they reach the age of *Rum Schpringe* (running around—about 16 for boys, a bit younger for girls) and for the next half-dozen years until each marries, Joe Stoltzfus and his sister Katie do much of their socializing at Sunday-night singings, usually held at the farm where the preaching service took place in the morning. Singings are functions of the church district, which helps keep dating and eventually marriage within the group. In Lancaster County young people from several church districts with similar interpretations of the Ordnung may get together for a joint singing. Although the main activity is singing hymns, these occasions are more social than religious.

At the more conservative singings boys sit on one side of a long table in the barn, and girls sit on the other, and between joking and teasing they take turns in the role of Vorsanger. The hymns they sing are the "fast tunes" (some of them familiar Protestant hymns) rather than the "slow tunes," or chants sung at the preaching service. At around 10 o'clock the singing ends, and the girls serve snacks. The siblings, now paired off—Joe is with Leah Zook, as usual, and Katie has somehow ended up with Reuben Beiler—start home.

Although outsiders believe that the social life of an Amish teenager begins with a singing and ends with a buggy ride home at a respectably early hour, Amish dating is actually much livelier. Among the more liberal groups, the old-fashioned singings can turn quickly into rowdy, foot-stomping hoedowns. A few bring out harmonicas, guitars, and other forbidden instruments; older boys haul in cases of beer. Few outsiders attend these events.

On the "off Sunday," when there is no preaching service, Joe and Leah and other young unmarried people go courting—but always in secret. Before they marry, they are never seen together in public as a couple except as they leave a singing or a barn dance.

Bundling, the practice of courting in bed fully clothed, is usually attributed to the Amish. Actually it is an English word with no equivalent in Amish dialect that comes from New England, where it had more to do with keeping warm in a cold house than with sex. No one is quite sure whether the Amish do or don't, but the consensus is that the girl's parents, rather than the Ordnung, have the final say. Leah's father and Jacob Stoltzfus have both said no.

THERE IS A SAYING that if a boy can persuade his girl to take off her prayer cap, she'll have sex with him. Evidently that doesn't happen often because the rate of premarital pregnancies among the Amish is quite low. Premarital sex is forbidden, birth control is taboo, and sex education is nonexistent. The Amish child growing up on a farm isn't ignorant of the reproductive process, but the facts of life usually remain a mystery until the age of marriage.

When Jacob's son Sam married Sarah Beiler, their wedding was held after the harvest in November. December is the second most popular month for weddings, and there are traditionally only two possible days in the week for the ceremony: Tuesday and Thursday. Sarah chose Thursday. There was no honeymoon, but every weekend throughout the winter the couple went to visit relatives. Now they're living on the Stoltzfus farm.

The average age at marriage of Amish couples has been rising because of the problems of accumulating enough money to establish a household and to acquire land. Many Amish parents retire while they are still relatively young, especially if they have a son who needs a farm. Sam and Sarah have moved into the "grandfather's house," a section of Jacob's farmhouse built to accommodate a second generation. In a few years, when Sam assumes full responsibility for the farm and has children, he and Sarah will move into the larger part of the house, and Jacob and Becky will move into the grandfather's house.

Recently Sam told his parents that a new little "woodchopper" or "dishwasher" is expected, the first grandchild of Jacob and Becky. A new generation of the Stoltzfus family and for the Amish community is on the way.

THE ROOTS THAT NOURISH Amish beliefs and bring vitality to Amish tradition reach back hundreds of years. Theirs is a complex story of persecution from without and division within. Remembrance of the past is a part of the present for the Amish every day of their lives, not something reserved for Sunday worship and special ceremonies.

To understand the Amish as something more than a quaint anachronism, turn back the calendar to 16th-century Europe. The poor, by far the majority, were exploited by the rich and powerful few. The Roman Catholic Church wielded tremendous influence, and many blamed the church for society's ills. When Martin Luther launched the Protestant Reformation in 1517, he had many opponents in addition to the Roman Catholic Church. One was Ulrich Zwingli, a radical Swiss Protestant, who also opposed Conrad Grebel. Grebel's followers wanted to establish free congregations of believers baptized as adults who made a confession of faith and committed themselves freely to a Christian life. Backing Zwingli, the Great Council of Zurich announced that babies must be baptized within eight days after their birth, or the parents would be exiled.

This marked the beginning of Anabaptism, which means "rebaptized." Regarded as radically left wing, the Anabaptist movement posed a threat to both the Roman Catholic and Protestant establishments. Anabaptist leaders were imprisoned, beaten, tortured, and killed; by the end of the 16th century nearly all the Anabaptists of Switzerland and Germany had been put to death.

But the movement spread through Central and Western Europe. Menno Simons, a former Roman Catholic priest, became one of those persecuted for Anabaptist preaching. His followers were called Mennonites (in Switzerland they were known as the Swiss Brethren). And although they were hounded by Catholics and other Protestants, dissension began to grow among the Mennonites themselves. A principal source of disagreement was the interpretation of the *Meidung,* the practice of shunning

church members who had broken a rule. Shunning was based on St. Paul's advice to the Corinthians to avoid keeping company and eating with sinners. The Mennonites interpreted this to mean the member was to be subjected to Meidung only at communion. But Jacob Amman, a young Mennonite bishop, insisted that the Meidung meant that the rule-breaker must be shunned totally; even his wife and family must refuse to have anything to do with him until he repented and had been forgiven.

The controversy grew, and in 1697 the stubborn and fiery Jacob Amman broke from the Mennonites. His followers, known as the Amish, were as stubborn and inflexible as Amman himself, and they became known for their unwillingness to change. Although the difference in clothing detail was not a primary issue, it did become symbolic of the split. The Amish became known as the *Haftlers* (Hook-and-eyers), while the more worldly Mennonites were called the *Knopflers* (Buttoners).

Meanwhile, King Charles II of England granted a large province in the American colonies to William Penn. A devout Quaker, Penn believed he could offer refuge, freedom, and equality to the persecuted. Penn arrived in 1682, and the following year Francis Daniel Pastorius of the Frankfort Land Company brought the first group of Mennonites to Pennsylvania. They established themselves in Germantown, northwest of Philadelphia. The first Amish immigrants left Switzerland and the Palatinate of Germany in 1727, settling near Hamburg north of Reading. When Indian raids threatened that community, the Amish moved toward the southwest.

By the start of the Revolutionary War, about half of the 225,000 Pennsylvania colonists were German, but only a small minority were Amish and Mennonite. Although the Germans were excellent farmers, Benjamin Franklin dismissed them as "stupid boors." The English scorned them and tried to anglicize them. But the Amish and Mennonites were determined to hold on to their religion, which was a way of life that included their language and their plain dress.

The Amish of Pennsylvania were all of one conservative mind until 1850, when a schism divided the Amish into two main factions. The more progressive group built meeting houses, which earned them the label "Church Amish," to distinguish them from the stricter "House Amish," who continued to worship in their homes. Since then innumerable splits have been caused by various interpretations of the Meidung (as happened in the days of Jacob Amman) or by different details of the Ordnung— by Haftlers who want to live more like Knopflers but still remain Amish.

Every society changes to some extent, and in every society there are a few people who cannot adjust. The Amish are no exception. Many leave; there is generally a shortage of young men in the Amish community because most of the dissidents who leave are male. But some exert pressure for changes in the Ordnung that result in splits. Today there are 8 Amish, 24 Mennonite, and 9 Brethren groups in the Lancaster area.

The ultimate control exerted by the Amish to keep the members in strict adherence to the Ordnung is the Meidung. No one will speak to the person, eat with him, conduct business with him, or have anything to do with him while he is under the ban. It can last for a lifetime, unless the sinner mends his ways, begs for forgiveness, and is readmitted to fellowship by a unanimous vote of the congregation.

Visitors are sometimes surprised to learn that "Pennsylvania Dutch" and "Amish" are not synonymous. Many of the early settlers of Pennsylvania came from Germany at Penn's invitation; many were farmers, most were Protestant, and they spoke the same dialect. Despite these similarities, the Amish refer to all non-Amish as "English." These English are the Pennsylvania Dutch who permit hex signs on their farms (the Amish do not) and whose ancestors decorated useful items such as furniture and dishes with colorful designs. The work of Amish craftsmen is competent but plain.

The Amish are generally friendly and hospitable people. Tape recorders and cameras are not welcome, but a visitor who is sincerely interested in the Amish people and does not act like an interrogator can quietly learn something about their unique way of life.

— *Carolyn Meyer*

BOOKS AND VIDEOS

Fiction

"Writing fiction set in Philadelphia is tough," says novelist Steve Lopez. "There is nothing you can make up that is any more unbelievable than what actually happens here." Nonetheless, Lopez succeeded with *Third and Indiana*, a hard-edged story set in Philadelphia's "badlands," and *The Sunday Macaroni Club*. *God's Pocket*, by Pete Dexter, *South Street*, by David Bradley, and *Payback*, by Philip Harper, also capture the grittier side of the City of Brotherly Love.

Michael Shaara's Pulitzer Prize–winning *The Killer Angels* is a gripping account of the battle at Gettysburg.

History and Background

Philadelphia: A 300-Year History, essays edited by Russell F. Weigley, is the best overall text. *1787: The Day to Day Story of the Constitutional Convention* and Catherine Drinker Bowen's *Miracle at Philadelphia* tell the story of the Constitution. For biographies of seven Philadelphians, read *Philadelphia: Patricians and Philistines, 1900 to 1950*, by John Lukacs. *Puritan Boston and Quaker Philadelphia* by the late E. Digby Baltzell, is a scholarly work that compares the two cities. Other selections are *Christopher Morley's Philadelphia*, edited by Ken Kalfus, and *Philadelphia—A Dream for the Keeping*, by John Guinther.

South Philadelphia, by *Philadelphia Inquirer* reporter Murray Dubin, is both a memoir and an oral history that describes a well-known neighborhood. Philip Stevick's *Imagining Philadelphia* looks at how visitors to Philadelphia since 1800 have perceived the city.

Sightseeing and Touring

Walking Tours of Historic Philadelphia, by John Francis Marion, though dated (1974 was the last edition), has wonderful walks by the late Philadelphiaphile. The Foundation for Architecture's *Philadelphia Architecture: A Guide to the City* contains maps, photos, biographies of noted Philadelphia architects, and descriptions of almost 400 sites. *Cultural Connections,*

Museums and Libraries of Philadelphia and the Delaware Valley, by Morris J. Vogel, has photos and text on sites throughout the region. *Frank Furness: The Complete Works*, by George E. Thomas, Jeffrey A. Cohen, and Michael J. Lewis, assesses one of Philadelphia's most original architects. *Eastern State Penitentiary: Crucible of Good Intentions*, by Norman Johnston, discusses the influence of the city's massive prison.

Guides to Philadelphia's spectacular collection of outdoor art include: *Sculpture of a City*, by the Fairmount Park Art Association, with text and photos; *Philadelphia's Outdoor Art: A Walking Tour*, by Roslyn F. Brenner, describing more than 50 works of art along Benjamin Franklin Parkway; and the comprehensive *Public Art in Philadelphia*, by Penny Balkin Bach. Garden lovers will want to study *Gardens of Philadelphia and the Delaware Valley*, by William M. Klein Jr., which has photographs. *Rediscovering the Wissahickon*, by Sarah West, gives mapped geology and history walks for this lovely area of Fairmount Park.

Other selections are *Country Walks Near Philadelphia*, by Alan Fisher; *Philadelphia One-Day Trip Book*, by Jane Ochevhausen Smith; *Philadelphia and its Countryside*, by Ruth Hoover Seitz, which has photographs; and *The Mid-Atlantic's Best Bed & Breakfasts*, by Fodor's Travel Publications.

Videos

Rocky, with Sylvester Stallone (1976), and its four sequels describe the adventures of an underdog Philadelphia boxer. *Philadelphia* (1993) stars Tom Hanks as a lawyer in a Main Line firm who is dismissed from his job because he is battling AIDS. In *Witness* (1985) Philadelphia police detective Harrison Ford has to live undercover with the Amish in order to protect the young witness to a murder. The four-hour movie *Gettysburg*, based on Michael Shaara's novel *The Killer Angels*, captures the intensity of the War battle.

INDEX

WHEREVER
YOU TRAVEL,
*H*ELP IS NEVER
FAR AWAY.

From planning your trip to providing travel assistance
along the way, American Express® Travel Service Offices
are always there to help you do more.

Philadelphia

American Express Travel Service
2 Penn Center Plaza
S.E. corner 16th & JFK
Philadelphia
215/587-2300

do more AMERICAN EXPRESS
Travel

http://www.americanexpress.com/travel
American Express Travel Service Offices are located
throughout the United States.
For the location nearest you, please call 1-800-AXP-3429.